A CROOKED LINE

*When there are obstacles,
the shortest distance between
two points is a crooked line.*
—Bertolt Brecht

A Crooked Line

From Cultural History

to the History

of Society

GEOFF ELEY

The University of Michigan Press   Ann Arbor

Copyright © by the University of Michigan 2005
All rights reserved
Published in the United States of America by
The University of Michigan Press
Manufactured in the United States of America
⊚ Printed on acid-free paper

2008   2007   2006   2005   4   3   2   1

A CIP catalog record for this book is available from the British Library.

Library of Congress Cataloging-in-Publication Data

Eley, Geoff, 1949–
      A crooked line : from cultural history to the history of society /
   Geoff Eley.
         p.   cm.
      Includes bibliographical references and index.
      ISBN-13: 978-0-472-06904-0 (pbk. : alk. paper)
      ISBN-10: 0-472-06904-7 (pbk. : alk. paper)
      ISBN-13: 978-0-472-09904-7 (cloth : alk. paper)
      ISBN-10: 0-472-09904-3 (cloth : alk. paper)
      1. Historiography.   I. Title.

   D13.E44   2005
   907'.2—dc22   2005016617

facing page: Photograph of the Great Blue Heron courtesy of Nova Scotia
Tourism, Culture and Heritage.

For Tim

CONTENTS

PREFACE

As a young person seeking change in the world, living through a time of excitements and upheaval, I wanted to become a historian because history really *mattered;* it was necessary for making a difference. I never thought that the connections from history to politics were easy or straightforward, whether in the grander way or just as a guide for personal behavior. Some homilies about the uses of history certainly invited simplicity, marshaling stock quotations made ever more facile by repetition. Orwell's "Who controls the past controls the future: who controls the present controls the past," for example, or Santayana's "Those who cannot remember the past are condemned to repeat it."[1] Learning from history was more complex than that—less transparent, less manageable, less reducible to a set of direct protocols or prescriptions.

But how exactly the past gets remembered (and forgotten), how it gets worked into arresting images and coherent stories, how it gets ordered into reliable explanations, how it gets pulled and pummeled into reasons for acting, how it gets celebrated and disavowed, suppressed and imagined—all have tremendous consequences for how the future might be shaped. All of the ways in which the past gets fashioned into histories, consciously and unconsciously, remain crucial for how the present can be grasped. For political purposes, history is constantly in play. I continue to believe that history matters in that sense. In negotiating the promises and possibilities, and the pitfalls and deceptions, of the past's disorderly presence in the difficult landscape of our social and political lives, the professional historian—someone schooled in the ways of the discipline, intimate with its practices, enabled by its epistemologies—has an essential role to perform.

While this book draws on biography, it makes use of the personal voice only sparingly and strategically. Readers expecting a detailed account of my own political involvements or outlook will certainly be disappointed. I've tried to avoid straying into the kind of self-referentiality that would collapse the last four decades of historiography into the experience of the historian, charting its movements by reference to an avowedly personal "I," and reducing the explicit object of inquiry to the implicit sensitivities—and dilemmas—of the inquirer. My book is far less than autobiographical in that sense. If it seeks to relate large historical debates, political changes, and social processes to the practices of the individual intellects that engage them, it presumes no pregiven logic to the connection. Indeed, while the political, the historical, and the personal form the triangulated streams of what I want to say, their relationship bespeaks contradictory pressures as much as confluence or collision. It's precisely at those moments of critical tension—involving the breaches between social processes and subjective experience, or between politics and the academy—that this book raises its central questions: What is history? Why do we do it?

My main motivations for writing this book are two. The first is to take stock; the second is to explore history's relationship to politics. With respect to the former, what follows is meant neither as a survey of current approaches and types of history nor as a guide to best practice. Nor is it quite a work of theory, in the manner of another familiar contemporary genre, in which the advocates of "new ways of telling the past," who celebrate the pleasures of experiment and transgression, face off against the champions of the tried and true as they circle their wagons "in defence of history."[2] As should become clear, I'm personally far more disposed to the first of these postures than to the second. But in providing my own take on the contemporary debates of historians about their discipline, I've chosen a rather different tack. Using my own experience as a point of departure, and returning to it allusively along the way, I've tried to present the disagreements among social and cultural historians of the second half of the twentieth century as a journey through a politics of knowledge defined by certain primary and abiding questions in their various forms: of base and superstructure, being and consciousness, structure and agency, material life and subjectivity, the "social" and the "cultural." In so doing, I've tried to see the genealogies of the historian's understanding in a continuous conversation between the main forms of historiographical inquiry and the succession of surrounding political conjunctures.

Here I've chosen the personal voice in order to emphasize precisely the *collective* rather than the individualized nature of how that happens. In my view, our ability to work through the most difficult questions and problematics—the respective challenges of social history and cultural history, in the terms of this book—almost always entails a collective and collaborative effort that too often goes unacknowledged. In traveling down new roads, in exploring new directions, and in engaging with new theories, methods, and ideas, we succeed best by dialogue, by cooperation, and by finding the points of connection beyond our immediate scholarly concerns—whether to other fields, to other disciplines, or to wider contexts of politics and the public sphere. In what follows I seek to relay back and forth between my own experiences as a historian and these larger contexts in a variety of ways. One of the most formative of those contexts was provided by the British 1968; another by the particular institutional environment of the University of Michigan in the 1980s and 1990s.

In telling my own story I'm aware of taking a risk. The perspectives are necessarily partial and subjective. As I take pains to acknowledge from time to time, there are obvious specificities of standpoint—of generation, nationality, geography, gender, sexuality, citizenship, political affiliations, and so forth—quite apart from my preferred kinds of history and theory, which structure and dispose my discussion. My overt presence in the text becomes submerged for quite long periods, then to resurface for the purposes of key discussions, usually at points of transition. Embedded in my account are also certain arguments about British-U.S. and British-German circuits of intellectual exchange which could certainly be developed into the subject of a book in themselves. At the very least I've tried to be explicit and self-conscious about the place from which at any one time I'm seeking to speak. I've certainly tried to deliver the kind of detailed historiographical narrative for our own present that no one else has yet provided. In that sense, the partialities of standpoint are less important: it's the form of the account that matters. In tracking myself as a young (and then not so young) historian moving through contemporary politics and historical studies, I've tried to model the necessary protractedness and arduousness of developing workable ideas. For those at their own beginning stage of becoming historians, I want to show the lifelong character of the process. Above all: we learn through dialogue with others.

I certainly want these reflections to play a part in shaping our understanding of what historians do, just as I'd like them to illuminate the intellectual-political histories that bring us to where we are now. But I see my book as seeking to *open* a conversation rather than aspiring to bring anything to closure. In that respect, by far the most important feature of the past four decades of historiography has been the huge tectonic shift from social history to cultural history that forms the subject matter of this book. I've been inspired in my outlook as a historian by both of those disciplinary movements. Moreover, despite the unsettlements and disappointments accompanying the impasse of social history, I experienced the so-called linguistic or cultural turn of the 1980s as a vital empowering of possibilities. Yet at the same time I've always been impressed by the obstacles to building a conversation across the resulting differences. The first purpose of my book, consequently, is to step back from the situation created by the "new cultural history" and to consider what the latter may not be accomplishing so effectively. Without in any way disavowing the processes of critique and labors of theory, or the kinds of cultural analysis these have enabled, I want to explore how and in what forms the earlier moment of social history might be recuperated. What has been gained and what has been lost by turning away from the salient commitments of social history? What in those earlier inspirations remains valuable for critical knowledge—and dissent—today?

As I've already said, my reflections on that question will be avowedly partial in all sorts of ways, limited both by my own particular knowledge and expertise—that of a modern European historian trained in Britain, working mainly on Germany, living in the United States—and by the kinds of history I'm mainly interested in writing about. But I've tried as far as possible to cast a very wide net, to educate myself in the concerns of other fields and areas of the discipline, and to reflect self-consciously on the partialities of my standpoint. More to the point, I'd like my own mapping of this territory—the forms of a politically engaged historiography during the past four decades—to resonate not only with those in my own immediate fields, but to speak comparatively or analogously to the experiences of others working elsewhere.

My second motivation comes from politics. In what follows, my concern is not with historiography in some entirely open-ended, capacious, or pan-disciplinary manner, but with a more delimited body of work. I'm interested in those historians since the 1960s who've sought to link their scholarly practice of the discipline to a politics of large-scale social and cultural change. Using my own passage through these years as a reticent but purposeful counterpoint, and while focusing on three especially notable or emblematic individuals—Edward Thompson, Tim Mason, and Carolyn Steedman—to exemplify and condense the argument, I've tried to capture the ways in which politics and the writing of history are constantly informing each other. *Politics*—whether in the grand, institutional, and macro-discursive dimensions or in the micropolitical, personal, and everyday—can profoundly influence the kinds of history we're able to think and do. *History* and *politics* bleed into each other all the time. Thus my book is about the politics of knowledge associated with social history and cultural history in the broadest of ways.

As I try to emphasize, this isn't a simple or one-to-one relationship. But inscribed in my account is a strong generational subtext centered on the political and ethical meanings of 1968. While Edward Thompson was much older and possessed of a very different political sensibility, his work and presence exercised extraordinary influence on the generations of historians coming of age during the 1960s and 1970s. Tim Mason was certainly among the latter, although just old enough to register a kind of distance. Carolyn Steedman's biography was entirely bounded by the parameters I'm describing, as indeed was my own formation. Again, no *particular* set of standpoints or identifications was entailed by that political conjuncture, and we'd be hard put to assimilate Steedman's heterodox, independently minded originality to any straightforward version of a generational narrative. The argument I'm making is far more about a certain kind of relationship between historians and the public sphere.

In talking about that relationship, however, I'm continually reminded of a double difficulty: historians and the works they produce are no more consistent, stable, or transparent than the practices of a public sphere and the passions and antagonisms that underlie even the most rationalist theories of its constitution. Not only does this book not aim to defuse this double difficulty. It does its best to provoke it. In seeking to illuminate the proliferating tensions in how we now approach the past, it is equally alive to the demands for recognition inhering among them. Only with an understanding of those tensions will history—and the twin categories of the cultural and the social—be made fully available for politics.

ACKNOWLEDGMENTS

THE IDEA FOR THIS book was hatched on November 18, 2002, when I gave my inaugural lecture as the Sylvia L. Thrupp Collegiate Professor of Comparative History at the University of Michigan. In naming my chair (local custom asks collegiate professors to choose their own title by honoring someone connected to the University) I wanted to make a double statement. First, as well as being a pioneer of medieval social history, Sylvia Thrupp was a main instigator of the openness of historians to interdisciplinary and comparative analysis. The journal which she founded in Chicago in 1958 and brought to Michigan three years later, *Comparative Studies in Society and History,* fostered a rare and challenging reciprocity between historical thinking and various kinds of social science. An unforced eclecticism, with a willingness to think comparatively across the disciplines, across fields, and across periods, was the hallmark of Sylvia Thrupp's editorship, and it came to describe the outlook of the Michigan History Department more generally. Her energy and acuteness of judgment made the journal into what it still remains, namely, the premier international showcase for historically inclined interdisciplinary scholarship across the social sciences. Second, Sylvia Thrupp came to Michigan as the first Alice Freeman Palmer Professor of History, a chair originally endowed for a distinguished woman historian in the pre-affirmative action era when the presence of women in the profession was still so sparse. Though she'd retired by the time I arrived in Ann Arbor in 1979, I was lucky enough to get to know her via *Comparative Studies,* and I'm proud to be associated with her name.[3]

Immediately after delivering my lecture, I was urged by Phil Pochoda, Director of the University of Michigan Press, to consider converting my thoughts into a book and I've been enormously grateful for that initial encouragement and subsequent support. In my immediate editor at the Press, Jim Reische, I've also been fortunate indeed. I wrote the book between October 2003 and April 2004 during a year's leave, which was made possible by a Guggenheim Fellowship and the associated support of the University of Michigan. Pete Soppelsa provided invaluable help at the final stage of the manuscript's preparation.

Still more crucial have been the various intellectual communities I've relied upon over the years, whose identity should be readily apparent from what follows below. Pride of place goes to the University of Michigan, both to my colleagues and graduate students in the Department of History and to the wider interdisciplinary culture fostered so uniquely by this University, whose crucible in many respects was the Program in the Comparative Study of Social Transformations (CSST) formed in 1987. I also thank my fellow German historians as well as my wider cross-disciplinary community in German Studies, who again include a remarkable group of colleagues and students at Michigan itself and an essential network of friends on either side of the Atlantic (and the North Sea). My final source of friendship, solidarity, and inspiration in this collective sense is the one absolutely crucial to the framing of the arguments for this book, namely, those who share my credo of engaged scholarship and intellectual work, who write the histories from which I learn the most (whether members of the historical profession or not), and who believe that history can and should continue making a difference.

In those three broad respects I owe so much that it becomes invidious to name only a small number of individuals. But for this particular book I'd like to acknowledge intellectual debts ranging from more recent exchanges to conversations now stretching across many years. I thank Lauren Berlant, David Blackbourn, Monica Burguera, Antoinette Burton, Kathleen Canning, Jane Caplan, Dipesh Chakrabarty, Vinayak Chaturvedi, Becky Conekin, David Crew, Nick Dirks, Jessica Dubow, Atina Grossmann, Julia Hell, Young-sun Hong, Kali Israel, Jennifer Jenkins, Robin Kelley, Mike Kennedy, Marjorie Levinson, Alf Lüdtke, Terry McDonald, Kristin McGuire, Bob Moeller, Gina Morantz-Sanchez, Frank Mort, Dirk Moses, Rudolf Mrazek, Keith Nield, Sherry Ortner, Kathy Pence, Moishe Postone, Alice Ritscherle, Sonya Rose, Bill Rosenberg, Adelheid von Saldern, Bill Schwarz, Bill Sewell, Peggy Somers, Scott Spector, Carolyn Steedman, George Steinmetz, Uli Strasser, Ron Suny, Dennis

Sweeney, and Susan Thorne. Each of these superb scholar-intellectuals (some of them historians by profession, some not) gave me indispensable help and guidance, whether by their general influence over the years or by their specific advice.

A number of people read the entire manuscript, including the two anonymous reviewers for the Press, whose readings were extremely helpful and discerning. The finished manuscript was read by Gina Morantz-Sanchez and Frank Mort, who were the very best of readers. They suggested many particular improvements, but most of all helped me believe in the usefulness of the project. If Frank kept my sights focused in Britain, Gina helped me keep my footing in the United States. Finally, Jessica Dubow read the book as I was writing it and proved the ideal interlocutor. From neither Britain, Germany nor the United States (but South Africa); not a historian by discipline, but with a range of historical knowledges very different from my own; not a sixty-eighter, but of a much younger generation—in each respect she brought differences of perspective that sharpened the clarity of what I wanted to say. I thank each of these readers for the generosity of their response to the spirit and purposes of this book

I would like to thank Ruth Rosengarten for her generosity in allowing me to use her drawings for the cover art of this book. They express perfectly the essence of my purposes.

It should already be plain that my book offers more than just historiographical commentary. The cadence of its organization—from optimism through disappointment to reflectiveness and finally defiance—gives the game away. It also aspires to politics. Above all, it presents a statement of personal conviction. It makes an appeal to my fellow historians, both within the profession and without. Practice the historian's classic virtues, of course. Ground yourself in the most imaginative, meticulous, and exhaustive archival research, in all the most expansive and unexpected ways the last four decades have made available. Embrace the historian's craft and the historian's epistemologies. But never be satisifed with these alone. Be self-conscious about your presuppositions. Do the hard work of abstraction. Converse with neighboring disciplines. Be alive to the meanings of politics. History is nothing if not sutured to a pedagogy, to a political ethics, and to a belief in the future. Otherwise, as Stuart Hall once said at the end of a reflection on the meanings of popular culture, to be perfectly honest, "I don't give a damn."[4]

I. BECOMING A HISTORIAN
A Personal Preface

W HEN I WAS DECIDING to become a historian, interdisciplinarity had yet to haunt the corridors of history departments. It was further from doing so in Britain than in the United States. I came to Balliol College, Oxford, in October 1967 coveting access to a new universe of knowledge, poised at the portals of scholarship and learning. To my chagrin, the first term brought only Gibbon and Macaulay, de Tocqueville, Burckhardt, and—last but not least—the Venerable Bede. Amid this chronically unimaginative Oxford pedagogy, which sought to dampen the intellectual ardor of youth in the cold shower of antiquated knowledge, by far the worst experience was plowing through Bede's eighth-century *Ecclesiastical History of the English People*. The inveterate archaism of this requirement beggared belief. As I made my way through that interminable chronicling of the Christianizing of England, whose relevance for historical education in the later twentieth century escaped me, I took consolation in the marauding exploits of Bede's nemesis, King Penda of Mercia, whom I always imagine rampaging his way across the monastic landscape as a ferociously bearded avenger of truly Pythonesque proportions, heroically defending England's last redoubt of vigorous paganism.

Oxford study of history was nothing if not consistent. In our second term, my fellow students and I began a long odyssey through the entirety of British history, beginning with the burial mound at Sutton Hoo. Five semesters later, we ended safely before the outbreak of World War II. Looking back, I'm reminded of how little of my excitement about history came from these formal undergraduate studies. Oxford's Modern History School seemed organized precisely for the purposes of restraining imaginative thought, keeping our perceptions tethered to the discipline's most conservative notations. Many students in the late sixties were moved by a strong and often passionate sense of history's relevance for the present, after all. We saw it not only as an aid to effective political thinking but also as a tool for honing a critical social consciousness and for making our way toward a workable political ethics. Yet Oxford's disciplinary guardians kept such things dourly at bay. My time there was spent living inside a paradox. Any excitement at becoming a historian grew in the interstices, after hours, or beyond the Modern History School altogether. Effective learning happened despite, rather than because of, the curriculum. Its custodians willfully closed their eyes to the changes occurring outside.[1]

This reminiscence can be chased a little further. I arrived in Oxford painfully green and ill equipped. At some point in my early teens, a bookshop had opened in Burton-on-Trent, five miles from where I grew up. Byrkley Books won no prizes for the richness of its inventory, but it did claim an extensive display of Penguins and Pelicans, which gave me a certain greedy access to the Western intellectual canon, contemporary social commentary, and serious fiction. For all its other virtues, the Swadlincote Public Library had precious little to offer in that respect, and my parents had neither the income nor the wherewithal to provide much at home. On my occasional visits to the Burton bookshop, therefore, I consumed its wares voraciously, extending my horizons in a very indiscriminate, hit-and-miss way. My first historical interests are now a source of embarrassment. I read variations on the pompous and sentimentalized nationalist history delivered by conservative patriots during the first two postwar decades in Britain, for which the grandiose multipart television documentary celebrating Churchill's war leadership, *The Valiant Years,* was the epitome.[2] I could count as an antidote only A. J. P. Taylor's weekly book reviewing in *The Observer,* together with his various television lectures.[3] On these bases, I made myself into an intellectually conservative, but modestly effective, autodidact.

At Ashby-de-la-Zouch Boys' Grammar School I had none of those formative mind-awakening encounters so often recorded in the memories of intellectuals. One history teacher definitely encouraged an early interest in medieval castles. A later history teacher was more attuned to the world of scholarship, opening my first window onto serious academic history. In my last year at school, he introduced me to the journal *Past and Present* and plied me with a series of historiographical controversies, including those surrounding Elton's *Tudor Revolution in Government,* Taylor's *Origins of the Second World War,* and the general crisis of the seventeenth century.[4] He also had me translate a text by Max Weber on the sixteenth-century price revolution, which helped my German, if not my knowledge of the history of social thought. An academic manqué marooned in a stagnant provincial backwater, my teacher clearly kept abreast of historical debates. He must have been a contemporary of Eric Hobsbawm and Raymond Williams in Cambridge before the war, I now realize, though certainly without sharing their politics.

I wasn't the only freshman historian to arrive in Balliol underendowed with cultural capital. Nonetheless, it was hard to experience the disparities. Most of my contemporaries simply seemed to know more—to have read more of the right kinds of books, to have traveled more widely, to speak more languages with greater facility, to have the right references at their fingertips, and generally to be sure they belonged. This preparedness didn't always correlate with the advantages of class. Roughly half of the group were from public (that is, fee-paying) schools, half from state schools. Of the two most disconcertingly knowledgeable of my twelve contemporaries, the first came from an elite public school, knew several languages fluently, and was already working on the Mexican Revolution (whose place in history came as complete news to me). The other, from a Merseyside comprehensive school, arrived for our first orientation bearing a copy of Fernand Braudel's *Mediterranean and the Mediterranean World in the Age of Philip II,* five years before it appeared in English translation.[5] Measured by this, I was definitely a late starter.

I recount these sometimes painful antecedents to make a general point. We become historians by many different routes. In my own case, nothing in my family or schooling pushed me in that rather particular direction. My early years contained no big experiences or set of affiliations driving my curiosity, no traumas or tragedies lodged in the collective memory or the family past. In grammar school, my relationship to history unfolded via pragmatics and a series of accidents— it was something I happened to be good at—with a logic not especially open to my own control. The official curriculum, whether in grammar school or at the university, never captured my imagination. What made the difference was the pressure of events in the wider political world. For many of my own generation, a relationship to history was ignited by the dramatic and exciting demandingness of the time, by the intrusion of its ethical and political urgencies. In that sense the "ordinariness" of my and many other working-class and lower-middle-class lives was made extraordinary by the educational chances we were given and by the large-scale political events that suddenly and unexpectedly supervened. And of course it's all the subsequent acquisition of knowledge—of theory, of politics, and of history— that now gives me, in Valerie Walkerdine's words, "the way to look from the vantage point of the present to the fantastic shores of the past."[6]

Fired by the desire for understanding, rather than merely an undergraduate earning a degree, I was propelled into being a historian by 1968. As we can now see, a series of quite different historiographies were already lying in wait, eager to ambush the complacencies of the British historical scene. Exactly how this happened remains a fascinating question of intellectual history in itself. But for those of us who were undergraduates at the time, the breakthrough to new kinds of history—even more, to a new vision of what doing history could mean—owed very little to what was happening in our classrooms. For my required work in the history of political thought, I may have been slogging through Aristotle, Hobbes, and Rousseau (actually I wasn't, because my reading for that part of my final examinations came wholly at the last minute), but my real mind was on Marx. The locus of most of my reading and thinking developed a quite contingent relationship to what was needed for my degree. About the importance of constitutions and the arbitrariness of unaccountable power, I learned as much from my encounters with college and university authorities as I did from studying the 1832 Reform Act or even the February Revolution of 1917. The works that inspired me were placed in my hands only partly by my appointed teachers. They came much more from what was happening outside academia.

I still remember how I first heard about Edward Thompson's *The Making of the English Working Class*.[7] Chatting with me in front of Balliol opposite the Paperback Shop, which had just received its new Penguin titles (a monthly moment of excitement in those days), Paul Slack, then a Balliol junior research fellow, pondered the purchase of the Pelican edition of Thompson's book—which, at more than one predecimal pound in 1968 prices, implied a serious budgetary decision.[8] That alone was reason to take notice. First published five years before, *The Making* was sniffily dismissed by the Industrial Revolution's mainstream historians—as I learned in 1968 from Thompson's new postscript, where he answered his critics. Shamed by ignorance—I had the dimmest understanding of the political and historiographical backgrounds for all this—I set about filling in the blanks. By the autumn of 1968, I was the owner of a copy of the Gollancz hardback edition and devoted a large part of the winter to reading it. At a time when my disillusionment with history in Oxford was bottoming out, it renewed my belief.

At one level, the present book lays out one person's journey through the shifting landscape of historical studies during the ensuing decades. I realize that to many readers, such a first-person account may seem self-inflating, possessing at best some minor curiosity value for a few immediate students, colleagues, and friends. But my real purpose goes far beyond this. I'm interested in charting the impact of some vital features of contemporary intellectual history on historians' thought and practice. For my own part, an ideal of politically engaged and theoretically informed history formed the lasting outcome of my Oxford time. I certainly believed strongly that history needed to meet the highest standards possible in conventional scholarly terms, based in the most creative and reliable empirical investigations and the most exhaustive archival research. But history also had to be relevant. Trying to balance that ideal has never been easy. Approaching history politically can lead to misplaced moralizing, off-putting didacticism, and unhelpful simplification. But history's usefulness can't be extricated from an appreciation of its pedagogy. Some broader ambition toward such appreciation has moved historians' best achievements during the past four decades.

This relationship of history to politics is not simple. History is more than either an instrument or a mirror. But the scholarly debates of historians are inseparable from politics in the widest sense of the term—all the partially visible philosophical, sociocultural, and strictly political baggage historians bring with them into the scholarly arena; the wider contentiousness implied by their position-taking within institutions and the public sphere; and the broader political issues and controversies that shadow their concerns. All these factors helped frame history's purpose during the past three decades. For those on the left, the new kinds of history inspired by feminism will spring readily to mind, as will the parallel challenges presented by the growing centrality of race for contemporary public life. Further illustrations can easily be multiplied.[9] The debates among historians have in each case been finely linked to wider developments in the public sphere, sometimes in direct response, but just as frequently via indirect influence or partial borrowings, whether from the political processes themselves or through related discussions in other academic disciplines. The resulting changes cannot be isolated from the ethical and practical dilemmas facing historians on the ground—in the decisions about what and how to teach, in conflicts about hiring and the setting of academic policy, in the handling of relations with colleagues, and in the general dailiness of departmental life.

The importance of this public world for the changing purposes of historians can't be gainsaid. Historians today think, teach, and write in an environment profoundly different from the one I entered in the late 1960s. They've been required to respond not just to the various transformations internal to the discipline, including the remarkable changes in the sociology of the profession, but also to the constant pressure of events in the wider social and political arenas. Those larger contexts have encompassed passionate debates about theory and methods across the academic disciplines, as well as far-reaching conflicts over the purposes of higher education.

Recounting my particular version of this story, in careful counterpoint with the general intellectual histories it partially reflects, may have some modest usefulness as a foil for others. My hope is that mapping a series of personal encounters between the tasks of historical writing and the surrounding political climate may make it possible for others to recognize their own analogous accounts, whether converging with mine or not. By thus using my experience to explore the complex back-and-forth between history and politics—between trying to be a good historian and trying to act politically in effective and ethical ways—I may be able to add something to the more familiar historiographical narratives of our time.

As I grapple with the meanings of the extraordinary changes in the discipline of history during my adult lifetime, I'm often struck by the orderly logics and implicit progressivism that so many of the existing accounts tend to display. This is far more a feature of historiographical commentary in the United States than in Britain, perhaps, and also very much a feature of retrospectives published since the 1960s.[10] Methods improve, archives expand, subareas proliferate, bad interpretations are junked, and better interpretations mature. Historians' understanding only gets better. Innovations are proposed, conflicts rage, breakthroughs are secured, changes get institutionalized, and new advances begin. Incorrigible upholders of earlier orthodoxies fade into the night; new priorities of teaching, research, and publication settle into place; a higher plane of sophistication ensues. Of course, I'm overstating this progression for effect. But in declaring their credentials during the 1970s and 1980s, the various schools of social historians certainly produced one genre of narratives like this. Since then, the "new cultural historians" speak another.

This "progressivist" effect has many particular forms. For those of us embracing Joan Scott's advocacy of gender history in the course of the 1980s, for example, gender swiftly graduated from being a "useful category of historical analysis" into a necessary one, whose benefits promised a higher form of understanding.[11] The same might be said of other associated recognitions, from the growing salience of ethnicity and race or the new work on diverse sexualities to the general endorsing of cultural constructionism and its pervasive languages of analysis. But in making the case for such advances, particularly through the more confrontational types of public disputation usually involved, certain risks are always entailed.

In the course of winning one's argument and thereby establishing some influence over resources, a certain measure of pluralism easily gets impaired. Unfortunately, the temptations of purism persistently intrude on contemporary historiographical debate. Sometimes less perceptibly, but often with full and explicit aggression, the exponents of any new set of approaches all too readily equate acceptance of their insights with an approved degree of intellectual sophistication. But whether we hold the classical ground of such now-questionable grand narratives as "the nation," "science," "emancipation," or "class" or prefer such emergent emphases as "identity" and "difference," we can surely acknowledge the degree to which one epistemological standpoint all too easily works preemptively against others.

These logics of advocacy and temptations of certitude, powered by the politics of commitment and the ethics of conviction, enlist us all. At various times, I've been as guilty of these habits and tendencies as anyone else, savoring the radicalism of controversies and sharpening the relevant differences to their best polemical edge. At the same time, I've always tried to keep some room for critical distance. Staying attuned to the public sphere of politics, as opposed to the isolated scholarly and intellectual arena, certainly helps in this respect. The chastening that results from so many repeated disappointments and unexpected reversals in the political world makes it easier to accept the impermanence of the changes occurring in intellectual life. Indeed, being a historian during the last third of the twentieth century has required learning to live with a condition of virtually continuous flux. On the most fundamental terrain of the various theory disputes successively waged by historians, I've personally always needed a generous pause for thought. I've been too conscious of the difficulty—of the persisting areas of disagreement and of the frequent transience of the latest best thing—to want to go all the way. Indeed, it's often precisely *inside* the remains of that ambivalence, it seems to me, that the most creative histories can be written.

Moreover, the impulse for such creativity invariably comes from outside the discipline. For that matter, it originates beyond the academy altogether. The boundaries between history's professional precincts and the wider realms of the public are far more porous than most academic historians might allow. Once we admit that porousness, we relativize our understanding of the professional historian's influence. If we ask where a society gets its sense of the past, for instance, only delusions of grandeur could induce historians into claiming much of the credit. For most people, knowledge about the past comes very rarely from its professional guardians and then usually at several times removed. Even those of us squarely inside the profession spend much of our time responding most urgently to questions coming from elsewhere, from beyond the safety of the archive, the library, or the seminar room.

Once we probe the provenance of our own motivations with any honesty, as I tried to do at the start of this discussion, the force of these observations comes through. Particularly if we examine the sources for our enthusiasm and the webs of early curiosity—the idiosyncratic mixtures of deliberation, desire, external influences, and pure serendipity that first move most of us into becoming historians—the unschooled or naive quality of our sense of the past ought to become extremely clear. It would be silly to suggest that historical education in the more formal or didactic sense never plays its part, though in most schoolteaching, this works as often to alienate or deter as to influence and inspire. Amid the larger turmoil of our images and assumptions about the past, it's the circulation of everything else that makes this question of the provenance of motivations so hard to sort out.[12]

In what follows, I track some of the most decisive changes in historical studies of the last four decades. Needless to say, this is not a comprehensive or full account. Large numbers of key controversies and agenda-setting debates and whole types of history are left out. Not all my friends and colleagues will find themselves or recognize their interests in the narrative I am about to lay out. But, for good or ill, the narrative describes some main directions of radicalism, intellectual excitement, and theoretical and methodological innovation between the 1960s and now. The story I want to tell opens, at the beginning of that period, with the dramatic new rise of social history, which in its turn was intricately connected to contemporary political events. As I intimated earlier, that convergence of historiographical and political developments also coincided with my own intellectual and political coming-of-age.

When I arrived in Balliol College, Oxford, in October 1967, the historiographical landscape was already in the process—although I little knew it—of being dramatically opened up. It's impossible to be too emphatic about just how inspiring and truly exhilarating the impact of social history turned out to be. In the English-speaking world more generally, this impact had three principal sources. First was the long-gestating influence of the group who became known as the British Marxist historians, together with the broader coalitions of economic historians, labor historians, and social historians they helped to build. Next came the more immediate impact of the social sciences, which began from the late 1950s to challenge the thinking and practice of many historians. Finally came the inspiration offered by the *Annales* school in France, whose key works became more systematically translated during the 1970s. In all three ways, social history aspired, with great and high-minded ambition, to deal with the big questions of how and why societies change or not.

Of course, there are many reasons for wanting to study history. After all, history's pleasures are many-sided. They include the pleasures of discovery and collecting, of exhaustiveness and pursuit, of the exotic and the unfamiliar, of serendipity, and—last but not least—of mastery. History is also a site of difference; in the loose sense of the term, it offers contexts for deconstruction. History is where we go for defamiliarizing our ideas and assumptions; it is our laboratory, where we question the sufficiencies of apparently coherent and unified accounts of the world, and where the ever-seductive unities of contemporary social and political discourse may also be named, de-authorized, and upset.

But for me, neither the pleasures nor the critiques of history can be complete without the seriousness of larger understanding—without the possibility of making the world more knowable in some overall or meaningful sense. Part of that condition is also making the world more changeable, not as a basis for actually changing the world itself necessarily (as these days that seems a little too much to expect), but at least to show how the changeability of the world might be thought or imagined. In that sense, history is about the critical recognition of given fixities, about exploring how the openings and closings of knowledge can occur, about examining the categories through which we understand our relationship to the world, about disturbing familiar assumptions and allowing us to see the unnecessities of closure. It can bring into focus the possible horizons of a different way. In my understanding, history can become both inspiringly and pragmatically prefigurative.

In relation to that larger ambition, there have been two massive waves of innovation since the 1960s, each drawing its momentum from exciting and contentious interdisciplinary conversations. The first of these, extending from the 1960s into the 1980s, involved the discovery of social history. The second wave, cresting during the 1990s, produced the "new cultural history." Both movements shared a relationship to the political debates of their respective times. They bore the desire for a kind of democratic inclusiveness, through which hidden and suppressed histories could be recognized and disempowered groups could enter the profession. While the main emphases differed—new social historians stressed material life, class, and society, while their culturalist successors refocused on meaning and on the forms of perception and understanding that people make and display—each wave brought a radical broadening of the historian's legitimate agenda. Over a thirty-year period, by means of these two movements, the practices, subject matters, and composition of the historical profession became dramatically pluralized.

But the movement out of social history into cultural history was no straightforward progression. It also entailed some losses. It was achieved through bitterly fought controversies over goals, theories, and methods. In embracing the contemporary skepticism about grand narratives, for example, and in substituting microhistories of various kinds for the macrohistories of capitalism, state making, revolution, and large-scale transformations, many historians also came to retreat from the ambitious social analysis and explanation that was so inspiring in the 1970s. In 1971, leading British Marxist historian Eric Hobsbawm published an enormously influential essay called "From Social History to the History of Society," in which he argued that the real point of the new approaches was not so much the recognition of previously "hidden" or marginalized subjects or groups (although that certainly was important) but the opportunities this now created for writing the history of society as a whole.[13] This meant partly a commitment to generalization and theory, to trying to keep the whole picture in view, and partly a particular analytical approach aimed at understanding all problems to some degree in their social context. Of course, in 1971—and certainly for Hobsbawm—that tended to imply that social and economic causes and explanations were primary.

One of my key contentions is that we don't have to reinstate the primacy of social explanation and a materialist model of social determination, or insist on the causal sovereignty of the economy and material life, in order to take seriously the tasks of social significance or social analysis. Now that much of the heat and noise surrounding the new cultural history has started to die down, it's time to reassert the importance of social history in the main sense advocated by Hobsbawm in his 1971 essay, namely, that we need always to keep relating our particular subjects to the bigger picture of society as a whole—whether we are social historians, political historians, cultural historians, or whatever. Hence come the terms of my title, which also seek to reclaim the relevance of Marxist approaches for this goal. I maintain that we can hold on to all of the gains of the new cultural history without having to abandon everything we learned as social historians. As it happens, I was trained personally neither as a social historian nor as a cultural historian, but that has never stopped me from learning how to be both; utilizing either approach is more a matter of general theoretical and analytical standpoint than of which card-carrying professional identity you embrace.

I offer a word of caution: the temporalities of these movements—the successive turnings to social history and to cultural history—were by no means as clear-cut as my scene-setting discussion implies. The high tide of the popularity of the new cultural history from the mid-1980s to the mid-1990s hardly prevented many social historians from doing their work, and many of those who embraced versions of the "cultural turn" also continued practicing what they had previously learned. The speed of the various transitions made an intermingling of approaches almost inevitable. Within only a handful of years, for example, my early excitements at discovering Marxism and other traditions of social theory during the late 1960s and early 1970s were followed by the new challenges of feminism and similar critiques. By the end of the seventies, the default materialism anchoring social history's novel ascendancy was already wavering, and during the 1980s and early 1990s, it gradually crumbled away. Social historians were edged out of the discipline's coveted center ground by "new cultural historians" and the advocates of the so-called linguistic turn. Yet by the turn of the new century, there were already signs that these freshly established culturalisms were themselves starting to fall under review.

Chapters 2, 3, and 4 of this book detail aspects of the changes in historical thinking during the last forty years, proceeding from what I call (with only a little self-irony) the utopia of social history, through a discussion of the latter's limits and disappointments, to the renewed possibilities opened up by the so-called cultural turn. Each of these three chapters closes with an example taken from different areas of historiography, intended both to illustrate the main trajectories of progressive historical writing and to capture my own intellectual passage. Without discussing their work exhaustively or in any complete and rounded sense, my purpose is to use each of three remarkable historians—Edward Thompson, Tim Mason, and Carolyn Steedman—to make an argument about the strengths and failings of social and cultural history. Their works provide snapshots of the best achievements of an ambitious and politically engaged history across the period I'm surveying: Edward Thompson's *The Making of the English Working Class,* published in 1963, remains one of the several genuinely great books of the big social history wave; Tim Mason's pioneering studies of Nazism during the 1970s took the explanatory ambitions of social history to the outer limits of their potential; Carolyn Steedman's *Landscape for a Good Woman,* published in 1987, represented the best edge of the emerging new cultural history. The present book closes, in chapter 5, with some thoughts about the circumstances faced by historians in the present.

II. OPTIMISM

Thinking Like a Marxist

For me, becoming a historian was intricately bound with an exposure to Marxism. At first, this was an extremely messy and piece-meal encounter. As I suspect is common for many of my particular generation, early familiarity with Marxist theory came only haphaz-ardly—not through much of a reading of Marx and Engels themselves, let alone from any systematic education or political socialization, but through various kinds of secondhand or vicarious translation. That meant partly the omnipresent political languages circulating through the student movement of the late 1960s, partly the burgeoning left-wing literatures of the same time, and especially the firsthand practi-cal scenes of my own political activity. Unlike some of my friends, I had no prior connection to Marxist ideas through family or party membership or some earlier intellectual epiphany. Like many children of 1968, I learned initially through doing. I acquired my Marxism on the job, collecting theory on the fly.

My most sustained acquaintance with Marxist theory came in a rather untheoretical manner, through the writings of the grouping now called the British Marxist historians—for example, Eric Hobs-bawm's *Primitive Rebels* and *Labouring Men*, George Rudé's pioneering studies of popular protest in *The Crowd in the French Revolution* and *The Crowd in History*, and (as already mentioned in chapter 1) Edward Thompson's *Making of the English Working Class*.[1] Perhaps the most exciting single new work to appear in this respect while I was a stu-dent was *Captain Swing* by Hobsbawm and Rudé, which reconstructed the agricultural laborers' uprising of 1830 through an inspiring combi-nation of empirical excavation, quantification, empathy, and critical

13

materialist analysis of the development of British capitalism.² My choice of undergraduate college wasn't irrelevant to this acquaintance, for not only was Balliol the active center of the student Left in Oxford, but it was also the college of Christopher Hill, one of the most eminent British Marxist historians. Without directly molding the intellectual culture of the Balliol undergraduate historians, Hill's presence gave a kind of legitimacy and encouragement for the kind of history I slowly realized I wanted to do.³

For the British New Left, however, this British Marxist historiography seemed scarcely on the map.⁴ Student radicalism's main home in Oxford was not history but philosophy, politics, and economics, which held the place sociology occupied in less archaic institutions. The emergent new Marxism flourished in social and political theory, anthropology, philosophy and aesthetics, literature and film, psychiatry and social work—anywhere, it seemed, but the corridors and seminar rooms of history departments. The emblematic handbooks for student radicals published by the mass paperback houses Penguin and Fontana between 1969 and 1972—*Student Power* (1969), *Counter Course* (1972), and *Ideology in Social Science* (1972)—treated history manifestly as a poor relation.⁵ The benchmark critique of established historiography by Gareth Stedman Jones, "The Pathology of British History" (later reprinted as "History: The Poverty of Empiricism" in *Ideology in Social Science*), held little place for the contributions of the older generation of Marxists, whose theoretical understanding seemed far too passé. The locus classicus for such disdain was Perry Anderson's brilliant indictment of English intellectual formations in "Components of the National Culture," originally published in the summer of 1968. Finding no indigenous basis for a viable social theory on the continental European pattern, Anderson saw history as one of the primary sites of that deficit. The British Marxist historians were not mentioned.⁶

My attention to Marxism during the late 1960s was initially not much more than a belief in the efficacy of "social and economic factors." If pressed, I'd have invoked a series of axioms to explain what I thought this meant—for example, the determining effects of material forces on the limits and potentials for human action or the linking of the possibilities of political change to what happens in the social structure and the underlying movements of the economy. If the goal was the analysis of whole societies and their forms of development or an understanding of what made them work, pass into crisis, and occasionally break down, this robust conception of the sovereignty of the economy and its associated class relations seemed a very good place to start. For these purposes, Marx's famous 1859 preface to *A Contribution to the Critique of Political Economy* was the touchstone: "The mode of production of material life conditions the general process of social, political, and intellectual life. It is not the consciousness of men that determines their existence, but their social existence that determines their consciousness." Equally well known is Friedrich Engels's statement "According to the materialist conception of history, the ultimately determining element in history is the production and reproduction of real life."[7]

Of course, writing history as a Marxist involved much more than this. In the grand Marxist scheme of things, human society advanced from lower to higher stages of development, demonstrating ever-greater complexity in the forms of organization of economic life and in securing the key transitions—between feudalism and capitalism and thence to socialism—through the upheaval of a social revolution. Moreover, the main motor of change was class conflict. Under capitalism, Marxists viewed such conflict as necessary and systemic, a permanent and irreducible feature of social life, deriving from the unavoidable antagonisms of mutually incompatible, collectively organized class interests centered around production. In a capitalist society, the core social relationship was defined by the wage, making the working class the most numerous social grouping and the indispensable agency for any movement seeking progressive political change. The workers' collective mobilization relayed to the political system pressures that created the openings for reform and even, in the most extreme crises, for revolution.

Under the circumstances of the late 1960s, for a young left-wing historian frustrated by the fact-grubbing theory-averseness of so much of the academic discipline, the Marxist approach seemed very attractive. Energized by the politics of the time—not just by the extraordinary ferment of ideas surrounding the explosions of 1968, but also by the remarkable wave of labor militancy sweeping Europe in the years that followed—I warmed to a body of theory capable of locating these events on a larger historical map. Marxism's objectivist aura—its claim to be a science of society—was also appealing. Furthermore, during the 1960s, the Marxist tradition had itself become the scene of

exciting debates, critiques, and innovations. Whether in international, party, or theoretical terms, Marxism was diversifying and
renewing itself. Its dogmatic retrenchment behind the arid and
churchlike orthodoxies of the Stalinist era was coming to an end. For
anyone seeking to fashion a general understanding of how societies
hold together or change, it offered a powerful combination of standpoints—a theory of societal development permitting the periodizing
of history, a model of social determinations proceeding upward from
material life, and a theory of social change based on class struggles and
their effects.[8]

With all hindsight, I can now recognize the second of these features—the foundational materialism—as especially arresting. Marxists classically reserved a first-order priority—ontologically, epistemologically, analytically—for the underlying economic structure of
society in conditioning everything else, including the possible forms of
politics and the law, of institutional development, and of social consciousness and belief. The commonest expression for this determining
relationship was the architectural language of "base and superstructure," in which the spatial metaphor of ascending and sequential levels
also implied the end point in a logical chain of reasoning. This
metaphor could be very flexibly understood, leaving room for much
unevenness and autonomy, including the discrete effectivity of the
superstructure and its reciprocal action on the base, especially for the
purposes of any detailed political, ideological, or aesthetic analysis.
But ultimately, such analyses still rendered account to the "final-
instance" social determinations emanating from the economy and the
social structure.

Amid all the other excitements and challenges I experienced while
learning to think like a Marxist, this metaphorical expression was the
recurring key. Yet here was a fascinating paradox. Marxism's fundamental materialist commitment to the primacy of social determinations formed both my most stable intellectual starting point—defined
by an almost bedrock certainty—and the place where all the most creative disagreements among Marxists could now be found. Inside the
hitherto closed worlds of Marxist theory, in fact, the 1960s opened a
time of rampant heterodoxy, as virtually all the most influential Marxist thinkers began grappling with precisely those questions of ideology, consciousness, and subjectivity that the tradition had previously
approached all too reductively, through an interest-based analysis cen-

tered around class. This was true whether the theorists concerned were inside the Communist parties themselves or around the edges of the various socialist parties, whether they moved in the intellectual netherworld of the burgeoning sects and groupuscules or lacked organized affiliations altogether. In other words, even as the power of Marxism's materialist analytic started to ground my understanding of politics, all the most exciting discussions among Marxists seemed preoccupied with the difficulties of making that classical materialism of base and superstructure work.[9]

In other words, Marxist ideas were finally breaking out of the self-referential isolation of the Cold War, a process hugely assisted by the great expansion of higher education in the 1960s and the associated boom in left-wing publishing. The student movements and wider political mobilizations of the time played the obvious role in helping this to happen, but two other kinds of impetus can be mentioned. One came from the increasingly systematic translation of continental European theory, both classical and contemporary, which encouraged a new internationalizing of Britain's isolated and parochial intellectual culture. For the first time, not just the Marxist canon but also the writings of Max Weber, Émile Durkheim, and other classic social theorists became more widely available in the English-speaking world, not just via translations and cheap mass-produced editions, but, more important, via critical commentaries and integration into undergraduate and graduate curricula. Likewise, there was suddenly increased access to a wide range of contemporary German, French, Italian, and Eastern European philosophy, aesthetic theory, sociology, and political theory.[10]

Equally important for me was a kind of broad-gauged cultural dissidence extending across large areas of British intellectual life and the arts, including cinema, popular music, literature, poetry, theater, and television. The directly politicized version of this history is rightly associated with one strand of the rise of the British New Left during the later 1950s. Its focus on aspects of youth culture, the consequences of postwar affluence, and the changing terms of social self-identification fed eventually, by the 1970s, into the invention of the new interdisciplinary field of cultural studies. In this sense, the left-wing intellectual radicalism surrounding 1968 fed as much off the transgressive rebelliousness within popular culture as off the freshly accessible French, German, and Italian theory. The resulting confluence was "a mixture of high French intellectual culture and low American popular culture," in which the latter was "epitomized by Hollywood cinema, preferably B movies, also of course American popular music—jazz and particularly rock 'n' roll."[11] The boundary-pushing experimentalism of much television drama, satire, arts programming, and social commentary during the 1960s was another part of this story. The plays of David Mercer, Harold Pinter, Ken Loach, and Dennis Potter exposed and denounced the injuries and injustices of class long before I'd read a word of Marx.[12]

Both movements of change—the often esoteric theoretical writings of continental European Marxists and the cultural criticism of the British New Left—converged on problems of ideology. Older Marxisms from the interwar years were either revisited or freshly discovered from this point of view—for example, in writings by Georg Lukács, Karl Korsch, the Frankfurt school, Walter Benjamin, and Antonio Gramsci—while such contemporary writers as Jean-Paul Sartre, Lucien Goldmann, and Louis Althusser were now extensively translated and addressed. In the process, as Perry Anderson argued in his anatomy of this distinctively "Western Marxism," the accent shifted from political economy to philosophy, culture, and aesthetics, thereby allowing a far more extensive engagement than before with questions of subjectivity (or "consciousness," as the language of the time preferred).[13] A powerful current of socialist humanism, inspired by readings of Marx's early philosophical writings of the 1840s emphasizing concepts of "freedom" and "alienation," further reinforced this trend. Bitterly fought disagreements about these readings—especially concerning the so-called epistemological break that may or may not have separated the "young" from the "old" Marx—were soon to divide Western Marxists into mutually hostile camps. But for a while, the concurrence was far greater than this impending divisiveness.[14]

These extremely abstract discussions of freedom and alienation within Marxist theory helped empower more practical efforts at concretely grounding an understanding of politics in the complexities of personal experience and everyday life. This is where the various "culturalisms" of the first British New Left had their important effects. Some of the New Left's driving political urgencies were more readily assimilable to the established Marxist frameworks—for example, the doubled critiques of Communism and social democracy arising from the 1950s, the analysis of the new forms of capitalist prosperity and the consumer economy, or the search for an antinuclear internationalism beyond the twin camps of the Cold War.[15] But that advocacy was also motivated by a set of concerns that resisted the given forms of class-based analysis. As Stuart Hall has explained, such discussions were calling the boundaries of politics themselves into question.

> We raised issues of personal life, the way people live, culture, which weren't considered the topics of politics on the Left. We wanted to talk about the contradictions of this new kind of capitalist society in which people didn't have a language to express their private troubles, didn't realize that these troubles reflected political and social questions which could be generalized.[16]

One figure who exceptionally united both sets of concerns, the philosophical renewal of Marxist thought with a cultural critique of life in the late capitalist present, was Raymond Williams. A specialist in modern drama, employed in the discipline of English, Williams was best known for his general works *Culture and Society, 1780–1950* and its companion volume, *The Long Revolution,* published in 1950 and 1961. In these books, he developed an avowedly "oppositional" account of the impact of the Industrial Revolution on British society, by using a history of the idea of culture. He showed with great subtlety how elitist fears for the defense of civilized values against the vulgarizing consequences of industrialism and democracy had always been disputed by more generous conceptions of culture as a faculty of the whole people. Combining close readings of the canonical English writers and social commentators with pioneering social histories of education, the reading public, the press, and other cultural institutions, he proposed an amplified and extended understanding of culture. This encompassed not only a society's formal values and highest artistic achievements ("the best which has been thought and said") but also the generalized commonalties of its "whole way of life" and the associated "structures of feeling."[17]

Williams moved amphibiously between the domains of high theory and popular culture. For my own part in the late 1960s, he epitomized everything that inspired me to become a historian but that had absolutely nothing to do with the influence of professional historians or with the authorized rules and practices of history as an already formed discipline.[18] It's worth saying something more extensively about this place Raymond Williams made for himself beyond the conventional boundaries of academic life (that is, outside the given institutional patterns of the disciplinary organization of knowledge in the universities), because the type of interdisciplinarity—or, perhaps better, "adisciplinarity"—he represented was another key ingredient of the intellectual conjuncture I'm trying to describe for the late 1960s and early 1970s.

In Williams's case, this included a biographical dimension that I also found appealing. As the son of a railwayman and trade unionist on the South Wales borders, he stood out among the 1930s generations of student Marxists by his working-class pedigree. He went directly from the university into the army during World War II; then, after resuming and completing his studies, he went straight into adult education, where he taught from 1946 to 1961. His journey through grammar school and Cambridge University as a "scholarship boy" prefigured one of the primary sociocultural narratives defining the promises of prosperity in postwar Britain, which joined working-class provincial origins to professional middle-class destinations in a bargain of assimilation and upward mobility. For Williams, negotiating this "border country" (to use the title of his first novel) was made still more complex by the extra dualisms of Wales versus England and Oxbridge university establishment versus adult education. He was part of the last generation of left-wing male intellectuals in Britain before the almost total professionalizing of higher education initiated by the big university expansion of the 1960s. In common with such historian contemporaries as Edward Thompson, Thomas Hodgkin, Henry Collins, Royden Harrison, and J. F. C. Harrison, who helped shape the emergence of social history (and most of whom were Communists for portions of the era between the 1930s and 1950s), he spent the first half of his career in adult education, on the fringes of the academic world proper, only receiving his first university appointment, at Cambridge, in 1961.[19]

During his earlier career, Williams developed a complex and hesitant relationship to Marxism. He was formed politically in three successive conjunctures—first, the period of Popular Front and antifascist campaigning closed by the international crises of 1947–48; next, the Cold War years, which, for Williams, were a time of political isolation and distance from the recognized contexts of Marxism; and finally, the heyday of the first New Left, extending from the crisis of

Communism in 1953–57, the Suez debacle of 1956, and the rise of the
Campaign for Nuclear Disarmament in the late 1950s to the explosion
of the student movement around 1968. With the appearance of *Culture and Society* and *The Long Revolution,* which made him into an
acknowledged standard-bearer of the New Left, Williams took up a
singular place in British intellectual life: a now fully credentialed academic, speaking from the central institutional spaces of the dominant
culture (including Cambridge University, the Arts Council, and the
British Broadcasting Corporation), he was yet an "unassimilated
socialist" in an "infinitely assimilative culture," who was simultaneously independent of the existing socialist parties, whether the Labour
Party or the Communist Party. This entailed an angular and uncomfortable stance. In Edward Thompson's words, it required "put[ting]
oneself into a school of awkwardness . . . [making] one's sensibility all
knobbly—all knees and elbows of susceptibility and refusal."[20]

The doubled nature of Williams's intellectual persona was crucial
for my generation's sense of our own possibility. On one front, in a
sustained critique that ran through the center of *Culture and Society,*
Williams challenged the legitimacy of the dominant culture's
entrenched description of itself—in the lineage of Matthew Arnold,
T. S. Eliot, and F. R. Leavis—as "the great tradition." Against that
"official" discourse of cultural value, which privileged the calling of an
austere and embattled minority of the high-minded in preserving the
authentic goods of life against the corrupting and destructive effects of
"commercial" or "mass" society, Williams countered with a democratic conception of a society's common pursuits, of culture's "ordinariness" in that sense. But on the other front, Williams rejected the available forms of a Marxist alternative during the 1950s, deformed as they
were by the consequences of Stalinism and the Cold War. He rejected
both the political culture of "manipulation and centralism" he'd come
to associate with the "style of work" of the Communist Party and the
economistic patterns of thinking characteristic of orthodox Marxism.

> As for Marx, one accepted the emphasis on history, on change,
> on the inevitably close relationship between class and culture,
> but the way this came through was, at another level, unaccept-
> able. There was, in this position, a polarization and abstraction
> of economic life on the one hand and culture on the other, which
> did not seem to me to correspond to the social experience of

culture as others had lived it, and as one was trying to live it one-self.[21]

This ambivalence notwithstanding, during the 1960s, Williams entered into continuous conversation with the full range of European theoretical Marxisms and produced in the process a diverse and original body of writing on the relationship between social history and cultural forms, whose standpoint he named "cultural materialism." His 1973 essay "Base and Superstructure in Marxist Cultural Theory," whose argument became hardwired into the 1977 book *Marxism and Literature,* was especially influential here.[22] Breaking decisively with older deterministic and functionalist readings of culture's relationship to the economy and its social interests, Williams developed an argument about culture's own materiality. Rather than seeing culture as separated from material life, simultaneously tethered by social determinations yet moving above them, he stressed the very practical and concrete ways in which culture was always lodged inside social relations and forms of material practice.

By "cultural materialism," Williams meant not only the precise social and institutional conditions and relations through which cultural meanings were themselves produced, but the constitutive presence of cultural processes for all other practices of a society, including not only politics and social interactions but also the complex operations of the economy. In that sense, according to Williams, the architectural metaphor of base and superstructure, with its imagery of the clear and physical separation of levels as well as its implications of logical priority, was actively misleading. However necessary it may be to separate cultural meanings from their social contexts for the purposes of abstraction, they can only ever be encountered together, fused and embedded in what Williams called "specific and indissoluble real processes."[23] Language, meanings, and signification should all be seen as "indissoluble elements of the material social process itself, involved all the time both in production and reproduction." In that case, culture's relation to other things—work, market transactions, social interests, practical activities, and so forth—is always already embedded. That relationship can only be theorized, by means of "the complex idea of determination," as the exertion of pressures and the setting of limits, in processes that run actively in both directions.[24]

The argument is getting ahead of me a little here: my own tentative reconnoitering of Marxism in the late 1960s hardly betrayed much inkling of the problems Raymond Williams was trying to attack. Yet looking back, I'm fascinated by how rapidly the climate of awareness seems to have moved. A key milestone, both for myself and for the broader discussions, was the publication, in the spring of 1971, of the first substantial translations from Antonio Gramsci's *Prison Notebooks,* which gave vital impetus for Williams's project of opening Marxism for more complex forms of cultural analysis—for "culturalizing" it, one might say.[25] This occurred during my first year in graduate school at the University of Sussex, by which time I was seriously reading Marx and Engels, properly discovering the Western Marxists, and subscribing to *New Left Review.*

In other words, even as I acquired my classical Marxist outlook, the most important Marxist discussions were already escaping from the old understandings grounded in the metaphor of base and superstructure. I choose Raymond Williams to exemplify this escape, partly because he addressed the problem through a body of original and creative historical work, partly because the latter converged importantly with the oeuvres of the British Marxist historians mentioned earlier. As the followers and sympathetic critics of that grouping came to appreciate, its underlying materialist credo had proved no impediment to producing social and cultural histories of great subtlety. Christopher Hill's work, in particular, centered on the intricacies of the relations among political conflict, popular piety, and social order in the seventeenth-century English Revolution, focusing on theological debate, literary history, and rival programs of spirituality rather than on sociologies of class interest per se, while moving ever further from the moorings of any straightforwardly "social interpretation."[26] It was no accident that Hill had reviewed an earlier selection of Gramsci's writings, published in 1957 as *The Modern Prince,* or that Eric Hobsbawm was an early English-language commentator on Gramsci's thought. For many years, the main guide to Gramsci's idea of "hegemony" in English was another British Marxist historian, Gwyn Williams, who had published a much-cited article on the subject in 1960.[27]

Interest in Gramsci's heterodox writings proved the hidden catalyst for much of the emergent social history at the turn of the 1970s. It was clearly behind Robbie Gray's contribution entitled "History" in the *Counter Course* volume, for example, even if that influence occurred mainly off the page.[28] Taking the older Marxist historians as a practical model, while learning from the new debates, my generation of left-inclined historians initially dealt with theory in an eclectic and embedded way. Yet we rarely escaped theory's reminders; they were in the air we breathed. I can think of two further examples. The first was a volume I stumbled on by accident in Blackwell's one afternoon in 1969, called *Towards a New Past,* edited by Barton Bernstein. It contained the essay "Marxian Interpretations of the Slave South," by Eugene Genovese, whose writings on the history of slavery I'd begun reading in the *New York Review of Books* around the same time. His call for "a break with naïve determinism, economic interpretation, and the insipid glorification of the lower classes," in the name of a more complex understanding of culture and ideology, was perhaps my first serious encounter with Gramsci's ideas, an interest I could then pursue through another of Genovese's essays, "On Antonio Gramsci," published in 1967.[29] The second example was a critique of radical historiography in the United States, published by Aileen Kraditor in *Past and Present;* it took a similar Gramscian standpoint.[30]

If Raymond Williams anticipated many of these theoretical departures, he also offered what was for the time a quite rare example of interdisciplinary practice. In this capacity, he was largely self-taught, lacking, through most of the 1950s, either the academic or the political contexts of collaboration that might have provided collective or institutional supports. Any historians of that time who were interested in giving their studies greater theoretical or contextual breadth faced the same problem. This situation was to change a little with the mid-1960s, when some of the new universities included interdisciplinarity in their pedagogical and curricular design.[31] Otherwise, historians looking for contact with sociologists, anthropologists, or literary scholars were generally on their own. Where not actively hostile, the bulk of the historical profession took a dim view of such ambitions.[32] For those of us trying in the late 1960s to become self-conscious about how we approached our work, whether by interrogating and refining our particular conceptual tools or by devising an overarching theoretical framework, the best help always came from the outside.

During my years as a student in Oxford, it was completely clear to me that history was insufficient by itself, that it needed "theory," and that other disciplines had to be enlisted for this purpose. In the context of the time (when claims for history's social and political relevance were invoked so irresistibly in materialist terms), this meant turning principally to sociology and political science, less frequently to anthropology, but at all events to the general repertoire of critical social science. There was a catholic quality to this commitment. For example, among my undergraduate contemporaries in philosophy, politics, and economics, Claude Lévi-Strauss and other French structuralists attracted a lot of interest; and the presence in Balliol of Steven Lukes ensured that traditions of thought descending from Durkheim were taken extremely seriously.[33] But there were no doubts about the main orientations: turning to theory meant, above all, turning to the great source of interdisciplinarity (or, more accurately, the great incitement to cross-disciplinary or, perhaps, pan-disciplinary knowledge)—namely, Marxism.

Three Sources of Social History

In 1971, Eric Hobsbawm ended a famous essay on the state of the discipline by saying it was "a good moment to be a social historian."[34] That was certainly my own feeling when embarking on graduate work in October 1970. The very scale of the developing activity was impressive—with new journals launched, standing conferences and subdisciplinary societies founded, curricula redesigned, special chairs established, and ever greater numbers of dissertations under way. Social history had certainly existed before. But the ambition was now enlarged. To call oneself a social historian in Britain no longer automatically spelled an interest in trade unions or the poor law or meant that one would be shunted off into obscure sidings of economic history departments or excluded from the main thoroughfares of the profession. Despite the persisting conventions of middle-brow coffee-table publications and a continuing genre of popular history, the term *social history* no longer necessarily implied the colorful and nostalgic evocation of "manners and morals," as the editors of the *Times Literary Supplement* still wanted to see it. During the coming decade, in fact, social history would fast outgrow its earlier subaltern status inside the historical profession itself. Indeed, there were few areas of the discipline to which the coming generations of social historians would neglect to lay claim.[35]

The most interesting feature of social history as it emerged into the

1970s, flagged in the title of Hobsbawm's essay ("From Social History to the History of Society"), was its new generalizing or totalizing potential. In the past, the term *social history* might easily have implied indifference to a society's political institutions or the business of government and the character of the state. Its sectional attentiveness to the "social" as a subspecialism of the discipline had not implied any necessary commitment to generalizing about society as a whole. Until recently, the category of the social historian had implied something specialized and narrow, even antiquarian. Thus, it became something of a novel departure when some social historians started claiming the totalizing possibilities as the specific virtue of their field. They began declaring an interest in particular practices (such as trade unionism or poor relief) less for their own sake than for their bearing on the character of the social formation at large. They talked increasingly of "structures" and "social relations." They now tried to situate all facets of human existence in the aggrandizingly materialist contexts of their social determinations. As the first editorial of the new journal *Social History* maintained, they wanted to "be as much concerned with questions of culture and consciousness as with those of social structure and the material conditions of life."[36] But there was little hesitancy about where the main lines of explanation began.

As I suggested in chapter 1, there were three significant influences on the growth of social history in the English-speaking world: the British Marxist historians, the *Annales* school in France, and post-1945 U.S. and British social science. All three converged on a materialist model of causality that might also be called "structuralist." Its terms implied a master concept of "society" based on the sovereignty of social explanation, in which the lines of determination ran predominantly upward and outward from the economy and its social relations to everything else. It also implied an integrated or holistic account of the social totality. All three approaches believed actively in cross-disciplinary fertilization. Each was certainly borne by a politics.

The British Marxist Historians

For me, the foremost of these three influences was the first. Considered from a vantage point inside the 1960s themselves, the British Marxists were not at all as cohesive or separated a group as the subsequent commentary can easily imply. As individuals, they were centrally connected to the various wider networks whose coming together had gradually solidified the basis for social history's emergence—above all, around the journal *Past and Present* and in the Society for the Study of Labour History (launched in 1952 and 1960, respectively), but also in the growth of new specialisms (such as the Urban History Group, formed in 1963), the founding of separate economic and social history departments at a number of universities, the progressive social science connections running through the London School of Economics, and so forth. Moreover, other individuals without the same Marxist affiliations—most notably, Asa Briggs—were equally important for social history's origins in the 1950s.[37] Nonetheless, drawing on the shared outlook they acquired from the Communist Party Historians' Group between 1946 and its disbandment in 1956–57, the Marxists exercised definite and disproportionate influence on the forms social history acquired in the course of its emergence.

Among others, the Historians' Group included Christopher Hill (1910–2003), George Rudé (1910–93), Victor Kiernan (born 1913), Rodney Hilton (1916–2002), John Saville (born 1916), Eric Hobsbawm (born 1917), Dorothy Thompson (born 1923), Edward Thompson (1924–93), Royden Harrison (1927–2002), and the much younger Raphael Samuel (1938–96).[38] Not many from the group taught at the center of British university life in Oxbridge or London. Some were not historians by discipline: for example, a book by the older Cambridge economist Maurice Dobb (1900–1976), *Studies in the Development of Capitalism* (1946), had focused a large part of the group's initial discussions. Others in the group held positions in adult education: Rudé and Thompson, for example, secured academic appointments only in the 1960s—Rudé by traveling to Australia to do so. The main impulse of the group came from politics, a powerful sense of history's pedagogy, and broader identification with democratic values and popular history. A leading mentor was the nonacademic Communist intellectual, journalist, and Marx scholar Dona Torr (1883–1957), to whom the group paid tribute with a now-classic volume called *Democracy and the Labour Movement,* published in 1954.[39]

Some of these scholars displayed extraordinary international range. This is well known of Eric Hobsbawm. His interests embraced British labor history, European popular movements, Latin American peasantries, and jazz, while also recurring to the study of nationalism, capitalism's successive transformations as a global system, the relationship of intellectuals to popular movements, the history of Marxism, and other grand themes. He became best known, perhaps, for his series of unparalleled general histories, which covered the modern era from the late eighteenth century to the present in four superb volumes.[40] Among his comrades, Victor Kiernan was also a true polymath, publishing widely on aspects of imperialism, early modern state formation, and the history of the aristocratic duel, as well as British relations with China and the Spanish Revolution of 1854, with an imposing wider bibliography of essays on an extraordinary range of subjects.[41] George Rudé was a leading historian of the French Revolution and popular protest.[42] Two other members of the group worked almost exclusively on British topics but enjoyed massive international resonance over the longer term—Raphael Samuel as the moving genius behind the History Workshop movement and its journal, Edward Thompson through his great works *The Making of the English Working Class* (1963), *Whigs and Hunters* (1975), and *Customs in Common,* the last of which incorporated agenda-setting essays and lectures originally written in the 1960s and 1970s.[43]

But this British Marxist historiography was also embedded in some very British concerns. Inspired by A. L. Morton's *People's History of England,* which had been published in 1938 at the height of Popular Front campaigning, the group's early goal was to produce a social history of Britain capable of contesting the pedagogical, cultural, and general ideological dominance of established or official accounts.[44] While this ambition was never realized as such, the oeuvres of the various individuals nonetheless came to aggregate by the end of the 1960s into an impressive collective contribution of exactly that kind—including, notably, Rodney Hilton on the English peasantry of the Middle Ages, Christopher Hill on the seventeenth-century English Revolution, John Saville on industrialization and labor history, Dorothy Thompson on Chartism, and, of course, Edward Thompson and Eric Hobsbawm on the general course of popular history in the nineteenth and twentieth centuries.[45]

In that sense, the legacy of the Historians' Group was intensely focused on national themes. For younger historians placing themselves on the British left in the later 1960s, this was most famously true of Edward Thompson's vigorous general essay "The Peculiarities of the English," published in 1965 as a counterblast against a general interpretation of British history advanced by two Marxists of the "second" New Left, Tom Nairn and Perry Anderson.[46] Thompson's writing in the aftermath of leaving the Communist Party had also converged with the cognate works of Raymond Williams (discussed earlier in this chapter), whose *Culture and Society* and *The Long Revolution* proposed their own general interpretation of modern British history. Both Thompson and Williams were seeking to recuperate the national past in self-consciously oppositional and democratic fashion, wresting control of the national story from conservative opinion makers of all kinds and rewriting it around the struggles of ordinary people in a still unfinished democratic project.

During the 1950s, these British concerns were centered most strongly on two areas. On the one hand, the Historians' Group decisively shaped the emergent phase of labor history, most obviously through Hobsbawm's foundational essays collected in 1964 in *Labouring Men,* but also via the influence of John Saville and Royden Harrison and in the collective setting established by the founding of the Labour History Society in 1960.[47] This rapidly burgeoning context of new scholarship became broadly organized around a chronology of specific questions about the presumed failure of the labor movement to realize the trajectory of radicalization projected by Marx's developmental model, laying out for labor historians and social historians an enduring problematic that dominated well into the 1980s.

Connected with this, on the other hand, the Historians' Group also shaped the historiography of capitalist industrialization in Britain, most notably through the standard of living controversy between Hobsbawm and Max Hartwell during 1957–63, over whether industrialism had improved or degraded the living standards of the working population.[48] Saville's first book on the social destruction wrought by the capitalist transformation of British agriculture provided a Marxist counterpoint to the depoliticized mainstream accounts of "landed society" offered by G. E. Mingay and F. M. L. Thompson, a project further continued by Hobsbawm and Rudé in their study of the 1830 agricultural laborer's uprising.[49] Both Edward Thompson's *Making of the English Working Class* and Hobsbawm's general British economic history, *Industry and Empire,* powerfully addressed the general question. At the same time, neither of these momentous contributions (to labor history and to the critique of capitalist industrialization) was thinkable without the prior labors of the earlier twentieth-century pioneers of social history in Britain—namely, the Webbs, G. D. H. Cole, R. H. Tawney, and the Hammonds.[50]

But the vision of these Marxist historians was the opposite of parochial. While doing his pathbreaking research during the 1950s in Paris, Rudé had worked with the grand old man of the history of the French Revolution, Georges Lefebvre, and his future successor Albert Soboul. Kiernan practiced an eclectic version of global history long before "world history" became a recognized part of the profession's organization and teaching. Hobsbawm enjoyed incomparably diverse connections across Europe and Latin America. Another Communist, Thomas Hodgkin (1910–82), not a member of the Historians' Group, vitally influenced African history in its nascent years, again from the margins of the profession, in adult education.[51] Hobsbawm's work developed in dialogue with colleagues in France—not only with the Marxist-aligned Lefebvre, Soboul, and Ernest Labrousse, but also with Fernand Braudel and his colleagues of the *Annales* school.

On an international scale, Hobsbawm and Rudé transformed the study of popular protest in preindustrial societies. Rudé meticulously deconstructed older stereotypes of "the mob," using the French Revolution and eighteenth-century riots in England and France to analyze the rhythms, organization, and motives behind collective action. In the process, he laid down a pioneering sociology of the "faces in the crowd." Hobsbawm analyzed the transformations in popular consciousness accompanying capitalist industrialization—in studies of Luddism and pretrade union labor protest; in his excitingly original commentaries on social banditry, millenarianism, and mafia; and in essays on peasants and peasant movements in Latin America. He pioneered an extraordinarily fertile and long-running conversation between history and anthropology. He helped redefine how politics might be thought about in societies that lacked democratic constitutions, the rule of law, or a developed parliamentary system.[52]

The biggest step undertaken by the Historians' Group—the step that ultimately had the widest professional resonance—was the development of a new historical journal, *Past and Present,* launched in 1952. Subtitled symptomatically *Journal of Scientific History,* it was an extremely self-conscious effort at preserving dialogue with non-Marxist historians at a time when the Cold War was rapidly closing such contacts down. The original editor and instigator of the initiative was John Morris (1913–77), a historian of ancient Britain, who was joined by Hobsbawm, Hill, Hilton, Dobb, and the archaeologist Vere Gordon Childe (1892–1957), all Marxists, together with a group of highly distinguished non-Marxists, including the ancient historian Hugo Jones (1904–70), the Czech historian R. R. Betts (died 1961), the Tudor-Stuart historian David B. Quinn (born 1909), and the complete generalist Geoffrey Barraclough (1908–84).

From the start, contacts with Europe were crucial for the outlook and success of the new journal. Connection with Eastern Europe brought articles from the Soviet historians Boris Porshnev and E. A. Kosminskii and from J. V. Polisensky and Arnost Klima in Czechoslovakia. The French connection brought articles not only from Lefebvre and Soboul but also from historians associated with the journal *Annales.* Six years later, in 1958, the journal's editorial board was broadened to dilute the original Marxist dominance, taking in the early modernists Lawrence Stone (1919–99) and John Elliott (born 1930), the medievalist Trevor Aston (1925–86), the archaeologist S. S. Frere (born 1918), and the sociologists Norman Birnbaum and Peter Worsley (born 1924). With this extremely important reconfiguration, the subtitle now changed to *Journal of Historical Studies* [53]

In the guiding vision brought by the Marxist historians to the intellectual project of *Past and Present,* the term *social history* referred to the attempt to understand the dynamics of whole societies. The ambition was to connect political events to underlying social forces. During 1947–50, the Historians' Group had focused on the transition from feudalism to capitalism and on a complex of associated questions—the rise of absolutism, the nature of bourgeois revolutions, agrarian dimensions of the rise of capitalism, and the social dynamics of the Reformation. Hobsbawm's 1954 two-part article "The General Crisis of the Seventeenth Century" prompted *the* salient discussion of *Past and Present*'s first decade, the various contributions to which were subsequently collected, under Trevor Aston's editorship, in the 1965 volume *Crisis in Europe, 1560–1660.* [54]

The debate energized historians of France, Spain, Sweden, Germany, Bohemia, Russia, Ireland, and the early modern era more generally, as well as historians of Britain. It connected the seventeenth-century political upheavals to forms of economic crisis graspable in pan-European terms, in what Aston called "the last phase of the general transition from a feudal to a capitalist economy." [55] It built a case for studying religious conflict in social terms, a more general project that also carried through a number of other early debates in the journal, including especially that on science and religion. It grasped the nettle of trying to conceptualize the histories of societies as a whole, with profound implications for how later historians were able to think about these various problems—best exemplified perhaps in the long-lasting resonance of J. H. Elliott's far-reaching contribution "The Decline of Spain." The debate reemphasized the convergence between *Past and Present* and *Annales*, because Hobsbawm's initial intervention had relied extensively on scholarly work sponsored under Fernand Braudel. Above all, the debate featured the exciting and constructive possibilities of the "comparative method."[56]

It's impossible to exaggerate the enduring contributions to the rise of social history made by *Past and Present* during its early years. While the journal was directly sustained by the particular Marxist formation grounded in the Historians' Group, the outlook of its editorial board translated into a series of commitments that shaped the most ambitious historical discussions in the discipline at large well into the 1970s. First, the journal was committed to internationalism. It brought new and exciting access to European work into the English-speaking world, aided by the editors' political networks and the direct exchanges with France and Eastern Europe, while building on the impetus provided by the 1950 International Historical Congress in Paris and its newly created Social History Section.

Second, Hobsbawm and his comrades urged the comparative study of societies within an overall framework of arguments about historical change, posed explicitly at the level of European or global movements and systems. This commitment grew directly from the classical Marxist perspectives learned during the 1930s and 1940s, crystallized from the working agenda of the Historians' Group, and recurred in the annual *Past and Present* conference themes from 1957. Some of those themes are reflected in the titles "Seventeenth-Century Revolutions," "The Origins of the Industrial Revolution," "Cities, Courts, and Artists (Fifteenth to Nineteenth Centuries)," "War and Society, 1300–1600," "Colonialism and Nationalism in Africa and Europe," "History, Sociology, and Social Anthropology," and "Work and Leisure in Pre-Industrial Society." *Past and Present* assembled an inventory of many of the most exciting areas of research and debate defining the attractions of the discipline for aspiring historians of my generation by the end of the 1960s.

Third, encouraged by the axiomatic Marxist recognition of the indivisibility of knowledge, *Past and Present* pioneered interdisciplinary collaborations with sociologists and anthropologists. While at one level simply a new form of the intellectual Popular Frontism of the journal's founding impulse, this dialogue with non-Marxist social scientists notably accelerated after 1956–57, when, with the exception of Hobsbawm, most of the Marxist historians left the Communist Party. Such discussions offered an alternative source of ideas and approaches, given the newly perceived incompleteness of a partially deauthorized Marxism. The model of open-minded materialism in this respect, grounded in a self-consciously cross-disciplinary synthesis of "historical sociology," was embodied by twenty-four-year-old Philip Abrams (1933–81), who joined Hobsbawm as an assistant editor in 1957. Educated during the 1950s in the intellectual-political universe of the first British New Left, rather than the Popular Front Communism of the 1930s, Abrams brought a very different generational formation to the journal, one shaped far more by the critical sociologies of postwar Britain.[57] In comparison, Peter Worsley, who displayed the most free-ranging and eclectic of cross disciplinary dispositions and whose historical sensibility accompanied a training in anthropology, field research in the Pacific and Southeast Asia, and a university appointment in sociology, had been in the Communist Party until 1956, formative years that continued to mold his many varied publications.[58]

Fourth, for the Marxist architects of *Past and Present,* social history went together with economics—whether via the master category of structures taken from the *Annales* school in France or via Marxism and the materialist conception of history. Within history as an academic discipline, where social history became disengaged from the "manners and morals" mode of popularizing or from projects of "people's history," it invariably became coupled with economic history, as in the new departments of economic and social history created in some British universities during the 1960s.

Finally, the Marxist historians' commitment to dialogue and debate—to bringing Marxist approaches not only into the center of discussions among historians in Britain but also into much broader intellectual circulation, as an essential bridge for both international exchange and generous cross-disciplinary explorations—profoundly enriched the intellectual culture of the discipline just at the point of the great expansion of higher education in the 1960s, which produced such a notable leap forward in the volume, range, and sophistication of scholarly historical research. In that sense, the conditions of takeoff for the late twentieth-century growth of historical studies were not simply assembled by the creation of national research bodies, the founding of new universities, and the growth of funding for research. Those conditions were also to be found in the hard and imaginative labors of the group involved with *Past and Present* and in the politics of knowledge they pursued.

The Annales *School in France*

It was no accident that the impetus for social history in its late twentieth-century form came from well outside the mainstream of the profession. In the case of the British Marxist historians I've just described, that momentum grew from the labors of a cohort of radicals mainly in their thirties, drawing inspiration from a set of political experiences in and around the Communist Party between the late 1930s and the aftermath of the World War II. Often securing at best an uncertain foothold in the profession, they nonetheless delivered much of the energy and ideas behind social history's emergence. By the 1960s, the lessening of the Cold War's ideological hostilities and the slow effects of institution building had gradually drawn these British Marxists into a much broader supportive milieu. But the force of the general point remains: social history's impulse came from the margins.

We can detect the same effect even more clearly earlier in the twentieth century. Because the discipline was founded in the later nineteenth century, statecraft and diplomacy, warfare and high politics, and administration and the law held sway over history teaching at the university level. The earliest social histories were written beyond the walls of academia altogether, either through the labors of private individuals or in the alternative settings of labor movements. After 1918, stronger potentials emerged from the more propitious political climate, once again usually abetted from the outside. In Britain, the key for that process was the creation of the Economic History Society and its journal, *Economic History Review,* in 1926–27. In Germany, it was an impressive flowering of sociology during the Weimar Republic.

France was a more complicated case. By the late nineteenth century, the French Revolution's centrality for the country's political culture had already created an institutional space for studying the revolutionary tradition, and the resulting attentiveness to popular politics and the presence of the masses was inherently encouraging to social history. Successive occupants of the Chair for the History of the French Revolution at the Sorbonne, from Albert Mathiez (1874–1932) through Georges Lefebvre (1874–1959) to Albert Soboul (1914–82), sustained a strong line of social-historical research.[59] Another key figure, Ernest Labrousse (1895–1988), pioneered the quantitative study of economic fluctuations as an essential condition for understanding the nature of revolutionary crises. By this work, he situated 1789 in an economic conjuncture for which the history of prices and wages, bad harvests, and unemployment delivered the key.[60] His general model compared the successive crises of 1789, 1830, and 1848. His analysis worked upward from price movements and the structural problems of the economy, through the wider ramifications of social crisis, before finally ending in the mishandling of the consequences by government.

As in Britain and Germany, an early impulse to social history in France came from economic history and sociology, but this occurred with far greater resonance among French historians than in the other two countries. For *The Great Fear,* his remarkable 1932 study of the countryside's popular turbulence on the eve of the 1789 revolution, Georges Lefebvre read the crowd theories of Gustav Le Bon, the social theory of Émile Durkheim, and the ideas about collective memory from his Strasbourg colleague Maurice Halbwachs. Going back to the turn of the century, the influence of the economist François Simiand (1873–1935) had been central to this distinctive French symbiosis of history and social science. In a seminal article of 1903 published in the new journal *Revue de synthèse historique,* Simiand disparaged the traditional *histoire événementielle* (history of events) and attacked what he called the historians' three "idols of the tribe"—politics, the individual, and chronology.[61] The journal concerned had been founded three years earlier in 1900, by the philosopher of history Henri Berr (1863–1954), in furtherance of an interestingly ecumenical conception of social science. Among Berr's younger supporters were Lucien Febvre (1878–1956) and Marc Bloch (1866–1944), who joined the *Revue* in 1907 and 1912, respectively.

Lucien Febvre's dissertation on Philip II and the Franche-Comté, published in 1912, was palpably indifferent to military and diplomatic events. In it, he located Philip II's policies in the geography, social structure, religious life, and social changes of the region, centering his account on the conflicts between absolutism and provincial privileges, nobles and bourgeois, Catholics and Protestants. He inverted the usual precedence, which viewed great events from the perspective of rulers and treated regional histories as effects. Region became the indispensable structural setting, for which geography, economics, and demography were all required. Appointed to Strasbourg University in 1920, Febvre collaborated there with Marc Bloch, who, before the war, under Durkheim's influence, had already rejected traditional political history. In 1924, Bloch published *The Royal Touch,* which sought to illuminate conceptions of English and French kingship by analyzing popular belief in the ability of kings to heal the skin disease of scrofula by the power of touch.[62] This remarkable study freed historical perspective from simple narrative time, reattaching it to longer frames of structural duration. It practiced comparison. It also stressed mentalité, or the collective understanding and religious psychology of the time—for example, against the contemporary "commonsense" question of whether the king's touch had actually healed or not.

These twin themes—structural history (as opposed to political history or the "history of events") and the history of mentalities (as opposed to the history of formal ideas)—gave coherence to the Febvre-Bloch collaboration. In subsequent books on Martin Luther and the bases of popular unbelief, published in 1928 and 1942, Febvre switched to studying the mental climate he thought specific to the sixteenth century.[63] Bloch, conversely, moved from an archaeology of mind-sets to the archaeology of structures, in his great classics *French Rural History: An Essay on Its Basic Characteristics,* published in 1931, and *Feudal Society,* which appeared in 1939–40.[64] His holistic account of feudalism, which aspired to a picture of the whole environment by combining analysis of the "mental structures" of the age with its socioeconomic relations, departed radically from prevailing work on the topic. He insisted on comparison, making Europe, not the nation, into the entity of study. He exchanged conventional chronologies based on the reigns of kings for a more challenging framework of epochal time, the famous *longue durée.* He shifted attention from military service, which provided the dominant approach to feudalism, to the social history of agriculture and relationships on the land. He moved away from the history of the law, landholding, kingship, and the origins of states in the narrow institutional sense. All of these moves came to characterize "structural history."

In 1929, Bloch and Febvre made their interests into a program by founding a new journal, *Annales d'histoire économique et sociale,* which began acquiring prestige with their move from Strasbourg to Paris. But not until after 1945—with the founding of the Sixth Section of the École Pratique des Hautes Études for the Social Sciences, with Febvre as its president—did *Annales* really take off, tragically boosted by Bloch's execution by the Nazis in June 1944 for his role in the Resistance. Bloch's indictment of French historiography's narrowness merged into the enthusiasm for a new start after the war, sharpened by his arraignment of the rottenness of the old elites, who capitulated in 1940 and collaborated with the Nazis under Vichy. The change of the journal's name to *Annales: économies, sociétés, civilisations* in 1946 signified this enhanced vision. The Sixth Section also placed history at the center of its new interdisciplinary regime, endowing it with a leading place among the social sciences, a place unique in the Western world. Sociology, geography, and economics—all vital influences for Bloch and Febvre—were joined by structural anthropology and linguistics in the guise of Claude Lévi-Strauss (1908–), Roland Barthes (1915–80), and Pierre Bourdieu (1930–2002). The term *histoire totale* (total history) became identified with *Annales.*

Febvre's assistant was Fernand Braudel (1902–85), who followed him into both the presidency of the Sixth Section (1956–72) and the directorship of *Annales* (1957–69). Braudel's career was framed by two monuments of scholarship: *The Mediterranean and the Mediterranean World in the Age of Philip II,* published in 1949 but mainly researched in the 1930s; and the three-volume *Civilization and Capitalism, 15th–18th Century,* completed in 1979.[65] In these great works, Braudel schematized his mentors' complex practice. His three temporalities or levels of analysis functioned as a materialist grand design, shrinking great men and big events into the sovereign causalities of economics, population, and environment. The causal logic moved upward from the structural history of the *longue durée,* through the medium-term changes of conjunctures, to the faster-moving narrative time of the traditional *histoire événementielle.* The ground floor contained landscape, climate, demography, deep patterns of economic life, long-run norms and habits, the reproduction of social structures, the stabilities of popular understanding, and the repetitions of everyday life. At the second level, the rise and fall of economies, social systems, and states became visible. Only at the third stage of the presentation could one find human-made events, comprising the familiar military, diplomatic, and political histories that *Annales* wanted to supplant. In this thinking, the "deeper level" of structure imposed "upper limits" on human possibilities for a particular civilization, while crucially determining the pace and extent of change. This was the historian's appropriate concern. "Events," in the old and conventional sense, were mainly epiphenomenal or a diversion.[66]

In a sense, Braudel's rendering of the ideals of *Annales* realized one of social history's default purposes—the dethroning of kings—while divesting it of all progressivist or "whiggish" narrative design. That uplifting quality was exchanged for a very different model of progress, seeking to render the world knowable through social science. In the Braudelian notation, that meant economics, demography, geography, anthropology, and quantitative techniques. In the French context of the politics of knowledge, moreover, during the Braudel era, *Annales* history became counterposed against the historiography of the French Revolution, where progressivism and the great event remained alive and well. Mentalité solidified into an implicit master category of structure. Braudel's project was imposingly schematic. His works were ordered into a reified hierarchy of materialist determinations, locating "real" significance in the structural and conjunctural levels and impoverishing the third level to the most conventional and unanalytic recitation of events. Reciprocity of determination—so challenging in Bloch's work on feudalism—now disappeared. The recessiveness of religious conflict and the other spectacular dramas of the early modern age was startling. Yet Braudel's magnum opus on the Mediterranean had few parallels in the sheer grandiosity of its knowledge and design.

If we consider the emergence of social history comparatively, country by country, *Annales* had a remarkable institution-building role.[67] Uniquely in Europe, it provided those efforts with a long continuity going back to the 1920s. It both established protocols of historical method and understanding and endowed a cumulative tradition of collective discussion, research, training, and publication. Interdisciplinary cohabitation was always essential, and—again uniquely—history was at the center. During the 1950s, quantification became soldered into this intellectual culture: one characteristically dogmatic statement declared, "from a scientific point of view, the only social history is quantitative history."[68] It emerged into the 1960s with several hall-marks: history as a social science; quantitative methodology; long-run analyses of prices, trade, and population; structural history; and a materialist model of causation. Certain key terms—*longue durée, mentalité,* and, of course, *histoire totale*—passed into the currency used by historians elsewhere.

Under Braudel, *Annales* became a magnet for "new" history in France. Its influence extended outward into Italy, Belgium, and Eastern Europe, especially into Poland, where many connections developed. The journal also opened dialogues with historians in the Soviet Union. Until the 1970s, however, the school's works were mainly known in English through Bloch's *Feudal Society,* which was translated in 1961—although Philippe Ariès's maverick history of childhood also appeared in English in 1962. Not until the 1970s did the real work of English-language transmission begin, with the translation of Braudel's *Mediterranean* in 1972 and of a selection of articles from *Annales* edited by Peter Burke in 1972.[69] Burke then became a principal impresario of the further reception—publishing commentaries, managing translations, reviewing the various works as they appeared, and publishing his own versions of the *Annales* approach. By the end of the seventies, a full-scale guide by Traian Stoianovich had appeared, and Immanuel Wallerstein had established the Fernand Braudel Center in Binghamton, with its new journal, *Review.*[70]

Between the 1930s and the 1960s, the dispositions of *Annales* paralleled those of the Marxist historians in Britain. Shared conviction in the value of materialist forms of analysis provided the obvious common ground, just as the Braudelian grand design contained obvious echoes of Marx's 1859 preface. Not only the common appeal of social and economic history but also the excitement of entering a common project of societal understanding could allow Marxists and the followers of *Annales* to converge, as the experience of Labrousse and Lefebvre in France itself implied.[71] In the prevailing ideological climate of the 1950s and under the dominant academic conditions of the time, this was in itself enough for some basic solidarity: "[T]here could be no History if it were not for Social History," Labrousse declared.[72] When the British Marxists launched *Past and Present* in the unpropitious circumstances of the early 1950s, Braudel and the *Annalistes* became their natural associates. The motivating commitments behind that enterprise were to be found not just in the guiding philosophical perspectives, which might seem rather prosaically orthodox when explicated, but far more in the detailed works of scholarship they produced, which might have a great deal in common with those of the non-Marxist colleagues across the English Channel. For this reason, any strict demarcations between the British Marxist historians and the historians of *Annales*—especially during the 1950s—make little sense.[73]

Social Science History

What was history's more general relationship to social science in the mid-twentieth century? Another feature of the intellectual conjuncture of the late sixties, I'd argue, was its ecumenicalism, a quality not disconnected from the distinctiveness—and efficacy—of the radical political movements of the time. Although dogmatisms of various kinds came quickly into play, I mainly remember the open-endedness of the intellectual discovery; the sense of experiment and assay; the readiness to explore, to pick and choose, to try any ideas that worked. While avidly sampling the Marxist historiography that happened to come my way, for instance, I initially made little distinction between Marxist and other kinds of materialist sociology. Precisely for the purposes that interested me most, such as an understanding of ideology or theories of power and the state, which orthodox Marxism had notably neglected, it seemed important to cast a wide net. This openness wasn't exactly indiscriminate. But for a while, many flowers bloomed.[74]

Both *Past and Present* and *Annales* had pioneered a certain practice of interdisciplinary scholarship. As suggested earlier in this chapter, the creation of the Sixth Section of the École Pratique des Hautes Études in 1946 registered the institutionalizing of traditions that had been part of French academic life from the start of the century. Uniquely, the prestige of *Annales* allowed history to be instated at the very center of the postwar social science complex in France, a placement further reinforced in 1962 by the founding of Braudel's Maison des Sciences de l'Homme. The interactions between history and social science in Britain were, by comparison, more piecemeal and pragmatic. As Marxists lost confidence in the self-sufficiency of their ideas during the crisis of Communism in the mid-1950s, for example, it became easier to seek sustenance elsewhere; the dialogue between historians and varieties of non-Marxist sociology and social anthropology became strengthened as a result. The involvement in *Past and Present* of Philip

Abrams, Peter Worsley, and the anthropologist Jack Goody was especially notable in that regard. Eric Hobsbawm's *Primitive Rebels,* originally given as the Simon Lectures under the auspices of the anthropology department at the University of Manchester at the instigation of Max Gluckman, was a pathbreaking demonstration of what talking and listening to other disciplines could enable.[75]

During the 1950s, the United States witnessed a peculiarly one-sided version of such a dialogue. A succession of Social Science Research Council reports—issued in 1946, 1954, and 1963, respectively—had exhorted historians to learn from sociologists, but the imagined conversation seemed annoyingly one-way: for admittance to the club, historians needed to adopt the social scientists' available theories and methods.[76] In this first phase of later twentieth-century interdisciplinarity, historians tended to be extremely self-effacing, to say the least. They wrote their own histories, but not always under conceptual conditions of their own choosing. In particular, the massive prestige of using developmentalist frameworks based on modernization theory to describe social change across time—indeed, the presumed superiority of such frameworks—reached a climax in the late 1950s and early 1960s, during the research boom of the postwar capitalist prosperity; it was abetted by Marxism's seeming atrophy as an intellectual tradition in the English-speaking world. For historians, the main sites of the resulting interdisciplinary conversation were a series of new journals. Aside from *Past and Present,* they included *Comparative Studies in Society and History,* founded in 1958 in Chicago and then taken to the University of Michigan by the British medievalist Sylvia Thrupp; the *Journal of Social History,* launched in 1967 by the generalist social historian Peter Stearns; and the *Journal of Interdisciplinary History,* founded in 1970 by the early modernist Theodore Rabb and the political scientist Robert Rotberg.[77]

Historians turned to sociology most successfully and self-consciously when borrowing techniques, rather than theory per se. Family history provided one of the best illustrations of this process, pioneered programmatically in Britain by Peter Laslett's *The World We Have Lost,* published in 1965. Demanding a new "social structural history" that embraced whole societies and focused on the "structural function of the family" in the transition from "preindustrial" to "industrial" times, Laslett (1915–2001) helped form the Cambridge Group for the History of Population and Social Structure (founded in 1964), which he proceeded to guide with evangelical zeal.[78] Imbued with the certainties of quantifying and the hubris of science, the new demographic historians aspired to recast the defining ground of the discipline. But despite impressive methodological sophistication, Laslett's main achievement paradoxically became an argument about the absence of change—namely, his so-called null hypothesis regarding the nuclear family's continuity across the caesura of industrialization. He used this hypothesis to lay one of the classic modernizing myths of postwar sociology—the belief that family forms followed a long-term pattern of progressive nucleation.

Demographic historians became masters of falsification, dismantling ungrounded claims in dialogue with contemporary sociology.[79] But their ability to retheorize social change beyond the technics of the immediate debates remained far more limited.[80] The strongest explanatory program for demographic history remained that of the leading voices of the third generation of the *Annales* school, for whom population had become the prime mover of social change, most notably in Emmanuel Le Roy Ladurie's study of the peasantry of Languedoc.[81] Ironically, given the default cautions of Laslett's null hypothesis, the first two general histories of the family in the 1970s, by Edward Shorter and Lawrence Stone, presented bold teleologies of modernization, as in Stone's thesis of the "rise of affective individualism."[82]

The larger promises of family history were realized more effectively in studies of "protoindustrialization," a concept that was capturing the attention of many social historians by the mid-1970s. The key work on this subject, by the German historians Peter Kriedte, Hans Medick, and Jürgen Schlumbohm, accomplished what Laslett and the demographers apparently shied away from—the reconnecting of family history and population studies to a larger argument about the origins of capitalism and the social history of industrialization.[83] By arguing that precisely the continuity of household organization facilitated the development of cottage industries through a process of protoindustrialization, the three authors showed how Laslett's "null hypothesis" might finally be put to work. They resituated it in the larger contexts of economy and society. In earlier criticism of Laslett's project, Edward Thompson had argued, "How is it possible to get very far with the discussion of household or family if we don't know whether the households were of serfs or freemen, fishermen or bakers, nomadic shepherds or miners,

were cultivating rice or silk or chestnuts, what kind of inheritance customs determined the transmission of land, what kind of dowries or
marriage settlements, what customs of apprenticeship or migrant
labor."[84] Measured against these necessary social-historical concerns,
the nuclear family debate, with its more specific terms, increasingly
appeared to be an issue of staggering unimportance.

Above all, therefore, Kriedte, Medick, and Schlumbohm suc-
ceeded in mobilizing the history of the family for social history's larger
totalizing ambition. In common with others interested in protoindustrialization—for example, David Levine, Wally Seccombe, and
Charles Tilly—they managed to bring the burgeoning field of family
history out of its self-made technicist and subdisciplinary ghetto.[85]
They drew creatively on the literatures in a wide variety of cognate
fields—the transition from feudalism to capitalism, peasant studies,
the history of popular culture, and so forth—to produce an unusually
rich and well-integrated account of the family and its shifting place in
society. The openness of their theory was especially refreshing. For
their specific purposes, the three coauthors drew eclectically on a varied repertoire of influences, producing an interesting mix of German
social theory; French, British, and North American anthropology; and
Anglo-Marxist social history (including, most notably, the work of
Edward Thompson). In this last respect, Medick's work, in particular,
edged toward the terrain of popular culture and the neo-anthropolog-
ical study of "plebeian" everyday life.[86]

I dwell at some length on the example of family history because it
offers a paradigm case for the emergence of the social science variant
of social history. Most obviously, it illustrates the analytical power and
excitement that merely appropriating the techniques and methodologies of the social sciences could confer. Family reconstitution, census
analysis, sophisticated quantification, the promise of computerized
technologies, the new divisions of labor enabled by elaborate research
teams, and the benefits of the associated infrastructure of long-term
and large-scale funding—all these factors opened unimagined possibilities for the study of ordinary social life. The historiography of the
family also revealed the materialist epistemology common to most
versions of the interest in social history as it accelerated toward the
1970s. It suggests, once again, how easily Marxist and non-Marxist
influences could converge for the early generations of enthusiasts and
practitioners.

In its frequent technicist predilections and tendencies toward narrowness, however, the field also contained one of social history's recurring tensions—that between the social historian's totalizing aspiration and the practical foreshortening of interest around more limited contexts and monographic concerns. Moreover, historical demography showed, in an extreme form, the dangers of privileging "quantitative" approaches to the study of social life, to the virtual exclusion of "qualitative" approaches. Despite everything else the Cambridge Group achieved during the sixties and seventies, we learned little from them about the texture of "family life and illicit love in earlier generations" (to quote the title of another of Laslett's books).[87]

Urban history provided a similar microcosm. Here, again, was a freshly invented subdisciplinary field that subsisted on methods and approaches learned from the social sciences and allowed interdisciplinary collaborations to thrive. It enabled the posing of fundamental questions concerning the nature of the changes producing the modern world. It was certainly vulnerable to narrowness and empiricism, but it provided an obvious bridge to general societal analysis. Its British pioneer, H. J. Dyos (1921–78), formed the Urban History Group inside the Economic History Society in 1963, then launched the field with an international conference at his academic home, the University of Leicester, in September 1966.[88] The associated *Newsletter* became institutionalized into the *Urban History Yearbook* in 1974, further transmuting into the journal *Urban History* in 1992. Substantively, urban history brought issues of place, environment, and setting actively into the orbit of social history, rather than passively, as they had been treated before.

Dyos was a tireless proselytizer, combining social science rigor with expansively eclectic thematics, whose compass embraced all aspects of the city's history: its changing political economy and spatial organization; the social histories of the built environment, land sales, mass transit, labor markets, slum dwelling, and suburbanization; and the architectural history and the cultural analysis of urban images and representations. Dyos purposefully approached the history of urbanization as a site where social scientists, humanists, and historians would all be able to meet. After his tragically premature death, a memorial volume in his honor impressively confirmed this transdisciplinary potential.[89] Quite independently, of course, the urban community study was also becoming established as the main vehicle for studying class formation and the rise of the working class.

The history of youth and childhood was yet another field invented by social historians during the 1960s, coalescing from the opportunities seeded by comparable transdisciplinary efforts. The impetus came from historians of population and family, especially among early modernists, who delivered on one of social history's most exciting promises, the calling into question and dismantling of established commonsense beliefs about the seeming naturalness of the most familiar social arrangements and institutions—in this case, the late twentieth-century understanding of childhood as a sharply demarcated stage of life or state of being. New research—with the extraordinarily influential *Centuries of Childhood,* by Philippe Ariès, at its head—showed the basic categories of the human life course to have actually been historical creations, defining childhood, in particular, as an artifact of the specifically modern era.[90]

An interest in youth subcultures was inspired by the student radicalism and general youthful rebelliousness of 1968. In freely cross-disciplinary ways, scholars drew partly on work at the Birmingham Center for Contemporary Cultural Studies, partly on radical criminology and the sociology of deviance.[91] Such work further intersected with new social histories of crime, punishment, law, and imprisonment, which, during the late sixties and early seventies, burgeoned into one of the most popular growth areas of research.[92] The attraction, once again, was the handle such studies provided for analyzing the larger questions of social and political order. Scholars entering this field were certainly moved by the positivist excitements of social science methodology, which promised the ability to measure change, establish patterns, and specify causal relations. But also at work was a powerful dynamic of populist identification through "history from below." Here, the British Marxist historians again provided inspiration. As so often, Eric Hobsbawm's writings—on "primitive rebellion," "social banditry," and "social criminality"—scouted the basic terrain.

The excitements and potentialities of social science history during the 1960s were epitomized in, above all, the person and work of Charles Tilly. Born in 1929 and trained in sociology at Harvard during the 1950s, Tilly stood for a vision of historically dynamic macrosociological analysis of societal change on the most ambitious of scales. His first book, *The Vendée,* published in 1964, was a pioneering achievement of archivally grounded historical sociology, which connected the distribution of political allegiance during the French Revolution to regionally specified patterns of socioeconomic life. One leading strand of Tilly's work concerned the changing interrelationship between capitalist development and state making, which he analyzed with attention both to the expansion of state capacities between the sixteenth and twentieth centuries and to the demographics of proletarianization. But by the 1970s, Tilly was best known as the preeminent sociologist and social historian of collective action, whose changing bases and forms of rationality he charted in relation to the impact and growing penetration of capitalist markets and national states.[93]

Tilly's most grandiose projects—on France between the seventeenth and twentieth centuries and on Britain from the 1750s to the 1830s—sought to uncover the key shifts in the long-term patterns of collective action, while reconstructing the coherence, rationality, interests, and conceptions of justice driving the actions of ordinary people. In response to the complex dialectic between the growth of capitalism and the national state's increasing penetration of social life, Tilly argued, popular actions moved away from older forms of protest—such as the food riots, tax rebellions, and *charivaris* (or "rough music") of the first half of the nineteenth century—and regrouped around industrial strikes, public demonstrations, and associated social movements. This epochal shift followed an earlier one in the mid-seventeenth century, through which collective action had refocused from primarily local arenas onto national ones, basically in response to the state's expanding efforts to extract taxation and other resources. By exhaustively and systematically examining the shared interests, forms of organization, and opportunities for action available to ordinary people across these changing contexts (conceptualized as varying "repertoires of contention"), Tilly brilliantly illuminated the rise of modern popular politics. His were also studies of almost industrial proportions, based on painstaking longitudinal research and requiring big resources, large teams of workers, and huge machineries of quantitative production.[94]

Taken as a whole, Tilly's work forms an extraordinary achievement. It was not always clear that the substantive results of the French and British studies justified the gargantuan efforts and expenditures involved or that the industrialized research methods met the exacting standards historians try to bring to the gathering and use of evidence.

More damagingly, those studies also remained notably blunt in relation to questions of popular culture, meaning, and ideology, whose importance received a low priority in Tilly's thinking.[95] But as the primary architect of historical sociology in the United States as it emerged from the 1960s, Tilly made lasting contributions that remained unimpeachable, doing more than any other individual to show historians how to use theory while simultaneously historicizing sociology. His impact on social historians trained in the United States since the 1960s is incalculable.

From a vantage point circa 1970, Tilly's achievement mapped very closely onto the distinctive contribution of the British Marxist historians. That he shared some of their basic commitments—for example, to internationalism, comparison, and interdisciplinarity—was obvious. His studies of collective action paralleled very closely George Rudé's work on the crowd. Their systematic quality complemented the aggregate achievement of Eric Hobsbawm's more essayistic analyses in *Labouring Men, Primitive Rebels,* and elsewhere. Tilly's interest in state making and the rise of capitalism mirrored the seminal *Past and Present* debates around those questions, as did his allied interest in revolutions. Tilly and the British Marxists clearly shared the same commitment to writing a theoretically driven history of whole societies changing across time. The doubled genealogies of social history during the 1960s—identifying with the people and learning from social science—were common to both of them. Above all, they shared the desire to ground an understanding of politics at the highest levels of government and the state in imaginatively and systematically conducted social histories of ordinary life. At the very end of *The Contentious French,* Tilly said:

[The] connection of the largest processes transforming France and the collective action of ordinary people exposes the fallacy of treating "violence," "protest," or "disorder" as a world apart, as a phenomenon distinct from high politics, as a mere reaction to stress. There lies the most important teaching of popular collective action: it is not an epiphenomenon. It connects directly and solidly with the great political questions. By the actions that authorities call disorder, ordinary people fight injustice, challenge exploitation, and claim their own place in the structure of power.[96]

Edward Thompson

One Communist Party Historians' Group alumnus not involved directly in the launching of *Past and Present* was Edward Thompson—although he did join its editorial board later, in the 1960s. Known first for his sprawling and energetic study of the life and thought of William Morris, published in 1955, and then for his leading role in the first British New Left, Thompson came to prominence as much for his public political stands as for his scholarly work, in an impassioned duality of commitments that the rest of his life further sustained.[97] Above all, he came to inspire several generations of social historians with his magnum opus, *The Making of the English Working Class;* published in 1963, it appeared in its Pelican paperback edition in 1968. A remarkable combination of historical retrieval, oppositional grand narrative, and moral-political crusade, this book was, in Hobsbawm's words, an "erupting historical volcano of 848 pages," or, as Gwyn Williams called it, "less a book than one continuous challenge."[98]

Remarkably (given the comprehensive professionalizing of scholarly historical writing well under way when it was published), *The Making* was researched and written entirely from outside the university, while its author was teaching in adult education in Leeds. Thompson was "[a] brilliant, handsome, passionate, and oratorically gifted activist" for the Communist Party until 1956;[99] on leaving the party in protest at the Soviet invasion of Hungary, he became a leading voice of the British New Left. For the rest of his life, he engaged zestfully and prolifically in various kinds of public polemics, most importantly in the international peace movement during the 1980s, of which he became an especially eloquent and charismatic voice. He created the Center for the Study of Social History at Warwick University in 1965, the only time he held a regular university appointment; he directed the center until 1971, when he resigned. His time there was notable not just for the intellectual excitement surrounding his seminars on the social history of crime, the customary cultures of rural England, and the commercial-capitalist transformation of eighteenth-century society but also for his political critique of the business model of the university, which he published in the midst of a major crisis at Warwick that rocked the British academic world more generally in the spring of 1970.[100] This combination of professional marginality, public upstandingness, and intellectual radicalism was essential to Thompson's aura.

A panoramic account of the self-making of the working class, *The Making* avowedly derived from Marx its concentration on the cultures, experiences, and political resistance of the working class in the half century before 1832. Thompson's work also advanced an eloquent counternarrative to gradualist versions of British history as the triumphal march of parliamentary progress, a conventional story from which popular uprisings, government coercion, and civil strife—all the rich and turbulent histories of democratic mobilization in extraparliamentary spheres—had largely been banished. Instead of this polite and complacent success story of the farsighted extension of voting rights to ever-widening circles of the population, Thompson sought to reground the history of democratic gains in an epic recounting of the necessary popular resistance against violence, inequality, and exploitation. In one of the most quoted lines by a historian in the late twentieth century, he famously declared, "I am seeking to rescue the poor stockinger, the Luddite cropper, the 'obsolete' handloom weaver, the 'utopian' artisan, and even the deluded follower of Joanna Southcott, from the enormous condescension of posterity."[101]

Thompson's book was also an antireductionist manifesto—attacking narrowly based economic history, overdeterministic Marxism, and static theories of class. For Thompson, class was dynamic, eventuating through history. It was a relationship and a process, rather than an inert description of social roles or the distribution of positions in a social structure. It resulted from a common consciousness of capitalist exploitation and state repression, graspable through culture. It implied a strong conception of collective agency, whose importance Thompson reasserted against the more deterministic versions of Marxism and other economistic sociologies then prevailing in the history of the Industrial Revolution. Playing deliberately off the "base and superstructure" couplet and the primacy of "social existence" over "consciousness" expounded by Marx in his 1859 preface, Thompson instated "agency" as the missing third term, upholding the necessary inventiveness of collective action beyond all the "conditioning" exercised by the economy and its social interests. The working class, as *The Making*'s fourth sentence so tersely put it, "was present at its own making."[102]

In emulating Thompson, the movement away from labor's institutional study and toward social histories of working people gained enormous momentum, rapidly encompassing the parts of life that historians of parties and trade unions had rarely tried to reach, except in antiquarian and colorful ways. Spurred by Thompson's achievement, younger generations of aspiring historians entering the profession during its growth years of the later 1960s and early 1970s found new subjects, while tackling the old ones in a radically innovative spirit. This heady recasting of the agenda, which was also a change of temper, became obvious from the evolving activities of the Labour History Society after its foundation in 1961, both through the pages of the Society's *Bulletin* and in the themes of its annual conferences. Labor history transmuted into an expansive version of its former self, in restless conversation with all the other emergent subspecialisms of social history. Its range now seemed unlimited—encompassing not just the workplace, in all its practices and customs, but housing, the family, nutrition, leisure and sport, drinking, crime, religion, magic and superstition, education, song, literature, childhood, courtship, sexuality, death, and more.

In the course of the 1960s, Thompson's work moved back in time. His social history of property crimes and the law in relation to the bases of England's early eighteenth-century political order, *Whigs and Hunters,* together with the work of his Warwick students gathered in *Albion's Fatal Tree* (both published in 1975), explored the transformations of customary culture beneath the onslaught of a rapidly commercializing capitalism and its forms of penetration into the countryside.[103] Two ground-laying essays, "Time, Work-Discipline, and Industrial Capitalism" and "The Moral Economy of the English Crowd in the Eighteenth Century," were published in *Past and Present,* whose editorial board Thompson joined in 1969, and a third, "Rough Music," appeared in *Annales.* Two others followed in the *Journal of Social History* and *Social History* during the 1970s, as did his legendary lecture "The Sale of Wives," which remained long unpublished. Though not finally assembled together as *Customs in Common* until shortly before his death in 1993, these works cumulatively transformed perceptions of the transition to industrial capitalism every bit as powerfully as had *The Making.*[104] In the process, they further defamiliarized the older grand narrative of the Industrial Revolution. Moreover, *Albion's Fatal Tree* argued that crime and punishment should be considered "central to unlocking the meanings of eighteenth-century social history," and a host of exciting new work soon vindicated this claim.[105]

Thompson's impact helped two vital initiatives on the margins to form, whose longer-term effects both mirrored the earlier dynamics of the influence of the Communist Party Historians' Group and crucially surpassed its substantive range, organized forms, and political intent. One of these was the Social History Group in Oxford, which convened on a weekly basis between 1965 and 1974, in the borderlands of the university's official life. This seminar's organizers were a younger generation of leftists, including the Marxist author of *Outcast London,* Gareth Stedman Jones (born 1942); a specialist on Spanish anarchism, Joaquín Romero Maura (born 1940); and a young and already highly respected historian of Nazism, Tim Mason (1940–90), who was, for a time, an assistant editor at *Past and Present.* These men were inspired by a fourth member, the somewhat older Raphael Samuel (1934–96), who had been a schoolboy recruit to the Historians' Group, had left the party in 1956 to become a key energizer of the New Left, and then took an appointment as tutor in history at Ruskin, the trade union college based in Oxford but not part of the university, where he taught from 1961 to 1996.[106]

Linked to the ambitions of the Oxford Social History Group and conceived initially to bring Ruskin students into wider contact with other historians, the annual History Workshops organized by Raphael Samuel and his students became a vital engine of social history during the coming period. Starting modestly with "A Day with the Chartists" in 1967, the meetings escalated within several years to become elaborate weekend events with international participation, given obvious momentum by the political radicalisms of 1968. By 1972, two thousand people were converging on Ruskin for the year's workshop. The first few themes fell recognizably within labor history, but the new expansiveness of social history was apparent by 1972 ("Childhood in History: Children's Liberation") and 1973 ("Women in History"). The first thirteen workshops met in Oxford at Ruskin College itself; after 1979, the workshops started migrating around the rest of the country. They inspired a series of pamphlets (twelve altogether during 1970–74) and an imprint of more than thirty books between 1975 and 1990. The group's flagship became *History Workshop Journal,* which began publishing in 1976.

In common with *Social History,* another new journal founded in the same year, *History Workshop Journal* sought to reenergize the commit-ments inaugurated by the earlier generation of Marxist historians through *Past and Present*.[107] But far more than a project of the politics of knowledge within the discipline alone, the History Workshops crystallized a wider set of ambitions, which were more akin to an ear-lier and unrealized goal of the Communist Party Historians' Group—producing a "people's history" capable of contesting the official or pre-dominant ideology of the national past. This meant partly attempting to democratize the practice of history, both by building on Ruskin's labor movement connections and by further embedding support of the History Workshops in a community-based network of local activities.

But the History Workshops also sought to establish a more visible public presence, both locally and nationally, by intervening politically where questions of history were in play—most substantially, for example, during the debate over the national curriculum in the 1980s. The annual workshops were more like popular festivals than academic conferences; they were attended by diverse contingents of nonacade-mics as well as university historians and were borne by an ebullient and iconoclastic political esprit. In Samuel's words, they were inspired by "the belief that history is or ought to be a collective enter-prise, one in which the researcher, the archivist, the curator and the teacher, the 'do-it-yourself' enthusiast and the local historian, the family history societies and the industrial archaeologists, should all be regarded as equally engaged." Samuel further explained:

> It has also stood by the idea of enlarging the vocation of the his-torian to take in perceptions of the past, arguing that the novel-ist and the story teller, the film maker and the caricaturist are at least as worthy of critical attention as the professional scholar. . . . At a time when we are bombarded with images of the past on all sides, when questions of the self and of subjectivity, of nationality and identity, clamor for inclusion on the scholarly agenda, historians cannot ensconce themselves in a problematic of their own making—least of all, those like socialists who are supposed to believe that knowledge is indivisible, and under-standing a creature of its time.[108]

Among all of the older generation of Marxist historians, Edward Thompson had been closest to practicing an earlier version of this ideal, during his seventeen years in adult education and in the successive political contexts of the Communist Party and the New Left. Less by direct example than by the momentum of the broader historiographical departures he inspired, as well as by individual encouragement, he also influenced the beginnings of the second new initiative needing to be mentioned, the emergence of women's history in Britain. Although the first initiatives for this occurred only in the course of tense and often angry contention, such pioneers as Sheila Rowbotham (born 1943), Anna Davin (born 1940), Sally Alexander (born 1943), and Catherine Hall (born 1946) all emerged from the History Workshop milieu in various ways, drawing important support and inspiration both from the workshops themselves and from involved older mentors, such as Thompson.[109] Plans for the first National Women's Liberation Conference, which met at Ruskin in 1970, had originated in discussions at the 1969 History Workshop, and the seventh workshop, in 1973, eventually took "Women in History" as its theme. In other words, the possibilities for social history's emergence—whether in general or for a particular area, such as women's history—were entirely bound up with the new political contexts of 1968.

Thompson's influence was also international. *The Making* shaped North American, African, and South Asian historiographical agendas—no less than it shaped studies of class formation in Britain and Europe. His eighteenth-century essays had perhaps even greater resonance in this respect, especially "The Moral Economy," which influenced scholars working across national histories in diverse regions of the world and formed the basis for a retrospective international conference held in Birmingham in 1992.[110] In the course of the 1970s, social history became internationalized in the full sense envisaged by the British Marxist historians who had founded *Past and Present,* through a growing proliferation of conferences, new journals, and active processes of translation. In one network of particular importance, for example, Thompson and Hobsbawm became central participants in a series of roundtables on social history organized in the late 1970s by Braudel's Maison des Sciences de l'Homme and the Göttingen Max Planck Institute of History, which brought together scholars from France, Italy, West Germany, and elsewhere.[111]

Thompson's first love was the English literature of the eighteenth and nineteenth centuries. The first time I saw him, with the Balliol student history society in 1969, he talked about Coleridge and

Wordsworth in "The Apostacy of the Poets"—having left on the train (or perhaps a plane) the talk on William Blake that he meant to give. He was the very polar opposite of a dry-as-dust archive-grubber or a shriveled policer of knowledge, yet his erudition stretched into arcane aspects of social and cultural history and recondite corners of the archive that were only captured for dissertations and monographs years later. He was extraordinarily charismatic. I remember him lecturing on "rough music" in the assembly hall of the Brighton Cooperative Society in 1971, filling the stage with his intellectual fire and largeness of presence, prowling occasionally away from the rostrum, passing a hand through a shock of hair, every gesture holding the crowd. A storyteller of brilliance, he passed effortlessly from poetics to analysis and back. He released phrases like lightning shafts and thunderbolts, calling up Jerusalem with the sheer compelling exuberance of his physical and moral eloquence. Thompson's intellectual impact was inseparable from this kind of magnetism and restlessness.[112]

How would I distill Edward Thompson's importance in the late 1960s and early 1970s for my personal sense of the generational breakthrough to social history then occurring? As I already mentioned in chapter 1, I first read *The Making of the English Working Class* in the winter of 1968–69, when my attention was very far from the official classroom and its curriculum. The desiccated and hollowed-out learning of the Oxford Modern History School was leaving me cynically unconvinced that becoming a historian was still a future I wanted to acquire. Discovering Thompson's book allowed me to reconstruct my sense of history's importance. It was so inspiring because it provided access to a potential counternarrative that was different from the story of national stability and successful consensus, of gradualist progression toward a naturalized present, that everything in the insidiously assimilative intellectual culture of postwar Britain invited me to accept. Thompson's book showed me the instabilities in that account, which could be retold against the grain in some very different ways. There were a number of particular aspects to this.

First and foremost, Thompson's was an oppositional history. It uncovered suppressed traditions of popular democracy that could be mobilized for the purposes of challenging the official version of the British past as the placid and gradualist romance of parliamentary evolution. His book also unearthed the existence of a revolutionary tradition. Forged in the radical democracy of the Jacobin movements of the

1790s, then driven underground by repression, this continuity sustained itself as an "illegal tradition," conjoined with the emergent labor militancies of the new industrializing economy, and resurfaced in the radicalisms of the 1810s. It showed that British society and its institutions had only ever been secured from popular struggles against injustice, violence, and exploitation. In so doing, it built on the achievement of Thompson's fellow Marxist Christopher Hill, who, during these same years, successfully redefined the seventeenth-century civil war as the English Revolution. For a young historian like myself, raised on the patriotic guff and John Bullism of Arthur Bryant's histories of Britain during the French Revolutionary and Napoleonic Wars, this insistence on the generative necessity of societal conflict for the realizing of progress was emancipating. Democratic goods, it seemed clear, came only as a result of collective action, mass politics, and insurrectionary resistance against a coercive, corrupt, and narrowly based political system.

Second, in a related effort, Thompson also reclaimed certain national cultural traditions for the Left—most notably, the visionary writings of William Blake and the major poets of the 1790s and early 1800s, together with the romantic critique of industrialism and other utopian moments of cultural criticism. Over the longer course of the nineteenth century, this critical countertradition also included the ideas of William Morris, to which Thompson had devoted an earlier enormous book. His work here converged with that of a fellow standard-bearer of the New Left, Raymond Williams, whose own comparable works, the hugely influential *Culture and Society* and *The Long Revolution,* had just been published. In those books, Williams's "primary motivation in writing" had been "oppositional." His goal was "to counter the appropriation of a long line of thinking about culture to what were by now decisively reactionary positions." Williams explained:

> There was a question for me whether I should write a critique of that ideology in a wholly negative way, which at one time I considered, or whether the right course was not to try to recover the true complexity of the tradition it had confiscated—so that the appropriation could be seen for what it was. In the end I settled for the second strategy. For it allowed me to refute the increasing contemporary use of the concept of culture against

democracy, socialism, the working class, or popular education, in terms of the tradition itself. The selective version of culture could be historically controverted by the writings of the thinkers who contributed to the formation and discussion of the idea.[113]

Third, Thompson opened up the ambiguities and complexities of cultural history.[114] *The Making* passionately pursued the ways in which large-scale experience—in this case, the doubled consequences of capitalist exploitation and political repression between the 1790s and 1820s—became handled by ordinary people in cultural ways, focusing, in particular, on the political beliefs and popular traditions available to them in everyday life. For its time, this enterprise was extremely daring. In the early 1960s, outside some discussions beginning around *Past and Present,* there was virtually no conversation between historians and anthropologists. Thompson's attention to ordinary values, ritual practices, and the symbolic dimensions of everyday life suggested a form of historical ethnography soon to be realized more richly in his writings on time and work discipline, "rough music," and the moral economy. Thompson later reflected that in focusing on such subjects as "paternalism, riot, enclosure, and common right, and on several popular ritual forms," he was seeking to understand the "non-economic sanctions and the invisible rules that govern behavior quite as powerfully as military force, the terror of the gallows, or economic domination."[115] More broadly, Thompson's work foregrounded the legitimacy of popular culture, which dominant historiographies had always refused to acknowledge and which the Left had also been surprisingly reluctant to see. Thompson's influence fed powerfully into the prehistories of cultural studies.[116]

Fourth, an important part of Thompson's foregrounding of culture was a kind of populism, a politics of empathy, borne by an intense and vehement valuing of the lives and histories of ordinary people. Identifying with the people in such a manner presupposed a readiness for entering their mental worlds, for getting inside past cultures, for suspending one's own context-bound assumptions. Thompson's discussions in *The Making* and, even more, in the eighteenth-century works often began from the close analysis of specific cases as symbolic moments, which he approached as the "crystallized forms of more general features of a social formation."[117] This was classically true of his essay "Rough Music," of the readings of anonymous threatening letters in *Albion's Fatal Tree,* and of his article "Moral Economy." Another example was the analysis of millenarianism in *The Making.* Retrieving the meanings behind such arcane and exotic appearances required reconstructing their hidden rationality, and in the staid and stultified climate of British historical studies in the earlier 1960s, this had the capacity for taking one by surprise, for defamiliarizing one's own assumptions and making them strange. Hearing Thompson do this in his lecture on "rough music" was utterly invigorating. Very few others were doing such work.[118]

Fifth, Thompson refused the "base and superstructure" model. His thinking here paralleled that of Raymond Williams. Where Williams spoke of "specific and indissoluble real processes" through which the economic and the cultural were always imbricated together, Thompson saw class as simultaneously "an 'economic' and . . . a 'cultural' formation," in which the one could never receive "theoretical priority" over the other.[119] For both men, "the cultural" worked directly inside the economic realm of production and market transactions. So far from being "natural" or unfolding accordingly to its own discrete logic, economic rationality of a capitalist kind needed to be historically constructed. It presumed the destruction of an earlier set of relations grounded in the customary practices of the moral economy. Thompson proposed the concept of a "plebeian culture" to capture this emplacement of popular culture "within its proper material abode":

> plebeian culture becomes a more concrete and usable concept, no longer situated in the thin air of "meanings, attitudes and values," but located within a particular equilibrium of social relations, a working environment of exploitation and resistance to exploitation, of relations of power which are masked by rituals of paternalism and deference.[120]

Sixth, Thompson's *The Making* belongs in direct lineage with the interest of the Communist Party Historians' Group in the history of capitalist industrialization and the transition from feudalism to capitalism. Beginning life in the later 1950s, as the putative first chapter of a general textbook on the history of the British labor movement, *The Making* picked up the threads of two unrealized projects of popularization initiated by the Historians' Group ten years before: a Marxist history of the British labor movement and a general history of British capitalism.[121] In this sense, its companion texts were Hill's and

Hobsbawm's volumes in the Pelican Economic History of Britain series, Hobsbawm's essays in *Labouring Men,* Saville's *Rural Depopulation,* and so forth. Thompson's angry and broad-gauged critique of orthodox economic histories of the Industrial Revolution particularly highlighted affinities of this kind. It leveled a double challenge to those conventional accounts. It decisively problematized the simplistic category of "traditional" or "preindustrial" society through which the transition to the modern world was then conventionally thought; and it was the first general social history of capitalist industrialization "from below"—that is, from the standpoint of its victims.

Finally, by pioneering research on popular protest, customary culture, and the transformations wrought by industrialization, Thompson opened out the understanding of politics. His studies of the new popular-democratic radicalisms generated between the 1790s and 1830s, followed by his patient reconstruction of the plebeian culture of the eighteenth century (in all its turbulent self-assertiveness), marked out a space in which "politics" could be found in all sorts of disconcertingly unexpected ways. *The Making* is full of such rereadings, finding the expression of collective values about the nature of the good society in a variety of practices and manifestations that the "enormous condescension" of conventional political historians had rarely admitted into their stories—from the desperately improvised "rituals of mutuality" on which community depended to the mass outbreaks of millenarianism and the direct action of General Ludd. In that sense, *The Making* belongs with two other key texts of the late 1950s and early 1960s that defined new ways of looking at popular politics, Hobsbawm's *Primitive Rebels* and George Rudé's *The Crowd in History.*

This is where Thompson's work as a historian connects most directly to the broader character of the period I'm trying to describe. His achievement in this particular respect was inseparably linked both to the cultural insurgencies of the 1960s and to the distinctive rethinking of politics already initiated by the first New Left. The efflorescence of social history about to occur, which Thompson's writings did so much to inspire, presupposed a radically deinstitutionalized understanding of politics, in which the possible sources of a popular oppositional impulse were now sought away from the recognized arenas of parties, polite associations, and parliaments, in a wide variety of noninstitutional settings. Among the latter, everything from street violence, rioting, types of criminality, and industrial sabotage to forms of mental illness and the general flaunting of social rules came to be claimed for their dissentient political meanings, including even "apathy" and indifference to politics itself.[122] This expanded conception of "the political," which was about to be blown even further apart by feminist critiques of domesticity, sexuality, and personal life, became one of the most important enduring consequences of the upheavals of 1968. Thompson's influence was a vital source of sustenance here as well.

Conclusion

What were the entailments of the "optimism" inscribed in this chapter's title? In the first place, they included, simply and straightforwardly, the belief in knowledge. This meant the desire—impatient and headstrong, but also ethically impassioned—to make the world knowable through history. This was perhaps the latest version of an aspiration going back to the pioneering social science of the mid-nineteenth century and continuing through the founding disciplinary consolidations of the early twentieth century, some of them (as in the prehistories of *Annales*) explicitly linked to the collaboration of a few innovative historians. The same ambition informed the strongest initiatives toward a social history in the 1950s and 1960s, which I've tied to the convergent efforts of three distinct tendencies—those of the British Marxist historians, the *Annales* school in France, and Charles Tilly and some other Anglo-American sociologists. In the second place, these intellectual developments conjoined with a series of political departures. The radical politics of the sixties were inseparable from the historiographical story. The breakthrough to social history was unimaginable without the sense of political possibility beckoning during the later 1960s, the excitement of a new political world beginning to open up. For me, at least, thinking these things together was an essential part of the time. Good history meant good politics, just as bad politics produced bad history.

All of this added up to a particular sensibility, which was also profoundly the sensibility of 1968. One of the most important things about Thompson was that he was a leading member of a left-wing intellectual generation in Britain who had not sold out but—especially in Thompson's case—continued to live truthfully within an ethics of commitment that seemed worth trying to emulate. Despite his incorrigible grandiosity and occasional bad behavior, Edward Thompson was a beacon of intellectual fortitude. He was a brilliant historian. He held a place for a certain kind of eloquent, troublemaking, disobedient, and creative disrespect for the rules and decorums that the hierarchies of power and prestige require us to perform. As a generation of young historians arguing for a new way of practicing our discipline, we were uniquely lucky to have had him.

III. DISAPPOINTMENT

Across the North Sea

THERE IS A GERMAN side to my story. In October 1970, I arrived
at the University of Sussex to begin graduate work in German history.
As an undergraduate, I'd spent much of my time on early twentieth-
century Germany, so there was some logic to this choice. My best
teacher had also been a German historian, Hartmut Pogge von Strandmann, who was now moving to a lectureship at Sussex.[1] But my interest in Germany went back much further. Growing up in the 1950s, I
couldn't help being impressed by the spectacular qualities of the
recent German past, its lurid and violent momentousness. World
War II had been all around me as a child: British culture—political and
intellectual, popular and polite—was suffused with its effects. My
most sustained historical reading before coming to Oxford had been
devoted to the war's origins and course.[2] But there was also a disorderly and accidental element in my decision making, another
serendipity. During my final year in Balliol, I toyed with various
potential doctorate fields, from nineteenth-century British social history to the Levellers in the English Revolution.[3] In the end, I allowed
myself to be steered toward Germany by Hartmut Pogge. I had excellent arguments for myself, which were more than rationalizations.
Emerging from an undergraduate degree with all the anticareerist
angst of a sixty-eighter, I needed good reasons to justify doing a Ph.D.
in history. In that respect, German history was easy. Big things had
happened there. It was an excellent laboratory.[4]

I arrived in graduate school with the usual set of German history
interests for the time, in such topics as the origins of World War II,
militarism and the role of the army in German politics, and the

strengths and weaknesses of the German Social Democratic Party (SPD). These interests were hard to move beyond, given the limited materials still available to an undergraduate in Britain. Looking back, I'm struck by how innocent my undergraduate essays were of the controversies then raging among German historians about the issue of continuities between the Nazi era and earlier periods of the German past. They also betrayed very little of the social history interests I was excited about more generally.

That quickly changed. The first book I read in German as a graduate student was Hans-Ulrich Wehler's freshly published magnum opus on Bismarck's imperialism.[5] I was blown away by the scale of its ambition—the extraordinary weight of its erudition, the imposing density of its empirical research (including the mountainous footnotes), the vast plenitude of its bibliography (twenty-four separate archives, sixty-five collections of private papers, some twenty-three hundred titles), and the impressive openness of its theoretical framing. The combined effect of economic theory, concrete analytical detail, density of political narrative, and overarching interpretation was daunting. It contained not only a challenging theoretical framework but also a comprehensive analysis of Germany's commercial and colonial expansion in all parts of the globe in the late nineteenth century and a detailed account of Bismarckian policymaking. Historians in Britain, I remember thinking, simply didn't write this kind of book.

In fact, the author of *Bismarck und der Imperialismus* was in the process of emerging during the 1960s as an inexhaustible campaigner for the modernizing of the West German historical profession, which, in Wehler's mind, meant transforming the discipline into a "historical social science." Strikingly, historians in West Germany couldn't rely on any equivalent of the Marxist historiography or *Annales* tradition that encouraged the earlier rise of social history in Britain or France. Indeed, a handful of pioneers notwithstanding, the conservative disposition of the discipline during the 1950s had combined with the dominant ideological climate to stifle innovation. The economic historian Wolfram Fischer (born 1928) and the historian of popular literacy Rolf Engelsing (born 1930) produced important work without much wider emulation, as did a few others in technically specialized fields—for example, Wilhelm Abel (born 1904), in agrarian history, and the demographer Wolfgang Kollmann (born 1925). In retrospect, both Otto Brunner (1898–1982) and Werner Conze (1910–86) might be seen to have developed notions of "structural history" cognate to the thinking at *Annales,* but this lacked any greater resonance at the time.[6] Only in the 1960s did a set of extraneous developments allow a breakthrough toward social history to occur.

But if the West German starting points for social history were badly underdeveloped after 1945 in comparison with Britain or France, the reasons were not hard to find. The catastrophic impoverishment of German intellectual life by the Nazi era left its mark in this way no less than in so many others. The special irony was that in many respects— for example, the pioneering achievements of German sociology in the early twentieth century, the institutional strengths of the labor movement dating from the 1890s, and the intellectual dynamism in Weimar culture—the earlier foundations for doing social history had been much firmer. In Germany, just as across the North Sea, important scholarship had already started to appear. But Nazism severed those potentials. It prevented any slow influencing of university history departments on the British pattern. The difference surely came from the violent political dislocation of the Third Reich, not from some unique and deeply embedded conservatism of the German historical establishment alone (as West German progressives of the 1960s were inclined to claim).

In both Germany and Britain, the way for social history was prepared mainly beyond the central bastions of the discipline of history per se. In chapter 2, I traced social history's British genealogies between the 1930s and the 1960s, through the influence of the Marxist historians and a range of allied tendencies and individuals. But the British story actually began somewhat earlier, at the start of the century, with a variety of pioneers, including the Fabian social investigators Beatrice (1858–1943) and Sidney Webb (1859–1947), the early modern economic historian R. H. Tawney (1880–1962), the radical journalists John (1872–1949) and Barbara Hammond (1873–1961), and the Oxford-based socialist academic G. D. H. Cole (1889–1959). The Webbs's multivolume histories of local government, trade unionism, and workplace relations already adumbrated the main themes social historians came to pursue after 1945, while the Hammonds's epic account of the human costs of the Industrial Revolution sustained much of the inspiration behind Thompson's *Making of the English Working Class.* Among Cole's many works on the history of labor and socialism, *The Common People, 1746–1938,* jointly authored with Raymond

Postgate, remained the best general account of British social history "from below" until after the 1960s.[7]

These people were institution builders: the London School of Economics (LSE), founded by the Webbs in 1895, became an early crucible for progressively inclined social and political science in Britain, while Tawney (also at the LSE) helped launch the Economic History Society and its journal in 1926–27.[8] More to the point, these precursors were all politically active on the left. Their particular bent varied: Tawney was a Christian Socialist, a Labour Party parliamentary candidate, a supporter of the Workers Educational Association, and a leading public intellectual who practiced ethical commitment no less in his scholarly than in his political work;[9] the Webbs were driven by a reforming belief in the "inevitability of gradualness" and by a high-minded administrative ideal of rational taxation, social provision, and public goods, which they eventually hitched to the electoral rise of the Labour Party. But they all inhabited the broadly progressivist political culture of the 1920s and 1930s in Britain, which was coalescing more firmly around the Labour Party and settled properly into place during World War II. In their approach to history, they shared a moral and political critique of the social consequences of industrialization.

My point here is that social history's origins in the early twentieth century presumed a set of left-wing political supports.[10] From a vantage point in the 1920s, those supports were arguably more favorable in Germany than in Britain. Before 1914, the SPD had already accumulated its own historiographical tradition, and the liberalized polity of the Weimar Republic created a climate in which forms of social history could further thrive, not least through the growing imbrication of the labor movement's cultural institutions with the activities of the new state. A good example was the Engels biographer Gustav Mayer (1871–1949), some of whose classic essays on labor's early relations with liberalism were already published before 1914, but whose university career in Berlin remained blocked by conservatives. In the changed conditions after 1918–19, the surrounding institutional constellation shifted; in 1922, Mayer was appointed to a new position in the History of Democracy, Socialism, and Political Parties. German empirical sociology flourished in a similar way. Typical in this respect was Hans Speier (born 1905), whose pioneering research on white-collar workers began during the later years of the Weimar Republic but went unpublished until 1977: after studying in Heidelberg with

Emil Lederer (1882–1939), whose own studies of white-collar workers dated back to 1912, Speier worked as an editor for a Berlin publishing house, was connected to the SPD's Labor Education Department and the city's social services, and was married to a municipal pediatrician.[11]

Until 1933, in other words, German and British historiographies were moving roughly in parallel. In neither country were university history departments open to social history, with its double connotations of popularization and political dissent. As I've already argued, German conditions were even somewhat better in this regard, given the extra supports offered for Marxist thinking and other kinds of progressivism in the national labor movement. The flowering of German sociology added a further positive factor.[12] But the disaster of Nazism during 1933–45 scattered these progressive potentials into a mainly Anglo-American diaspora. Moreover, while the British foundations for social history were being assembled, the historical profession was restored on mainly conservative lines in West Germany after 1945, and social history was able to make few inroads there before the 1970s. In contrast to the early twentieth century, consequently, a gap in the two countries' receptiveness to innovative historiography started to open. In Britain, the democratic patriotisms of World War II had moved some historians out of the narrower state-focused forms of political and diplomatic history dominating their profession; in West Germany, that older dominance endured. The effect of West German emigration over the longer term was to exacerbate the national divergence: the scholarship of the émigrés enriched the historiographies of the host countries and further widened the gap.[13]

West German *Gesellschaftsgeschichte*: Modernizing the Discipline

When things changed in the course of the 1960s, they did so for the usual complicated reasons, including the longer gestating influence of certain individuals, the favorable mix of circumstances at particular institutions, and the purer happenstance of a charismatic personality, an exciting seminar, or an especially resonant publication.[14] But the dramatic political events of the sixties once again were the key. The West German ingredients of this political conjuncture ranged from the slow dissolution of the political conformities of the Adenauer era and the Cold War to the fallout from the great expansion of higher education. As the cohesion of the so-called CDU-state (a shorthand for the single-party dominance of the Christian Democratic Union in the Federal Republic) unraveled during the mid-1960s, the universities also came undone, with student numbers expanding, academic orthodoxies loosening, and the radicalism of 1968 waiting in the wings. Of course, historians were directly involved in many of the resulting conflicts, both through embittering confrontations with their own students and in response to the New Left's demand that the unresolved legacies of the Third Reich finally be faced. Amid all these other fights, a particular controversy that had been raging among West German historians since the start of the decade did much to open the way for social history's early gains.

The celebrated "Fischer controversy" surrounded the work of the Hamburg historian Fritz Fischer (1908–99) on Germany's war aims during World War I.[15] This is not the place for a detailed commentary on this affair's ins and outs. For my purposes here, I need only note how dramatically it brought the problem of continuity in modern German history into intensive debate. By exposing the similiarities between German expansionism during 1914–18 and the later imperialism of the Nazis, Fischer's work located Nazism squarely within the deeper German past. Against the overwhelming weight of existing West German interpretation, which treated the events of 1933 as a kind of *Betriebsunfall,* or "accident in the works," Fischer drew attention toward the longer-term patterns of development through which Nazism could arise.

Interest quickly focused on the sociopolitical system of the German Empire, or *Kaiserreich,* between 1871 and 1918. Fischer and his allies sought to ground an argument about persisting structures of authoritarianism—and forms of opposition against democracy or liberalism—in a heavily materialist analysis of ruling socioeconomic interests. The argument ran that among the advanced industrial nations, Germany alone produced a fascist outcome to the world economic crisis after 1929, a susceptibility spelling deeper weaknesses of the political culture, which could only be explained in social terms. Germany's peculiar "backwardness" in that sense became attributed to the political continuity of a ruling cluster of interests—the "alliance of iron and rye," or the political bloc of heavy industry and big agriculture, which had originally come together under Bismarck's guidance

during the 1870s. That coalition impeded the growth of liberal democratic institutions before 1914, while surviving the 1918 revolution to
fight another day. It destabilized the Weimar Republic and hoisted the
Nazis into power.

The debates surrounding this interpretation gave impetus to an
exciting transformation of West German historical studies. The
Fischer controversy's impact went far beyond Fischer's own, rather
straightforward type of political history and helped clear the way for a
wide-ranging root-and-branch self-examination within German historiography as a whole. Linking the continuity in Germany's twentieth-
century foreign expansionism to a more basic continuity of ruling
interests inside German society at home stimulated an intensive period
of conceptual innovation. The main outcome was a powerful logic of
social explanation. This logic's distinctive understanding of the political process—as being primarily constituted from the interaction of
organized interests—remained the enduring legacy of the Fischer controversy and shaped prevailing approaches to the *Kaiserreich* and the
Weimar Republic. It was accompanied by polemical advocacy of the
"primacy of domestic policy," a formula originally advanced to counter
an older geopolitical determinism that explained German policy by the
vulnerabilities of the country's central European location. All in all, by
fixing attention on the interrelations among economy, politics, and
social structure, these debates around the continuity question gave
decisive momentum to the emerging interest in social history.

Hans-Ulrich Wehler's drive to modernize the discipline took shape
in this context. In the absence of some indigenous equivalent of the
lineages I've described for the emergence of social history in Britain
and France—some counterpart, that is, to the sedimenting of research
and discussion represented by the British Marxist historians and the
Annales school—Wehler set about inventing one. He did so by two
routes.

One route Wehler used was to go back and systematically retrieve
the work of dissenting or marginalized precursors from the early
twentieth century, whose scholarship had either been ignored or suppressed due to the prevailing conservatism of the German profession
(known to its critics as the *Zunft,* or "guild"), before being banned by
the Nazis altogether. The key names included Eckart Kehr (1902–33),
George W. F. Hallgarten (1901–74), Alfred Vagts (1892–1986), and
Hans Rosenberg (1904–88), all of whom adhered to a liberal outlook

of varying radicalism and an interest-based model of social causality, composing a loose intellectual network and finding their way to the United States during the 1930s. To them were added the Marxist Arthur Rosenberg (1889–1943), the left-wing liberal Veit Valentin (1885–1947), and Gustav Mayer (mentioned earlier in this chapter). Having left Germany upon the Nazi seizure of power, most decided not to return after 1945. They continued to receive little recognition inside the *Zunft* until Wehler's generation rediscovered them: Wehler published various editions of their work between the mid-1960s and early 1970s; he also edited a multivolume series of paperbacks (the German Historians series) that integrated these former dissidents into the general pantheon of recognized or recovered voices.[16]

Much as the British Marxists had striven for an oppositional counternarrative capable of challenging the authorized version of national history, Wehler set out to invent a liberal–cum–social democratic countertradition using earlier generations of outsiders. For a while, between roughly the mid-1960s and the early 1970s, this tradition retained a broader political edge—notable during the years of the Brandt-Scheel government (1969–74), when the so-called *Ostpolitik* (eastern policy) for normalizing West Germany's relations with the German Democratic Republic (GDR) and Eastern Europe focused the public engagement of left-of-center intellectuals. During this period, within the universities, the demands of the student Left for relevance and democratization also became briefly connected to the disciplinary discontents of progressive historians. Among Wehler's generation, there was much talk of "emancipation," a "critical science of history," and the discipline of intellectual relevance. This encouraged a wide-ranging eclecticism of theoretical reference, an opening of new subjects (notably toward social history), and a general mood of experiment. Above all, this period was driven by an unbending commitment to *Vergangenheitsbewältigung* (coming to terms with the past), so that Nazism's deeper rootedness in the German past could be laid bare. The new "critical history" was perhaps characterized most of all by this strong sense of pedagogical political purpose, a principled determination that uncomfortable realities of the German past should properly be faced.

The German historiography of the 1970s—including my own entry into the field—was formed in this highly politicized moment. That historiography featured the fleeting convergence of very different intellectual tendencies on the same ground of the "continuity question": advocates of social science history (such as Wehler) worked alongside many scholars who were moving into other kinds of social history closer to historical anthropology and "Anglo-Marxism" (as they called it), and during the later 1960s, broader currents of the West German New Left unfolded an intensive discussion on the subject of fascism. Ultimately, the idea of a "historical social science" made the deepest inroads, and this "Western" orientation eased an affinity with British and U.S. German historians of a similar age and background. Wehler said of his own cohort (namely, "the advanced students and doctoral candidates, assistants, and lecturers who were active in [West German] history departments around 1960"), "An interested and approving opening to the West European and American world was for them as self-evident as was a liberal-democratic point of view."[17]

This was the second route Wehler traveled in equipping his new ideal of *Gesellschaftsgeschichte* (societal history) with a pedigree. At the core of the new openness to theory were more precise affiliations, aligning West German social historians with the mainstream of U.S. social science. The program Wehler (born 1931) and his younger ally Jürgen Kocka (born 1941) laid out was to be based on the explicit use of theory; it required competence in quantitative methods and all the other proficiencies of empirical-analytical social science and was always to be comparative. The underlying master concept of "modernity" implied a classically "whiggish" and progress-oriented reading of the epoch since the late eighteenth-century democratic revolutions, whose meanings were vital both to the values avowedly guiding the intellectual or "scientific" project—its *erkenntnisleitende Interessen,* or "knowledge-constitutive interests" (in the talismanic phrase of the time)—and to the associated larger interpretation of German history it sought to develop. The case Wehler and Kocka made for social history always reflected this duality of epistemological and substantive ambition. The Enlightenment's foundational values (universalism, rationalism, civility, individual emancipation) provided not only an idealized description of the good society that theories of modernization entailed but also a yardstick for measuring the disastrous "misdevelopment" Germany had actually experienced between Bismarck and the Nazi seizure of power.

Wehler and Kocka made their case for a "historical social science" in a stream of programmatic writings, as well as in their respective historical works, calling into service the copious resources of empirical social science relevant to problems of social inequality, industrialization, economic fluctuations, and so forth, while drawing on theoretical traditions descending from both Weber and Marx.[18] They heavily prioritized—as the defining ground of social history—structural analysis of patterns, trends, and large-scale collective forces. Kocka demonstrated the value of Weberian ideal types in his major books on white-collar workers at the Siemens company during nineteenth-century industrialization and on the significance of class conflict during World War I: for the purposes of one, he deployed Weber's typology of bureaucracy; for the other, a model based on Marxist class analysis adjusted for the autonomy of the state. By analyzing the sociopolitical attitudes of U.S. white-collar workers between 1890 and 1940 in a third major study, Kocka then used the comparative method to specify the distinctiveness of white-collar consciousness in Germany. In each of Kocka's studies, the vaunted superiority of social science methods was simultaneously harnessed to showing Germany's peculiarities of historical development, the so-called special path, or *Sonderweg,* that explained how and why German history had culminated in Nazism.[19]

Following the trail of the Fischer controversy, a great deal of the work inspired by the new call for social history focused on the German Empire of 1871–1918. Instead of the older fixation on Bismarck's achievements in unifying the national state, the new authors foregrounded the "authoritarian and anti-democratic structures in state and society" that they argued became locked into place during German unification before descending in disastrous continuity down to 1933.[20] An impressive battery of books appeared during the late sixties and early seventies to secure this interpretation. All of them focused on the success of the imperial system's ruling elites in blocking the pressure for modernizing reform, and all incorporated the interest-based model of social explanation alluded to earlier. Furthermore, the authors concerned strongly associated themselves with Wehler's program for modernizing the discipline. Both drives were intimately linked together—on the one hand, for making history into a critical social science (indeed, for promoting "societal history" as the discipline's new integrative paradigm); on the other hand, for locating the origins of Nazism in a set of nineteenth-century political developments as part of a new overarching interpretation of the German past.

Building on much older lines of comparative understanding among sociologists and political scientists (extending as far back as Weber and Marx), the new West German historians insisted on the uniqueness of Germany's historical development. They viewed German history as an instance of failed, blocked, or distorted modernization. As such, it fundamentally diverged from the history of "the West." Indeed, Nazism could only happen because Germany's earlier history lacked the healthy pattern of development that sustained stronger and more resilient democratic traditions elsewhere. The new historians argued that in contrast to successful instances of political modernization further to the West (in Britain and France), the defining feature of German history under the empire was an extreme discrepancy between the dynamism of its economic growth and the obdurate backwardness of its political institutions. In recurring to such an argument about Germany's so-called *Sonderweg,* the new scholarship was always guided by the larger questions framed around the Third Reich. If the pre-1914 authoritarianism was a primary explanation for German society's later availability for Nazism, Germany's failure to replicate a British or French pattern of liberal democratic evolution during the nineteenth century turned out to have terrible costs from a standpoint in 1933.

How might this West German story of social history's emergence in the late sixties and early seventies be summarized? Where did it converge with the British and French versions described in chapter 2? Where did it differ?

First, it contained the same synthetic ambition. Wehler and Kocka sought both to integrate the different areas of the discipline within a common project—extending from social histories in the more technical subdisciplinary sense, through economic and business history, to labor history, political history, history of ideas, and the rest—and to do so by organized cross-disciplinary collaboration. The goal was synthetic in the further sense of producing an integrated account of the German past. For Wehler, "the unity of history" was at issue.

Societal history in this sense aspires to an analysis of society in its entirety, which is constituted by three equally important dimensions: economics, power, and culture. Its synthetic capacity is to

be proven in terms of its ability to accommodate the complexity
and connection of diverse dimensions of reality more adequately
than do older concepts of integration.[21]

This was the West German version of the totalizing wish. Wehler's
"societal history" had obvious affinities with Hobsbawm's "history of
society"—if less so, perhaps, with Braudel's *histoire totale*. Compared
with Hobsbawm's conception, though, this societal history was heavily social-scientific in orientation, and in the coming years, the Web-
erianism implied by Wehler's trinity of "economics, power, and culture" became ever more pronounced. But at all events, all three
national variants converged on the most decisive common commitment—namely, the search for an overall account of social change,
managed by the primacy of social explanation, directed toward "society as a whole," conceptualized on the ground of material life.

Of course, Kocka and Wehler spoke for a wider network of scholars interested in promoting social history, not all of whom shared all
aspects of their program. During the 1970s, there was much debate
over whether a definite "school" existed and about the degree of its
influence over the West German historical scene.[22] Other individuals
were highly active behind the drive for more "empirical-analytical"
social science history, for example, while being far less involved in
debates about the political history of the *Kaiserreich* and its relationship
to the events of 1933.[23] While endorsing the general desirability of
more social history, another key figure, Wolfgang Mommsen
(1930–2004), didn't regard *Gesellschaftsgeschichte* as a necessary paradigm shift in the same way as Wehler and took a more skeptical stance
on the issue of the *Sonderweg*.[24] Moreover, large areas of scholarship,
including work on the Third Reich or labor history and social histories
of the working class, had a more oblique or partial relationship to the
full program evinced by Wehler and Kocka: while the thinking of people in those fields may have been broadly congruent on the topic of the
Sonderweg, the nature and degree of their commitment to the new
social history was more uneven and diverse.

Second, by the mid-1970s, Wehler had nonetheless carried off a
remarkable feat of institutionalization. Much of this was accomplished
from his base at the new University of Bielefeld, where he arrived in
1971, being joined there two years later by Kocka. His systematic
campaign of retrieval, which fashioned the works of precursors into a

convincing historiographical countertradition, has already been mentioned. He proceeded just as methodically in establishing the groundwork for history's collaboration with the social sciences, anthologizing a succession of bilateral encounters—between history and psychoanalysis, history and sociology, and history and economics—and making Bielefeld into a major center for interdisciplinary research.[25] In 1972, he also started a book series at the Göttingen academic press Vandenhoeck and Ruprecht; the Critical Studies in Historical Social Science series quickly became the leading showcase for the new history. As well as publishing the fresh scholarship of Wehler's and Kocka's students and colleagues, that series became the vehicle for republishing older works and for collecting the essays of others whose mantle Wehler wanted to claim.[26]

During the 1970s, Wehler maintained a prodigious level of organizational, editorial, and publishing activity. Together with Kocka and other close allies—for example, Hans-Jürgen Puhle (born 1940), Reinhard Rürup (born 1934), and Heinrich August Winkler (born 1938)—he occupied center stage among West German historians, not least at the biennial meetings of the national *Historikertag* or historians' association.[27] His publication of a new general history of the *Kaiserreich* in 1973, in effect a practical manifesto for the new social science history, provoked an apoplectic response from conservative political and diplomatic historians and successfully rallied West German historians into opposing camps.[28] In 1974, he edited a massive volume entitled *Social History Today,* honoring Hans Rosenberg; its thirty-three contributors composed a veritable who's who of German social history's leading practitioners.[29] In 1976, he launched a series of bibliographies, the first two volumes (*Modern German Social History* and *Modern German Economic History*) under his own name.[30] Most important of all, the new journal *Geschichte und Gesellschaft* (History and Society) began publishing in 1975, with Wehler very much at the core of its editorial group. Subtitled *Journal for Historical Social Science* and intended as a flagship for the new societal history, it aspired to do for the discipline in West Germany what *Annales* and *Past and Present* had done, in their own time, for France and Britain.

Third, if societal history was far more beholden to U.S. social science than was social history in either Britain or France, its distancing from Marxism also became extremely pronounced. After a brief period of intellectual pluralism during the later 1960s, a discouraging decline of tolerance for Marxist ideas set in. By the mid-1970s, Wehler and his friends were equating Marxism per se so crudely with the self-evidently dogmatic and unappealing orthodoxies of the GDR that any more creative uses of Marxist theory became effectively ruled out. They invoked the sterility of the official Marxist-Leninist historiography of the East to disqualify the claims of Marxist approaches tout court. Yet the very charges they leveled against Marxism—that its approach to social analysis was economistic, reductionist, crudely deterministic, and disrespectful of the autonomies of ideology, politics, and the state—were ironically the very same critiques Marxist historians in the English-speaking world were already conducting among themselves. By ignoring these debates, which (as I argued in chapter 2) reflected a more general ferment within the Marxist tradition, Wehler and Kocka deflected the more interesting challenge and imprisoned any potential dialogue with Marxism inside the provincialism of an inner-German exchange.[31]

In effect, the battle lines for a modernized "historical social science" were drawn for a two-front war—not only against the conservative dinosaurs of the *Zunft,* but also with one eye on the East German historians across the border. The advocates of "societal history" negotiated a middle path, exposing the limitations of traditionalist history of whatever stripe, while strictly demarcating themselves against the official historiography of the GDR.[32] In practice, this effected an unfortunate intellectual closure. It was paralleled and partially encouraged inside West Germany by the attacks launched on "radicals" in public employment by means of the infamous *Berufsverbot,* which potentially rendered the expression of Marxist or equivalent "extremist" opinions reasonable grounds for dismissal or exclusion from the public professions for most of the 1970s.[33] The West German historical profession was not immune against those developments, and in contrast to their earlier engagement for progressive political causes, few of the new "critical historians" seemed willing to come out publicly in defense of this particular cause of academic freedom. Here, the unwillingness to credit the possibility of an independent or critical Marxist historiography began to acquire very tangible meanings. In contrast to Britain and France (and also Scandinavia, the Mediterranean, and North America), there was virtually no Marxist presence in the emerging West German movement for social history.[34]

Fourth, just as in Britain, the turning to social history in West Germany had an essential political dimension. In West Germany even more so than elsewhere, social history's appeal was directly informed by a public climate of superordinate political conflicts, in which contested images of the national past were weightily in play. The rhetoric of social history in West Germany was always heavily didactic. It was openly driven by a politics of knowledge in that sense. But while the political conjuncture of the late 1960s in West Germany bore clear similarities with what I experienced in Britain (particularly in the turmoil of the universities, the broader cultural radicalisms, and the surrounding intellectual ferment), it also involved powerful specificities that came from the painful and unresolved legacies left by Germany's earlier twentieth-century past.

From the start, the drive for a new kind of history was intimately linked in West Germany to a contemporary discourse about history's political relevance. The interest in social history was always linked to a substantive argument—about the long-run course of the German past—that carried profound implications for the ethical probity of West German democracy in the present. At one level, this West German story was simply the local variant of "a broad international movement of historiographical renewal in Europe and North America"; at another level, its character was much more national and specific, involving both the imperfections and fragilities of West German political culture and a new generation of historians desiring that these problems be honestly faced. However indirectly, Chris Lorenz rightly observes, Wehler, Kocka, and their cothinkers were permanently preoccupied with "the question of how it was possible that Germany started two world wars within three decades and how it had organized a mass murder without precedent in history." Lorenz maintains, "This so-called problem of the German *Sonderweg* structured the research agenda and the debates of the *Gesellschaftsgeschichte* from the 1960s to the 1990s."[35]

Social History as the Critique of Backwardness

Where were my own thoughts during all of this? My first reaction to the new approaches pressed by Wehler and stimulated by the Fischer controversy was excitement. After reading Wehler's big book on Bis-

marck's imperialism in the autumn of 1970, I greedily devoured the
new scholarship on the *Kaiserreich* then appearing in such rapid profusion. Another thick book, by Helmut Böhme, one of Fischer's senior
students, rewrote the history of German unification as the advance of
dominant socioeconomic interests, replacing the old story of Prussian
aggrandizement and Bismarckian statecraft ("blood and iron") with a
new narrative of the making of the national economy, whose main axis
was the lasting coalition of heavy industry and big estate agriculture
("iron and rye").[36] Hans Rosenberg's extraordinarily influential book
on the political consequences of the so-called Great Depression of
1873–96 also appeared, elaborating an argument he'd originally made
in the 1940s and further solidifying the interpretation proposed by
Böhme and Wehler.[37] There were pathbreaking monographs on
agrarian politics, on the political influence of the main industrial
lobby, on the interests behind fiscal policy in the pre-1914 decade, on
the politics of the "big navy" after 1897, and on the interest-based
dynamics of party politics in the same period; and Eckart Kehr's
works were revived.[38] Three benchmark volumes of essays, edited by
Böhme, Wehler, and Michael Stürmer, were especially influential in
laying down this ground.[39]

These works had in common an interest-based understanding of
how politics worked under the empire. They contended that a dominant bloc of the most powerful agrarian and industrial interests in the
economy ("iron and rye"), further linked to the social power of the
ruling elites, was fashioned by Bismarck during the 1870s into the
main support of his politics and had remained the reliable parliamentary basis for governing the empire ever since. Böhme called the first
solid appearance of this coalition, during Bismarck's break with the
liberals and his turn to the right in 1878–79, a social refoundation of
the *Reich*. Despite brief oscillations, later governments cleaved consistently to the same ground. It was the political scaffolding behind the
persistence of the empire's prevailing authoritarianism.

As an approach to the period's political history, this scholarly effort
also stressed the elites' successful manipulation of popular support.
Wehler and the other post-Fischerites argued that the undemocratic
provisions of the 1871 constitution weren't enough by themselves to
guarantee the preservation of the status quo; Bismarck and his successors needed strategies for mobilizing the electorate's allegiance. These
strategies were found in various forms of popular nationalism, aggres-

sively exploited for electoral purposes under the pressure of alleged crises of national endangerment, whether the main issue was a strengthening of the army (as in the election campaigns of 1887, 1893, and 1912), the navy (1898), or colonies (1907). In one of his boldest and most seductive conceptual moves, Wehler proposed a generic definition for this plebiscitary mechanism: "social imperialism."

In Wehler's understanding, "social imperialism" meant "the diversion outwards of internal tensions and forces of change in order to preserve the social and political status quo," helping sustain a "defensive ideology" against "the disruptive effects of industrialization on the social and economic structure of Germany."[40] Using Bismarck's colonial policy and mass support for overseas expansion as his model, Wehler described a consistent attempt to use popular nationalism as "a long-term integrative factor which helped stabilize an anachronistic social and power structure."[41] Social imperialism of this kind was an effective "technique of rule" applied by Bismarck, by his main successors under Wilhelm II, and, later still, by Hitler for the purposes of defeating "the advancing forces of parliamentarization and democratization."[42] It was responsible for reconciling the working class to the status quo and containing the rise of the labor movement. Its consequences reached so far that the distinctiveness of German history from Bismarck to Hitler could be defined by this "red thread of social imperialism."[43]

Wehler's approach sharply restated the meaning of the Fischer controversy. "If there [was] a continuity in German imperialism," Wehler declared, it consisted in "the primacy of social imperialism from Bismarck to Hitler."[44] The resulting system of ideological manipulation became endemic to the empire's governing practices, pervasively targeting sundry "enemies of the Reich," as in the *Kulturkampf* against the influence of the Catholic Church during the 1870s, the anti-Polish policies in Prussia's eastern provinces, or the running battles against the SPD.[45] The popular conformities needed for the continuous "stabilizing of the system" were reproduced more generally by the empire's key socializing institutions—namely, schooling, conscription, and the churches.[46] Yet at the same time, in Wehler's view, this amounted to no more than "secondary integration," capable only of provisionally and artificially papering over the cracks. The ensuing desperation encouraged ever more extreme recourse to foreign affairs, leading to the ultimate "social imperialist" escalation of July

1914. This continuity burdened the Weimar Republic with a "long catalogue of historical handicaps," including

> the susceptibility to authoritarian politics; the hostility to democracy in education and party politics; the influence of pre-industrial leadership groups, norms, and ideals; the tenacity of the German ideology of the state; the mystique of the bureaucracy; the manipulation of political antisemitism.

After 1918, these continuities "ensured at least one thing: the traditional power elites could hold the stirrups for Hitler." Without the stirrups, "he could never get into the saddle."[47]

At the time, this approach was exhilarating for me. The new history in West Germany seemed to have exactly the same qualities that were so exciting in the emergence of social history in Britain. Its advocates were passionately committed to theory, much more explicitly so, in fact, than the British Marxists, whose own use of theory was extremely understated by comparison. The West Germans' sense of theory was likewise both interdisciplinary and comparative. In the name of "societal history," they sought equally to draw connections between the social transformations accompanying industrialization and changes in politics, government, and the state. They fundamentally accepted the superiority of materialist social explanation. Their model of determination was heavily structuralist, building from the movements of the economy and large-scale social patterns and trends to careful appraisals of political opportunities and constraints. In all of these ways, the new history had affinities with Marxism. Last but not least, its politics were avowedly progressive. Its foregrounding of the continuity problem and insistence on facing up to the Nazi past were admirable.

I developed big reservations quite quickly. Some of these were about particularities of interpretation in a classic historian's way. My very first article disputed one of the leading post-Fischer arguments about the precise salience of the alliance of "iron and rye" for German politics, by looking intensively at one of the contexts in which it was supposed to have been forged, namely, a key political realignment in 1897–98; disconcertingly, what I'd found in the archives hadn't seemed to fit.[48] From there, I explored doubts about other organizing concepts of the new work, especially Wehler's "social imperialism."[49] Again, these doubts came from the classic historian's concerns.

Exactly how did these concepts function, both by their internal logic and in their wider theoretical ramifications? What larger interpretive work were they doing? How and in which concrete settings should their explanatory claims be assessed? What kind of evidence would show their validity? How did they stand up to the actual evidence of the relevant archive once I'd found it?

My serial unease with the concepts employed by Wehler and his colleagues eventually brought me to the idea of the *Sonderweg* itself. The very grandness of this concept's claims started to seem a very mixed blessing. On the one hand, it captured what appealed to me in the ambitions of social history—namely, the ability to conceptualize the developmental paths of whole societies, in ways that connected big political outcomes to social explanations and required an explicitly comparative approach. The *Sonderweg* thesis likewise offered a deep structural explanation for the origins of Nazism, which, like all German historians, I certainly wanted to understand.

On the other hand, the *Sonderweg* historians gave this deep-structural approach a powerful extra twist. In their view, the absence of a nineteenth-century breakthrough to liberalism on the French or British models allowed the old "preindustrial elites"—the military, the bureaucracy, and the big aristocratic estate owners usually known as the Junkers—to carry on exercising their dominance. Lacking democratic legitimacy, they had to do so repressively and manipulatively, thereby blocking any progressive reform of the polity. As a result, Germany's "modernizing" process was thrown out of kilter: the fundamental clash between economic modernity and political backwardness cast the empire into repeated instability, even a "permanent structural crisis," which grew from the anachronistic primacy of "preindustrial traditions." The resulting "structural syndrome" of German authoritarianism made Germany into a site of "misdevelopment," compared with the healthier societal trajectories further to the West.[50] This continuity of backwardness was the seedbed of Nazism.

In this way, the *Sonderweg* approach encouraged a teleological line of argument, which inscribed Nazism's origins in the depths of the nineteenth century, when German history supposedly failed to take a "Western" turn. In effect, the quest of West German historians, such as Wehler, for an explanation of the "German catastrophe" of 1933–45 had inspired a chain of reasoning that led them into an extraordinarily deterministic reading of the history of the *Kaiserreich*. They believed that the undeniable uniqueness of Nazism, the peculiarly vicious and violent resolution of Germany's interwar crisis, implied a deeper-rooted pathology that made German history in general different from the history of the West. But this teleology of German exceptionalism—of the German *Sonderweg*—increasingly gave me doubts.

For one thing, it seemed to begin the explanation for Nazism from the wrong time, shifting focus away from the immediate fascism-producing crises of 1929–33 and 1918–23 and toward the deeper conditions of backwardness under the empire. Wehler and the others believed that these conditions really separated Germany from, say, Britain, France, or the United States and that they explained why Germany produced fascism and the others did not.[51] Yet to my mind, this focus hopelessly exaggerated the pre-1914 instabilities of the political system. The German Empire was the very opposite of a backward state equivalent to czarist Russia or the underdeveloped European periphery. For good reason, contemporaries saw it as the most compelling case of a modern state and the very model of national efficiency, sustained by the most dynamically growing capitalism in Europe. Moreover, German society was hardly any more unstable or violently conflict ridden than Britain or France during the same pre-1914 years, and the forces of discord were managed just as successfully within the given constitutionalist system. In these terms, both the internal conflicts of imperial German society and its restless foreign expansionism could just as easily be seen precisely as expressions of its modernity, as the symptoms of an exceptionally dynamic modernizing society pushing against its limits.

This unease about the teleology of the *Sonderweg* was also connected to my Marxism. For my generation of Marxists, the particular notions of "modernity" and "modernization" proposed by modernization theory had themselves come to seem extraordinarily problematic—ahistorical, Eurocentric, technocratic, and horribly compromised by their imperialist affiliations.[52] Such approaches were predicated on highly schematic unilinear and inevitabilist assumptions about where history was headed. They postulated a complex of functionally interrelated desiderata, whose development could be disaggregated in economic, social, political, and cultural terms, but which were also integrated at a level of "values."[53] Modernization theorists also implied an end to history, a point of functional integration at which society could become stabilized in some progressively realized and terminal sense.

For most exponents of modernization theory—including the West German advocates of "historical social science"—the model of such successful integration was provided by the post-1945 societies of "the West." Wehler, in particular, saw the modern ideal as having triumphed in "the Western societies of the past two hundred years, step by step, with varying tempo and varying intensity and reach, first in the United States, then after the French Revolution in Europe."[54] It projected "the end utopia of a society of legally equal, educated and propertied, freely competing, possessively individualist, politically capable citizens, oriented toward the eliciting and implementing of the 'rational' common good."[55] Of course, pre-1914 Germany was precisely the case that fell out. German history was the site of omissions and failures, of "ruinous manifestations and pathological developments," of "devastating defeats," and, ultimately, of the "betrayal of bourgeois society."[56] Indeed, the main story of German history under the sign of 1933 was precisely the failure to create a "modern society" in any full and satisfying sense, the failure to traverse "the long hard road to modernity."[57]

But rather than seeing imperial Germany's authoritarianism—and the possibility of Nazism beyond—as coming from the legacies of a "feudal" and "absolutist" past, I preferred to regard them as the complex effects of the turbulently evolving early twentieth-century capitalist present. I thought that historical perception of the conflicts of the imperial period was being distorted by Wehler's narratives of stagnation and rigidity, of "backwardness" and the dominance of "preindustrial traditions," because Germany was already in the throes of full-throttle capitalist transformation. In that sense, change itself, rather than some reified status quo, supplied the strongest continuity. In light of the explicitly anti-Marxist thrust of the *Sonderweg* advocacy, moreover, the insistence on explaining Nazism's origins by "feudal" or "preindustrial" holdovers seemed to me increasingly like a way of freeing capitalism from the odium of any causal responsibility for Nazism. By these means, capitalism was being let off the hook.

Class Analysis from Below

My skepticism of Wehler had a further political aspect. The belief in popular agency so vital for social historians and others inspired, like myself, by Edward Thompson collided with Wehler's kind of history on a double front. On the one hand, it clashed seriously with Wehler's social science predilections. It was no accident that Bielefeld's British connections favored the more classically materialist Hobsbawm over the more "culturalist" Thompson, for example, while a figure like Raymond Williams barely registered on their radar screen at all.[58] On the other hand, Bielefeld's top-down model of political action was also in tension with a Thompsonian commitment to "history from below." Emphasis on long-term structural changes, large impersonal forces, and measurable social trends wasn't incompatible with the latter, and Wehler's manipulative model of popular politics couldn't fail to seem highly uncongenial and problematic. Both these aspects of the West German approach left a very reduced place for popular agency. One early critique of the post-Fischer "new orthodoxy" spoke for many of us by pointing to this particular problem.

> Political processes, changes, and influences are perceived as flowing downwards—though now from the elites who controlled the State, rather than from the socially vaguer entity of the State itself—not upwards from the people. The actions and beliefs of the masses are explained in terms of the influence exerted on them by manipulative elites at the top of society. The German Empire is presented as a puppet theater, with Junkers and industrialists pulling the strings, and middle and lower classes dancing jerkily across the stage of history towards the final curtain of the Third Reich.[59]

In other words, the *Sonderweg* thesis, in all its ramifications, severely discouraged us from taking popular politics in imperial Germany seriously. Claims about the importance of popular mobilization and the potentials for popular citizenship could always be trumped by insisting on the empire's prevailing backwardness, the continued dominance of the preindustrial elites, and the successful defense of authoritarianism. Any evidence of popular activity could be dismissed as the effects of manipulation. Accordingly, neither the vigorous normality of popular politics before 1914 nor the real meanings of the conflicts in German society were likely to be grasped.

On realizing this, my own response was to work at developing a more complex picture of popular political involvement before 1914, one that sought to explain the new mass movements of the period by the effects of social and political changes at the grass roots rather than by manipulative interventions from above. By reconstructing the coherence, rationality, and self-activating qualities of popular mobilization, I wanted to restore a better sense of popular agency. My immediate work concerned popular politics on the right—more specifically, the role of nationalist pressure groups in radicalizing right-wing politics before 1914.[60] But there's absolutely no question that I owed much of my skepticism about Wehler's manipulative model to what I'd learned from Thompson, Hobsbawm, and Rudé about the nature of popular protest. I also kept a close interest in German labor history, where the impact of the new social science history was especially revealing.

To some degree, the recent growth of labor history across the North Sea had paralleled that in Britain. A yearbook that began publishing in 1961, the *Archiv für Sozialgeschichte*, initially focused rather austerely on the socialist tradition's internal past, but within a decade, it branched out toward a wider vision of social history. The *Internationale Wissenschaftliche Korrespondenz zur Geschichte der Deutschen Arbeiterbewegung* (*IWK*)—an academic newsletter containing articles, documentations, guides to archives, and inventories of research—was launched in 1965. But whereas the *IWK* followed closely the format of the *Bulletin* of the Labour History Society in Britain, the pattern diverged in other respects. Backed officially by the SPD's institutional resources, the annual *Archiv für Sozialgeschichte* reaped the benefits of a political relationship that the Labour History Society could never enjoy. This contrast was confirmed in 1969 with the opening of the SPD's official archive in Bad Godesberg, linked to the party's research arm, the Friedrich Ebert Foundation, which sponsored an impressive flow of publication and research.

It was no accident that the founding works in West German labor history came from the period when the SPD officially repudiated its Marxist heritage and declared itself a "people's party" at the Bad Godesberg Congress of 1959. Those key works included a reading of the influence of Karl Kautsky by Erich Matthias; an intellectual history of the Social Democratic tradition by Susanne Miller (born 1915); a series of studies focusing on the 1860s and 1870s by Werner Conze and his students at the University of Heidelberg; a detailed account of the SPD subculture under the empire by the Weberian sociologist Guenther Roth; and a pioneering study, by Gerhard A. Ritter (born

1929), of the SPD's growth, during the 1890s, into a mass move-ment.[61] As the Godesberg Program ratified the SPD's long march through the existing institutions of West German society toward its destiny as a "responsible party of government," a new academic histo-riography emerged to ground those same claims. The convergence was splendidly manifest in the labor movement's centenary celebra-tions in 1963.[62]

Because its mentor was such a key forerunner of social history in the West German profession, the Conze school is especially interest-ing from the point of view of the present study.[63] The argument revolved around the fateful consequences of the split between labor and liberalism in the mid-1860s, during the conflicts over unifi-cation—or "the separation of the proletarian from the bourgeois democracy," in Gustav Mayer's arresting phrase of 1912.[64] The result-ing recriminations debarred the SPD from its rightful place in the democratic wing of an integrated national consensus, where it might have become something more akin to British labor in the post-1867 Gladstonian coalition. For Conze, that implied "an independent party of labor, allied with the Democrats but organizationally distinct, with-out revolutionary hostility to the state, and committed to participating in a generally accepted democratic-monarchical constitution."[65] Indeed, "until 1871," he argued, "the labor movement in Germany was part of the national movement."[66] Workers became alienated from their patriotism only by Liberal readiness for compromise with Bismarck. Liberal disparagement of democracy preempted labor's "readiness for cooperation in state and society." Their democratic hopes spurned, socialists retreated into revolutionary rhetoric and class-based isolation.[67]

The Conze school's influence was complemented by works dealing with the solidarities of the Social Democratic subculture and with the effects of illegality under the Anti-Socialist Law (1878–90), each of which had deepened the labor movement's isolation from the rest of society, while heightening the integrative importance of the move-ment's new Marxist creed. By the 1970s, the first spate of mono-graphs formed in the image of the new "historical social science" was also coming to fruition. As well as the next generation of Conze stu-dents, their authors included younger scholars working with Kocka and Wehler in Bielefeld, with Ritter in Münster and then in Munich, with Hans Mommsen and others in Bochum, and in a variety of other centers. Especially important in bringing this work to print were Conze's Industrial World series, published by Klett-Cotta; the Critical Studies series edited by Kocka, Wehler, and others; and the publishing house of the Friedrich Ebert Foundation.[68]

Even as a consensus began coalescing during the late seventies and early eighties, new critiques and counterreactions were already emerging. Challenges came from women's history and gender history in particular, although the ascendant social science historians proved no less adept at sidelining the resulting scholarship in West Germany than elsewhere. From more generalized discontents, a new standpoint of cultural history was beginning to crystallize; its most radical West German version was *Alltagsgeschichte,* or the history of everyday life. I'll explore the nature of these departures in chapter 4. Here, I want to say something more about how societal history approached the history of the working class. For my own hopes of social history's possibilities, the goal of fashioning an oppositional narrative of popular-democratic agency capable of contesting the authorized accounts of the national past was always at the core, in a materialist analysis of the working class under capitalism—an analysis best exemplified, in their differing ways, by Edward Thompson and Eric Hobsbawm. The pre-1914 German labor movement, so much more socialist, better organized, and apparently more class conscious than its moderate and pragmatic British counterpart, offered ideal materials for such an enterprise. So how far did the West German critical historians deliver the goods?

One answer can be found in the multivolume series History of Workers and the Labor Movement in Germany since the End of the Eighteenth Century. Edited by Gerhard A. Ritter for the Friedrich Ebert Foundation, the series started appearing in 1984. For its respective volumes, this project enlisted the most prestigious West German practitioners, including Jürgen Kocka (nineteenth century), Heinrich August Winkler (Weimar Republic), Michael Schneider (Third Reich), Klaus Tenfelde (*Kaiserreich* and World War I), and Ritter himself (*Kaiserreich*).[69] These authors confidently avowed their indebtedness to the historical social science shaped by Wehler, Kocka, and others since the 1960s—if not as a full-blooded programmatic declaration, then as an operational commitment that was simply axiomatic, intermittently brought to visibility by the footnotes, as though now self-evidently the form that good history would take.[70] In other words, this imposing project's overt framing, including the visible architecture of the chapter organization of the individual books, was entirely assimilable to an established discourse of West German societal history as it emerged from the 1970s. What were the results?

The overall approach was heavily materialist in the now classical social-scientific sense. The foundational context of the labor movement's history was established by aggregating a series of structural analyses, built up in the course of the overall account. These covered the demographics of labor migration and recruitment; aspects of the labor process, productivity, and changes in the divisions of labor; the organization and dynamics of labor markets; the movements of wages and prices; living standards and the material conditions of social life in families, households, and neighborhoods; housing, health, and nutrition; sexuality and reproduction; and the access to welfare and social security. Holding this framework together was the directional logic of long-term processes of development, linked to changes in the social structure and their grand-scale periodization. The underlying theoretical reference points tended to be drawn from Max Weber. The assumptions about long-term societal change were organized into a Western-derived paradigm of modernization.

This was nothing if not "structural history," whose implied understanding of causality delivered the organizing principle behind the boundaries and scope of each of the books in the series.[71] In the dynamics of class formation, the authors fundamentally prioritized structures and processes over human agency; they focused on changing market relations, the character of the labor market, the expansion of wage labor, the spatial growth and concentration of industry, the distribution of incomes, and the "stabilizing of the proletarian milieu" via family, neighborhood, and associated social mores. Furthermore, the history of the labor movement per se, in the form of parties and trade unions, was cleanly separated out—either for entirely freestanding volumes, such as Kocka's on the nineteenth century and Tenfelde's and Ritter's for the prewar *Kaiserreich,* or in distinct parts of the book, as in Winkler's trilogy on Weimar.[72] With the partial exception of the "subcultural" clubs and associations, which the established wisdom considered a part of the structural working-class milieu, all the organizations and events that gave the German working class its active history under the *Kaiserreich* became formally isolated from the experiential contexts of everyday material life. Everything that made the German working class visible as a collective agency—the SPD, the unions, the cooperatives, the major strikes, the election campaigns, the imposing demonstrations and rallies, the internal controversies, the charismatic personalities—became bracketed from class formation per se.

Thus, the place of politics in the pre-1914 volumes was inconsistent and not a little paradoxical. These authors presumed a model of normal development, a process of class formation deriving from the capitalist economy's structural conditions and relations, to which, over the longer run and given the chance, German workers would also have produced a "normal" response—namely, entering the legitimate public sphere through their organizations, winning support from other social groups, and becoming gradually integrated into the political system. But the reactionary political backwardness of the imperial state and its ruling elites stopped any normal evolution in its tracks. By repressing the German workers' legitimate self-organization, the government and the big employers forced the labor movement back into a posture of defensive militancy. That intransigence allowed the entrenchment of a radical Marxist leadership, who would otherwise have disappeared and made way for the pragmatists and moderate reformers who supposedly characterized the labor movement in, say, Britain.

This critical approach had been refined over a number of decades, not least by Ritter himself, whose first book helped pioneer the argument.[73] But it's worth noting how this political explanation is handled relative to what otherwise seems like a textbook case of socioeconomic determinism. In Ritter's and Tenfelde's account of the situation of workers under the *Kaiserreich*, the imperial state was installed at the very front of the book, assuming a foundational explanatory equivalence with the industrializing economy: in effect, the antimodern behavior of the traditional ruling elites was thereby freed from the book's machinery of structural determination and allowed to operate autonomously, acting on and against the labor movement (to block its emancipation), distorting its aspirations into self-isolating radicalism, and limiting its agency. Yet the labor movement's own political actions were given nothing like the same determinative importance in shaping the collective dispositions of the working class. Instead, by being consigned to the subsequent (and still to be written) volumes, the politics of labor received more of an epiphenomenal meaning, becoming very much "superstructure" to the earlier account's "base."

This simultaneous diminishing and overburdening of politics—the argument that politics is not part of the process of class formation but external to it, that politics distorts the collective agency and cultural dispositions that class formation would otherwise produce—has been a hallmark of the German labor history interpretation represented by Ritter and Tenfelde. Yet this was precisely where the social science materialism behind that interpretation bothered me the most. During the seventies, I'd become ever more drawn to the kind of culturalist Marxism practiced by Raymond Williams, which seemed far better suited for capturing the subtleties and indirections that characterize transfers between "the political" and "the social." The social and cultural theory I found most helpful was seeking to understand ideology and politics inside the manifold practical settings of social and cultural life, whether in the more accessible sites of the workplace or party and trade union organization; in informal spaces, such as the family or the street; or in dynamic experiential contexts, such as an election campaign, a strike, or a riot. Yet, in contrast, the social science historians continued to approach politics and ideology as discrete levels or spheres, proceeding either according to their own logics and rhythms or else connected to the economy and social structure in mainly functionalist and instrumentalized ways—at all events, as warranting a dependent and second-order reflection.

In other words, within social theory at large, the kind of structuralism presumed by *Gesellschaftsgeschichte,* which made politics external to the economy and social life, was becoming harder and harder for the more self-critical practitioners to defend. It involved a highly suspect procedure—first bracketing politics out of the discussion of class formation, then reintroducing a political explanation after an exhaustive empirical-sociological analysis has established the determinative power of the economy and its social relations in the more fundamental and underlying sense. But as Peggy Somers has pointed out, "Politics, laws, cultural practices, and belief are not external to the economy; they are the mechanisms through which human livelihood operates, they *are* the economy no less than the accumulation of capital or the attempt to overcome scarcity."[74] Far from acting externally on the working class as an already completed structure, politics and the state should be seen as involved directly—constitutively and inextricably—inside the very processes of class formation themselves.

In that case, we are back once again to the central flaw in the master concept of the *Sonderweg*. In support of their approach within labor history, the latter's exponents always pointed to the repressive labor relations of so much of Germany's large-scale industry before 1914, together with the associated debarring of the SPD and trade unions from the legitimate political nation. By maintaining such a system of exclusion, the reactionary attitudes of the *Kaiserreich*'s most powerful capitalists were to be regarded as the redundant holdovers from a "preindustrial" or traditionalist mentality. But in response, I came to argue that we might just as well see the illiberal political outlook so prevalent among the big industrialists—their banning of unions, their heavy-handedly authoritarian approach to relations on the shop floor, and their company-based welfare paternalism—as a resourcefully modern response to the distinctive labor problems encountered during an exceptionally rapid, large-scale, and dynamic type of industrialization. In fact, rather than being pathologies or survivals intruding from a "preindustrial" past that ought to have been superseded, both the imperial polity's distinctive authoritarianism and the forms of the SPD's radicalism might be traced perfectly well to the extreme modernity of German society. Before 1914, Germany was not following an aberrant or "exceptional" path but offering a particularly extreme version of "normality."

At the heart of the problem was a lack of readiness to treat historical agency seriously enough—to honor its own terms and time while always bringing the appropriate comparative and theoretical criteria to bear, within longer-drawn perspectives of historical locatedness and change. In my view, we would never get much closer to an understanding of short-term and longer-term historical outcomes (which here meant all the complicated historical reasoning needed for a more successful positioning of the meanings of the events of 1933), unless we got further inside the political subjectivities produced by the distinctive conflicts of the different periods between the 1860s and the 1930s. In this respect, during the late seventies and early eighties, I was more and more preoccupied with the challenge of bringing my own two historian's identities more consistently together—of bridging between, on the one hand, a British historiographical scene where I was most interested in the complexities of working-class culture and the intricacies of popular ideology and, on the other, a West German one where the dominant school of social historians thought in such relentlessly structuralist ways.[75] The dilemma was posed particularly tellingly by the new West German histories of the working class. In their stress on large-scale structures and objective processes, these studies narrowly cramped the space for any element of popular agency. They offered the opposite of a Thompsonian account. In the works of Kocka, Ritter, and Tenfelde, the German working class was decidedly not present at its own making.

On the Edge

The mid-1980s brought to a head the tensions I'm trying to describe. It's notoriously hard to date changes in the history of ideas very exactly, especially those we've lived through ourselves. Put a dozen historians around a table, and they'll each have a slightly differing version. But most will agree on this significant watershed in the life of the discipline: beforehand, social history gave the main impetus for innovation; afterward, it came from cultural history, certainly in the attention-grabbing debates and controversies. The *Sonderweg* discussion remained powerfully focused on the reasons for Nazism and the unique enormity of the genocide of the Jews, and my German interests had their own "local" momentum, but my thinking was constantly informed, challenged, and troubled by the wider debates surrounding this big transition.

The temporalities of the change varied from field to field and country to country. Among Europeanists, it occurred most rapidly in French history as opposed to other national fields, such as the British or German, and more easily among early modernists than modernists. It gathered greatest momentum most quickly among the profession in the United States, elsewhere growing far more on the margins and in the interstices. In large part, the main pressure for change in West Germany came from outside university history departments altogether, in the grassroots activism of a History Workshop movement modeling itself partly on the British forerunner. Likewise, from outside the university profession, the History Workshops remained a vital source of new ideas in Britain, establishing a much stronger presence in the polytechnics and other second-tier institutions eventually given university standing in 1992. In the British case, many cultural historians initially found a home in cultural studies rather than history departments per se. In most fields, the changes took a long time to percolate. In my own cohort of German historians, the transition began among a few of us during the later 1980s, but even after a decade, arguments for the "new cultural history" were still meeting angry or dismissive resistance.

Unease crept up on us slowly, a gradual doubt in the sufficiency of social history's totalizing claims, a slight fraying of the optimism about what it could be expected to deliver. The early debates also developed inside social history's new frame, for by the later 1970s, this was, to a great degree, hegemonic. There was a confidence that, whatever one's particular topic or specialism, the power of social explanation would still provide the establishing rules. In the wryly repeated phrase of the time, we were "all social historians now." Even as we acknowledged—in fact, relished—the continuing difficulties (however much we struggled with the complexities of culture and ideology or with the never-ending need for still more sophisticated ways of theorizing the relationship of politics and society or the state and the economy), we still assumed the permanence of the underlying turn to social history itself. Even as we stepped tentatively into the forbidden zone of subjectivity and the unconscious, this held good. "In the final instance," the sovereignty of the social would prevail. Nothing else was yet thinkable. Too many hopes, intellectually and politically, were invested. Its legitimacy was too dearly bought.

My own immediate work on the radicalization of the Right in pre-1914 Germany found me grappling firsthand with the emerging predicament. I wanted to explain the rise of radical nationalist ideology without either succumbing to a simple continuity thesis focused on 1933 or resorting to stereotypical claims about the "German mind" or a peculiar "German ideology." Yet having started with the assumption—naturally—that this would require mainly a sociology of patriotic activism, I learned, during the distance separating my dissertation (1974) from my book (1977–78), that this wouldn't work. Instead, I needed an improved theory of ideology, one better attuned to the experiential dynamics, self-contained logics, and independent efficacy of the radical nationalist appeals and rhetorics than the materialist analytic of the available social history approaches allowed—one capable of capturing ideology's "relative autonomy" (in the important phrase of the time).

I found this in a number of intersecting influences, few of which troubled the thinking of many German historians. One was Gramsci, whose prison notebooks had been anthologized in 1971, followed by translations of his prison letters in 1974–75 and by increasingly extensive commentaries, reaching a climax around 1977.[76] Close in importance was Raymond Williams, whose 1973 article "Base and Superstructure" gave me a constant point of reference, leading to his more elaborate *Marxism and Literature,* published in 1977. Beginning in early 1975, I struggled with the implications of Louis Althusser's influence, which increasingly preoccupied British Marxists. This wrestling with Althusser's ideas did more than anything else to release thinking about ideology from its older tethers in ideas of "false consciousness," just as the agonies of reading Nicos Poulantzas enabled a more complex grasp of the relations linking the state, political power, and social classes.[77] Most far-reaching of all over the longer term, the consequences of the new feminism, working away still somewhat beneath the surface of these other discussions, were increasingly unassimilable and a source of ever-widening disturbance.[78] Finally, two influences especially moved the thinking that went into my book: *On Ideology,* a volume of papers published by Stuart Hall and others at the Birmingham Center for Contemporary Cultural Studies, and Ernesto Laclau's essays in *Politics and Ideology in Marxist Theory.*[79] (Both works appeared in 1977 and prefigured later elaborations that came during the 1980s.)

Such discussions pushed on the edges of the materialist consensus without wanting to leave its terrain. They saw the problems with "base and superstructure" materialism while seeking to stay within a rethought structuralist Marxist idiom. As social historians turned their minds in this same direction, moreover, the second half of the 1970s brought much taking of stock. Polemical essays published in 1976 by Stedman Jones and the Genoveses were quickly taken as signs of a "crisis" in social history, for example.[80] But these were still far more the self-confident expressions of forward momentum than any sign of uncertainty. They were a further instance of the desire to recast the whole of the discipline rather than merely creating another specialism. If achieving the latter left older specialisms, such as political history, simply intact, they argued, little in the overall discipline would change.

Thus, social history now needed to make good on its totalizing promise. It should lay materialist claim to the analysis of politics, too, rather than remaining content with "the social" narrowly conceived.

There were plenty of differences among social historians. Those between Marxist-inclined Thompsonians and social science historians of various stripes, from West German advocates of "societal history" to North American admirers of Charles Tilly, come first to mind. But social historians mainly explored varying versions of a common materialist paradigm—whether pushing toward the more anthropologically inflected conception of a society's "whole way of life" in the manner of Raymond Williams's "cultural materialism" or looking toward more structuralist directions grounded once again in the economy or mode of production. In perhaps the most significant British debate of this kind in the late 1970s, "structuralists" inspired by the ideas of Althusser faced a broad front of social historians (dubbed "culturalists") taking their stand with Edward Thompson, whom the author of the original intervention, Richard Johnson, had described as not taking the economy seriously enough. Each side bridled against what they saw as the other's reductionist proclivities, whose procedures were inflating either the mode of production's structural determinism or the explanatory reach of culture.[81]

But these were, again, conflicts over a common materialist goal. Cracks in the project itself appeared only more slowly. By using a decidedly nonmaterialist form of linguistic analysis to attack the validity of social interpretations of the failure of Chartism, for example, Gareth Stedman Jones questioned the class-analytical orthodoxies of British social history in one of their main nineteenth-century heartlands. His critique called into doubt the received assumptions of social history and was an early stalking horse for what became known as the "linguistic turn." But while versions of his argument were presented in papers beginning in 1977–78, the larger implications weren't fully apparent until his essay on the topic appeared in 1982–83.[82] Similarly, William Sewell, who mixed with anthropologists and a few sympathetic historians during a five-year stint at the Institute for Advanced Study in Princeton in the late 1970s, was clearly in the process of revising his commitments as a social historian and getting ready to take the linguistic turn (as he now puts it). But this bent wasn't widely visible until 1980, when he published his book *Work and Revolution in France*.[83]

These dispersed signs of change were only partially perceptible to most people before the early 1980s, including even the few pacesetters themselves. Yet, in seeking to grapple with the conceptual difficulties I've been describing, social historians were encountering the limits of what had so far remained a broadly consensual project. The process of rethinking an approach to questions of culture and ideology, meaning and subjectivity, was taking some people to the edges of what social history was usually thought to allow. In the interests of a nonreductionist approach to such questions, some were pushing so insistently on the boundaries of the materialist paradigm that it started to come apart.

In West Germany, for example, a scattering of individuals—Alf Lüdtke (born 1943) and Hans Medick (born 1939) at the Max Planck Institute for History in Göttingen, Lutz Niethammer (born 1939) at the University of Essen, Karin Hausen (born 1938) at the Technical University in Berlin, Adelheid von Saldern (born 1938) at the University of Hanover, and Dieter Groh (born 1932) at the University of Konstanz—were pursuing new directions that pushed deliberately past the structuralism of Gesellschaftsgeschichte. Though from the same generation in terms of birth, these figures differed markedly from the social science historians in their outlook, bringing political dispositions influenced less by the modernizing reformism of the SPD and liberal democratic veneration of the United States than by the student movement and the New Left, by the new feminism, and by the resurgent extraparliamentary radicalisms shortly to culminate in the Greens.

Just as societal history declared its credentials with the new journal Geschichte und Gesellschaft, these alternative voices began to be heard. In 1976, for example, Lutz Niethammer joined with Franz Brüggemeier (born 1951) to publish a remarkable study of working-class housing under the Kaiserreich. They developed an argument about patterns of working-class solidarity running through social life beneath the levels of party, union, and club activity normally associated with the shaping of working-class political consciousness. They urged that to understand the distinctive forms of that consciousness and, still more, its potential strengths and weaknesses, the informal settings of workers' everydayness needed to be explored. Then, in 1977, Alf Lüdtke edited an issue of the journal SOWI (Sozialwissenschaftliche Informationen für Unterricht und Studium) entitled "Needs, Experience, and Behavior," which gave the first systematic indication of what an emerging interest in the history of everyday life might mean. In the next year, Jürgen Reulecke and Wolfhard Weber (both born 1940) took this a step further, in an edited showcase of empirical research with fourteen essays on "the social history of everyday life in the industrial age," covering aspects of work time, family, and leisure.[84]

Each of these initiatives had in common a pronounced shifting of social history away from the prevailing definitions of *Gesellschafts-geschichte,* without a return to the older institutionally or politically bounded approaches of traditional labor history. The purpose was to reach a more qualitative grasp of ordinary people's lives by exploring the circumstances of daily existence at work, at home, and at play, thereby entering the inner world of popular experience. Lüdtke and the others argued that by exploring social history in those experiential or subjective dimensions, conventional distinctions between the "public" and the "private" might be overcome; the interior complexities of ordinary lives and the possible forms of political subjectivity might be opened up; and a better way of making the elusive connection between the political and cultural realms might finally be found. In the works of social science historians, precisely these "insides" of the "structures, processes, and patterns" of social analysis, "the daily experiences of people in their concrete life-situations, which also stamp their needs," were usually left out.[85] *Alltagsgeschichte,* or the history of everyday life, was excellently fitted for bringing them in.

These new West German proposals emerged at the end of the 1970s as a radical solution to the problems of "base and superstructure" that, in so many ways, had preoccupied my own generation of left-tending social historians since the advent of Thompson's *Making of the English Working Class.* Certainly for those influenced by Marxism, those years had seen a sustained series of encounters with a persisting dilemma—that of finding more subtle and sophisticated ways of making connections between "the social" and "the political" (or between the ground of material life and the spheres of ideology and politics) while simultaneously providing a better strategy for conceptualizing the forms of individual and collective human agency. Beyond this larger theoretical task, moreover, was the more particular historiographical problem of connecting the increasingly rich knowledge generated by social historians with the conventional narratives that political historians were still busily reproducing.

Of course, most social historians influenced by Thompson approached agency via the dynamics of the production of class consciousness. But by the late 1970s, a belief in that model of class political agency was becoming much harder to sustain. Misgivings about the "base and superstructure" metaphor were linked by now to an increasingly generalized ferment within theory itself, reflecting critiques of economic determinism, doubts about the foundational materialism of Marx's 1859 preface, feminist attacks on the monomania of class, and the retheorizing of ideology associated with the reception of the ideas of Althusser and Gramsci.[86] The resulting debates pulled Marxists further and further away from deterministic forms of thinking and toward a concern with matters of culture, meanings, and subjectivities in their own right. The entire logic of discussion among British Marxists during the 1970s was toward one kind of antireductionist critique or another, and these certainly had their effects on how Thompsonians now thought about the model of class formation contained in *The Making*.

Furthermore, the impact these intellectual debates had on social historians was intimately connected to developments in politics. Just as the political excitements of 1968–69 lent momentum to new kinds of history (inspiring huge self-confidence in the explanatory power of the materialist paradigm), equally severe political setbacks at the end of the next decade helped take the wind from social history's sails. The new period opened by 1968 had fired belief in the potency of class as a prime mover in politics, not least because it also brought the last great transnational wave of Western European industrial militancy in 1967–76 and the unprecedented influence of an academic Marxist intelligentsia. For a while, the signs were conflicting. By 1978, the Eurocommunist experiment may have run into the sand, but socialists were still riding the democratic transitions in Spain, Portugal, and Greece into office, just as the French Socialists were also forming a government for the first time. In Poland, the extraordinary success of *Solidarnosc* (Solidarity) seemed to reaffirm the efficacy of class as a powerful source of political agency. But for anyone writing in the Marxist tradition in Britain, the years 1979–85 were a dismaying shock to the system. Amid two Conservative election victories and the escalating rhetoric of a New Right, masses of workers deserted the Labour Party, and the Left slid into disarray. Unemployment, deindustrialization, and capitalist restructuring gutted working-class communities with brutal and alarming speed, while the crushing of the great miners' strike in 1984–85 brought the old class-based politics to an especially demoralizing impasse.

The effect for social historians was maximized by a series of prestigious commentaries that set out specifically to historicize the meanings of this new conjuncture.[87] Most resonant for British historians was a commentary by Eric Hobsbawm, who initiated widespread debate with a 1978 lecture called "The Forward March of Labour Halted?"[88] Hobsbawm argued that class had decisively changed its valency as a source of alignment and motivation in politics. Persuasively pulling together the contemporary evidence of fragmentation, he contrasted the new patterns of disintegration with the histories of class concentration from the end of the nineteenth century, which had originally sustained the labor movement's progressivist momentum. The older infrastructure of class-political allegiance and identification was falling apart, and Hobsbawm averred that if the Left wanted to retain its primary bearings in a class analysis of the inequalities of wealth and power, it needed to think creatively about how new forms of political coalescence might occur, both at the level of coalition building among old and new constituencies and at the level of rhetoric and ideas. Simple reflex to the "unity of the working class," relying axiomatically on its progressive collective agency, wouldn't suffice.

This argument about the present was soon picked up and applied historically, forcing historians to think more searchingly about all the processes of coalition building and concentration needed to sustain forms of working-class political agency at different times in the past. If the working class could be dethroned from its natural or automatic centrality for the thinking of the Left now, what would happen to our analysis if it also became dethroned for the past? It now became easier to see that, far from a natural or "objective" unity growing sociologically from the material conditions of life in the economy and flowing logically into politics, the forms of working-class political agency had to be deliberately and creatively worked at and produced, whether in Thompson's period or in any other. Over time, a certain set of class-political traditions obviously acquired durable continuity from the end of the nineteenth century. However, the popular persuasiveness of the associated political languages—their capacity to go on doing their work—could never be taken for granted, whether in national campaigning or in the microsettings of local community life. Moreover, if

sonance of the languages of class could certainly be enhanced, it
lso, under other circumstances, undergo damage.

what case, the social historian's decisive questions started to
change. Rather than asking about the conditions under which a set of
assumed working-class interests could or couldn't become expressed
in their natural or appropriate forms of action and belief, perhaps we
should be questioning the ascriptive modeling of class consciousness in
the first place. When so many actual workers were always left out and
whole categories were only partially or unevenly present in the
achieved manifestations of class consciousness, what did it mean to
expect workers to behave "as a class"? Which operative categories of
workers were embraced—rhetorically and practically—in any particular collective action, and which were not? How did the prevailing
imagery and assumptions about what constituted the working class
come to be produced? How did particular practices, ideas, and institutions encourage or hamper particular attributions and interpretations of working-class interest? How did one particular complex of
images about the working class become accepted and entrenched over
another? Through this kind of questioning, working-class interests
seemed to be far more a contingent effect than an underlying cause.

These new doubts about the class concept increased under the
impact of other political developments with equally far-reaching theoretical consequences, which then also worked their way into historians' debates. By far the most important challenge came from feminism. Feminist insistence that vast categories of work and workers
should no longer be marginalized from working-class history and that
fundamental areas of social life simply couldn't be subsumed into the
analytical terms class provided increasingly damaged the integrity of
the established materialist outlook. To the disruptions and difficulties
of gender would soon be added the implications of other differences:
race, ethnicity, sexuality, nation and region, space, generation, religion, and so forth. All the resulting historiographies were shadowed
during the 1980s by the related pluralizing of progressive political
agendas, as women's movements became joined by peace movements, environmentalisms, sexual radicalisms, antiracist agitations,
and the wider repertoire of identitarian and new social movement politics. In all of these ways, a wedge became driven between the analytics of class and the progressive political possibilities they had previously been used to explain.

In the late seventies, these gathering uncertainties became dramatized in a variety of ways. Most powerfully of all (in retrospect), the public political climate began lurching to the right, in ways that bruised and impaired the accustomed routines of commentary and debate, creating an excess of political anger and anxiety that the available class-political standpoints couldn't easily address. The "German Autumn" of 1977, a dismaying climacteric of ultra-left-wing terrorist futility and state-repressive response, brought one such drama, mirrored six months later in Italy by the spectacle of the Aldo Moro kidnapping and murder. These were both indications of an acute difficulty for anyone relying on the usual materialist compass. Politics was manifestly running beyond the reach of the latter and its class-analytical bearings. Then, in Britain, the hardening of workplace militancy, the radicalizing of community-based activism, and the strengthening of the Left inside the Labour Party were all trumped by the electoral outcome of 1979. The polarizing of British political life under the aegis of Thatcherism between 1975 and 1983 began concentrating energies for a political assault on the entire infrastructure of class-based popular-democratic identifications that the Thompsonian vision had so optimistically presupposed.

In other words, no sooner had a younger generation of social historians heavily influenced by Thompson begun consolidating themselves than the surrounding political conjuncture abruptly changed. In the Britain of the seventies, with industrial militancy radicalizing, unions growing in influence, the Left apparently much stronger in the Labour Party, and new radicalisms flowing from 1968, class analysis had seemed to offer a way forward, building on the social democratic gains of the postwar settlement and the strengthened civil liberties of the 1960s, while assembling the signs of returning social conflict into an oppositional political narrative of some persuasive power. But I well remember the shift from that more optimistic reading of social crisis to a mood of uneasy foreboding. During 1977–78, the New Right waxed confidently into the emerging neo-McCarthyite tones of its rhetoric, mobilizing the language of "freedom" against dissent, sharpening its hostility against the unions, and playing the race card of populist anger against immigration.

I vividly remember two episodes in particular. In September 1977, together with several hundred representatives from the various left-wing periodicals then proliferating across the disciplines and associated professions, I went to a conference entitled "Left Intellectual Work" at the Birmingham Center for Contemporary Cultural Studies. The day was divided into parallel topical sessions under two overarching themes—"Problems of Ideology" and "Problems of Left Intellectual Work"—but the event was ultimately dominated in the final plenary by an understandably nervous and sometimes overwrought discussion of the hot-off-the-press publication of the so-called Gould Report, the latest in the Black Papers on Education series, which had been spearheading the right-wing counterattack against progressive education. Titled *The Attack on Higher Education: Marxist and Radical Penetration* and edited by the conservative sociologist Julius Gould, this survey of Marxists in the universities appended lists of participants at left-wing conferences of various kinds, if not with the intention of a blacklist, then clearly for the purposes of instilling fear.[89] Several months later, I spoke in a public meeting in Cambridge on the subject of the *Berufsverbot,* which was already damaging civil liberties in West Germany in the manner Gould was now intimating for Britain.[90] The sense of contracting opportunities—of politics shrinking around more limited and defensive needs— hung in the air. Both these occasions portended a very different political climate, one in which the tones and dominant terms would be set by the Right.[91]

In effect, class was weakening in its persuasiveness as a master concept. By the mid-1980s, battle lines were becoming very bitterly drawn, with the most forthright revisionists among the social history generation calling for the flat discarding of the old materialist standpoint, while its diehard defenders charged the former with backsliding and betrayal. Faced with such a polarity, most social historians found themselves not exactly "in the middle," because that phrase usually implies a fudged and compromising moderation or type of confusion, a disablement before difficulty or reluctance in taking a stand. My memory of those years is rather different. However upsetting the discouragements of politics, the undoubted disappointments could also translate into a productive uncertainty, a willingness to think through difficult things. The diminishing purchase of the old explanatory materialism opened a space of fruitful indeterminacy, in which other kinds of thinking might grow. As the sovereignty of the social became challenged, other claims could be raised.

In the meantime, of course, social historians were still busy with their own work while launching journals, building institutions, and generally benefiting from all the existing momentum. In July 1978, back in my German historical scene, I went to the University of East Anglia in Norwich for the first meeting of the Research Seminar Group on German Social History, organized by Richard Evans (born 1947). Ten of these workshops would eventually be held by 1986, leading to seven volumes of essays whose themes—the family, the working class, religion, peasant society, unemployment, the "underworld," and the bourgeoisie—nicely encompassed the new ground of social history assembled in the course of the seventies.[92] The purpose was to present new research from the German and English-speaking worlds in a spirit of collaboration and debate. As it happened, the seminar's main links to Germany bypassed both the centers of partisanship for social science history and the emergent circles of *Alltagshistoriker* (historians of everyday life),[93] and German women's history was also not notably present. Generationality was very clear: with the exception of the East German contingent for the volume on rural society, nearly all the participants were born in the 1940s, most of them after World War II. The group's meetings were crucial in allowing the British community of German historians to cohere.

As I recall them, the group's earliest discussions expressed all the sense of discovery and ambition so essential to social history's excitements at the time.[94] But they also afforded a snapshot of the changes I've just described. Provoked by discussions on the history of the family in the seminar's first meeting, I wrote a paper arguing why its subject should be made central to the next meeting, in January 1979, on the history of the working class. My purposes were certainly political. I'd spent much of that time educating myself in feminist theory (with all the severity that the reading-group culture of those years prescribed), focusing especially on critiques of the family and domestic labor but also on theories of "sexed subjectivity," the early borrowings from Lacanian psychoanalysis, and the ideas of Michel Foucault. However, the relation of politics to history remained indivisible. The whole point of calling on such discussions was to follow through on social history's totalizing claim—its ambition to integrate different kinds of analysis within a common history of society. I wanted to show that if we took that charge seriously, the new specialisms identified with social history's ascendancy couldn't be left by themselves. Once brought together, they'd illuminate the larger questions we still wanted to pursue about politics and ideology.

However, the axis of integration for radical historians was about to change. Feminist theory, for example, turned rapidly away from the Marxist terminology of women's material oppression under capitalism—with its language of patriarchy, domestic labor, social reproduction, and the sexual division of labor—toward theories of lived subjectivity centering on language and influenced by psychoanalysis, poststructuralism, and literary deconstruction. The intended collaboration of "feminism and materialism" slid from the "unhappy marriage of Marxism and feminism" into predictable divorce.[95] Since the 1960s, feminists had, in any case, consistently troubled the old "base and superstructure" thinking, and many now broke wholly from the materialist frame. In so doing, they both responded to and set the standard for a more general crisis of materialist thought. My 1979 paper remains a trace of the earlier self-confidence, chasing the ideal of a totalizing analysis just as it started falling apart. It's one of the few substantial papers I've written that never found their way into print. There it sits in my drawer almost a quarter of a century later, rather like a piece of bulky and exotic flotsam beached by an especially broad and powerful wave that crested impressively and then broke.

Tim Mason

Tim Mason (1940–90) was the premier social historian of the Third Reich in the 1970s. The author of a monumental 1971 Oxford dissertation on Nazi policies toward the working class, he was known for his brilliant essays and for an imposing volume of documentation and a book-length accompanying analysis on the creation of the Nazi system. For my generation of German historians, he was an inspiring and unforgettable presence. He pioneered the archivally based social history of the Third Reich from a clear stance of politically committed scholarship. An independent Marxist energized by the example of *The Making of the English Working Class,* he embodied the best of the social history produced in the Thompsonian tradition. Twenty-three years old when *The Making* was published, he was formed in the distinctive intellectual-political culture created by the British Marxist historians, becoming an assistant editor of *Past and Present* during 1967–70 and serving on its editorial board until 1971. A close friend and collaborator of Raphael Samuel and Gareth Stedman Jones, Mason then became a key member of the collective who launched *History Workshop Journal* in the mid-1970s.

While believing passionately in history's moral-political purpose, Mason set the highest standards of meticulous empirical research. He was determined never to sacrifice the complexities of interpreting the documentary record to the demands of theory or to the anti-Nazi moral imperative. Thus, when West German conservatives began accusing social historians of "trivializing" Nazism by allowing their complex explanations to efface issues of individual responsibility and the need for moral condemnation, Mason rightly rejected that charge. "[C]omplex historical arguments are not indifferent to moral issues just because they are complex," he responded. The ethical injunctions of working on Nazism could never absolve historians from other kinds of difficulty. Indeed, he argued, "[i]f historians do have a public responsibility, if hating is part of their method and warning part of their task, it is necessary that they should hate precisely."[96]

Mason was one of the first to tackle the question of working-class resistance against Nazism by going beyond the straightforwardly celebratory or heroizing approach so familiar from the orthodox Communist historiography of the GDR. His analysis likewise differed from the dominant views in the West, which had always cleaved obsessively to the aristocratic and military opposition associated with the July 1944 assassination plot against Hitler. Looking beyond the courageous, but ultimately isolated, resistance of the Communist and Social Democratic illegal undergrounds, Mason asked how else the dissidence of workers might be conceptualized under circumstances where the usual forms of collective organization were denied: "In what sense can one speak of class conflict in a situation where the class had been deprived of the possibility of organizing itself and of educating itself politically?"[97] This was an exciting departure in itself. Studying a time when popular freedom seemed to have been most violently and comprehensively taken away, Mason sought to restore agency to the working class. His work affirmed the necessity of doing social history even where conventional types of political, military, biographical, and related kinds of history most powerfully held sway. It affirmed certain basic Marxist commitments by giving history back to the German working class under the Third Reich. It affirmed certain values of socialist humanism as they appeared to the British New Left of the late 1950s and early 1960s.

For those who became German historians at the time, Mason's work was an invaluable support. I first read him in my last year at grammar school, in 1966. Learning my history through a series of current controversies and modeling myself on A. J. P. Taylor, I read Mason's *Past and Present* essays "Some Origins of the Second World War" and "Labour in the Third Reich, 1933–1939" and immediately discovered new ways of asking the pertinent questions.[98] I neither was taught by him while a student in Oxford nor even worked in his own period or field, but his presence was a vital fixture for history undergraduates active on the Left. The Social History Seminar he ran from St. Antony's College with Joaquín Romero Maura, Raphael Samuel, and Gareth Stedman Jones was a beacon of alternative history in a university whose official curriculum offered so little. It opened a window onto ways of doing history differently. In launching a similar seminar in Cambridge in 1975, I had very much this ideal in mind. Tim Mason was a model of critical and committed scholarship. He worked in a field where being a historian really mattered, where the issues of relevance that occupied so many of us in the late 1960s could patently be addressed. One obituary appreciation called him a "comet among his contemporaries."[99] For me, he was a lodestar.

In some ultimate sense, Nazism brought most of us into German history at that time. It was the dark secret that history could empower us to unlock. It shadowed our thoughts and conversations, whatever our particular periods and topics. We found ourselves recurring there all the time—facing up to its grotesque moral enormities, referring it to social explanation, locating it in the longer German past, probing the failures of the Left and the disabling of opposition, and puzzling over what exactly had brought Germany to the Third Reich. No one did more than Mason to help clarify those issues. He was one of the first on the Left to grasp the nettle of the autonomy of politics and to loosen the causal nexus of Nazism and the economy far enough to allow the links and mediations to come better into view.[100] He was the first to reformulate the questions of popular resistance and accommodation that motivated the best work on the social history of the Third Reich. While his peers buried their heads firmly in the sand, he insisted that women's history be taken seriously.[101] In the last period of his life, he began comparing Nazism with Italian fascism.[102]

More than anyone else, Mason rendered Nazism vulnerable to social history—not by "normalizing" it into a subject like all others

(divesting Nazi ideology of its horror or the Nazi terror of its brutality), but by showing as carefully as possible how Nazism remained subject to social determinations. He insisted on the class-political context of Nazism's emergence, its origins in the field of conflict defined by the German revolution of 1918 and the polarized political culture of the Weimar Republic. Nazism, he argued, was originally about the destruction of the working-class movement in Germany. Whatever else it may have been—and he always knew it was much more— Nazism had antisocialism inscribed at its very center. Everything else—from the political modalities of the economic recovery to the racialized ideology of the *Volksgemeinschaft* (the community of the race-nation-people), the drive to the East, and the dynamics of the Final Solution—flowed from the regime's founding acts of violence. To produce the regime's freedom of action, the forces of democracy organized around the labor movement had to be rooted out and destroyed.

Social historians, such as Mason, were highly skeptical about the effectiveness of Nazi ideology. Mason claimed that German workers, both underrepresented in the Nazis' ranks before 1933 and solid in their own Communist and Social Democratic allegiances, proved relatively resistant to the Nazi political message. Even after the labor movement's violent destruction in 1933, he argued, the regime only exercised its political control within certain practical limits, frustrated by the workers' strong residual and defensive class consciousness. In fact, the potential for class conflict remained structural and endemic even under the Third Reich, a permanent and irreducible feature of social life under capitalism, giving working-class culture an opacity and imperviousness to certain kinds of ideological persuasion, which neither the Nazis' repression nor their propaganda offensives could ever completely penetrate or sweep away.

Mason took pains to distinguish between, on the one hand, the political resistance of the labor movement's illegal Communist and Social Democratic undergrounds, which were isolated from wider support, and, on the other, the slow reemergence of class conflict in industry, which he termed the workers' "opposition." Coerced and deprived of their historic legal representation, the mass of ordinary workers pragmatically accepted the Third Reich's delivery of material improvements, he suggested, while still withholding their positive allegiance. But that "opposition" was essentially nonpolitical. It was a

silent refusal of the regime's ideological message, a withholding of active consent, either by pulling back into the relative safety of private life or by holding onto an economistically defined self-interest. The residual resourcefulness of working-class culture kept the full demanding voraciousness of the Third Reich at bay. Yet while the "workers' opposition" posed big problems for the regime during 1936–40, it did so, in Mason's view, without any explicit political challenge: "It manifested itself through spontaneous strikes, through the exercise of collective pressure on employers and Nazi organizations, through the most various acts of defiance against workplace rules and government decrees, through slowdowns in production, absenteeism, the taking of sick-leave, demonstrations of discontent, etc."[103]

Most influential social histories of the 1970s followed some version of Mason's logic. In the work of Martin Broszat, the doyen of Third Reich historians inside West Germany itself, the analogue to Mason's concept of "opposition" was the more qualified idea of *Resistenz*. Broszat used this term to capture not the forms of a translated or displaced authentic opposition whose actions thwarted the regime's fundamental goals, as Mason sought to suggest, but, rather, a category of behaviors that exercised only a limiting effect on its totalizing ambition.[104] Yet the implications reached no less far. The fine social histories published under the auspices of Broszat's Bavaria Project during 1977–83 had the effect of shifting attention away from the failed assassination plot of July 1944, which had long monopolized perceptions of the German Resistance, and refocused it instead on the level of everyday life. Broszat and his colleagues insisted that the efficacy of the Third Reich's governing system needed to be judged through the experiences of ordinary citizens, who lacked the conspiratorial resources, social privileges, and languages of ethical heroism available to the elite participants in the July plot but faced no less acute moral and practical dilemmas in their working, social, and familial lives. Broszat and his colleagues claimed that a more subtle idea of resistance as nonconformity or nonpermeability would allow us to grasp those quotidian realities of social life far more effectively. It could show us "how people behaved during the Nazi dictatorship, how they compromised with the regime but also where they drew the line—sometimes successfully—at the regime's attempts at interference, penetration, and control."[105]

This approach markedly downplayed the power of Nazi ideology. To put it another way, such historians as Mason and Broszat acknowledged the practical complicity of the ordinary population in the regime's daily working, only to counterpose this complicity against German workers' apathy and practical indifference toward the Nazis' specific ideological claims (their "opposition" or *Resistenz*). It was no accident that the accent of this work was on the Left. In a complicated sense, the argument about nonpermeability seemed to become a way of honoring the integrity of the German working class and its ability to keep the Nazis at bay—in a subtle counterpoint to the celebratory antifascism of East German Marxist-Leninist historians, as a kind of fallback position once the beleaguered and isolated qualities of the actually existing Communist and Social Democratic undergrounds had been admitted.[106]

In fact, Mason was very much inspired by Thompson's *Making of the English Working Class*. He wished to rescue the honor and dignity of the German working class from the defeat and humiliation inflicted on it by the Nazis. He approached Nazism with an underlying master category of "society" as his guide: while he accepted the breadth of the Third Reich's social support, he wanted to preserve the existence of this "society" as an intact and separable domain, as a source of viable agency that, however limited and compromised, still allowed Nazism's impact to be contained. In that sense, society remained a damaged but recuperable resource. Its resilience allowed the "effective warding off, limiting, damming up of the NS rule or its claims," whatever the particular "motives, reasons or strengths" of individuals may have been.[107] Mason also proceeded from the continuing sovereignty of German capitalism and the primacy of class as determinants shaping and constraining the ability of the Nazis to realize their goals, certainly in the years 1933–39. Even during the war, when militarist expansion and the racialist frenzy of genocide overwhelmed everything else, the integrity of the "social context," however battered and reduced, could still be analytically upheld. Indeed, Mason's grand ambition was to build a general analysis of Nazi rule from the ground up in that way, deriving both its driving force and its continuing constraints from the shape-shifting dynamics of class conflict and class relations.

This was the apogee of the social history ambitions emerging into the 1970s. Yet, twenty years later, German historians have almost

entirely jettisoned that attempt to explore the subtle and submerged ways in which society's autonomy was preserved. They now concentrate instead on showing how the bases of the social order were comprehensively disorganized and then remade. Different social groups may have kept some defenses against Nazism's explicit ideological message or protected some remaining privacy against Nazi coercion, but their behavior was influenced more insidiously by the spreading of racialized discourse across all the shelters and crevices of ordinary life. Moreover, that hegemony of racialized thinking—across social groups, in multiple sites of policymaking and knowledge production, in state and nonstate institutions, in academic and popular culture— can only be grasped by returning to the study of ideology, which social historians adamantly left behind. This has become the new orthodoxy for historians of Nazism, irrespective of the complexities of social differentiation in that older, 1970s sense.

In fact, in the thinking of most Third Reich historians these days, Mason ascribed to the working class an immunity against Nazi influences that has definitively gone. Whether colluding in the exploitation of coerced foreign labor in the war economy, wearing the uniforms of the genocidal army on the Eastern Front, or generally joining in the "good times" of the Nazi era from the mid-1930s to 1942–43, German workers could no more withdraw themselves from the consequences of Nazi rule than any other group. Their complicity ensued whether those consequences were structural, in the racialized labor market and its rewards; social, in the new patterns of discriminatory sociality; or cultural, in the new public mores and their sanctions.[108] In regarding the working class as Nazism's principal antagonist, moreover, Mason had used an overarching framework of fascism for understanding the Nazi regime, and that, too, has gone: "Theories of fascism have been replaced by models of the racial state, in which biological rather than social categories are preeminent."[109] As the main organizing category of Third Reich historiography, "class" is now trumped by "race."

These new patterns of thinking began developing in the course of the 1980s, as Mason gradually receded from the discussions of German historians and turned his attention to Italian fascism. The ground of social history from which the best minds had sought, since the sixties, to confront the enormities of Nazism was—at first gradually and then decisively—left behind. Like the earlier turning to social history,

this change was shaped by broader trends in the discipline, whose character forms the subject matter of chapter 4 of this book. Among German historians, those trends included the vital impact of women's history and gender analysis; the remarkable upsurge of *Alltags-geschichte;* a burgeoning interest in "biological politics," or the histories of medicalization and racialization in the social policy domain; and—last but certainly not least—the new centrality of the Holocaust for how German historians began thinking about their field.

Each of those developments brought ideology back into the very center of discussion. In the course of the 1980s, historians stopped being mainly interested in Nazism's variable social contexts in the classical materialist or sociological sense, which, almost by definition, had encouraged them into doubting or relativizing the efficacy of Nazi ideological appeals. They turned instead to exploring the deeper, more elaborate, and often submerged genealogies of Nazism's big ideas. In so doing, they didn't so much abandon social history's underlying commitment as attempt to build further on its gains. They retained the skepticism about how far the continuing exogenis of "Hitler's worldview," in the immediate sense, could take us. But they concentrated on the broader societal settings where thinking sympathetic or conducive to Nazi policies could be found. Emphasizing the practical circulation of racialized styles of thought, they examined the instantiating of Nazi ideals in the basic social intercourse of everyday life, in the ordinary behavior of institutions, and in all the more insidious kinds of ideological diffusion. The powerful implication of this new approach—that for anyone facing the spread of Nazi ideology, there was increasingly no safe place—began to corrode Mason's default belief in the damaged but resilient intactness of society and in the survival of the working class as a continuing source of agency, the place from which "opposition" could begin.

Mason also held passionately to a belief in the historian's ethical responsibilities, to the paramount necessity of keeping the larger picture in view. It mattered decisively where one chose to end and begin a particular historical account, he reflected. Which processes or possibilities were brought to an ending in 1945, and where might they have begun? Even more important, how definitive was the closure? What continuing lessons might there be? The importance of these questions grew if the story remained unfinished.

The imperative to assess the whole is above all a moral and political imperative. The suffering and destruction of life that the
Nazi regime brought about was on so vast a scale and of such
novel quality, that any study of a part of the story that fails to
confront this central fact must, at least by implication, trivialize
the whole. If this study of the working class in Germany were a
piece of labor history in the conventional sense, it would be an
intellectual, moral and political evasion, however accurate it
might be in detail. This obligation to attempt to interpret the
whole through one of its constituent parts is not, in the end, different in kind from that which faces all historians working on all
subjects. It is just more massively obvious. Casting a small, finely
finished stone onto a heap which might one day transform itself
into a mosaic is here an unmistakable capitulation. Elsewhere
this is just less obviously the case.[110]

From this point of view, Mason had wanted to use a study of the
working class to produce a general history of the Third Reich—not by
presenting the view "from below," in some populist perspectival sense,
but as a way of opening up the tense and conflicted dialectic between
the regime's driving objectives and its ability to enlist the resources of
Germany's class-divided society. He convincingly argued that varying
versions of this implied dilemma—involving the negotiation, focusing,
and containment of the political tensions resulting from the class divisiveness of the period—formed the common ground of Europe's interwar political history. He devoted great resourcefulness to reconstructing "the story of working-class insubordination" under the Third Reich,
oscillating "between depicting it as the quasi-spontaneous expression of
class conflict on the one hand, and, on the other, as the muted echo of
working-class traditions of political militancy which even the Nazis
were unable to stamp out until the intensified terror of the wartime
regime."[111] To the end of his career, Mason stood by the view that
"class conflict remained endemic in Nazi Germany." Given the brutal
specificity of Nazi rule, "which denied the working class its own organizations," the forms of that class conflict could "only be understood as
a diffuse, dynamic, relational phenomenon (lived experience)."[112] The
Thompsonian resonances in this view are very clear.

But the stronger contention that "class relations are *the* constitutive
element in the history of industrialized capitalist states," the Marxist

social historian's axiomatic wish, was given up.[113] Reaching such a recognition involved the profoundest disappointment. The extremes of that disappointment also had an acutely gendered quality because the slow collapse of the hopes invested in a class-based analysis by social historians was to prove far more disorienting for men who were on the Left than for women. Feminists had already grasped the insufficiencies of class-centered thinking after all, but made women's history their alternative ground for holding politics and social history together. Absent some comparable positivity, the frustrations and failures acquired a more painful emotional register—even where male socialists were making themselves into feminists too, as Mason himself certainly did.[114] Despite all Mason showed about the centrality of class conflict to the thinking of the Nazi leadership and the dynamics of policymaking in the 1930s, he came to acknowledge that for certain vital purposes, the class-analytical framework simply couldn't suffice. Indeed, precisely Nazism's worst violence and atrocities—the genocidal project of the Holocaust, which he urged the historian never to evade—most exceeded the social historian's reach.

At the end of his life, Mason reflected brilliantly and movingly on this insufficiency. In important aspects, he now saw, the original argument he'd tried to make about "the interlocking crisis of domestic and foreign policies" in 1939—the relationship of the decision for war to a putative general crisis of the regime—was flawed. In particular, contrary to his earlier thoughts, the plentiful evidence of industrial discontent couldn't be used to "indicate a wide-scale, hidden political discontent" of the working class.

> At bottom [that view] rested on the unsustainable proposition that a passive, latent loyalty to the class organizations destroyed in 1933 was still widespread in 1938–39. I greatly underestimated the disillusionment and fatalism which the policies of the parties and the trade unions caused among their supporters in 1933, and the depoliticization that followed the crushing of the first waves of underground resistance. More recent local studies and oral history research underline . . . the degree to which some elements of Nazi attitudes made inroads into popular consciousness from the mid-1930s on.

He didn't withdraw his arguments about the severity of the Nazi policymaking dilemmas on the eve of war or their rootedness in economic dysfunctions and the associated popular discontents. Yet he argued that "rejection of Nazi social and economic policies where they hit people's immediate material interests did not *necessarily* imply a disguised rejection of the regime in general, even though such partial rejections were often resolute and sustained."[115]

Everything implied by Mason's reference to Nazi "inroads into popular consciousness" caused the most damaging doubts. The best work on the Third Reich during the 1980s started exploring the histories of popular complicity, still using Mason's and Broszat's frameworks of negotiation and accommodation, but now seeing as the leitmotif collusion and co-optation rather than "opposition" and *Resistenz*. By the nineties, such work was focusing overwhelmingly on 1939–45, when the war economy's massive enslavement of foreign labor combined with the conscription of German workers into the genocidal army disorganized once and for all any remaining traces of the labor movement's older countervailing solidarities. Even the class-cultural resilience of workers when left to themselves, in the mutualities of the shop floor or the pride taken in work, presupposed forms of adjustment to the *Volksgemeinschaft*'s ideological power, in both its beneficial and coercive dimensions.[116]

By the end of the 1980s, Mason had abandoned his original goal. He no longer believed it was possible "to move outwards from the 'core area' of class relations towards a potentially all-inclusive political social history of Nazism and the Third Reich." His work stopped in 1939, so on two of the most decisive fronts for such a general history (the regime's lasting popular allegiance during the war years and its pursuit of genocide), it had nothing to say. This came partly from emotional choice. Before the horrifying actualities of biological racism and genocidal extermination, Mason felt "emotionally, and thus intellectually paralyzed": these were "facts which I could not face, and therefore could not understand and not give a proper place to."[117] Actually, he did reflect very acutely on the meanings of this absence. When, in his closing summation at a 1988 conference in Philadelphia, he described the main theme of the new research on Nazism as "biological politics," it was the first time I heard that now familiar argument.[118] But if "murderous biological politics of all kinds" was indeed "the great legacy of National Socialism," the class-analytical standpoint of Thompsonian social history clearly had its limits. As Mason came to acknowledge, "no clear path" could "be traced from class conflict to the fundamental projects of the Third Reich." Under Nazism, in fact, the "constitutive element" was not capitalism or its class relations at all but, on the contrary, the political regime of the Third Reich itself.[119]

In this sense, Tim Mason's project of writing a general class-based account of National Socialism's relationship to German society failed. His project hit an impasse, in an extreme and tragic case of materialist social history running up against its limits. By the early 1980s, Mason was doubting his ability to carry his book to an end. He resigned his teaching position in Oxford and moved to Italy in 1984, turning to the study of Italian fascism. Right to the last, he continued publishing extraordinarily important and suggestive essays. His final writing on Nazism remains among the best we have. But he never returned to his magnum opus. In fact, in March 1990, impossibly weighed down by a sense of personal, scholarly, and political difficulty, he killed himself, quite carefully and deliberately, in a weekend hotel room in Rome.

IV. REFLECTIVENESS

Crossing the Atlantic

As I left Britain for the United States in the summer of 1979, some weeks after the election of Margaret Thatcher's Conservative government, the world may have been changing, but the intellectual bearings seemed secure. With hindsight, we can see the solid ground of materialism cracking and shifting. As I suggested in chapter 3, between 1977–78 and 1982–83, such influential individuals as William Sewell and Gareth Stedman Jones were already breaking ranks, though not yet disavowing what came before. Most social historians certainly didn't perceive any crisis in what they were doing. The process of institutionalizing, country by country, was still young. In Britain, for example, the freshly established Social History Society and the new flagship journals for the emerging generation of thirty-somethings, *Social History* and *History Workshop Journal,* weren't yet four years old.[1] By the end of the seventies, the disciplinary battles for social history's legitimacy—in terms of hiring, curriculum, graduate training, and the general mood of the profession—had only recently begun. Troubling the underlying project with fresh fronts of self-criticism, querying gains that were still under contention, was hardly high on the agenda.

There were certainly declarations of complaint. I mentioned some of these toward the end of chapter 3, including an article by Elizabeth Fox-Genovese and Eugene Genovese and another by Stedman Jones, both published in 1976. But such voices spoke in the name of social history, rather than wanting to supplant it. For the Genoveses, this seemed to imply a cantankerously reductionist form of class-analytical Marxism based on interest ("who rides whom?"), in a deliberate provocation anticipating the future appearance of the short-lived U.S. journal *Marxist Perspectives*.[2] From his side, Stedman Jones urged social historians to have the full courage of their convictions, becoming theorists in their own right rather than relying on the concepts and categories of sociologists. They needed to escape from that dependency into a higher and more confident plane of consciousness.[3] At the end of the seventies, an extreme version of these injunctions appeared, an angry jeremiad against what its author called a "progressive dementia" in the discipline. "Now is truly a bad time to be a social historian," Tony Judt's article concluded counterintuitively, belying the buoyant momentum of the time. After a scattershot denunciation actually aimed against North American social historians of France, Judt called on "that minority of social historians who remain committed to the proper pursuit of history" to restore "the centrality of politics." Only by "re-emphasizing, on every occasion, the primacy of politics," he insisted, could a "history of society" really be pursued.[4]

But these were all pleas for the betterment of social history, not its rejection. On coming to the University of Michigan in fall 1979, I joined a department certainly moving in that direction. The Michigan History Department's commitment to comparative social science contended at most with a kind of good-natured skepticism, rather than recalcitrance or any outright hostility. The leading journal *Comparative Studies in Society and History* had been edited from the department since 1962, first by the medievalist Sylvia Thrupp (1903–97) and then by the nineteenth-century Europeanist Raymond Grew (born 1930). The Michigan department took for granted intellectual conversation across the more usual geographical and subdisciplinary boundaries. It valued non-Western histories extremely highly, a commitment practiced in the curriculum under the rubric of "comparative" and strongly encouraged by the university's support for area studies. Michigan's reputation in the social sciences, centered around the Institute for Social Research, also played a part. The main hub for social historians was the Center for Research on Social Organizations in the Sociology Department, where Charles Tilly (born 1929) held sway. Inside the History Department per se, particularly for graduate students and younger faculty interested in social history, Louise Tilly (born 1930) was the main figure. As a departmental milieu, social history crystallized around the Tillys' Sunday evening salon, where food was brought and papers were read. But the History Department at large fully reflected the prevailing disciplinary climate: in a playful poll of departmental preferences, Marc Bloch emerged as the late twentieth century's most influential historian.

At the same time, a sense of difficulty and fermentation—the growing awareness of the sheer range of new ideas waiting to be dealt with—was definitely building. At the turn of the eighties, by far the most important source of disturbance was feminism, as opposed to questions of race/racism, postcolonialism/postcoloniality, histories of sexuality, and the other proliferating multiculturalist and identitarian standpoints presenting themselves later on. But Foucault's ideas were slowly beginning to circulate, as were discussions of psychoanalytic theory, cautious borrowings from literary criticism, the slow subterfuge of Hayden White's *Metahistory* (published in 1973), and influences from cultural anthropology beyond the early essays of Clifford Geertz.[5] For those of us with a British connection, Raymond Williams remained central, as did the broader discourse of cultural studies gradually attaining stronger institutional shape. Stuart Hall's essays were acquiring greater resonance, while the distinctively "Gramscian" thrust of these British discussions was approaching its peak. In all of these British contexts, the tenor was still avowedly Marxist. In a further dimension, 1978 was also the year of Edward Said's *Orientalism*.[6]

In retrospect, we can see a new set of affinities coalescing. Soon after I came to Ann Arbor, Mick Taussig, then in the Michigan Anthropology Department, suggested we form an anthropology-history reading group from a few younger faculty and graduate students, which duly met on a regular basis during the next couple of years.[7] Faculty participants included my fellow German historian Michael Geyer, who left for the University of Chicago in 1986; Keith Hart, a British anthropologist specializing on West Africa, then visiting in the Michigan department; the U.S. urban historian Terry McDonald, who, like myself, had just arrived; and the Cuban historian Rebecca Scott, likewise freshly appointed in the History Department and the Michigan Society of Fellows. The graduate students included Friedrich Lenger, then a German Fulbright visitor and master's student in history, now teaching at the University of Giessen; the modern French historian Tessie Liu, now teaching at Northwestern; and the Romanian historian Irina Livezeanu, now teaching at Pittsburgh. We took turns in presenting from our own interests and research, but

I mainly remember the exploratory touching down on a wide variety of unfamiliar grounds. For a while, a local chapter of MARHO, the Mid-Atlantic Radical Historians Organization affiliated with the *Radical History Review,* also flourished in Ann Arbor, with its main axis among younger faculty and graduate students in American Culture and history. Again, the main interest was theory across the disciplines.

The most powerful sign of change I remember from soon after I arrived in the United States was an event improvised by Charles and Louise Tilly to coincide with the first North American Labor History Conference, which occurred in October 1979 at Detroit's Wayne State University. The conference drew a number of younger social historians, mainly in their thirties, from elsewhere in the country, and the Tillys took advantage of their presence to stage a one-day conference in Ann Arbor, to take stock of where things were in social history. Besides a sizable contingent of graduate students and faculty from Michigan itself, the incomers included James Cronin, a historian of twentieth-century Britain; David Levine, a scholar of the social and demographic history of industrialization; Edward Shorter, whose focus was the history of the family; and three leading French historians of the younger-to-middle generation—John Merriman, Joan Scott, and William Sewell. To help discussion, the Tillys proposed an advance reading of the recent articles (mentioned earlier) by the Genoveses, Stedman Jones, and Judt, plus an article in which Lawrence Stone surveyed the relationship between history and the social sciences.[8] As the theme, they chose "Whence and Whither Social History?"

The day was organized into three sessions: "Has Social History Gone Awry?" "What Choices Face Us?" and "What Should We Do?" Short (one-page) position papers were invited. The Tillys' call to the conference foregrounded the degree to which existing practices of social history were now being vigorously questioned.

Complaints about the crassness, arrogance and naiveté of those social historians who draw heavily from the social sciences have erupted in history since the econometricians burst upon the historical scene. But recent criticism contains some new elements: a desire to substitute cultural analyses and anthropological perspectives for the harder-edged sociological work which became popular in the 1960s; increased questioning of the epistemological bases and implicit political orientations of social history, especially as it is practiced in North America and particularly as it is influenced by the social sciences; a tendency of historians who had previously pushed for a rigorous, autonomous brand of social history to develop doubts about the feasibility or desirability of that program.[9]

What struck me instantly at the time was a silence on the obvious common denominator of the three precirculated critiques—their Marxism. My own one-page paper saw the rise of "a more self-confident and self-conscious Marxism" as the real source of the current divisions. While the call to the conference implied the apostasy or desertion of those who'd previously wanted a "rigorous, autonomous brand of social history," it seemed to me that Marxist critiques were themselves calling "for greater rigor, a more self-confident independence, and a more consistent theory—i.e., for more rather than less autonomy." So far from "cultural analyses and anthropological perspectives" now being freshly imported, moreover, such approaches had long been constitutive for the kind of social history enabled by Edward Thompson and other British Marxist historians but not encompassed in the Tillys' social science paradigm. In fact, I doubted whether recent polemics amounted to a general crisis at all. Rather, they described "a field of *internal* disagreement" among social historians, directed not against social history per se but toward competing visions of its future. Marxists wanted social history to follow through on its "totalizing potential" and actually deliver on the ideal of a "history of society." That was the meaning of the call for a return to politics.[10]

Of course, measured by similar discussions a decade later, much else was missing from this conference. Despite the presence of Louise Tilly, Joan Scott, and others, for instance, feminism and women's history were notably absent from the event's formal architecture. Race was entirely missing as a category, as were studies of colonialism and empire and the histories of non-Western societies—although, like questions of women's history, these arrived intermittently in discussions on the day. But most striking of all was the antinomy constructed by the event's organizers between anthropology and other kinds of cultural analysis, on the one hand, and the true ground of social history, on the other. The Tillys implied, in no uncertain terms, that turning to culture would be a serious loss, even a betrayal, after all the hard work of social science credentialing during the past two decades. They maintained that a social history based on the methods, theories, and procedures of the social sciences was "rigorous," whereas a social history based on cultural analysis was not; the latter could only be soft, loose, insubstantial, more elusive, and simply not as serious in its credentials and claims.

For me, the occasion of this conference was fascinating. It was my first encounter with an important network of North American social historians in collective action. It soon became clear that much of the energy came from understandable irritation against Tony Judt's personalized polemics. But as the discussion unfolded, there was much careful and exploratory self-positioning. Talk recurred to the insufficiencies of "vulgar Marxism," which seemed to be shorthand for quantitative studies of everyday social relations and material life in all the familiar social historian's ways. To make good the shortfall of understanding, speaker after speaker agreed, a "more sophisticated kind of cultural history" was now needed. The anthropologists present—notably, Mick Taussig and the South Asianist Bernard Cohn (then visiting from Chicago)—offered their own provocative counterpoint. There was also much reference to European theory and to the British battles among Althusserians and Thompsonians. Initially known across the Atlantic via the debates surrounding Richard Johnson's critique of Thompson and Genovese in *History Workshop Journal,* these battles were ratcheted forward by Thompson's intemperate anti-Althusserian tract *The Poverty of Theory.*[11]

As it happened, those British theory debates were about to reach one particularly unpleasant and chastening climax. At the thirteenth History Workshop in Oxford, on 1 December 1979, Thompson demolished Johnson in the Saturday evening plenary, shocking even his intellectual allies with the angry theatrics of the attack. That Oxford occasion showed many things, but one was certainly the limited usefulness of the sharp binary between "structuralism" and "culturalism," which Johnson applied to history's possibilities. Neither Thompson and his allies nor their opponents had foreseen the infinite creativity and greater epistemological radicalism of the coming cultural histories of the 1980s, which eventually broke from the still-shared materialist problematic altogether. So-called culturalists and structuralists had each retained materialist bearings that the new cultural historians would largely disavow. Johnson himself originally declared, "Neither structuralism nor culturalism will do." The logic of a way forward pointed somewhere beyond each. In Britain, the changed political climate produced by Thatcherism and the rebooting of the Cold War during the early 1980s rapidly relativized those bitterly fought theoreticist battles.[12]

From the Tillys' conference in Ann Arbor, I took an enduring impression of uncertainty and flux. I'd seen an apparently rather cohesive group of social historians, formed around a set of generational friendships and solidarities (both political and intellectual), who were previously convinced of their choices but were now far less sure. While British Marxism and Marxist feminism were called on for part of a possible solution, moreover, this hope was more the vicarious imprint of a partially digested and still emerging antireductionist critique, whose further unfolding across the Atlantic would eventually dissolve the given Marxist problematic altogether. While the conference discussions had generally embraced a spirit of openness and generosity, the closing session was blighted by Charles Tilly's angry intervention directed against various statements in William Sewell's initial presentation, which had referred to their personal disagreements over the desirability of a turn to anthropology. Measured by the good humor of the rest of the day, the effect was shocking. The room was stunned. Interrupting and overriding Sewell's efforts at reply, Tilly wielded all the personal authority of a presiding intellectual patriarch. He reasserted, in no uncertain terms, the primacy of "the harder-edged sociological work" that the conference had clearly been called to defend. "Show me the alternative," he kept demanding. Big things were obviously at stake.[13]

Taking the Turn

Looking back, I find the Tillys' conference a prescient occasion. Within the year, Sewell's *Work and Revolution in France* had been published; Joan Scott had moved from Chapel Hill to Brown, where she began a sustained encounter with poststructuralist thought; and Charles Tilly continued to hold the line. Simply to speak these three names is to register the dimensions of the change. Attached to Tilly during the 1960s (Scott formally so, under the terms of a Social Science Research Council training fellowship), Scott and Sewell were probably the leading progeny of the union of history and sociology among European historians. Yet here they were, declaring the new social history to be no longer enough. The discourse of social historians was beginning to disobey, outgrowing its disciplinary containers, spilling across the boundaries its practitioners had thought secure. In a published statement for the Tilly symposium, Francis Couvares said (in language still innocent of the coming times): "The new harlots of cultural anthropology, 'thick description,' and semiotics threaten daily to shift the focus, to alter the terms of the discourse."[14]

Yet the published trace of "Whence and Whither Social History?" conveyed virtually nothing of the immediacy of the intellectual breaking point. Charles Tilly noted the challenge of "anthropological work, . . . the study of *mentalités,* and . . . more rigorous Marxist analyses," but he then proceeded on the assumption that the existing project— namely, "collective biography, quantification, social-scientific approaches, and rigorous studies of everyday behavior"—could go on much as before. The trick was simply connecting it to "the established historical agenda" in language historians could understand. As far as it went, Tilly's description of social history's "two callings" was unexceptionable: "asking how the world we live in came into being, and how its coming into being affected the everyday lives of ordinary people; asking what could have happened to everyday experience at major historical choice points, and then inquiring how and why the outcomes won out over other possibilities."[15] But so long as the cultural construction of those processes was ignored and such categories as "everyday experience" and "ordinary people" weren't put into question, the formulation would continue not to satisfy. Likewise, Louise Tilly's problematizing of "work" and "politics" was all to the good: she averred that "to talk about changes in women's work over time, more rigorous definitions, words, categories are needed"; she further maintained that politics must also be reconceptualized, "so we can talk about the politics of those without formal rights."[16] But that conceptualizing, it was clear, would happen only on the old materialist ground. In that sense, the book Louise Tilly published jointly with Joan Scott in 1978 (*Women, Work, and Family*) and Scott's later *Gender and the Politics of History* were separated by far more than a matter of years.[17]

This story of the Tillys' Ann Arbor conference stands in for a much larger and more ramified set of intellectual histories, with many local variations. It suggested the fracturing of the generational consensus that sustained social history's popularity during the previous decade and a half. The confrontationalism of the resulting debates threatened to divide the profession just as angrily as the earlier struggles for social history had done before. Sometimes, these conflicts were over theory per se, as in the acrimonious attacks on "structuralist Marxism" referred to earlier, which dominated left-wing intellectual life in Britain in the later 1970s. In the next decade, Foucauldian approaches and other poststructuralisms elicited comparable fear and loathing in the United States. Within wider fields of cross-disciplinary innovation, the turning to forms of cultural history was also related to the changing climate of political life. The associated dynamic of generational reflexivity pushed left-wing scholars of my broad generation into bringing their intellectual and political life choices under review. As beneficiaries of the great expansion of higher education, trained during the 1960s and 1970s, we were also the last cohort to make it more easily into secure positions before the academic job market dried up. By the 1980s, the resulting career paths were bringing us tenured access to institutional influence. Increasingly, we were training graduate students, managing research projects, organizing conferences, and editing journals.

The salience of this particular generational voice, its tones, and its preoccupations was magnified by the relative paucity of its successors. The later 1970s and early 1980s saw both a contracting job market and a depletion of the numbers of history graduate students, so that the resulting cohorts of doctoral graduates were less able to build a distinctive generational presence. The divisiveness of the public skirmishing between older social historians and the new cultural historians during the later 1980s heavily overshadowed the intellectual choices available to younger people entering the profession. Only the most courageous and idiosyncratic—or the most conservative and narrow—easily avoided enlistment into the rival camps. This contrasts yet again, in my view, with the later cohorts qualifying after the early 1990s, who were already publishing their books and entering tenured positions by the turn of the new century. By virtue of the revival of an extremely forthright politics of knowledge in the U.S. universities, in an atmosphere infused by the consequences of the so-called linguistic turn, these historians would have a great deal to say about gender history and cultural studies in the course of claiming their own distinctive voice.

It's hard to plot with any precision the movement out of social history into cultural history. As I've argued, the first wave of stocktaking essays usually tied to a "crisis" in social history—by the Genoveses, Stedman Jones, and Judt—still spoke from familiar materialist ground. They were notably innocent of the poststructuralist and allied theories already driving innovation a few years later. The same innocence applied to other programmatic statements, including the founding editorials of such new journals as *History Workshop Journal* and *Social History* (both launched in 1976) or the compendium of U.S. historical writing edited by Michael Kammen for the American Historical Association in 1980, *The Past before Us,* whose essays were commissioned in 1977–78 in the same climate of the midseventies. All of these examples were borne by the momentum of social history's expansion rather than reflecting the coming uncertainties. A systematic survey of more established journals—such as *Past and Present,* the *Journal of Interdisciplinary History,* and the *Journal of Social History,* plus general journals with social history content, such as the *Journal of Modern History* or *American Historical Review*—reveals a similar absence of the literary or linguistic theoretical influences soon to characterize the cultural turn. Whereas the latter two journals started noticing the new influences through review essays and discussion forums by the end of the eighties, the older social history journals kept their distance well into the next decade, as did another journal in the vanguard of the earlier exchange between history and social science, *Comparative Studies in Society and History.*

The shift can be tracked through the newer journals, such as *History Workshop Journal, Social History,* and *Radical History Review.* We might juxtapose *History Workshop Journal*'s very first editorials, "Feminist History" and "Sociology and History" (1 [spring 1976], 4–8), together with the slightly later "British Economic History and the Question of Work" (3 [spring 1977], 1–4), against the editorial "Language and History" published several years later (10 [autumn 1980], 1–5). If the earlier statements were firmly continuous with the critical materialist departures of the 1960s (evidently connected with the influences of Thompson, Hobsbawm, and the other Marxist historians), the 1980 editorial marked some distance from that founding materialism. *History Workshop Journal* then renamed itself *Journal of Socialist and Feminist*

Historians, simultaneously publishing the guide "Foucault for Historians," by Jeffrey Weeks (14 [autumn 1982], 1, 106–19). This was followed by the editorial "Culture and Gender" (15 [spring 1983], 1–3). The new feminist literary criticism arrived in review essays by Mary Poovey and Joan Scott (22 [autumn 1986], 185–92). We can note the gradual entry of psychoanalysis via essays by Sally Alexander (17 [spring 1984], 125–49) and Laura Mulvey and T. G. Ashplant (23 [spring 1987], 1–19, 165–73), further confirmed by the full-blown special feature "Psychoanalysis and History," which showcased four articles (26 [autumn 1988], 105–52), and by the follow-up response by Jacqueline Rose (28 [autumn 1989], 148–54).[18] Another special feature, "Language and History," included an extremely severe article by Peter Schöttler, "Historians and Discourse Analysis" (27 [spring 1989], 1–65). The same year's bicentenary issue on the French Revolution then took an almost entirely "culturalist" tack, in what was becoming the prevailing literary-cum-linguistic sense (28 [autumn 1989], 1–87).[19]

In the world of historians, this was the much vaunted "linguistic turn"—a general discursive shift in the rhetoric and practice of the profession from "social" to "cultural" modes of analysis. In the course of the 1980s, social history became one site of a more general epistemological uncertainty characterizing broad areas of academic-intellectual life in the humanities and social sciences of the late twentieth century. That flux affected some disciplines more radically than others. It became more central more quickly in literary studies and anthropology, for example, than in the "harder" social sciences, such as sociology. It was also no accident that the furthest-reaching discussions occurred in the new and nominally "un-disciplined" areas of women's studies and cultural studies. Exactly why such a pointed and powerful convergence of new thinking should have occurred across fields and disciplines at this particular time will require much more careful study across many more types of contexts than I have room for here.

In particular, I want to avoid any suggestion that the new departures occurred entirely within thought or that changes for historians were somehow caused by debates within theory or by the impact of a set of philosophical interventions. As with any history of intellectual transition, the ideas concerned will need to be tracked through many particular debates and biographies, numerous individual projects and institutional sites, and all the relevant chains of influence for collaborators and disciples. Intellectual changes also intersect in complex ways with the policy worlds of governmentality and education, with the public spheres of politics and the media, and with nonacademic types of engaged intellectuality. When a fuller or larger history comes to be written, all these aspects will have to be addressed.

Nonetheless, the process included a specifically theoretical dimension, through which certain bodies of thought offered historians resources and strategies they hadn't possessed before. Through the transition I'm describing, certain conditions of possibility became opened or enabled. Certain new languages were proffered. As I argued toward the end of chapter 3, by the end of the seventies, social history was encountering frustrations and insufficiencies for which it had no self-generated solution. This was the impasse from which the cultural turn promised escape. It did so not least by furnishing the tools for self-reflexive examination of the history of social history itself. By focusing on the disciplinary pedigree, it alerted social historians to the forms of their own critical practice. In that sense, the cultural turn offered a way "out" precisely because it opened a way "in." From my own, rather specific vantage point as a modern Europeanist of British extraction living in the United States, that was how I experienced the changes.

First and foremost, the cultural turn enabled a theoretical understanding of gender whose effects transformed the ground of thinking about history. Whether as a dimension of analysis or as an area of empirical work, women's history had been absent from Hobsbawm's benchmark 1971 survey, and simply to reread such older accounts is to experience just how crucial the change has been. This was still true in 1979: none of the four symptomatic essays flagged by the Tillys as the reading for their conference (by the Genoveses, Stedman Jones, Judt, and Stone) grasped the transformative significance of the new women's history, if they acknowledged its existence at all. Only in the later 1970s did a substantial body of monographic work in this area begin to appear. Even then, quite aside from the politics of surmounting the discriminatory practices and prejudices of the profession's given disciplinary regime, much of that new work proved relatively easy to sideline, either because of its conceptual framework of "separate spheres" or because it subsumed the history of women within the history of the family.[20] The theoretical move to gender analysis reduced this self-neutralizing effect. Only with the conceptual shift from the history of women to the history of gender did the protected central precincts of the discipline start to give way. Aside from the resulting histories of sexuality and sexual representations as such, the histories of work, of class formation, of citizenship and the public sphere, and of popular culture were all being reshaped by the close of the eighties.[21]

Second, by the end of the 1980s, the influence of Michel Foucault had become unavoidable. The speed of the reception shouldn't be overstated. His books were available very quickly, but Foucault's ideas remained entirely absent from the earliest pioneering works on the social history of crime, the law, and imprisonment, published in the 1970s. At that time, the English-language reception was conducted around the margins of academic life—in such journals as *Telos* and *Partisan Review* in the United States and by a self-conscious avant-garde of post–New Left journals (such as *Economy and Society, Radical Philosophy, Ideology and Consciousness,* and *m/f*) in Britain.[22] Only by the early 1980s were historians explicitly taking note. After that time, work on prisons, hospitals, asylums and other places of confinement, social policy and public health, and all forms of governmentality became shot through with Foucauldian arguments about power, knowledge, and "regimes of truth." Looking back at this entire burgeoning field of social and cultural histories during the seventies and eighties, we can see Foucault's ideas less as the direct instigator than as a classic illustration of his own arguments about the shifts in discursive formations. By the 1990s, for example, early pioneers of the social history of crime were taking a strong cultural turn, with superb results—from Peter Linebaugh's *The London Hanged,* through V. A. C. Gatrell's *The Hanging Tree,* to Richard Evans' gargantuan *Rituals of Retribution.*[23] At a level of intentions, Foucault may have been inessential to these authors' new directions—for instance, an excellent sampling of German research edited by Evans revealed little of Foucault's explicit presence.[24] But their works couldn't be imagined without him.

Furthermore, Foucault's reception vitally redirected thinking about power, away from conventional, institutionally centered conceptions of government and the state and from the allied sociological conceptions of class domination, toward a dispersed and decentered understanding of power and its "microphysics." It sensitized historians to the subtle and complex forms of the interrelationship between power and knowledge, particularly in its forms of disciplinary and administrative organization. It delivered the exceptionally fruitful concept of discourse as a way of theorizing the internal rules and regularities of particular fields of knowledge (their "regimes of truth") and the more general structures of ideas and assumptions that delimit what can and can't be thought and said in specific contexts of time and place. It radically challenged the historian's conventional assumptions about individual and collective agency and their bases of interest and rationality, forcing us instead to explore how subjectivities are produced within and through languages of identification that lie beyond the volition of individuals in the classical Enlightenment sense.

Not least, Foucault encouraged a rethinking of what historians understood by "the archive." He sought to break history out of its desire for the exclusive specificity of the origin and the sequential linearity of progressive time, aiming to reconstitute, instead, the forgotten places where new ways of understanding the world came to be imagined. His "genealogical investigations" helped historians review their given attitudes toward evidence and the empirical. Against the grand explanatory designs of the birth of the modern world, he sought to foreground the disparaged and overlooked; against the wish for a revealed continuity, he stressed interruption and dispersion, "the accidents, the minute deviations . . . the errors, the false appraisals and faulty calculations that gave birth to those things that continue to exist and have value for us."[25] In Foucault's distinctive usage, genealogies retrieved the marginal, the disadvantaged, and the lowly from the suppressed and occluded "ahistorical" corners where conventional historians tended to banish them, demanding a different kind of archive for the story to be told. This could show that

> things "weren't as necessary as all that"; it wasn't as a matter of course that mad people came to be regarded as mentally ill; it wasn't self-evident that the only thing to be done with a criminal was to lock him up; it wasn't self-evident that the causes of illness were to be sought through the individual examination of bodies.[26]

None of this redirection came easily. For some years after Foucault's writings entered currency, scarcely a meeting of historians passed without dismissive jokes or irritated complaints about his "unhistorical" procedures. But for those bridling against the dry and disembodied work of so much conventional historiography, an extended encounter with Foucault's writings resuscitated the archive's epistemological life. Far from supplanting or discarding an older empirical approach, discursive analysis became its complementary and coexistent partner. By engaging the archive as a "material event," Foucault offered a kind of "radical empiricism." Rather than approaching the archive merely through critique, he exposed its principles of construction. In so doing, he revealed the space of communication between the thought and the time of culture, or between knowledge and the weight of history. He found the "root" ground where the empirical might come to representation, the enabling structures that allowed the category of the empirical (and its authority) to speak itself. Put another way, if we understand Foucault's critique of epistemology as essentially an interrogation of its conditions of possibility, those conditions themselves become a form of materiality. By restating the archive as a question, Foucault challenged historians to think about the very ground from which history could be written.

A third aspect of the cultural turn concerned the fate of one of the main existing approaches to cultural analysis among social historians, that of the *Annales* tradition in France. For much of the 1970s, the history of mentalités functioned as a panacea for many social historians. It seemed a compelling alternative to the canonical, high-cultural, and formalistic-exegetical kinds of intellectual history; it promised access to popular cultures of the past; it provided ground for the application of quantitative methods and of approaches from anthropology; and it was animated by the enticing vision of a "total history." For a while, the translation and reception of the major *Annales* works, orchestrated by a few well-placed admirers, was virtually uncritical: "social history seemed to turn around the *Past and Present-Annales* axis."[27] Then the climate seemed to change. The tone of the symposium inaugurating the avowedly Braudelian new journal *Review,* in 1978, was still largely celebratory, but by the mid-1980s, a series of prominent and extremely searching critiques had appeared.[28]

Together with the unwillingness of the *Annalistes* themselves to theorize their understanding of culture, those critiques successfully exposed the reductionisms and unspecified determinisms at the core of the work of Braudel and Ladurie. Critiques by Dominick LaCapra and Roger Chartier also recuperated the ground that intellectual history seemed to have ceded earlier to the history of mentalités. Neither of those developments ultimately compromised the achievements of

Bloch and Febvre or precluded the potential ongoing production of cultural history in the classical *Annales* mode, suitably rethought in the light of contemporary ideas. But on the whole, historians' discussions of culture moved elsewhere, either outside the main early modern locations of *Annales*-influenced work or onto the ground of language where the running was being made by feminist theorists and intellectual historians, either untouched by the *Annales* paradigm or directly critical of it. Now, the more interesting readings of early modern culture were tending to come not just from social historians inspired directly by *Annales,* who'd set the pace in the 1960s and 1970s, but from literary critics interested in Mikhail Bakhtin.[29]

Fourth, another body of cultural analysis, that of contemporary cultural studies, exerted extraordinary influence, without yet having produced very much specifically historical work. A still emergent cross-disciplinary formation during the 1980s, cultural studies comprised a miscellany of eclectic influences—sociology, literary scholarship, and social history (but not, interestingly, anthropology) in Britain; communications, film studies, literary theory, and reflexive anthropology in the United States, where strong institutional support would also come from women's studies, American Culture, African-American studies, and ethnic studies programs more generally. The U.S. momentum came from the humanities, without much convergence with the concurrently proliferating interdisciplinary initiatives in social science. In Britain, in contrast, where the prevalence of qualitative sociologies blurred the severity of the divide between social science and the humanities, developments ran in the opposite direction. On both sides of the Atlantic, feminist theory was to record decisive influence, as would the gathering post-Saidian critique of colonial and racialized patterns of thought inside the Western cultural tradition. By the early 1990s, the two national discussions had definitely converged.

The range of topics pioneered in cultural studies reads like an inventory of the new areas gradually opened up by historians in the wake of their own "cultural turn." Cultures and economies of consumption and entertainment, whether approached in mass or luxury terms, became one of the first of these, generating elaborate projects from the eighteenth century to the present. For both funding and critical purchase, this interest fed patently off the processes of capitalist restructuring driven so relentlessly forward during the 1980s, as did serious work on the visual technologies of film, photography, video, and television, extending into commercial media (such as advertising, comic books, and magazines).[30] Feminist scholars explored the relationship of women to popular reading genres (including romances, family sagas, and gothic novels), to television soap operas and sitcoms, and to popular cinema through film noir, melodrama, science fiction, and horror.

Before the 1990s, any presence of historians within this emergent universe of cultural studies was extremely thin: among the forty-four contributors to the benchmark volume *Cultural Studies* (the published record of a spectacular international gathering of the field at Urbana-Champaign in April 1990) were only four historians, none of whom taught in a history department.[31] But the territories being charted were eventually occupied by great numbers of historians. In addition to the topics already mentioned, thematics pioneered in cultural studies increasingly dominated history's disciplinary landscape by the end of the nineties. Examples include the use of autobiography and the personal voice, postcolonial cultural critiques, the reopening of debates around high versus low culture, explorations of popular memory, and the study of representations of the national past. Whereas most concrete research initially focused on the era since 1945 (the "long present" of cultural studies), interest soon transferred to earlier times.

Fifth, with the cultural turn came an acceleration of the dialogue between history and anthropology. Versions of this accelerated dialogue could already be encountered at the height of the social history wave in the 1970s, notably in the ubiquitous citations of Clifford Geertz's advocacy of "thick description" or in Edward Thompson's reflections on "anthropology and the discipline of historical context."[32] The conversation appeared in the pages of *Past and Present* during the early 1960s and went back earlier still to such isolated works as Hobsbawm's *Primitive Rebels*. In certain historiographical contexts—notably, the pioneering scholarship on colonialism and decolonization in South Asia, Africa, and Latin America—the closeness of historical and anthropological work had always been clear. But during the 1980s, a big fracturing that occurred in anthropology's main understandings of "culture" changed, from a historian's point of view, the valency of the ethnographic epistemology associated with Geertz. As a result, the mere "opening of difference to sympathetic cross-cultural understanding" became called radically into question as a sufficient description of the anthropologist's charge.[33] Again, this story varied from country to country. In the United States, anthropology's disciplinary coherence became disordered by an explosion of new thinking about agency and action. There, the discipline's boundaries were blown completely open by the impact of poststructuralism, feminist theory, literary theory, and Foucault.[34]

For historians already engaged in rethinking their approach to culture, the resulting debates had big implications. Anthropology's inscription into colonial and broader imperialist relationships during the nineteenth and twentieth centuries had made it part of the machinery of values and belief that helped structure Western forms of modern subjectivity. It not only became a source of colonial knowledge in the more obvious technical ways but also rendered the non-Western world "knowable" in the more basic sense, by delivering the theories, categories, and constructs that shaped the metropolitan West's own self-understandings. The same process translated the practices, beliefs, and social relations of indigenous peoples into terms of comparison.

In these connections, accordingly, the new anthropologies of colonialism both revivified the historiography of European colonial domination and invited a less encumbered study of the colonized peoples themselves. Such work deauthorized the canonical standing of earlier theorists of the ethnographic encounter. Most important of all, the new critiques turned the "colonizing gaze" back in on itself, making the metropolitan world's constructions of the colonial Other into themselves an object of study. As Edward Said's insights became worked through, anthropologists and historians began to examine the pedigrees of their own disciplines. In the spirit of Said's "contrapuntal" analytic, the history of empire became revealed not as the stage where those disciplines had performed themselves but as the condition for their possibility in the first place. As Franz Fanon had put it, "Europe is literally the creation of the third world."[35]

The ethnographer's standpoint has been radically deconstructed. The most influential early intervention was undoubtedly the sustained analysis of anthropological texts in the 1986 collection *Writing Culture,* by James Clifford and George Marcus; after it, the innocence of the ethnographer's procedure could never be quite the same again.[36] A generation of studies proceeded to explore the ways in which ethnographies "make use of various tropes, literary conventions, and narrative devices to establish ethnographic authority and/or certain kinds of unstated visions of the world." Whereas fieldwork had always sought to show how "'native' categories are culturally and historically constructed," the privileged standpoint of anthropology itself had survived, because the ethnographer's own categories had never been subject to the same close scrutiny.[37] However, once the objectivity of the ethnographer's gaze was brought under exhaustive critique (within a new paradigm of situatedness and self-reflexivity), the previously accepted protocols of fieldwork started to come apart.

Each of these developments—the problematizing of fieldwork, the critique of the ethnographic encounter, and the self-questioning of the anthropologist's place in the colonial relationship—have produced a turning back into the anthropologist's own society. Encouraged by the breaking down of disciplinary boundaries, anthropologists began the serious investigation of the contemporary United States. Similarly, kinship, family, religion, and ritual were toppled from their natural dominance of the cultural anthropologist's research agenda, which on the contrary became radically opened up. That agenda could now include everything from the forms of legitimacy of the Latin American state, representations of history in Andean popular culture, and the contemporary dynamics of genocidal violence in Rwanda and Sri Lanka, to the patterns of transnational migration in the post-Fordist economy, the scandals of televangelism of the late 1980s, and the experience of a New Jersey high school graduating class between the 1960s and the present.[38]

Two Disruptions

Two further aspects to the cultural turn of the 1980s don't fit cleanly into any integrated narrative of unfolding individual and collective change but certainly had a vital presence—sometimes as a productive incitement, but more often as an uncomfortable supplement, a kind of continuous second-guessing. One of these involved questions of "race"; the other concerned the related problems of colonialism and postcolonialism. Of course, historians, especially those on the left, were painfully aware of these issues long before the arrival of the cultural turn. Indeed, certain fields were centrally concerned with them, most obviously in large parts of U.S. history, in studies of slavery and

ipation, or in the history of colonized societies. But before the
ality of social historians could begin properly seeing the impor-
of "race" (above all, for the study of Europe's metropolitan soci-
), some sustained political encounter would be needed, a jolt or a
k, much as the earlier acceptance of "gender" had required a similar political process of recognition.

Taking such concerns into one's default grasp of the shape of the
social world and how it works, rather than treating them as discrete
and demarcated subjects of interest to specialists, was something new.
For social historians of classic materialist bent, class had always supplied the main lens for studying the behavior and attitudes of particular social groups, whatever the precise definitions of class position and
class belonging preferred. Where racism was most palpably present in
the practices and outlook of a particular working class, as in the
United States, social historians struggled with finding some basis for
distinguishing "class" from "race" in the explanatory framework being
used; for the answer, they invariably cleaved to the "harder" or "more
objective" rootedness of class in the actually existing social relations of
property and workplace. Lacking any comparable objective basis in
biology or scientifically founded differences, "race" could then be presented as "entirely socially and historically constructed as an ideology
in a way that class is not." The varying forms racist ideology took—
including its material existence and instituted practices, all the ways in
which it became a basis for action as an "ideological" category—could
then be tackled using the familiar social historian's methods.[39]

As Barbara Fields pointed out in one of the best statements of this
view, approaching race as an ideological construct certainly didn't
imply that it was "illusory or unreal."[40] Fields explained: "Nothing
handed down from the past could keep race alive if we did not constantly reinvent and re-ritualize it to fit our own terrain. If race lives
on today, it can do so only because we continue to create and re-cre-
ate it in our social life."[41] But despite this acknowledgment of ideology's social materiality, such approaches tended to treat racial ideology as mainly a mask for interests located elsewhere, as a language
devised to secure and reproduce a superordinate structure of interests
and authority, whose vocabulary directly reflected the society's
unequal distribution of wealth and power. Even while specifically
emphasizing the "realness" of racial ideology, therefore, these
approaches implicitly referred it to the underlying sovereignty of

social explanation. They invariably related "race," in some ultimately determining sense, to the more decisive structural facts of property ownership, job competition, access to social and cultural goods, distribution of community power, and so forth.

David Roediger observed of this syndrome, "The point that race is created wholly ideologically and historically, while class is not wholly so created, has often been boiled down to the notion that class (or 'the economic') is more real, more fundamental, more basic, or more *important* than race, both in political terms and in terms of historical analysis."[42] This was especially a problem for historians working in U.S. labor history. But much more generally, unpalatable ideologies, such as racism or xenophobia, tended to be externalized or otherwise relativized from treatments of working-class formation during the 1960s and 1970s, much as Tim Mason's work had stressed the limited success of Nazism in breaking down the defensive resilience of the German workers' class-conscious culture. No matter how rich and sophisticated its detailed analyses or empirical instantiations, "base and superstructure" materialism ultimately tended to sell the complexities of ideological analysis short. Even the most sophisticated such analyses tended to reduce "race" to one kind of "ideological device" or another, emphasizing its origins and functions in some larger system of mystification where it serviced a dominant structure of "political, economic, and social power."[43]

Seeking to understand racism's efficacy culturally by getting inside the appeals of racial thought—trying to grasp how "race" worked as a lived identity or as a credible source of meaning, as a persuasive strategy for bringing imaginative order to the material world—challenged these existing practices of social history. Gradually during the 1980s, though, some historians began exploring racial thinking in its own terms like this. They approached it as a type of subjectivity requiring more than a readily legible relationship to benefits and privileges or a calculus of interest in order to achieve its purchase. Fully cognizant of both the power-related aspects of racist practices and the violence associated with maintaining racialized systems of inequality and exploitation, such an approach argued for cultural analyses of racial distinction as well. In this view, racism subsisted on combinations of explicit, partially articulated, and unconscious assumptions and beliefs, while engendering more insidious forms of collusion and complicity than violent coercion could deliver alone. This was the difficult step in question: being able to see racialized forms of understanding as comparable in importance, cognitively and ontologically, to a person's social provenance and class location in helping shape her/his sense of belonging in the world. As well as being a system of coercive power and violent inequality, in other words, "race" also needed to be understood as a discursive formation.

By the early 1990s, this context produced Roediger's *Wages of Whiteness*.[44] This book, clearly incited by the transatlantic version of the new rightward political conjuncture (it was written "in reaction to the appalling extent to which white male workers voted for Reaganism in the 1980s"), bespoke a loss of materialist confidence in the sufficiencies of social history similar to the one I've been describing.[45] It certainly presented a bleak view of the alleged opportunities for cross-racial labor solidarity in the nineteenth-century United States, although, by this time, a rich and nuanced historiography on the subject hardly made this very controversial. More damagingly, it queried efforts to salvage nineteenth-century labor republicanism as the distinctive U.S. form of a generic process of working-class formation: though the democratic élan of this working-class political culture may have been impressive, its racist and exclusionary features had been too easily effaced, as was the absence of black workers from the story provided.[46] Still more searchingly, Roediger raised the question of the psychic compensations workers derived from acquiring a "white" racial identity under the simultaneous impress of becoming proletarianized: "[T]he pleasures of whiteness could function as a 'wage' for white workers. That is, status and privileges conferred by race could be used to make up for alienating and exploitative class relationships, North and South."[47] New languages of racialized class identification, postures of assertive masculinity, the ambivalent pleasures of such popular entertainments as blackface and minstrelsy—all these inscribed whiteness with a set of powerful meanings whose particular virulence came from negative definitions of slave or free blacks.[48] In this way, Roediger argued, "race studies" became a necessary tool of self-analysis for dominant North American subjectivities.

With the *Wages of Whiteness,* we are back once more to the social historian's old difficulties with culture, ideology, and consciousness. Roediger and historians of his bent started to argue that the social historian's existing repertoire dealt poorly with the insidiousness of racial thinking in the forming of working-class subjectivities. Drawing modestly on psychoanalytic theory and a "socio-ideological" approach to language based on Williams and Bakhtin, Roediger shifted focus decisively to the "cultural," paying creative attention to such sources as folklore, popular humor, street language, song, and popular entertainment. Most important of all, he forthrightly returned to the study of ideology as such, offering a novel perspective on how to analyze dominant ideological forms. Under this perspective, "whiteness" was an invitation to participate in the benefits of a dominant culture whose principles of access were all the more efficacious for being unstated. In a public culture so relentlessly focused around race and its languages of distinction, the primary term of privilege, authority, and general potency went unnamed and unmarked: "race" belonged to the non-white minorities; the normal condition of being American was "white." If the nation was "a structure of power that circumscribes and shapes the identities to which individuals and groups can aspire," whiteness became crucial not only to social goods and psychic well-being but also to political faculties of citizenship and belonging.[49]

How did this impinge on the awareness of a modern European historian? However widely one reads or discusses, there's a difference between noticing important departures in other fields and moving from such abstract and detached encounters into one's own work—especially in this case, when the other context in question was the United States, whose histories and legacies of slavery, Jim Crow, migration, and immigration seemed so self-evidently different. The temporality of this particular intellectual history was also "off," post-dating the other developments I'm describing by about a decade: Roediger's impact came at the start of the 1990s, when the cultural turn was already in full swing. So how were Europeanists thinking about these questions? Why didn't "race" join "gender" earlier during the 1980s on the leading conceptual edge of the cultural turn?

In fact, since the late sixties, the confrontational dialectic of racist and antiracist actions had been violently troubling public life in Britain (and elsewhere in Europe). Escalating anxieties about immigration, dramatized in Enoch Powell's notorious "rivers of blood" speech in April 1968, brought issues of race into the centerground of political awareness; indeed, a mass demonstration against Powell at the Oxford Town Hall in 1968 provided my own initiation into direct-action politics.[50] During the seventies, questions of race and immigration formed one main crucible for the right-wing radicalization that culminated in the Conservative election victory of 1979 and the rise of Thatcherism. What interests me in retrospect, though, is the intactness of the separation between the disturbing presence of these political developments and my own historical interests. Actually, the two were bleeding into each other fairly continuously, but bringing this fact to consciousness took a much longer time.

One important marker was the 1978 publication of *Policing the Crisis,* by Stuart Hall and a collective of authors from the Birmingham Center for Contemporary Cultural Studies (CCCS).[51] During the seventies, the CCCS housed an intensive exchange between British traditions of cultural criticism and social history, on the one hand, and European grand theory, on the other. In effect, Williams and Thompson were encountering Althusser, Gramsci, and Foucault.[52] Taking off from the moral panic in August 1972 surrounding an instance of "racial mugging" in Handsworth, an important Birmingham center of black British population, *Policing the Crisis* showed how the issue of "law and order" had recast the agenda of British politics to become the centerpiece of an emergent racialized imaginary for the New Right. In an argument, reaching back over two centuries, about the British state and its legitimacy, the state was seen to be losing its capacity for organizing popular-democratic consent, leading to a political crisis in which racialized anxieties eased the passage to a more coercive and authoritarian period. But whereas racism was clearly a central term of the crisis this book diagnosed, "race" still figured mainly as a signifier for other things. Though the "race text" ran right through the center of the analysis, it receded, in a way, into the broader argument about the state, hegemony, and class.

The publication four years later of *The Empire Strikes Back: Race and Racism in 70s Britain,* by another CCCS collective, angrily protested this earlier effacement of race.[53] Paul Gilroy and his coauthors insisted that recognizing the pervasiveness of racial ideology had to become central to the analysis of contemporary British politics, because notions of British identity (and notions of the "Englishness" at their heart), were structured around powerful assertions of racial difference. These fed partly on the imperial past, partly on the postimperial social antagonisms of Britain's decline. Contemporary national identity was centered around an unmarked and unspoken whiteness, while marginalizing the presence of Afro-Caribbean, South Asian, and other minority populations. Indeed, the silencing of one population was an entailment of the primacy of the other. For all its crucial oppositional importance, furthermore, even the radical reworking of British traditions in the thought of Raymond Williams, Edward Thompson, and the New Left had reinscribed the same latent ethnocentrism. By bringing these assumptions into the open, *The Empire Strikes Back* sought to force the "Britishness" or "Englishness" of cultural studies into self-consciousness and voice.

In some obvious ways, this approach presaged the coming U.S. critiques of whiteness. It also reflected the incipient movement away from older habits of class-centered analysis, toward a recognition that consciousness, identity, and subjectivity are formed in other ways, too. As Gilroy wrote elsewhere, this analysis "challenge[d] theories that assert the primacy of structural contradictions, economic classes, and crises in determining political consciousness and collective action."[54] The argument drew its urgency from the political times: if more self-conscious subcultural identities were beginning to coalesce around British blackness during the seventies, these were more than matched by a mainstream Conservative drive for the recentering of national identity around an aggressively exclusive vision of Englishness, for which race held the key.[55] During the 1980s, the continuing eruption of racialized conflicts into public life slowly unsettled scholarly approaches to British history and allowed the earlier histories of racial attitudes to be brought into prominent focus.

Over the longer term, this shift encouraged a new appreciation of the empire's constitutive importance in delivering the operative bases of social and cultural cohesion for modern metropolitan Britain, particularly via its impact on popular culture and the dominant sociopolitical values. But for present purposes, the most striking thing about this new registering of the empire's centrality was the degree to which card-carrying historians themselves were not involved. The role of CCCS—a deliberately transdisciplinary organization, whose innovative historical work was conducted precisely away from the surveillance of a history department—has just been cited. But more generally, the challenge came from the margins even of cultural studies—for example, in the critiques of an emergent black arts movement and its interest in "diaspora aesthetics" or from outside Britain altogether, in literary studies in the United States.[56] In this period, a benchmark volume on definitions of Englishness, produced by historians, left imperialism out entirely.[57]

Of course, there was no shortage of monographic research either exploring the political, military, and economic histories of the empire's creation or assessing the importance of colonies for the home country in those same respects. In the 1970s, social historians also turned in large numbers to the local histories of the colonial encounter, where they examined the establishment of British rule in particular places. As long as culture continued to be regarded as "superstructure" or was set aside for the specialized attention of anthropologists, it was easily bracketed from these accounts. But once culture became rethought as residing in practices as well as ideas (in Benita Parry's words, "as itself a material practice producing representations and languages that embody active forms of power and is constitutive of a social order"),[58] no work had more impact in helping that awareness along than Edward Said's *Orientalism*. Said's work

> assert[ed] the indispensable role of culture as the vital, enabling counterpoint to institutional practices, demonstrating how the aggrandisement of territory through military force and the bureaucratic exercise of power in the colonies was sustained by the ideological invasion of cultural space, while at home the fact of empire was registered not only in political debate and economic and foreign policy, but entered the social fabric, intellectual discourse, and the life of the imagination.[59]

Concurrently with the new work on race, therefore, histories of colonialism also began registering an extremely far-reaching transformation. Awareness of the issues made swiftest headway in literary criticism, cultural studies, anthropology, geography, and historical fields with an existing anthropological presence (as in South Asia). But European historians also came gradually to see the point—namely, the degree to which the social relations, cultural practices, and axiomatically racialized discourse of national superiority that were generated overseas in the subordinated extra-European world became powerfully reinserted into European metropolitan frames.

"Colonial knowledge"—forms of colonial representation through literature, photography, museums and exhibitions, mass entertainment, commercial advertising, and all areas of popular culture—became an especially fruitful field of inquiry. The gendering of national identity, whether through militarism and warfare or in the more general ordering of nationalist representations around images of

masculinity and femininity, was also explored in its colonialist dimensions—as, for example, in the anxieties surrounding colonial inter-
marriage and all manner of affective attachments in colonial settings,
including the management of sexuality, child-raising arrangements,
and the forming of friendships. These areas of intimate life were intricately related to matters of colonial governance and affairs of state.
They accumulated huge bodies of discourse around gender inequalities, sexual privilege, class priorities, and racial superiority, which, in
turn, became subtly rearticulated into nationalist talk at home.[60]

If the complex back and forth between Europe and its "Others" has
been constitutive for the possible understanding of political identities
since the late eighteenth century, as Said and other critics of Enlightenment traditions claimed, such unequal reciprocities have also been
replicated inside European societies themselves—between metropolitan and peripheral cultures, between town and country, between
high and low cultures, between dominant and subordinate nationali-
ties and religions, between West and East. This has been clearest, perhaps, in the perceptions and consequences of the nation form. An
awareness of nationalism's negative codings, of the ways in which
even the nation's most generous and inclusively democratic imagin-
ings entailed processes of protective and exclusionary centering
against others (often extraordinarily subtle, but also including the
most violent versions of direct colonial rule), has been one of the most
important gains of the last two decades. In colonizing the world, metropolitan nations also created hegemonies of possible meanings. Even
the most radical and self-conscious of oppositional, anticolonial, or
minority movements have necessarily mounted their emancipatory
demands from a ground of identity that colonialism's power had
already laid down.

One of the most important bodies of historical work engaging these
questions developed around the Subaltern Studies project, initiated at
the end of the 1970s by a group of younger South Asian historians
from India, Australia, and Britain, who were inspired by the more
senior Ranajit Guha (born 1922), a Marxist historian of rural society
in colonial Bengal who was teaching at the University of Sussex. In the
series Subaltern Studies: Writings on South Asian History and Society,
including eleven volumes from its beginning in 1982 to the time of
this writing, this group sought to intervene in Indian historiography on
three distinct fronts, in each case contesting the influence of a power-

ful adversary in the politics of knowledge. They opposed, first, the celebratory historiography of the nationalists, who subsumed popular politics in the progressivist master narrative of the creation of the Indian nation-state; second, the "Cambridge school" of British South Asianists, who preferred an interest-based interpretation of Indian politics emphasizing elite factionism rather than mass-based mobilization; and finally, the class-based economic determinism of an Indian Marxist tradition.[61]

The project took its name self-consciously from Antonio Gramsci, who used the term *subaltern* for subordinate social groups lacking organized political autonomy. Growing from Guha's earlier Communist Party background and an impressively early discussion of Gramsci's ideas in Indian Marxist circles (going back to the late 1950s), this also suggested affinities with the work of Thompson, Hobsbawm, and other British Marxist historians drawn to Gramsci.[62] As such, the project had all the same resonances of the "history from below" familiar from the British social history wave already in progress. It signified a valuing of "the politics of the people" that established historiographies had variously suppressed. Guha's original preface declared that the study of the subaltern, connoting the "general attribute of subordination in South Asian society whether this is expressed in terms of class, caste, age, gender, and office or in any other way," could allow the forms of popular resistance to be recovered and reassessed. Gramsci's category of the "organic intellectual" was also important for the self-understanding (and affective pleasure) of these politically engaged historians.

I encountered Subaltern Studies personally early on, when I noticed the first volume in an Oxford catalog and ordered it blind, partly because of the Gramscian intimations, partly because of an interest in forms of peasant political action. Unsurprisingly, given the discipline's prevailing demarcations, I'd been unaware of Ranajit Guha's presence at Sussex; the university's chosen interdisciplinary organization by regions of the world made it unlikely that the paths of a graduate student in European history and a South Asian historian on the faculty would ever cross. Later in the 1970s, I spent much time dabbling in the historiography of peasant movements in various parts of the world, and by the early eighties, I claimed a passing familiarity with the work of several of the Subaltern Studies authors, yet I had no real inkling about the focus and intent of this new initiative. Similarly, I knew enough Indian historiography from my Cambridge years

(1975–79) to recognize a new body of oppositional work when I saw it, yet I had little sense of how this added up.

Things fell into place much later, when a powerful jolt in the public intellectual climate of the U.S. universities in the later 1980s brought "Western" and "non-Western" historiographies into direct conversation in quite new ways—sometimes smoothly, sometimes jaggedly, always with great and lasting intensity. The complexities of that encounter far exceed the bounds of what I can deal with here. The impetus came partly from the contemporary politics of multiculturalism and race, partly from all the sociocultural and political fallout from the transnationalized restructuring of the world capitalist economy we now call globalization, and partly from the autonomous course of interdisciplinary discussions inside the academy itself. Once certain kinds of academic debate got under way, powerfully driven by the pedagogies of multicultural exchange and coexistence (for which the universities acquired such overwhelming responsibility in the United States), the influence of Edward Said and other theorists of the "postcolonial," such as Gayatri Chakravorty Spivak (born 1942) and Homi Bhabha (born 1949), soon kicked in.

By the early 1990s, "postcolonialism" had begun defining the center ground for scholars working in cultural studies, providing those interested in connecting Third World and metropolitan histories with a challenging new frame. But once again, historians—especially historians of Europe—became only haltingly involved. Some may have been reading the relevant theory during the intervening years, but any transference into concrete and discernible research projects, in ways that changed how European history could be written and taught, took much longer to occur. Moreover, for theorists, too, this process was more protracted. For those living in Europe, the main ground of priority during the 1980s—theoretically and politically—remained an older sense of European priority. For instance, Stuart Hall had been writing about questions of race brilliantly and consistently since the 1970s, but as one term of a wider theoretical repertoire and often in parallel to his main concerns, which included successive episodes of "wrestling" with theory, the critique of Thatcherism, and the engagement for "New Times."[63] "Race" acquired primary salience only toward the end of the 1980s as the wider political priorities shifted and the discourse of postcolonialism coalesced.[64]

During the initial stages of the cultural turn, in the first half of the

1980s, awareness of "race" and colonialism crystallized for European historians somewhere beyond their main immediate scholarly preoccupations. The active processing of Said's ideas proceeded at first almost exclusively among literary scholars and, to some extent, anthropologists.[65] But sometime between the later 1980s and the early 1990s, a conjunction was made. Literatures that had previously stayed apart began to speak to each other, across disciplinary and international boundaries.[66] Clearly, there were particular local and institutional contexts for how that happened.[67] By 1992–93, a spate of major works—still rarely authored by historians in the formal disciplinary sense—signaled the arrival of colonialism on the Europeanist's historiographical map. These works included Paul Gilroy's retheorizing of modernity via the histories of black migration, in *The Black Atlantic;* Mary Louise Pratt's study of travel writing and the aesthetics of transculturation, in *Imperial Eyes;* a special issue of *History Workshop Journal* entitled "Colonial and Post-Colonial History"; a pathbreaking volume on *Nationalisms and Sexualities;* Michael Sprinker's critical anthology on the work of Edward Said; and Said's own new work, *Culture and Imperialism.*[68] At this point, discussions concerned with the extra-European colonial worlds looped back to reshape understandings inside Europe in very powerful ways.[69]

Among the authors of those imported extra-European historiographies, the Subalternists were an especially coherent and influential grouping. Increasingly noticed outside the immediate South Asian field by the early nineties, their approach was also being worked into a program for frankly oppositional popular histories elsewhere, most notably in Latin American studies.[70] Really striking in retrospect, though, is the degree to which Subaltern Studies negotiated, within its own trajectory, all the aspects of the transition from social history to cultural history experienced by historians of Europe in these same years. Under Guha's inspiration, the group had begun with a primary commitment to histories "from below," aiming to recuperate the suppressed importance of the Indian masses for the history of anticolonial struggles. While strongly grounded in the Marxist tradition, this ambition likewise patently paralleled the heterodox features of post-Thompsonian social history in Britain, developing an equally creative analysis of the forms and limits of domination in the Indian countryside and seeking to restore a strong and coherent sense of agency to the behavior of the peasantry. Retrieving and elaborating the complexities of the peasantry's presence in the anticolonial movement was the leitmotif for the group's early work, as was a searching review of Marxism's relationship to anticolonial sentiment or "critical nationalism."[71]

Like Edward Thompson, for instance, the Subalternists focused on the ramified ambiguities, as well as the straightforward oppressions, in the relations of domination and resistance in the countryside, insisting, with Gramsci, that "subaltern groups are always subject to the activity of ruling groups, even when they rebel and rise up." Their writing also displayed the same pull toward culture, focusing not only on "the history, politics, economics, and sociology of subalternity" but also on "the attitudes, ideologies, and belief systems—in short, the culture informing that condition."[72] To reassemble the submerged coordinates of peasant agency, Guha and his colleagues proved exceptionally creative at reading colonial archives "against the grain," broadening the social historian's usual repertoire toward literary criticism, Sanskrit philology, linguistics, folklore, and structural anthropology. Guha's own pioneering works evoked something of the "patrician society/plebeian culture" framework that Thompson's eighteenth century essays had been exploring around the same time.[73] It postulated

> two domains of politics in Indian modernity, the elite-domain based on European/bourgeois grammar of constitutionalism and organized public life, and a relatively autonomous domain of subaltern politics, both coming together in the workings of Indian democracy but operating on distinctly different understandings of power and rule.[74]

But by the time the group was being noticed seriously in Britain and North America (in response to the fifth Subaltern Studies volume, published in 1987), its complexion was already shifting. Early awareness of Foucault quickened easily toward theories of colonial governmentality and the critique of post-Enlightenment systems of knowledge, with inevitable damage to the earlier belief in an authentic peasant consciousness. Such doubts in the subaltern's resistive autonomies, together with the associated loss of confidence in historical materialism, exactly paralleled the uncertainties building up among British and North American social historians during the same period. Openings toward literary criticism, oral history, and anthropology emphasized the distance from the starting points even more.

Most searchingly of all, a poststructuralist critique published by Gayatri Spivak in 1988 under the title "Can the Subaltern Speak?" took the group to task for their highly gendered presuppositions, rejected the centered model of the sovereign subject their project seemed to imply, and, on that basis, questioned the very possibility of retrieving subaltern political agency in the first place.[75] As the group clarified its thinking in response—engaging seriously with gender, broadening its own ranks, and taking a pronounced "textualist" direction, while devoting more attention to the specificities of India's differences from the West—divisions began to open. Just as Subaltern Studies emerged into the international limelight during the early nineties, some voices began accusing the group of forgetting the politics entailed in the earlier materialist mission.[76]

In a double sense, however, these later trajectories can be found inscribed at the start. The culturalism embraced in the 1990s was neither the postmaterialist betrayal alleged by its detractors nor its mirror image, the upward progression toward ever greater sophistication or superior antireductionist recognition. On the one hand, the vital departures driving the cultural turn were quite visible in the earliest Subaltern Studies volumes, from the striking synergies of Gramsci and Foucault, through the favoring of microhistories, to the insistence on Indian specificities and a very acute sense of just how difficult recovering popular agency would be. While encompassing real diversities of approach, the early essays already struggled with the perspectival dilemmas now so familiar from current debates. Guha's reflections on the relation between ideas of history and the forms of domination, drawing on distinctions between mythical and historical time, anticipated later concerns with indigenous idioms of thought, just as his essay "Chandra's Death" marked out the methodology of the fragment.[77] Rather than advancing from a lower to a higher level of inquiry—as a simple progressivist model of the transition from the "social" to the "cultural" might suggest—such moves were built into the founding intervention. Thus, the later discussions required less the disavowing of a social history origin than the clarifying of an always detectable ambivalence.

On the other hand, this South Asian historiography both presaged and paralleled the course of the "linguistic turn" in the West. The new culturalist preferences of Subaltern Studies in the nineties were not a corruption resulting from access to the luxuries of postcolonial theorizing in the privileged academies of the United States, as some of the angrier opponents implied. The new culturalism wasn't something that had to be "learned" in the West in that sense at all; its incitements were constitutive from the beginning. Moreover, while, for their part, Europeanists certainly learned a very great deal from the Subalternists as they entered wider circulation, they also had their own points of earlier connection, which, however, were harder to see by the nineties. Like the embittered salvos fired against Subaltern Studies, the field of fire in the West between "new cultural historians" and self-styled Thompsonians was obscuring certain lines of descent. Yet, whether in South Asia or the West, social historians during the 1980s had been responding with theoretical and moral urgency to a set of common problems—those concerning the relationship between social pasts and political futures, between material life and cultural meanings, between the structural ordering of the experienced world and the accessible forms of subjectivity, between history and politics. In this sense, for a Europeanist of my generation, much of what the Subalternists offered linked back through the debates of the 1980s and 1970s—through Foucault, feminism, and Gramsci to the thinking of Raymond Williams.

This is what I meant by claiming earlier that postcolonial historiographies "looped back" to the earlier moments of radical innovation where this book began. On the one hand, as Said acknowledged, Raymond Williams had surprisingly little to say on the subjects of colonialism and empire as such.[78] Though a traverser of borderlands, he was otherwise the most rooted and ethnocentered of thinkers; and if determinedly internationalist in his European theoretical range, he wasn't notably inspired by the late twentieth-century florescence of postcolonial literatures, already so exuberantly under way when he died.[79] On the other hand, his later writings about modernism, with their intense back-and-forth between the novel uprootedness of metropolitan consciousness and the older and more parochial modes of national or regional belonging, echoed powerfully in the efforts of contemporary postcolonial thinkers to struggle through the contradictions of an intelligible cosmopolitanism, on one side, and an affective cultural nationalism, on the other.[80] So many of the concerns now considered coterminous with postcolonial thought—ideas of subject positionality; of the locatedness of identity; of the lived particularities of place, region, and the body; of the in-betweenness of actually existing community; and, indeed, of the complex relationship of all those things to the more universal formations of class—were subtly preempted in Williams's writings, particularly in the incomparable *The Country and the City,* but also in his fiction.[81] Precisely the problematic relationship between universalism and cultural alterity underscores the Subalternists' most recent work.[82]

If we see the cultural turn as, in part, enabling a renewed consideration of broad theoretical and methodological purposes (as opposed to validating of any particular empirical and textual content), the influence of Williams was clearly apparent in the first wave of postcolonial analysis. Said recognized that "even one or two pages by Williams on 'the uses of Empire' in *The Long Revolution* tell us more about nineteenth-century cultural richness than many volumes of hermetic textual analysis."[83] Said invoked *Culture and Society* when, at the end of his introduction to *Orientalism* (that first ground-breaking interrogation of the Western intellectual tradition), he asserted the need to work toward "the process of what Raymond Williams has called the 'unlearning' of 'the inherent dominative mode.'"[84] I'm certainly not trying, here, to restore His Majesty's metropolitan theory to a rickety and tarnished old throne, as the preeminent theoretical model that later non-Western thought could only emulate. On the contrary, if the postcolonial critique of the West's bad old binarisms means anything at all, it's to catch the convergences and contingencies of cultural (and theoretical) genealogies and, indeed, to rescue these "impure" spaces as the very site where critical thought might occur.[85]

History in Public

I'm here trying to flag the degree to which debates among historians during the 1980s were shadowed by the wider politics of intellectual change in the public sphere—ranging across the analogous conflicts in other academic disciplines; the commentaries of writers, journalists, and other public intellectuals; all the broader sociopolitical divisiveness of what came to be known as the "culture wars"; and the increasingly transnational or "globalized" dimensions of all such exchange. As a Europeanist, I did not exactly experience the urgency of conflicts over "race" and the "postcolonial" as "noises off"; I was too acutely aware of them for such a metaphor to work. But for most of the decade, they unfolded somewhat removed from where I did most of my scholarly work.[86] Even though my sense of being a historian was always formed by a politics, the grounds for that commitment were shifting in vital ways behind my back. Some of the consequences took me by surprise. Moreover, there were other ways in which academic historians were losing control of their subject.

Thus, in wider public arenas, we are now constantly bombarded by all manner of references to history and appeals to the past. All forms of public "memory work," remembrance, and commemoration— official, commercial, private—have acquired extraordinary momentum, accelerating during the 1980s into a veritable "boom in memory." The appeal to memory has become promiscuous, an unavoidable feature of the landscape of ideas for anyone interested in grasping the dynamics of social change at the turn of the new century. For historians themselves, moreover, "history and memory" has become an *idée fixe* of the discipline. But that interest massively exceeds any professionalized discourse, saturating large sectors of entertainment, popular reading, commercial exchange, and many other parts of the public culture. What is going on here?

In Fredric Jameson's view, this intense interest in the past signifies a "nostalgia for the present."[87] It bespeaks an anxiety about the loss of bearings and about the speed and extent of change, in response to which the narration and visualizing of history seem to promise a surrogate architecture of continuity. Representations of the past—personal and collective, private and public, commercial and uplifting— become both therapy and distraction, a source of familiarity and predictability while the actual ground of the present turns unstable. Such nostalgia spells the desire for holding onto the familiar even as it dwindles from view, for fixing and retaining the lineaments of worlds in motion, of landmarks that are disappearing and securities that are unsettled.

But by the 1990s the memory boom was also marking the return of "the local" to a central space in contemporary political thinking. This derives in part from the post-1960s revival in Europe and North America of a direct-action politics based on smaller-scale communities and grassroots solidarities. But it also bespeaks the "Think globally, act locally" rhetorics of Green activism and opposition to globalization, which in turn reflect the transnationalizing of contemporary history and the challenge to sovereignties based on the nation-state. This is precisely the ground of the postcolonial historiography discussed in this chapter's preceding section, a historiography defined by the complex struggles around place and ethnic particularism generated in the wake of empire in its decolonizing and newly revivified forms. In each of these contexts, encouraged by the logic of Jameson's "nostalgia for the present," memory work offers a way of resuturing individual stories to collective narratives of belonging and accomplishment at a time when the old models for imagining a political future, especially the socialist ones, no longer persuade. As contemporary disaffection from the conventional political process continues to worsen, such alternative modes of public self-recognition expand their appeal. The possibility of mapping personal experiences onto a public landscape of known and common events by using the memorializing repertoire (autobiographies, oral histories, museums, monuments, anniversaries, media celebrations, and national holidays) as the medium for alternative recuperative histories may allow a different ground of memory to be reclaimed.

Memory work as such has no specific political valence. In this sense, Pierre Nora's remarkably popular multivolume project *Les lieux de mémoire,* on French national history, provides one of the most grandiose of recent illustrations. It can be read as wanting to shift national identity decisively away from its older obsessions with the national state, in a spirit more in keeping with European integration, the postnational future, and the idea of a common European home. But Nora's paradigm of the "sites of memory" markedly depoliticizes the national question. For the highly centered national consensus of the old French Republican tradition, it substitutes a fragmented and discrete mélange of disparate topics, which nonetheless accomplish their own concentration of French national memory in a more insidiously ethnocentric manner. That more oblique recentering affirms an aggregated sense of common cultural identity, while excluding those parts of contemporary French society—Islamic, North African, migrant—who can't find themselves in the national past's assembled mosaic.[88]

There's a potential left-wing stake in this new discourse of memory and locatedness, for which the crisis of socialism in the post-1989 political conjuncture blazed the path. By shocking the Left out of its accustomed thinking about political futures, the end of Communism compelled a revisiting of earlier histories—not least in Eastern Europe itself, where the discourse of loss, dispossession, and displacement could be mapped most directly, if most painfully, onto the retrieving of earlier lived (that is, remembered) experiences of actual dates, events, places, names, and forms of historical agency. Through this complicated process of return, the concept of memory itself can be loosened from its earlier toxic connotations of right-wing "blood and soil" philosophy, encouraging the Left to think more positively about the nation in this finely located way. Such possibilities also resonate with postcolonial efforts at theorizing the emplacement of struggles for independence, social justice, and human rights in very particularized contexts of locality and ethnic recognition. Despite its growing identification with migrancy, diaspora, and hybridity, postcoloniality is a condition only ever experienced through its localized modalities, even as its subjects find themselves being relocated to the multicultural social scenes of the metropolis. In these terms, a language of recollection can become a language of recognition. The Left's classic utopian telos of a placeless futurity becomes replaced—for good and ill—by an image of the good society remembered in time and grounded in place, mapped onto specificities of history and experience. "Memory" supplies the language of this move.

In these terms, "memory" offers a crucial site of identity formation under our contemporary predicament, a way of deciding who we are and of positioning ourselves in time and place, given the hugeness of the structural changes now so destructively remaking the world—in the new era of capitalist restructuring defined by globalization, the end of Communism, and the "post-Fordist transition." It became a commonplace of the 1990s to speak of the "postmodern condition," while another claim placed us more tendentiously at the "end of history." Whatever the merits of these particular arguments, the memory boom seems related in one way or another to this "cultural logic" of a contemporary transition.[89] The new information technologies and electronic mass media are also involved. Processes of commodification and the commercialization of culture, in the consumer economies of entertainment and stylistic display, produce a postmodern economy of signs in which the mobile arbitrariness of historical imagery and citation becomes rampantly unavoidable. In that way, too, the contemporary sensibility becomes a memorializing one. We are constantly being invited to place ourselves in relation to one kind of "past" or another. The contemporary public sphere issues constant incitements to memory in that sense.[90]

An endless procession of anniversaries provides another part of this story. The national referents vary. The great extravaganza of 1989 in France, which sought to declare the French Revolution finally "over," was only the most dramatic of these culturally particular events. The most spectacular cross-national commemorations involved the extended and ramified remembering of World War II, beginning with the fortieth anniversary of the European peace, in 1985, and continuing through the sequence of fiftieth anniversaries from the outbreak of war in 1939, D-day, and the liberation (six years later). That public calender spawned an extraordinary degree of commemorative excess, overrunning the spaces of public representation and the television screens in particular, while triggering a plethora of private recollections.[91]

Once again, the meaning of all this activity—of so much obsessional public remembering—lies beyond the formal occasion and the immediate contents themselves. In Europe, surely, the sense of an ending— both internationally (with the end of the Cold War, the strengthening of the European Union, and the transnational shrinkage of the globe) and domestically (with the definitive dissolution of the postwar settlement and the recomposition of the social landscape of class)—sent us back to those earlier moments. In effect, we were returning home, revisiting the origins, reopening the history that produced the contemporary world, even as the latter turned out to be lost. This is what sensitizes us so easily to the past as a field of meaning.

Developments within history as a specialized activity—as a discipline—further explain memory's salience as a kind of thematics. Claiming the postwar era for teaching and scholarly research has played its part, so that historians are now able to write about the years when they were themselves biographically formed. Until very recently, 1945 acted as a boundary of the present in a limiting way. Oral history's slow acceptance as a subdisciplinary area since the mid-1970s has made a difference—again with its own journals, professional associations, conferences, institutional bases, individual classics, agreed methods, technologies, and evolving traditions. The power of interdisciplinarity, with its early institutional bridgeheads from the 1960s and more recent flourishing, likewise created homes for sophisticated intellectual work on memory. Until historians' suspicions toward anthropology, psychology, psychoanalysis, and other theoretical traditions became allayed, discussions wouldn't escape the narrowly drawn technical debates about the problems of using oral sources.

In this last respect, cultural studies certainly provided the main framing and impetus for the growth of memory as an intellectual priority. Treating memory as a complex construct shaped within and by the public field of representations, which needs to be approached via forms of interdisciplinary collaboration, owes everything to the analytical languages developed in cultural studies during the past three decades.[92] Those languages have recast our perceptions of the past in the present, pointing us to all the ways in which history becomes evoked and addressed. It alerts us to the wide range of sites and media through which remembering (and forgetting) take place in a public sphere, consciously and unconsciously, through film and television, photographs and advertisements, radio and song, theater, museums and exhibits, tourist spots and theme parks, fictions, ceremonials, school curricula, political speeches, and more. In this way, the wider domain of ideas and assumptions about the past in a society has been claimed for historical study, so that the historian's customary ground—that is, the boundaries of accepted historical analysis, the definition of what counts as a legitimate source and an acceptable subject—falls more and more into question.

The resulting possibilities are either extremely unsettling or extremely exciting, depending on the defensiveness of one's disciplinary standpoint. They confuse many of the older ways of defining the historian's distinctive practices and identity, freeing up the established disciplinary constraints and opening the imagination to a far more mobile agenda with a much wider repertoire of legitimate approaches and methods. This produces an extremely fruitful indeterminacy. It upsets the customary approach to the boundary between "memory" and "history," where the one was once straightforwardly the professional organizing and contextualizing of the other. History literally "disciplined" memory in that older approach. It shaped and educated the raw and unreliable rememberings of individuals as it called into action the superior languages of objectivity, facing their partial and subjective accounts with the truth of the archive, the "reality" of the historical record, and the "facts."

Precisely along that fault line, a certain de-professionalizing of historical knowledge has been at work. We're now used to finding historical thinking and historical research in places other than university history departments—partly elsewhere in the academy, but partly in the culture at large, in various amateur and lay pursuits. For Raphael Samuel, one of the most eloquent chroniclers and theorists of the implied process of redefinition, this shift made history into "an organic form of knowledge," "drawing not only on real-life experience but also memory and myth, fantasy and desire; not only the chronological past of the documentary record but also the timeless one of 'tradition.'" Samuel explains:

> History has always been a hybrid form of knowledge, syncretizing past and present, memory and myth, the written record and the spoken word. Its subject matter is promiscuous. . . . In popular memory, if not in high scholarship, the great flood or the freak storm may eclipse wars, battles and the rise and fall of governments. As a form of communication, history finds expression not only in chronicle and commentary but also ballad and song, legends and proverbs, riddles and puzzles. Church liturgies have carried one version of it—sacred history; civic ritual another. A present-day inventory would need to be equally alert to the memory work performed (albeit unintentionally) by the advertisers, and to the influence of tourism. . . . As a self-conscious art, history begins with the monuments and inscriptions, and as the record of the built environment suggests, not the least of the influences changing historical consciousness today is the writing on the walls. The influence of video-games and science-fiction would be no less pertinent in trying to explain why the idea of chronological reversal, or time traveling, has become a normal way of engaging with the idea of the past.[93]

Some of the favorite subject matters of cultural studies—exhibitions and museums, cinema and photography, magazines and popular fictions—have been ideal for exploring the porousness of the boundaries between academic history and the wider universe of knowledges about the past, described by Samuel. This is also where history's relationship to memory is being rethought. The relatively new journal *History and Memory,* the main standard-bearer for such work inside the profession, displays exactly this range of influences. Film, both as a visual record of the past and as a form for the production of history in its own right, is attracting widening attention. The critical and eclectic appropriation of psychoanalytic theory of various kinds has played a key role, whose potentials historians have begun only slowly to explore. Photography likewise affords rich opportunities, particularly for the social and cultural history of the family and personal life. Finally, in all of these areas, the impact of feminist theory and politics has been simply enormous, clearing the path for new initiatives and directly inspiring many of the most creative departures. Feminism's challenge has legitimized the study of subjectivity, eventually forcing historians to deal with such questions. The analytical uses of autobiography and various combinations of cultural theory, psychoanalysis, and history have been especially exciting.

Backing Away from the Social: History's New Borderlands

Being a historian at the start of the twenty-first century can mean a wide variety of things. In all of the ways previously mentioned (and many others besides), the boundaries have been coming down. As a result, history's borderlands are now far less defended against other disciplines or types of knowledge than they were forty or even twenty years ago. The traffic is two-way: historians visit the other places of understanding far less furtively than before and are also far more receptive to intrusions from the outside, whether these spring from other disciplines and fields of knowledge or from everyday life, popular culture, and parts of the public sphere. This double broadening of history's horizons, toward other parts of the academy and toward the wider social and cultural contexts of historical thinking discussed by Raphael Samuel, enables a new starting point for exploring the images of the past circulating through a society's public and private worlds.

This novel multiplicity of possible histories and the porousness of the boundaries between the inside and the outside of the academic discipline were a vital part of the crisis experienced by social historians. As the earlier part of this chapter argued, a new caution developing during the 1980s in relation to social analysis and the history of society led many to back away from the more grandiose ambitions of an earlier period and the confident materialism sustaining them. Concurrently, greater interest developed in questions of subjectivity and all aspects of personal life, for which feminism certainly supplied the most far-reaching and sustained inspiration. Both these developments were associated with what became commonly known as the "linguistic turn" or "cultural turn," namely, the interconnected controversies that were exploding around the given theories, methods, and epistemological standpoints of the human sciences by the turn of the 1990s.

Writing the intellectual history of that extraordinarily complex intellectual upheaval—in a manner commensurate with all its unevenness and diversity and with the broader cultural, social, and political forces partially explaining it—has so far eluded most commentators. It becomes ever clearer that the favored shorthand descriptions—"cultural turn," "linguistic turn," and "postmodernism"—were coined in the heat of relatively short-lived, but extremely polarizing, initial battles, disguise as much as they clarify, and conflate manifold variations. Announced in a 1989 volume of essays that blurred distinctions in just that way (foregrounding certain approaches of lesser staying power while neglecting or ignoring others), "new cultural history" became another of these talismanic descriptions. It helped a disparate miscellany of new approaches and subjects to be broached during the 1990s, allowing a motley assortment of radicals, innovators, and outliers to assemble under its banner. But in retrospect, it begged a great many questions as well.[94]

Turning to "culture" was the rather vague common denominator for heterogeneous discontents. By offering a label of convenience for an emergent skepticism about the study of "society," it brought to voice the gathering unease with an existing paradigm. It bespoke the growing appeal of smallness of setting, a moving away from big-scale structural histories of whole societies. During the earlier social history wave, the desire for an integrated account of society as a whole, sometimes voiced through a concept of "total history," usually implied the even larger comparative frameworks of development theory drawn from the social sciences. Such frameworks emphasized "big structures, large processes, and huge comparisons," whose pursuit pervaded the metadiscourse of social science historians during that time.[95] But by the 1980s, country by country, some disillusionment with those ambitions was beginning to set in.

One example of this disillusionment was the interest in "microhistory," a program proposed by Italian historians grouped around the journal *Quaderni Storici,* who were inspired by anthropology more than sociology, by the idiosyncratic or deviant anomaly rather than the sta-

tistically predictable or representative norm, and by a mor
tural" than "scientific" method. Dissatisfied with social scienc
because it imposed the standard of the large scale and the lon
and insisted on the superiority of quantitative methodolo
group sought to bring historical study down to the everyday l
lived experience of concrete individuals, as the best way of ren
the same large questions intelligible.[96]

This Italian grouping was certainly not the only example of a developing skepticism about the grand ambitions of social history in its reigning sociological or Marxist forms. A similar movement was under way by the late 1970s in West Germany. It converged with the Italian departures and adopted some of the same language, while flying its own banner of *Alltagsgeschichte,* or the history of everyday life.[97] In French history, Natalie Zemon Davis held a similar place since the late 1960s, with a series of pioneering essays. With the publication of *The Return of Martin Guerre* in 1983, she made much wider waves in the profession at large, a disturbance further reinforced, around the same time, by Robert Darnton's *The Great Cat Massacre and Other Episodes in French Cultural History.*[98] Across the English Channel, in Britain, social historians had been less swept up in the ambitions of social science history in its more robust and dogmatic guise. The ebullient critiques coming from Edward Thompson and others provided strong countervailing inspiration in that regard.[99]

One of the biggest new departures subsumed beneath the sloganeering of the "new cultural history" during the 1980s was feminist advocacy of gender history. Perhaps the single most influential—and necessarily contentious—early prospectus for the new approaches in general was Joan Scott's 1986 article "Gender: A Useful Category of Historical Analysis," which became a benchmark text for any historian seeking to grasp what was at stake in the linguistic turn. A brilliant work of lucid advocacy defined by eclectic poststructuralist affiliations, Scott's essay presented gender as the variable and contested construction of sexual difference, which was also "a primary way of signifying relations of power."[100] As such, it demanded the attention of historians at large rather than just those who happened to be working on gender relations per se.

Using a "deconstructive" method borrowed from the writings of the philosopher and literary theorist Jacques Derrida and a theory of power based on the ideas of Michel Foucault, Scott argued that the interrogation, breaking down, and opening out of accepted categories should be one of the historian's leading tasks. Doing this could make clear the contingent or constructed history of seemingly natural or stable terms of distinction, such as sex and gender, but also race, class, nation, and any other modern term of agency and belonging, including the very idea of the subject or the self. Moreover, in addition to its more purely methodological challenge to historians, this effort always carried a highly charged political meaning. If such "naturalized" systems of meaning could be shown to have been negotiated and contested in the past, they might become similarly vulnerable to questioning for the present and the future.

Scott's proposals proved hugely controversial, in ways that can't be gone into here.[101] They formed one central item in the so-called culture wars of the late 1980s and early 1990s as those "wars" affected the discipline of history. In that time, the bitterness dividing the adherents of the opposing positions was angry and intense. For a while, the space for effective thinking about genuinely difficult questions became gratuitously narrowed by the mutually exclusive epistemological choices that supporters and enemies of poststructuralism alike now sought to impose. The fixing of discussion to theories of language and textuality seemed to present feminist historians of gender with a strict polarity of options between "cultural" and "social" approaches, so that the disputes reproduced much the kind of restrictive binary opposition that Scott herself had originally wanted to refuse. But beneath all the turmoil of such positioning, a much greater diversity of work was always being done.

While the partisans of the linguistic turn and the defenders of social history were seeking to drum their respective allies into camps, a contingent of mainly younger historians were patiently exploring how both approaches might be joined. Undertaking such a work of synthesis, even at the level of generous-spirited and experimental conversation, was always a fraught thing to attempt. The pervasiveness of the debates at the height of the fighting in the early 1990s usually ruled out the option of simply absenting oneself from the fray. Wrestling with the issues required enormous energy and time—for the purposes of reading, arguing, writing, and thinking. Between the overwrought intensity of the polemics and the production of seriously grounded historical studies, either some time needed to elapse or other kinds of distance had to be present.[102]

But if troubling in their divisiveness, the polemical extremes also pushed back the boundaries and clarified the differences. If the space for publicly refusing the starkness of the choices took a while to open up, the practical coalescence of more hybrid possibilities has now become much easier to see. Behind the surface tumult of the linguistic turn, historians in a variety of areas were creatively subjecting the best of the older approaches to the exciting challenges of the new, across a wide variety of periods and themes—in labor history; in analyses of the welfare state; in histories of medicine, the law, and other professions; in studies of schooling and pedagogy; in readings of popular culture; in work on sexuality; in histories of empire, colonialism, and race.

Moreover, this process of fermentation was not occurring exclusively inside the discipline, sealed off from the outside. For one thing, the dynamism and excitement were intimately linked to the spread of an interdisciplinary consciousness, which can be charted institutionally between the late 1980s and mid-1990s, leading, by the end of the nineties, to significant consolidation—through journals, conferences, debates, and key publications and eventually within particular universities, by the launching of seminars, initiatives in curriculum, the founding of institutes, the allocation of funding, and the creation of new departments and programs. In a number of major universities, including my own, the very texture of scholarly, pedagogical, and general intellectual exchange became interdisciplinary through and through. For historians, accordingly, the bundle of theoretical influences shaping such texts as Joan Scott's 1986 article or circulating more broadly through the discipline was always generated elsewhere, either in other disciplines (such as anthropology, psychoanalysis, and literary theory) or among typically "adisciplinary" thinkers, such as Stuart Hall, Nancy Fraser, or Michel Foucault. Where innovative work is being produced, it's hard to find historians who are not in conversation with other disciplines by now, whether through collaborative research, in their teaching, in their conference attendance, or simply in whom they read and cite.

This is where the relationship between academic history and the rest of the world becomes particularly hard to disentangle. As the preceding reflections suggest, the sense of the past in a society embraces far more than merely the activities of the scholarly discipline, just as academics are themselves constantly interacting with a society's wider images and ideas of the past, whether consciously or in less reflected ways. As a field of meaning, history is always beset by these doubled understandings—on the one hand, of history as past time, as a distinct set of subject matters and all the ways historians seek to work on them; on the other hand, of history as a sign in and for the present, a container of contemporary meanings, with all the complexities that produces in the representational arena, enabling the constant and disorderly back-and-forth between a deceptively finished "then" and a patently active "now."[103] What makes the historian's predicament so interesting these days is precisely the intensity of the interaction between these two types of understanding. The relationship in itself is nothing new. But the willingness of historians to see it may be.

Ideas Change—but How?

Joan Scott's essays of the mid-1980s were certainly a central item in this repertoire. But a much wider range of debates were in play, varying field by field and country by country. With respect to gender history per se, the narrative I know best at firsthand— from my perspective as a Marxist historian educated in Britain, working on Germany, and migrating in 1979 to the United States—began in the mid-1970s, with Marxist-influenced analyses of women's oppression under capitalism, while moving rapidly to critiques of what the available Marxisms were able to offer. To grasp the ways in which women lived their oppression, feminists then turned quickly to theories of ideology and subjectivity, so that barely a few years had elapsed before psychoanalysis seemed to replace Marxism as the main point of orientation. In the resulting mix, literary theory and theories of language—shaped both by readings of the French feminist theorists Julia Kristeva, Luce Irigaray, and Hélène Cixous and by the wider reception of Foucault, Derrida, and Jacques Lacan—converged with an emerging interest in film, popular reading genres, and other aspects of popular culture across the burgeoning territories of cultural studies.[104] But again, if the ensuing theory debates could often be divisive, the lasting outcomes for historians materialized behind these more visible and sometimes grandstanding polemics, as the more focused and concrete historical projects gradually took shape. However constructive—and

indeed unavoidable—the debates over theory may have been, the ultimate payoff came in the actual histories they enabled.

Allowance also has to be made for serendipity. Certain texts
excited historians during the eighties, not because they were consciously adopted as an avant-garde, but because they worked symptomatically by bringing together disparate needs and discontents, by
answering questions barely waiting to be posed, and by feeding
nascent desires for change. Each individual text of that kind has a history, of course. The conditions of possibility for its production—by a
particular author, in a particular institutional scene, with particular
resources and supports, surrounded by all the determinate circumstances (intellectually, socially, culturally, and politically) that historians are used to exploring—can certainly be defined. With sufficient
perspective, using all the appropriate tools and strategies of contextu-
alization, historians can bring these complicated intellectual patterns
into focus, endowing them with persuasive coherence. In retrospect,
as the genealogy of any radical intellectual departure becomes convincingly historicized in that way, the interconnectedness of the relevant texts, ideas, and movements can then be established, and their
earlier pedigree can be identified. But for those who are living through
a particular process of intellectual change at the time, the sheer unex-
pectedness of the relevant influences can seem far more impressive.

The authors of the works I want to highlight here were only
ambiguously historians in the usual accredited sense. They came from
the margins of the profession, were writing outside the normal conventions of monographic or similar scholarship, or were working as
historians in other disciplines. Everyone will have their own preferred
candidates for such a list. My own choice necessarily reflects the particularities of my own standpoint and were among the most widely
read and discussed in the way I'm suggesting. They unlocked possibilities for new ways of thinking among historians. They took such thinking outside the proverbial box.

I give first mention to a trio of works (in descending order of resonance) whose imaginative methodologies, radical epistemology, originality of subject, and general quirkiness placed them self-consciously
at odds with the prevailing conventions of social history in their fields:
Carlo Ginzburg's study of the heretical cosmology of the sixteenth-
century miller of Friuli, Menocchio, in *The Cheese and the Worms;*

Jacques Rancière's *The Nights of Labor: The Worker's Dream in Nine-teenth-Century France,* which called into question the projections of proletarian authenticity only recently constructed by social historians around the figure of the radical artisan; and Wolfgang Schivelbusch's extended reflection on the cultural meanings of "the railway journey" for the nineteenth century's transformed understandings of the new technological modernity of the industrializing world.[105] The syn-chronicity of the influence of these works isn't exact. Ginzburg's book was published in Italy in 1976 and appeared fairly rapidly in translation four years later; the 1981 French edition of Rancière's work was extensively discussed among English-speaking social historians ahead of its translated publication in 1989; *The Railway Journey* enjoyed an altogether more subterranean influence, appearing in Germany in 1977 and New York two years later, but entering social historians' consciousness much more slowly.[106] Yet each of these works chal-lenged social history's presuppositions in a similar manner, encourag-ing a different vision of evidence, subject matters, and the writing strategies historians could entertain.

These historians were all mavericks operating on the edges of the profession, with a variety of eclectic and esoteric knowledges in their training and background—from philology, art criticism, and literary theory to drama, philosophy, and general cultural analysis. The next works I'll cite reemphasize the same type of connections, with further admixtures of psychoanalytic thought, anthropology, and British cul-tural studies, within the overall framing provided by the interest in poststructuralism. They included Benedict Anderson's extraordinar-ily influential reflections on "the origins and spread of nationalism" in *Imagined Communities* (1983); Ronald Fraser's oral history of his own childhood in the English Home Counties during the 1930s and 1940s, *In Search of a Past* (1984); Patrick Wright's *On Living in an Old Country* (1985), which explored the refashioning of the national past in Britain during the 1980s and its embedding in the experience of everyday life; *The Poetics and Politics of Transgression,* by Peter Stallybrass and Alon White (1986), which deployed readings of "the high and the low" to construct an argument about the shaping of bourgeois sensibilities between the seventeenth and twentieth centuries, using Mikhail Bakhtin's idea of "carnival"; Carolyn Steedman's *Landscape for a Good Woman* (1986), which used the author's own autobiography and the life of her mother to call some of the main tropes of British social history into question; and Denise Riley's extended reflection on the shifting historical indeterminacy of the category of "women" in *"Am I That Name?"* (1988).[107]

None of these works was by a historian in the fully credentialed professional sense—that is, someone teaching, researching, and writing inside a university history department. Only one of the authors, Carolyn Steedman, was even trained in history as such, but she worked first as a schoolteacher, before being appointed to a post in arts education at the University of Warwick. Otherwise, these eminently recognizable historians were trained in political science (Anderson), literature (Fraser, Stallybrass, and White), cultural studies (Wright), and philosophy (Riley). Those with full-time or permanent academic positions taught in departments of government (Anderson), cultural and community studies (Stallybrass), European studies (White), and arts education (Steedman). The rest taught in universities at various times but worked as much or mainly outside the academy altogether, whether as a writer and novelist (Fraser), a journalist (Wright), or a philosopher and poet (Riley). They were all—if highly complicatedly and, in Anderson's case, rather tenuously— British. Fraser (born 1930) and Anderson (born 1936) were older, but the others had a distinctive history in common: they were born between the late 1940s and early 1950s, shaped by the postwar culture of the welfare state, and formed by both the radicalisms of the 1960s and 1970s and the ensuing disappointments.

As the explicit framing of each of these books makes abundantly clear, the politics animating this generational experience was vitally implicated in the new vision of history beginning to emerge. By no means all the key elements in the intellectual politics of the 1970s and 1980s are captured by this particular selection of people and texts. Their range is heavily Eurocentric and falls patently short of the radical changes in thinking about questions of race, ethnicity, colonialism, and empire (described earlier in this chapter) that were gathering pace during the same time. A different kind of list might easily begin from the publication of Edward Said's *Orientalism* in 1978 and the earliest of the Subaltern Studies volumes in 1981. It could then continue through the Birmingham CCCS's collective volume *The Empire Strikes Back* (1982) and Paul Gilroy's *"There Ain't No Black in the Union Jack"* (1987), gathering up along the way essays by Gayatri Spivak, Homi Bhabha, and Stuart Hall or such books as James C. Scott's *Weapons of the Weak*

(1985), before culminating in Said's later *Culture and Imperialism* (1993).[108] But as I've already argued, the impact of these departures began materializing in comparable works of history only somewhat later, more in the 1990s than in the 1980s. Moreover, the arguments concerned were far less historically grounded in formal terms than those of the books I've preferred.[109] For a historian mainly working on Britain and other parts of Western Europe, their impact took longer to mature.

What do my preferred works have in common apart from their provenance in the borderlands of the discipline? For one thing, none conform to the historian's conventional genres of writing, such as the scholarly research monograph or the general survey. They all experiment with method and form. Some work through a series of essayistic reflections, whether ordered in rough and overlapping temporal sequences (Anderson, Riley, Stallybrass and White) or offered simply as an interconnected cluster of analytical vignettes (Wright). Others—notably, Fraser and Steedman—play more radically with writing strategies and literary forms, challenging our expectations with a very different kind of design, one that joins the structure of the psychoanalytic case study to the explanatory architecture of the work of history, or "stories" to "interpretations," in Steedman's words.[110] All of them depart from the more familiar rules of evidence. None rely on the archive in the stricter sense often attributed to professional historians—certainly in the early dissertation stages of their careers or in the official hierarchies of disciplinary attainment and prestige, for which a proven standing as an "archival scholar" is the necessary ticket. None would pass the test urged by Geoffrey Elton's *The Practice of History,* with its austere and arid insistence on the primacy of traditional and narrowly based archival research.[111]

These authors certainly show no disregard toward archival scholarship itself. Elsewhere, Carolyn Steedman has written eloquently about the challenges and pleasures of working in the archive in the practical dusty old sense.[112] These works promote not the abandonment of the professional historian's archival calling or of the established protocols of archival research but an imaginative broadening of what these can entail. This partly involves recognizing what the conventional archive is not, or seeing all the things it can never contain. Actually existing archives aren't exactly the neutral storehouses of the entirety of the past record implied by a traditional "objectivist" stance, preserving history whole or providing direct transmissions from a vanished time. On the contrary, archives are extraordinarily partial and contingent things. Whether in the official repositories of state-sanctioned record keeping (such as the National Archives or the Public Record Office), in the many other places where institutional records are kept, or simply in private collections, they are organized around habits and programs of selectivity, through which certain kinds of documents are privileged while others are rejected or transformed. Through archives, the past is damaged and spoiled as much as preserved.

> The Archive is made from selected and consciously chosen documentation from the past and also from the mad fragments that no one intended to preserve and that just ended up there. . . . It is indexed, and catalogued, and some of it is not indexed and catalogued, and some of it is lost. But as stuff it just sits there until it is read, and used, and narrativized.[113]

Thus, conventional archives are not only partial and selective; they are also inert. This dual insight unsettles all the traditionalist assumptions about the sovereignty of the archive in the classical objectivist sense. During the 1980s and early 1990s, the resulting implications caused no end of trouble for the organizing principles and orderly routines of the professional historian's imaginary landscape of knowledge. On the one hand, the archive's documentary contents—the physical traces of past times—mean nothing until historians actually set to work on them. Otherwise, the records sit there unused, either unknown or the guardians of an assumed understanding, hidden monuments to an already established account. On the other hand, archives possess their own story, embedded in the processes that created them, in the rules and practices governing their administration, and in the aggregate decision making of their staff. Archivists are as much the authors of what they keep as its preservers. How the documents got into the archive—who selected them, how they were organized, how they were guarded, how they were made available—is every bit as complex a question, requiring all the same sophisticated techniques of deconstruction, as how the words got onto the page. All the poststructuralist prescriptions, regarding the instabilities of texts, the complexities of authorship, and the contingencies of presentation, apply.

The next step in this argument is equally crucial, because "the

archive" is no longer found only in the physical and discrete institutional spaces to which we have usually given the name, the buildings
where the bundles of files are kept. In the wake of the reception of the
ideas of Foucault, the archive has also come to function as a metaphor.
In the most abstract versions, it refers indefinitely to the evidentiary
foundations for the knowable world. More manageably, it directs us
to all the materials surrounding the processes and techniques that
make the world available for knowledge, that render it graspable or
reducible as such. For Foucault, this approach began with his studies
of prisons, asylums, hospitals, and the general "order of things," but it
soon progressed to an overarching thesis about "governmentality,"
embracing the plenitude of practices developed by states for the purposes of managing and ruling their populations.

If we start thinking of the archive not just as the physical buildings
where documents are stored but also as encompassing the wider
processes—institutional, political, social, cultural, even epistemological—that defined and produced what the documents contained, some
interesting possibilities emerge. Amid the resulting technologies of
surveillance and control, statistical knowledge and processes of
classification acquired special importance, as did the coalescence of
the academic disciplines later in the nineteenth century. The argument can then be applied to the institutional domains of policing,
schooling, and social administration; it can be pushed further, into the
intermediate spaces of the professions and the public sphere; and it can
be extended, thence, to the ground of civil society itself. The imaginative realms of literature, the arts, and popular culture may also be
gathered in. Through all the resulting histories came the invention of
"the social" or "society" in its distinctive modern sense.

Once we think of the archive like this, as the traces left by the
desire for an intelligible and controllable world (or, more ambi-
tiously, by the drives of states for "the ordering of the world and its
knowledges into a unified field"),[114] the possible forms an archive
might assume for a particular topic or question can dramatically
expand. Even considered simply (in practical terms) as places where
documents can be stored, archives now greatly diversify in form.
They might include "a sound or film library or a collection of post-
cards or a filing cabinet of oral history interviews" as well as the
older types of record keeping or registry.[115] But even more, our
understanding of what counts as an important or legitimate source

can become blown wide open. Not so long ago, for example, the mainstream of the profession kept the practices of oral history resolutely at bay, on the grounds that oral testimony failed to meet the evidentiary protocols for the integrity of the archive as conventionally understood. But in the meantime, that epistemological boundary, which defined what I called earlier the sovereignty of the archive, has been decisively breached. The road has been extremely rapidly traveled from *The Cheese and the Worms,* through, say, *The Return of Martin Güerre* and Natalie Davis's later work *Fiction in the Archives,* to the extremely exciting methodological free-for-all of the present.[116]

This questioning of the conventional archive's objectivity and simultaneous broadening of the definition of a permissible source were two of the decisive gains for historians since the 1980s. They were intimately connected: being able to recognize the inventiveness and selectivity in the official keeping of the record, or its necessary arbitrariness, makes it easier to look elsewhere for the archival basis of one's research. This widening of the inventory of possible sources was brilliantly captured by Raphael Samuel in *Theatres of Memory* (quoted earlier in this chapter). Once the historian's agenda was opened up, the way was cleared for all kinds of research topics, often requiring a great deal of inventiveness in the search for sources and an ingeniously creative approach in reading them.

Thus, the topics available for historians have grown with dizzying profusion, to include fashion, shopping, and all aspects of taste, style, and consumption; art, photography, iconography, and visual culture; architecture, landscape, and the environment; drinking, eating, and cigarette smoking; music, dancing, and popular entertainment; histories of gender, tilted more and more toward masculinity; all aspects of the history of sexuality; travel and tourism; clothing, furniture, toys, and other objects of commodification, usefulness, and pleasure; collecting and museums; hobbies and enthusiasms; occultism; psychology, psychiatry, and all areas of medical practice; histories of the body; and histories of emotions. Most of these topics involve contact with other disciplines. Conversely, scholars in anthropology, literature, art history, film studies, and all parts of cultural studies have turned massively to history during the past two decades—certainly by historicizing their perspectives, whether or not they compose their own archives in ways historians would approve or expect.

The Subjective Element

While the key works on my list hardly engaged today's diverse topics in any detailed or grounded fashion, they challenged us to think differently about history. They allowed the established terrain of historical research of the social, political, or intellectual historian to be broken down and recomposed. They made possible its decentering. These books were also joined substantively by a number of common interests. Benedict Anderson and Patrick Wright were centrally concerned with the complexities of national culture, for example, as were the other authors more obliquely. The terms of modern political identity formed a similar common thread, although only some of the authors dealt explicitly with the category of modernity per se. More than anything else, though, the shared commitment to a history of meaning, focused around questions of political subjectivity, linked these six works together. This signaled the passage from social history into cultural history, in a number of ways.

First and most obviously, this turn to subjectivity has enabled a resurgence of interest in biography. The writing of individual biographies was one of the earliest casualties of the rise of social history during the 1960s and 1970s. With much justification, social historians dismissed the biographical approach as an example of everything in the discipline that needed modernizing, deriding it as either the benighted traditionalism of old-fashioned political historians or the trivializing and frivolous recourse of the nonprofessional. The pursuit of structural or broadly contextualized materialist analysis of various kinds, in contrast, became equated with a necessary degree of scholarly seriousness. By the 1980s, however, with feminist scholars in the lead, some historians were rethinking this stance. Rather than continuing to see biography as a simplification, they reclaimed it for complexity. Individual lives might now be revisited as complex texts in which the same large questions that inspired the social historians were embedded. Only a different range of theory and techniques would be required. The intersection of elaborate and multiform forces might be traced through and inside a particular life, allowing the generalized and the abstract to be focused through the personal and the particular. The resulting histories might take the form of a full-scale biography, or the biographical might take its place in a wider repertoire of analysis. The individual life became one of the sites where microhistory could be practiced.[117]

Second, the incipient culturalism of the 1980s exhausted existing theories of ideology. Again, my particular version of this story is personal and begins in the British Marxist debates of the 1970s, as certain classical and pragmatic applications of the "base and superstructure" metaphor among historians began collapsing under the pressure of sustained theoretical critique. That critique proceeded from the ideas of Louis Althusser, moved rapidly through an intense engagement with the thought of Antonio Gramsci, and began responding to the challenge of feminism. In escaping from a resulting impasse at the end of the 1970s, British Marxists turned increasingly to versions of Foucault, psychoanalytic theory, and cultural studies, while many feminists struggled toward theories of sexed and gendered subjectivity.[118] Until that time, most social historians tended to approach ideology through antinomies of coercion and consent or domination and resistance, addressing questions of popular conformity and rebellion from a class-analytic point of view. Under the impact of the new debates, however, the received materialist paradigm of class experience and class consciousness began to break down. By the mid-1980s, social historians were no longer so confident about the potential translations from oppression and exploitation into forms of collective action. They stressed instead the contradictory meanings through which class tended to be lived. Whether in exploring the ambivalence of individuals or grasping "how patterns of dependency, paternalism, [and] deference were reproduced in other contexts in the wider society," the classical Marxist causalities of class relations and class consciousness no longer held.[119] Other approaches to subjectivity came due.

Third, the turn to subjectivity was borne by the ur-feminist axiom of the late 1960s and early 1970s, "the personal is political." At one level, it registered the latest stage in the working through of one of the primary problems in women's history—namely, the relationship between family, domesticity, and intimate life, on the one hand, and the public worlds of politics, on the other. If the marginalizing of women from political power had always encouraged feminist historians to seek female voices elsewhere—in family and household, in the education of children, in religion, in the pleasures of consumption and entertainment, in all the unspectacular spaces of the everyday—the

same linkage of the personal to the political now formed the key starting point for each of the works under discussion. How could individual subjectivities be sutured to larger political identities and loyalties,
such as the nation or a class? Again, this was a two-way street: through
such processes, individuals might be constrained and imprisoned as
well as enabled or set free. We might invent identities from our own
immediately lived experiences or fashion agency through our intimate
encounters with the concretely experienced social actualities of
inequality and difference. But we could do so only by living out and
appropriating the consequences of scripts written and codified elsewhere.

Fourth, psychoanalysis vitally influenced the theorizing of exactly
these questions. At an early stage of the discussions, in the 1980s,
Timothy Ashplant usefully summarized this starting point: "Two
points in particular stood out: the relationship between the inner psychic realm studied by psychoanalysis and the external world studied by
history; and the role of language as mediating between these
moments."[120] Of course, even as the validation and critique of language by psychoanalysis was being upheld, linguistic analysis itself was
becoming problematized via deconstruction and the resulting "crisis of
interpretation."[121] Such emerging complexities notwithstanding, psychoanalysis promised strategies for dealing with a number of social
history's abiding problems. It answered the lack of a theory of the
individual subject, which neither Marxism nor other materialist sociologies had managed to address. It recognized the power of the emotional drives and resistances behind social and political movements.
Most important of all, it acknowledged the elusiveness and opacity of
the relationship between an originating event and the resulting circumstances or putative outcomes. This emphasis on "undecidability"
and the associated dialectics of memory and forgetting helped under-
mine the social historian's given assumptions about causality. This
applied most palpably to the books by Fraser, Steedman, and
Riley.[122]

Fifth, conceding the elusiveness of the relationship to the originating event expands the instigating role of the historian's own questions
and the relevance of the standpoints from which they are asked. This
brings the historian into his or her own text, while emphasizing the
present tense of the historian's voice.

To begin to construct history, the writer has to do two things, make two movements through time. First of all, we need to search backwards from the vantage point of the present in order to appraise things in the past and attribute meaning to them. When events and entities in the past have been given their meaning in this way, then we can trace forward what we have already traced backwards, and make a history.[123]

This is not really a "presentism" in the earlier and more directly politicized 1960s sense, in which the sloganeering of a "usable past" sought to erect "relevance" into an ethical prerequisite for historians wanting to place themselves on the left. Rather, it invites a certain self-reflectiveness when faced with the raw and unmediated inertness of the past, including an honesty in openly constructing one's standpoint and a willingness to acknowledge the shifting and provisional bases from which the questions can only ever be asked. This perspectivalism is not exactly without precedent, and there are many foretastes in the classics of historiographical commentary. But since the 1980s, more working historians have become more conscious of its force for more of their time than ever before. It is scarcely possible to avoid encountering the practical and theoretical dilemmas it brings. In some history departments, it supplies the very air we breathe.

Finally, for all of these departures, feminism was absolutely crucial. The pioneering women's histories of the seventies were rarely noticed by the leading social historians, who were issuing their classic manifestos of advocacy and crisis. But feminist histories from the eighties were unavoidably at the forefront of the cultural turn. This was something fundamentally new. Earlier, women's history had been so effectively sidelined into a discrete subfield, conceptualized via "separate spheres" and subsumed into the history of the family, that even such avowedly feminist syntheses as Tilly and Scott's *Women, Work, and Family* did little to break it out. If one's field happened to be specific kinds of labor history, the history of the family, or certain kinds of social reform, feminist critiques could hardly be ignored; otherwise, women's history could be left safely to its own devices. However, once feminists started insisting on gender as a dimension of all human transactions, collective and individual, the situation decisively changed. It started to seem that if sexual differences were variably and contingently ordered, in contestable as well as stable and normalizing ways, always implicating differences of power, with relevance across all the fronts of social, cultural, and political life, then the feminist challenge could no longer be quite as easily contained.

Carolyn Steedman

In many respects, Carolyn Steedman (born 1947) seems to exemplify the arguments I've been making about the changes in the discipline between the 1960s and now. She certainly began with her feet planted firmly in the post-Thompsonian social history of the late 1960s, attending the University of Sussex as an undergraduate in 1965–68 and completing a Cambridge doctoral thesis entitled "The Formation of English Provincial Police Forces, 1856–1880," published in 1984 as *Policing the Victorian Community*.[124] Yet ever since *Landscape for a Good Woman* and later works appeared, she's been known mainly as a leading cultural historian.[125] With respect to another part of my argument, moreover, she worked as a historian completely on the outside. While joining the editorial collective of *History Workshop Journal* in 1984 and moving in the associated circles of women's historians, feminist educators, and history workshoppers, she did so with no connection to any university history department. She worked as a primary school teacher during 1974–81, spent two years at a research project on bilingualism in early education at the London Institute of Education, and took an appointment in arts education at the University of Warwick in 1984. For ten years, she researched and wrote as a historian, with widening international resonance but no relationship to her own university's history department. Only in 1994 did she join the latter, with a personal chair. In other words—not unlike other feminist historians of this generation in Britain—she became a leading historian entirely outside the institutional and professional precincts of history as a discipline.[126]

Landscape for a Good Woman shaped Steedman's reputation as a historian. By now, the book has already been much written about and discussed, not only by historians, but also by scholars in literature, anthropology, women's studies, and gender studies—indeed, across the whole cultural studies map. The book holds appeal for anyone interested in the history of autobiography and the forms of writing; in histories of class and childhood; in the lives written for women and girls (and boys and men) by the main scripts of a culture; in the post-1945 histories of welfare and improvement; in the receding historical imaginary of an older Left; in the still unwritten histories of desire, envy, and longing; or in the enormous complexities of writing a history of the self and subjectivity since the eighteenth century. At the same time, *Landscape* is a highly personal and idiosyncratic work. It functioned for its author as part of a certain learning process that allowed big questions to be worked through, though more epistemologically than in the therapeutic terms we might assume. Steedman was interested, above all, in clarifying the difference between history and the other kinds of stories we tell.

As with the treatments of Edward Thompson and Tim Mason that close the previous two chapters of this book, my reasons for here focusing on Carolyn Steedman's book are autobiographical. Reading it played a key part in my own encounter with the intellectual shifts I'm describing. I could also tell my own convergent set of stories. Like myself, for example, *Landscape*'s author belongs to the generation inspired by Thompson's *Making of the English Working Class*. I might likewise describe parallel journeys through the safe but dispiriting social and cultural landscapes of the long postwar, whose genealogies of migration and marginality, validation and denial, would look quite familiar. I was also a child of the welfare state. The book's reflections on English childhoods could, to a great extent, be mine. In other respects, of course, our stories would be quite different. Most obviously, I was a boy and not a girl, and through that particular difference, Steedman elaborates an original and searching series of arguments about the gendered narratives of class disadvantage and aspiration. Among these, she composes a kind of "counter-counternarrative" of impaired popular democracy, intended to work deliberately against Thompson's oppositional counternarrative of the male labor movement, offered so eloquently in *The Making*. If, in the end, Steedman destabilizes and reenables the latter rather than overturning it, her critique is no less far-reaching for that. Moreover, I choose Steedman's book precisely because of its gendered standpoint: by far the most effective challenge to the given materialisms of social history during the 1980s came from feminists.

Steedman's book used her own and her mother's stories to challenge some of our main scenarios of modern British history and, indeed, to argue against some of the primary ways in which histories tend to be written—not only the historical presentation of particular topics (such as childhood, motherhood, or class), but also the very process through which historical accounts are conventionally put together. As a formal structure, her book disobeyed all the rules. It ranged back and forth between different parts of the nineteenth and twentieth centuries, between historical works and types of fiction, between history and psychoanalysis, between the personal and the political, and between individual subjectivity and the dominant available narratives of a culture, whether in historiography or politics, grand theory or cultural beliefs, psychoanalysis or feminism. Rather than relating the many particular arguments in the book, though, I want to highlight four specific features.

First, the book's use of the personal voice was immensely liberating. This was partly due to its freedom of form, its refusal of linear narrative; it moved back and forth between Steedman's personal history, the extensive repertoire of historical knowledges needed to shape it, and the forms of grand theory and types of determinism that would otherwise have fixed its available meanings so easily into place. In method, Steedman assembled a case history, giving us what she called "the bits and pieces from which psychological selfhood is made."[127] Among historians, her use of the personal voice was highly unusual. For those on the left, it struck a particular chord. It authorized reflectiveness at a time when my generation was experiencing a range of uncertainties and disappointments—concerning both the forms of social history we'd expected might explain the world and the types of politics we thought could change it. As I've argued throughout this book, both kinds of optimism were always intimately yoked together.

Second, those disappointments were about the collapse of grand narratives—or, rather, about the inability of existing grand narratives to capture either the directions of contemporary societal change or the diversity of past historical experience. In this respect, Steedman offered a history radically and disconcertingly at variance with the accounts we knew. She told a story of working-class lives that didn't fit; that didn't belong in the available scripts of socialism, the postwar democracy of opportunity, and the solidarities of working-class culture; and that couldn't easily be reconciled with the familiar frameworks of social history and cultural studies. Steedman's story was about a mother who didn't want to mother, a patriarchy without a patriarch, and forms of longing and desire, envy and exclusion, that spilled outside the acceptable frames of class and gender consciousness. Even more, it was about historians' inability—and unwillingness—to develop a language for dealing with personal longings. It was about what she called "lives lived out on the borderlands . . . for which the central interpretive devices of the culture don't quite work."[128]

Third, at the same time that it focused a rhetorically "personal" self, Steedman's book constantly reengaged the terms of the "big picture." In making the argument for the value of a case history—for one version of a microhistory, perhaps—she remained committed to the largest ideas of societal persistence and change, to the most abstract theses about modern subjectivity, and to the biggest of the overarching frameworks of capitalism and its social relations. She refused to dwell exclusively inside the minutiae of personal experience and individual lives instead of moving out to the larger-scale questions of human history (where the present book began, with Edward Thompson and Tim Mason). On the one hand, Steedman focused on those places where history and culture meet subjectivity, to explore how such encounters could be converted into a sense of the self. On the other hand, she showed the ability of the given social and cultural environment to consign some types of selfhood to the margins. In showing us "the fragmented and ambivalent nature of experience and self," Steedman's case study exposed "the precariousness of theory and class consciousness when it fails to incorporate the wants and needs of the individuals—especially the women—within it."[129]

Fourth, *Landscape* contains a meditation about "history" in precisely the disciplinary sense—as a type of intellectual practice, a mode of inquiry with materials and rules, a process of cognition, a genre of writing. This is partly an issue of "the archive" in the sense I've already discussed, involving "the massive authority" bestowed on "a storyteller" by history's "appeal to the evidence"—meaning, as Steedman puts it, "the pleasures of the plot shaped according to what the documents forbid, or authorize, but which they never contain in themselves."[130] But Steedman also asked what distinguishes history as a kind of writing from other literary or narrative forms, including letters and diaries, novels, autobiographies, and Freudian case studies. What does it permit, and what does it impede or disavow? Her answer explained history as a mode of cognition based on temporality, whose narratives are ordered around "time and causal connection." It rests on a "basic historicity," where "knowledge of chronology and time" inhere.[131]

Two additional arguments followed from this claim. One concerned the indefinite and unattainable plenitude of "the way it really was," or the abstract generality of everything the past theoretically contains, the totality historians can never hope to retrieve.

> It seems probable that history cannot work as either cognition or narrative without the assumption on the part of the writer and the reader . . . that there is somewhere the great story, that contains everything there is and ever has been—"visits home, heartbeats, a first kiss, the jump of an electron from one orbital position to another," as well as the desolate battlefield, the ruined village—from which the smaller story, the one before your eyes now, has simply been extracted.[132]

From the same indefiniteness, then, comes the argument of historical writing's openness and instability. Unlike stories claiming completeness, such as autobiographies or novels, historical writing is based on "a recognition of temporariness and impermanence." Historical inquiry "is constructed around the understanding that things are not over, that the story isn't finished: that there is no end." Desires for exhaustiveness and finality notwithstanding, new evidence and arguments will always be found; new accounts can always be made. Thus, histories allow for change. Indeed, they have the *idea* of change inscribed in them: "The telling of a life story is a *confirmation* of that self that stands there telling the story. History, on the other hand, might offer the chance of denying it."[133]

In the two decades since *Landscape* appeared, Steedman has continued exploring these themes, returning with particular consistency to the history of the modern idea of childhood, or, rather, to the epistemological work such an idea has been asked to perform. That work is intimately connected to ideas about history. In the course of the nineteenth century, she argues, the desire to see an individual's childhood "as the buried past, the place that is *there,* within us, but never to be obtained," acquired epistemological equivalence with the equally modern idea that history could be captured through the documentation assembled into an archive. This homology then perdured, even as the discipline of history began securing its own increasingly separate institutional credentials: "This understanding of the individual human subject was examined and expressed in many forms of writing in the nineteenth century, from the scientific treatise to slush fiction, though it was growth studies—the popularized physiology of the mid-century—that put new formulations of human insideness—of having an inside, a space within: an interiority—on the cultural agenda." This understanding of the self—of human subjectivity, its inner constitution, its developmental coordinates, and its burial beneath experience, requiring forms of archaeology to be retrieved—shaped a vital field of interconnections between the modern idea of childhood and thinking about social and political identity. It delivered an "imaginative structure" that allowed individuals to explore the sources of their own self while connecting the resulting descriptions and insights to the larger social world and, thence, to the world of public affairs.[134]

This way of understanding childhood, as "a mapping of analogy and meaning for the self," which simultaneously inserted actual children into the symbolic landscape of the social world, not only offered a kind of template for reflecting on the pastness where individual presents were embedded ("history" in commonsense and everyday meanings) but also stood more generally for the nineteenth century's evolving ideas about the origins of the self.[135] Throughout, as her recurring trope of the "Little Watercress Girl" suggests, Steedman is interested less in the real worlds of children than in the place required of the child in the social thought, moral philosophy, and political theory of the capitalist West.[136] From Rousseau to Freud, the figure of the child became emblematic for the entailments of the effort at imagining the good society, a central organizing metaphor for how we think about the possibilities of shaping or transforming the social world and, therefore, about the movements of history. No one has written more brilliantly than Steedman—analogically, hermeneutically, or epistemologically—about this complex field of meanings crystallized by the idea of childhood.

When considered with another of her main themes—the relationship of modern forms of writing to the making of the self and to the allied concept of interiority—this focus helps engage precisely those questions of political subjectivity that proved so troubling for social history's earlier optimism. Indeed, during the past three decades, Steedman has returned consistently to the histories of modern subjectivity, focusing, in particular, on the possibilities for self-fashioning allowed by various kinds of writing and public performance.[137] The latter include not only particular genres—novels, diaries, the epistolary form, private copybooks, conduct books, political tracts, social reportage, speaking from public platforms, storytelling, the *Bildungsroman,* biographies, guides for teachers—but also very exceptional texts Steedman happens to have encountered, from John Pearman's autobiography and the story of *The Tidy House* to a nine-year-old English Punjabi girl's singing of a storybook.[138] Some of the resulting narratives proved productive for larger public scripts, feeding (for good or ill) into the Left's progressivist political programs during the twentieth century.[139] Others, like the "radical soldier's tale" or "Amarjit's song," were either not noticed, directly disregarded, or silently co-opted—expropriated, in fact—by the dominative scripts of others.

As Steedman observes, this uncertain process of narrative absorption applies also to works of history, including even—or perhaps especially—such great inspirational epics of social history as Thompson's *Making of the English Working Class,* around which Steedman develops a typically original and dissentient reading. The time-bound partialness of Thompson's account wasn't only a matter of the absence of women or his masculinist conception of class. Thompson's more serious omission, Steedman argues, concerned the constitutive importance that a specifically feminized story of sensibility, sexual relationships, and suffering held for the social relations and political theory of the very process of class formation he wanted to describe. This is precisely the story—archetypal, scripted, diffused into a sensibility, discursively elaborated as ideology—that the collective agency imagined for the workingman-as-citizen fundamentally presupposed. For this claim, Steedman draws not only on her own arguments about the history of subjectivity, with its growing eighteenth-century associations of cultivated interiority, but also on a broader historiography concerned with the power of a popular "melodramatic vision" and its empathy for the "suffering self."

As Thompson wanted to tell the story of *The Making,* Steedman averred, "men come to new political subjectivities in community and collectivity through understanding the meaning of the suffering and exploitation they have experienced."[140] His telling took an avowedly heroic form that was intended to inspire and did. Yet how do we deal with those workers—men as well as women—who would never have found themselves in his version of the story, or how do we deal with those parts of life it omitted to describe? While *The Making* "is indeed an epic tale," it's also one "which most experience of the men who act as its heroes cannot actually have fitted (or cannot actually have fitted all of the time)."[141] At the heart of Thompson's account remains a startling lacuna: in this period, "the structures of feeling that Thompson delineates, the melodramatic mechanism by which social and self knowledge promotes political revelation, was bound up with the feminine and was almost exclusively figured by a woman and her story."[142] At some level, Thompson knew this. Yet within the coordinates of the time—the materialist sensibility, the registers of significance and recognition, the learned idioms of politics, the available languages of social history—he wasn't able to tell that story.[143]

Some years ago, as Steedman suggested to the 1990 Urbana-Champaign Cultural Studies Conference, Thompson's book had already begun entering that "transitional stage" in the life of a work of written history, when it ceases being used primarily for "its overt subject matter" and starts acquiring a documentary status of its own. It began turning more and more into the repository of the complex sequence of contemporary intellectual, social, and political histories it had partly enabled, becoming a kind of palimpsest of all the intervening hopes and disappointments—"an epic telling of a history that we watch with wonder and pity, that is also now, in our reading, about *us,* and our lost past." Of course, the book retains a great deal of its earlier substantive value—as "a quarry of information about class formation, the actual meeting of actual men under cover of darkness on moors six miles beyond Huddersfield, and the language they used in consciousness of their making a new political world." But at the same time, *The Making*'s impermanence now ineluctably supervenes.

> Too much has happened for this to operate as a simple historical source; there are too many new items of information—about what women were doing, at that moment, back in Huddersfield, about all the men who were not present at their own class formation, all those who did not "specially want it to happen . . ."; about recent events in Eastern Europe; about all our lost socialisms.[144]

Steedman's corpus—from *The Tidy House* and *Landscape,* through her writings on John Pearman and Margaret McMillan, to *Strange Dis-*

locations and *Dust*—struggles continuously with this legacy of Thompson and the wider ensemble of associated progressivist thought.[145] Her work challenges those received understandings by seeking to recuperate all the subjectivities they've neglected or disavowed; she uses these other stories—for example, her mother's or John Pearman's (and, of course, her own)—to subvert the older narratives. Still more, she reconstructs the overall "structures of feeling" (to use Raymond Williams's term) through which a certain ideal of interiority, associated ideas of femininity and childhood, and a set of presumptions regarding family, sexuality, and personal life were able to ground dominant ways of thinking about culture and politics since the mideighteenth century. At the same time, she remains constantly attentive to the processes that can bring individuals to a change in their self-understanding, in particular to the point where they can see through the power of the "prefigurative script" in order to craft the narratives of their lives.[146] She asks: How do we find ourselves in the landscape? How do we place ourselves historically inside our own story?

Does this make Carolyn Steedman into a "new cultural historian"? If that designation is earned by an interest in questions of meaning, language, and subjectivity, the answer is clearly yes. But none of Steedman's books actually depart the ground of social history, and most make a point of reaffirming it. Most of them specifically combine interpretive approaches with the contextualizing analysis and archive of the social historian. Do Steedman's essays "Englishness, Clothes, and Little Things" or "What a Rag Rug Means" deliver cultural history, social history, literary history, intellectual history, or something else entirely?[147] The question seems immaterial. In answer to her own critique of Thompson, moreover, Steedman is now working on the problem of service, servitude, and servants in exactly the period covered by his book. In the most basic of social historical terms—by any criteria, domestic servants formed one of the key working categories of the later eighteenth century—this subject is patently essential to both the history of working-class formation and the new discourse of political economy.[148] Does that spell "cultural history" or the "history of society"? What is the force of the distinction?

Steedman is better described as a historian who understands the theoretical and philosophical implications of doing historical work. She pushes edgily on the boundaries of what historians think they do, but she manages to combine social and cultural history without turning the results into some risk-free and reassuring middle way. She addresses the insufficiencies and exclusions of a class-centered approach to social history, but she does not abandon the standpoint of "class" altogether. She makes the "cultural turn" without waving good-bye to "the social." She resists the tyranny of grand narratives without succumbing to an excessively deconstructed identity. Finally, by acknowledging the very historicity of all subjectivities, she exposes the falseness of the dichotomy between the "social" and the "cultural" in the first place. That is what we should take away from reading Steedman's work: between social history and cultural history, there is really no need to choose.

V. DEFIANCE
History in the Present Tense

Where We Began

WITHIN THE VAST CORPUS of the social history accumulated since the 1960s, it's possible to find two distinct impulses or directions (though this is not the only way of telling the story). One impulse has been the desire to grasp the development of whole societies—sometimes discretely, by analyzing the forces shaping a single country's experience; sometimes internationally, by arguing about global or comparative change. The history of social structure—whether approached through class formation or through the study of social status, social inequality, social mobility, and social trends—is one context of such research, with its familiar emphases around employment, housing, leisure, crime, family and kinship, and so forth. Finding the long-run patterns and regularities of social organization and social behavior was an early passion of the social historian. The transmission from these to the great questions of early modern and modern political change provided the inspiration for many of social history's founding debates.

A second impulse has been toward studying particular locales. Village or county studies and studies of individual towns became the familiar building blocks of British historians for the big questions of Reformation and post-Reformation religious history, the origins and course of the seventeenth-century civil war, and histories of poverty and crime. Analogous tracks can be found in the historiographies of France, Germany, and other societies, too. For the modern era, the urban community study became the main practical medium for investigating class formation. The impact of Edward Thompson's *Making of the English Working Class* certainly encouraged a strong "culturalist" turn in such work, but the older materialist concerns—with wages, labor markets, apprenticeship systems, workshop regimes, mechanization and de-skilling—still remained, as did the quantitative study of strikes. Urban community studies also emphasized questions of social and geographical mobility. Such work converged on the stabilities and cohesion of working-class communities and their ability to sustain—or not sustain—particular kinds of politics.

With time, the closeness and reciprocity of these two kinds of impulse—between the macrohistorical interest in capturing the directions of change within a whole society and the microhistories of particular places—pulled apart. The two ambitions became disarticulated. Social historians didn't necessarily jettison an interest in the "big" questions, but they increasingly drew back to the intensive study of the bounded case, in which a particular community, category of workers, or event stood in for the "whole-society" argument. Such studies might deploy the full repertoire of the social historian's methods and techniques but held off from the aggregative account of what might have been happening at the level of the society as a whole. Indeed, the very logic of the community study tended toward the specificity of the local account, generalizing its relationship to larger social processes via claims of exemplification rather than aggregation.

In my own immediate field of German history, for example, these contrary impulses—the macrosocietal and the microhistorical—produced an especially strong polemical standoff. This resulted from the enormous popularity of *Alltagsgeschichte* (history of everyday life) from the end of the 1970s, pioneered by a small number of innovative scholars within academic history, but with extensive resonance in a wider variety of popular and semiprofessional contexts, embracing oral histories, school projects, local compilations, memory work, museums, exhibitions, and so on. If social history in West Germany had taken off in the sixties by modeling itself as "historical social science," the new *Alltagshistoriker* now challenged this focus on impersonal forces and objective processes, calling instead for histories of popular experience that privileged the local, the ordinary, and the marginalized.[1]

In the face of this challenge, the older and only recently established generation reacted aggressively in defending their own project of a systematic and "critical" social science—or *Gesellschaftsgeschichte* (societal history), as they called it. They upheld the paramountcy of structures and large-scale processes as the only level on which the trivial and isolated status of the local case could be overcome. They insisted on the use of quantitative and other social science methods. They reasserted the commitment to generalization and the production of social-scientific knowledge that could be called objective. Against them, the *Alltagshistoriker,* broadly corresponding to the "new cultural historians" coalescing during the 1980s in the United States, argued the importance of "historical miniatures" and small-scale contexts of historical research. Contrary to the social science historians' claims, they insisted, these contexts formed the ground on which the full complexity of ordinary experience could be captured, requiring an interpretive and ethnological approach. The resulting debates raged especially fiercely during the 1980s, and although some *modus vivendi* may have been edged toward more recently, the battle lines have by no means been surrendered.[2]

This German debate sharply illustrated the gaps opening between the practitioners of different kinds of work. By the mid-1980s, the cutting edge of innovation was shifting away from social history to the so-called new cultural history, in its various forms. One aspect was again the opening up of new subject matters social historians hadn't explored, such as the history of sexuality or histories of art and aesthetics, histories of popular culture, and histories of "strange" and exotic beliefs. Another aspect was a different interdisciplinary borrowing—no longer from the "hard" social sciences, but from anthropology, literary theory, and linguistics instead. Most important of all, social explanation and social causality were losing their hold on the imagination. Historians became ever more skeptical about the answers social analysis seemed able to deliver. "Materialist" explanations based primarily on the economy and social structure now seemed to oversimplify the complexities of human action. Previously attractive structuralisms now seemed "reductionist" or "reductive" in their logic and effects.

Instead, it became important to concentrate on meaning and the forms of perception people make and display. Above all, language and the complexities of reading required attention, because in trying to understand past actions, historians have only very limited documentary traces available. Only extremely partial and arbitrary descriptions happen to have survived, forming a thicket of representations between now and then. Those surviving traces of the past are really "texts" requiring interpretation. In other words, rather than being a social scientist collecting, counting, and measuring data and placing everything in its social context to explain it, the historian should become an anthropologist or ethnographer, a literary critic, a linguistic analyst, and so forth. Out of this shift in focus came the so-called linguistic or cultural turn, which proved as influential as the turning to social history twenty years before. This was especially clear among new graduate students entering the profession—in the subjects and approaches that got them excited, in the kinds of dissertations they wanted to write. Angry battles raged around all of this during the 1990s, field by field, in the journals and conferences and, of course, in relation to hiring decisions and the main directions history departments wanted to take.

In telling my own version of this story—of the complicated intellectual history of the shifting interests of historians between the 1960s and now—I've tried to avoid rehashing the details of the polemics assailing the public sphere of the profession from the later 1980s to the mid-1990s. Those debates—the discipline's variant of the "culture wars"—raged with particular ferocity across women's history and labor history, reaching a variety of climaxes, sometimes protractedly, national field by national field. Some individuals and certain books and articles tended to focus the passions. Joan Scott's 1986 article "Gender: A Useful Category of Historical Analysis" probably attracted more discussion than any other single intervention. An especially ill-informed squib from Lawrence Stone ignited one set of exchanges in *Past and Present,* and a more extensive airing of differences occurred in *Social History.*[3] Most journals registered the new divisiveness to some degree. National meetings, such as those of the American Historical Association or the Berkshire Conference on the History of Women, staged important debates, as did the various area and subdisciplinary meetings, not to mention lots of smaller conferences field by field, and countless local seminars and other events. If *postmodernism* had initially been used as the all-purpose boo-word by the opponents of the linguistic turn, *postcolonialism* was starting to take its place by the early 1990s.

These polemics were always shadowed by politics. From the late-Reagan and late-Thatcher eras into the heightened divisiveness of the 1990s, they hummed with the wider enmities we call the "culture wars." Their tones and terms were continuous in important ways across other disciplines. Their fallout frequently spilled into a wider public sphere.[4] They came to a head among historians with the publication of Bryan Palmer's *Descent into Discourse* in 1990, which, in the midst of much careful explication, nonetheless ended by caricaturing the cultural turn into the self-indulgent pretensions of a left-wing intellectual cohort who'd lost their way. Spinning self-serving rationalizations to justify their own ivory-tower isolation, while seeking substitutes for a lost materialist faith, Palmer argued, these "linguistic turners" simply lacked the staying power for the new hard times. His book reasserted the standby sufficiencies of historical materialism and social history—the class-analytical version of the ascendant social history of the 1970s centered around the collective agency of the working class—against the new prioritizing of subjectivities, identity, and discourse. In disavowing the old master categories and the classic grand narratives, he charged, the new cultural historians were also vacating the need for a critical analysis of capitalism, abandoning the very ground of a history of society per se. Their alternative amounted to an abdication, a "hedonistic descent into a plurality of discourses that decenter the world in a chaotic denial of any acknowledgment of tangible structures of power and comprehensions of meaning."[5]

Palmer was right in one thing, for in the course of the 1980s, the Left's traditional class-political optimism clearly became exhausted.[6] My own argument in this book has sought to use the political transitions of the past four decades as an essential counterpoint for the changing interests of historians. Political purposes exert a constant pressure on how those interests can be thought. Those purposes sometimes nudge and harass, sometimes jolt and inspire, but always structure and inform the questions we ask—indeed, the very questions that occur to us in the first place. In that respect, the dispiriting political experiences associated with the crisis of a class-centered socialist tradition from the late 1970s, under the combined effects of capitalist restructuring, deindustrialization, class recomposition, and right-wing political assaults, have profoundly shaped how I've been able to think about the kinds of history I do. For me, the cultural turn was appealing because its implications translated across these different sites—not only my teaching and writing, but also my political knowledge and social understanding, including the everyday settings of personal life. If the work of Edward Thompson and Tim Mason, for example, had seemed empowering for an earlier time, that of Carolyn

Steedman and others helped me think about a new and emergent set of needs.

In those terms, "politics" and "history" remained locked together—sometimes in mutuality, sometimes in contention—no less in the 1980s and 1990s than they had been before. At the fin de siècle, the intellectual perspectives associated with the cultural turn acquired a pertinence for politics that matched the earlier passions of the social historian every bit of the way. Their necessity for the tasks of finding a politics better fitted for the prevailing social relations of the restructured capitalism of the impending new century was to my mind incontestable. Amid the palpable wreckage of statist socialisms of all kinds, furthermore, the appeal of such perspectives for anyone seeking a viable basis for left-wing renewal had to be informed by a knowledge of the damage done to older assumptions about class-political agency by all the social and political changes of the preceding three decades. As a primary and sufficient basis for understanding and acting on the world, those earlier ideas of the 1960s and 1970s no longer carried conviction, at least in their already available forms. Of course, that also became the space into which the plentiful variants of contemporary localist and identitarian politics tended to settle.

Backing away from the older socialist metanarratives of capitalist critique, many of these new radicalisms emphasized the primacy of fragmentation and difference, diversity and pluralism. This isn't the place for any extensive reflection either on the character of this contemporary political conjuncture within and among societies or on the new forms of Left politics struggling, inchoately and stutteringly, to be born. I simply want to mark the now empty space that both the political forms of the socialist tradition and the analytics of an ambitious social history used to command. For more than a decade now, the emergent forms of resistance against the consequences of globalization have been learning how to coalesce. At hand since the end of the 1980s have been new structural analyses of this emergent conjuncture—of post-Fordism, of postmodernity, and of the transnational restructuring of the global capitalist economy. Yet these different registers of analysis, the "local" and the "global," are rarely thought of together as effectively today as they were under the earlier class-analytical dispensation. One of the few recent efforts at doing so, Michael Hardt's and Toni Negri's Empire, specifically refuses anything close to a concrete social history of a redeployed kind.[7]

But to call our understanding back (in an act of materialist faith) to an older conception of the social—and thereby to make harmless the complex and difficult questions this book has been seeking to raise— would be perverse.[8] "Social history" simply isn't available anymore, whether in its most coherent and self-conscious materialist versions (Marxist, *Annaliste,* social-scientific) or in the more amorphous, but still aggrandizing, forms of the 1970s. In the form of the original project, "social history" has ceased to exist. Its coherence derived from the sovereignty of social determinations within a self-confident materialist paradigm of social totality, grounded in the primacy of class. But since the early eighties, each part of that framework has succumbed to relentless and compelling critique. In the process, its prestige as the natural home for the more radical, innovative, and experimental spirits dissolved, particularly for younger people entering the profession. The "new cultural history" took its place.

What Kind of History?

When I became a historian, I really believed the world was changeable into a better place. I never fully expected this could mean socialism, although, occasionally, events in the wider world (Salvador Allende's election, for example, and the Portuguese revolution and the liberation of the Portuguese colonies) made the pulse quicken. Sometimes, events closer to home did that—such as the occupation of the shipyards on Clydeside in 1971, the defeat of the Heath government in 1974, and the promise of the Italian Communist Party's Eurocommunist strategy. But my own political hopes were really far more modest: belief in a propitious conjuncture, confidence in democracy's recorded achievements, conviction that the boundaries could be pushed outward further and further. My own childhood and what I knew of my parents' and grandparents' generations hardwired my outlook to an ethic of improvement in that sense, a belief in attainable futures based on the expansion of collective provision and the strengthening of public goods—modest futures, but futures available for the visiting. In that sense, politics was about imagining a modestly expanding structure of possibility—finding the openings, building the coalitions, redrawing the horizons. And, of course, "Sixty-Eight" was a key part of this too, creating the knowledge that history does, after all, move—that it moves forward, in fact, by sudden, unexpected, dangerous, and inspiring jumps. My political education contained a synergy of prosaic and utopian hopes, converging in the image of society's betterment. Now, I don't expect Jerusalem ever to be built.

To call my earlier outlook the optimism and naïveté of a much younger person, consigning it to an archive of misplaced idealism, would be a self-serving act of condescension. Such a knowing and complacent gaze backward would blithely ignore the vastness of all the actually occurring changes in the world since the 1970s, especially since 1989–91, changes whose effects render nugatory the optimism of an earlier kind. Using my own story as a foil, I've tried, in this book, to explore some of the uneven reciprocities between "history" and "politics" that played a part in bringing us "here" from "there"—"uneven" because, whereas historians may try to think through and process the meanings of events in the political world and, hopefully, translate them into better bases for action, those reflections rarely have much direct political effect. But for clarifying our political questions, at least, history supplies the ground where we need to think.

I became a historian because I thought history could make a difference. This was never a naive belief that doing history by itself could become a transformative act. But how the past gets recuperated does have consequences for how the present can be perceived. In this book, I have discussed historians who practiced an active version of history's pedagogy in this sense—Edward Thompson and Eric Hobsbawm, Sheila Rowbotham and Tim Mason, Joan Scott and Carolyn Steedman, and such social science historians as Hans-Ulrich Wehler and Charles Tilly. Their work inspired the successive moments of social history and cultural history. In a stronger notation, one can argue that the knowledge of past struggles, collective or individual, can itself shape resistance of the present tense. Depending on how the story is told, the past provides potential sites of opposition. It allows us to say: it didn't have to happen like this. And in the future it could be different.

My first answer to the question "What kind of history?" is a history that's engaged. Second, for me, writing an engaged history always presupposed something more than just history alone. For a socially and politically engaged historian of the late 1960s, that usually meant turning to social science, in what I have called the first phase of history's interdisciplinarity. That, in its turn, meant Marxism. I've no doubts here: having access to Marxism—to the generous and eclectic florescence of thinking produced by the Marxist revival, in all its varied idioms and encouragements—made me into a far better historian. Beyond the default materialism and the bedrock belief in social determination, which proved unable to withstand subsequent critique, the Marxism of the late sixties and early seventies enabled more enduring commitments. It was all about the interconnectedness of things. It gave me the confidence to tackle big problems. Even more, it promised strategies for theorizing their bigness. It offered ways of joining small questions to large and important ones. It was fundamentally about interdisciplinarity. Marxism cajoled and incited one to the best interdisciplinary ambition, to the belief that all knowledges were useful, all of them could be put to work. Usefulness observed no limits.

As I've argued for the period under consideration in this book, history's renovative energy—its new influences, new approaches, and most inspiring works—always came from the outside. That energy sprang from broader intellectual departures (ferments of theory, philosophical interventions, changes of fashion, discursive shifts), which were effective across disciplinary boundaries and traveled promiscuously through the public sphere. It came partly from other disciplines—from the social sciences in the 1960s and 1970s; from literary theory, anthropology, and cultural studies in the years that followed. It also came from outside the profession. In Britain, the most creative historians often worked outside the universities, whether in adult education and, later, the polytechnics or beyond higher and further education altogether (except in the most tenuous of unofficial and part-time ways). Only after many years did the feminist pioneers of women's history find footholds in university history departments, if at all. Even if historians by formal training, new cultural historians could just as easily be found elsewhere—in the fields of cultural studies, sociology, and literature and in a variety of interstices and enclaves.

If we write the intellectual history of the discipline honestly—not just for the last four decades, but more generally—we'll find the new impulses coming from the outside. Though a discipline with an institutional infrastructure, professionalized credentials, and a consensus of methods and epistemologies, history became defined only fitfully and incrementally between the late nineteenth and late twentieth centuries. The boundaries separating it from other academic disciplines, from the lay interests of "amateurs," and from wider influences in the public sphere have been far more porous than the curmudgeonly defenders of history's integrity can ever allow themselves to see. In any case, such know-nothing rejectionism will never actually manage to keep the intrusions of "theory" at bay, whether from the "Marxism" or "sociology" of the 1960s or from the "postmodernism" and "postcolonialism" of the 1990s. As I have argued through this book, if we really want to keep history alive and active, we should be welcoming this cross-border traffic rather than trying to close it down. Instead of policing the borderlands "in defense of history," we should be bringing history's defenses down.[9]

Why, then, should one stay a historian? What makes me a historian rather than something else? At one level, the question is academic (in both senses of that word). In practice, disciplines and departments continue to exist and won't go away, especially for purposes of hiring and tenure—even in a university like my own, where interdisciplinary programs and cross-departmental appointments have become so rampant. Backing interdisciplinary studies institutionally soon poses questions about the disciplinary "core," but to a great extent, these can be matters of pragmatics. Moreover, we know best we're historians precisely when conversing with others—with anthropologists and literary critics, with sociologists and political scientists, and certainly with philosophers and economists. The place where we do our distinctive thinking is the past, and the historian's mark has everything to do with time and temporality, with the associated modes of cognition and narrativity, with Carolyn Steedman's "basic historicity." This includes what Steedman calls history's "impermanence," its openness and changeability. The epistemology of the archive can be added, including the practical experience of dirtying one's hands with all those documents. Then come the pleasures of detection and pursuit, collecting and mastery. At the end, there's the exponential thickening of contextual understanding, what Thompson called "the discipline of historical context."[10] In all of these ways, I'd rather be a historian than not. But ultimately, an ambivalence remains—between knowing I'm a historian and knowing it isn't enough, between the security and the risks, between having a home and venturing out.

Finally, where do the clashing purposes of social and cultural historians, "postmodernists" and "materialists," leave us? What kind of history do they allow? The most acrimonious fights of the early 1990s seem to have abated by now, but a more important division tended to outlast them, that between the older prioritizing of large-scale processes of societal development and change—Charles Tilly's "big structures, large processes, huge comparisons"—and the new preference for more modest and individualized sites of social and cultural investigation.[11] As we've seen, the latter require a very different kind of analytic, one culturally, rather than socially, derived. As I've argued, the resulting shift came as much from cumulative logics of collective practice in the profession as from conscious choice; it came from more complex trends of contemporary intellectual life in the university, as opposed to deliberate discrimination or the systematic favoring of some kinds of research over others; it came from political developments and broader discursive shifts in the wider society. Whatever the process, the 1980s witnessed a growing tendency among many social and cultural historians—for example, the main constituency of such journals as *Social History* and *History Workshop Journal* (as opposed to the *Journal of Interdisciplinary History* or *Social Science History*)—to disregard the more social-scientific kind of approach.

Historiographical developments of the past two decades have strengthened that drift away from social history in the ambitious 1960s and 1970s guise—as the "history of society," in the second part of Eric Hobsbawm's famous couplet.[12] We have witnessed the dissolution of social history's totalizing aspiration—of the insistence that all aspects of human life be situated in relation to social determinations, whether politics, thought and the exchange of ideas, sexuality and intimate relations, cultural meanings, the interior dynamics of institutions, economic processes, the international relations among states, or whatever. Yet, interestingly, the new forms of cultural history haven't lacked their own logics of totalization, which can also be equally aggrandizing. These are most apparent, perhaps, in the broad domain of postcolonial studies, where some of the angriest and most intemperate of the polemics among social and cultural historians continued to occur in the course of the 1990s.

From Cultural History to the History of Society?

The new totalizing wish takes various forms. First, in seeking to relativize or historicize the standpoint of "the West" in the epoch of colonization—by dethroning its self-arrogated superiorities, by rethinking the bases for global comparison, by dismantling Eurocentrism, by "provincializing Europe"—post-Saidian historians sometimes imply an overabstracted and homogenized conception of the West and its internal histories.[13] Thus, we may certainly agree with Dipesh Chakrabarty that in the prevailing academic discourse of history, "'Europe' remains the sovereign, theoretical subject of all histories, including the one we call 'Indian,' 'Chinese,' 'Kenyan,' and so on." We can also see the functioning of what Chakrabarty calls the "mythical" or "hyper-real Europe" within a set of dominant social and political imaginaries, as an idealized origin of thought and practice about the state, citizenship, and governmentality, whether for the colonies or the metropolis itself.[14] Yet at the same time, this insight hardly disposes of the immensely complicated histories inside European society that still need to be written. This particular abstraction ("Europe") functions not so differently for the argument about comparative modernities than the earlier abstraction of "society" did for social historians two decades ago. In each case, certain big questions are enabled at the potential cost of leaving others unsaid. Subjecting this "Europe" to necessary critique still leaves unaddressed many other meanings of Europe, including the interior relations of very particular European societies.[15]

Second, "culture" itself easily acquires overtotalizing explanatory importance. Under Thompson's influence, social historians themselves had long inclined to the classic anthropological sense of culture as the realm of symbolic and ritual meaning in a society's overall ethos and forms of cohesion—or its "whole way of life," in Raymond Williams's notation. That sense became further extended by cultural studies toward "the whole complex of signifying practices and symbolic processes in a particular society," or what Williams called the "ordinariness" of culture, as opposed to the high-cultural domain of aesthetics and the arts.[16] A kind of minimalist consensus has crystallized around the "production and construction of meaning" as the best way of thinking about culture's relationship to social life. Yet the practice of the new cultural history can leave one uneasily wondering what culture is not. As Carolyn Steedman observes, many historians have come to rely "on the notion of 'culture' as the bottom line, the real historical reality."[17] While embraced as an answer to the overobjectified materialism of the social science historian, "culture" can sustain its own logic of holism. As Steedman says (citing Dominick LaCapra), this implies a trance-like reliance on the concept of culture . . . , where everything connects to everything else and "culture" is the primordial reality in which all historical actors have their being, do their thing, share discourses, worldviews, "languages," where everyone (I repeat the joke because I enjoy it so much) "is a *mentalité* case"; and where it is not possible to write the exception: to write about the thing, event, relationship, entity, that does not connect with anything else.[18]

Third, the concept of "empire" is also acquiring analytical—or perhaps epistemological—equivalence with the older category of "society." The concept's current popularity implies a number of historiographical referents. One might be the post-Orientalist and postcolonial impulse exemplified by the Subaltern Studies project (discussed in chapter 4); another could be the new recognitions accorded "race" in the thinking of historians of Western Europe and North America; a third would be the impact of contemporary globalization, which encroached steadily on historians' awareness during the 1990s—until the appointment of the Bush administration in 2001 marked the arrival of a more directive and unilateralist form, driven by the United States. Thus, from at least the early 1990s, a set of intensively grounded arguments about imperialism's importance—meaning both the acquiring of colonies and the informal dynamics of the West's coercive and exploitative impact on the rest of the world—have been slowly transforming the questions British historians bring to the study of national history; and comparable challenges are more recently developing in French, German, and other national historiographies.[19] This has particularly become true for the United States. Since the mid-1990s, programs in American studies and in American Culture have become entirely suffused with recognitions of empire's importance.[20]

This reviewing of national histories through the lens of empire has predictably drawn much hostility from a variety of political standpoints, whether from older-style imperial historians or from those working on society, culture, and politics at home.[21] But we don't need to share that negative response in order to worry that some versions of the argument about empire run the risk of subsuming too much complexity inside its overabstracted framework. It becomes important precisely to delimit the explanatory reach of "empire"; otherwise, we can easily replicate the syndrome created earlier by the overinvested materialist category of "the social," from which the cultural turn was originally an escape. Properly acknowledging imperialism's general imbrication with the social relations, popular culture, and polite thinking of the metropolis has certainly become one of the key challenges for current historiography, particularly with respect to the histories of race. But we need not gather everything beneath this same unitary framework before we can accept that empire's conse quences became constitutive in key ways for the main languages of national affiliation in the Western metropolis.[22]

These fresh totalizing logics deserve some pondering. The problem with the ambitious social histories of the 1960s and 1970s was their tendency to occlude certain kinds of difficulty. While being immensely complex and sophisticated for some purposes, they tended to be too simplified for others. Quite aside from the deeper critiques of the materialist analytic and its model of social determination, those available forms of class analysis were proving manifestly ill-equipped for dealing with class restructuring at the end of the twentieth century, whether in the deindustrialized post-Fordist economies of the metropolis or in the global arenas of transnationalized capitalism, where the working class of production was more and more to be found. Likewise, the social historian's desire to integrate the history of politics and the state was very unevenly realized. As I've argued, social history found it especially hard to deal with questions of ideology, consciousness, and subjectivity.

"Cultural history" (in the varied respects explored in chapter 4) provided ways out of this several-sided impasse. In this fundamental sense and in the many particular respects I've tried to explore, the cultural turn was hugely enabling. The initial debates and challenges were unsettling; thinking oneself out of familiar and valued intellectual standpoints was sometimes agonizingly hard; translating the new critiques into workable projects wasn't always easy. But for the reasons I've tried to describe, the move out of "social history" was both necessary and fruitful. With the loosening, during the 1980s, of the hold of "society" and "the social" on the analytical imagination—and of the determinative power of the social structure and its causal claims—the imaginative and epistemological space for other kinds of analysis could grow. The rich multiplication of new cultural histories ensued.

But there were also costs. The large-scale debates reaching their climax three decades ago—over state making and comparative political development, the social bases of absolutism, the transition from feudalism to capitalism, the origins of capitalism and the industrial revolution, the comparative study of revolutions, the logics of collective action, and so on—no longer exercise historians in the same way. The earlier impetus carried over into the 1970s—for instance, with the Brenner debate or the grand designs of Perry Anderson and Immanuel Wallerstein.[23] Combinations of modernization theory and neo-Braudelian vision inspired other attempts at capturing the structural transition to the modern world, from such authors as Charles Tilly and Keith Thomas.[24] Moreover, a large body of historical sociology continues to be organized around those problematics and indeed seems to have claimed this ground as its distinctive terrain. Such work elaborates its theoretical ambitions around grand narratives of an unapologetically classical kind, in some cases even seeking to rebuild social theory by writing the history of the world.[25]

Some historians remain fully engaged on that level of generality, addressing the biggest questions of cross-societal comparison on the largest possible scale. Ken Pomerana's study of the divergent developmental paths of the Chinese and European economies since the later eighteenth century is one extraordinarily rich example; Victor Lieberman's comparative analyses of commerce and state formation in Southeast Asia are another; Chris Bayley's synthetic account of the global origins of the modern world could be a third.[26] But it's no accident that each of these works has an extra-European vantage point. With a few exceptions, such as Eric Hobsbawm, European historians rarely participate in those discussions anymore. In its European heartlands, the large-scale or comparative study of whole societies moving through time ("societal history," in that sense)—which provided the founding inspiration for so much of the social history of the 1960s—has lost its hold on the imagination.

It's not clear why "taking the cultural turn" should require ignoring this different order of questions. Doing so has serious effects. Not only are the social sciences continuing to generate large bodies of historical work predicated around exactly these concerns—state formation, nation building, revolutions, the development of whole societies, the relationship between markets and democracy, all the sundry aspects of "modernization" and "development"—but in the post-Communist era of globalization, this corpus of work remains as intricately embedded in policymaking as ever.[27] Moreover, unless critical historians can find ways of joining this fray—by offering persuasive frameworks for understanding the contemporary dynamics of international conflict and societal change—the latest pack of recklessly and hubristically aggrandizing master narratives will continue enlisting popular imaginations, shaping the political common sense, and generally sweeping the globe.

In their very simplicities, those recharged master narratives are being both straightforwardly instrumentalized for political purposes and pressed into more elaborately legitimating service. But they also consist in less consciously secured patterns of belief and consent. With the advantages of our new "postculturalist" sophistication, we're immeasurably better equipped for subjecting this discursive architecture to effective critique. But the continuing purchase of neoliberalism's distressing ascendancy in the public culture rests on potent simplifications and grand reductions that aggressively conflate "politics" and "society," "values" and "interests," "democracy" and "markets"— closing the gap between the bedrock legitimacy of a capitalist market order and any remaining space for pluralist disagreement. Unless the ruling ideas can also be challenged and contested at this level of their efficacy, left-wing historians will be stranded without a public voice, whether watching powerlessly from the sidelines or clinging, knowingly but fearfully, to the wings of Benjamin's Angel. There's no reason why contesting these new master narratives has to entail leaving the ground of the cultural turn or reverting to a now unworkable idea of "the social." Why isn't it possible to think and talk in different ways for the purposes of conducting different intellectual, pedagogical, and political conversations?

Occasionally, for example, even the most fervent advocates of the linguistic turn, while arguing around the dinner table about the widening extremes of social inequality, might find themselves reaching for analyses of income disparities, the restructuring of labor markets, and even the distinctive forms of the labor process produced by the new information and service industries. They may yet find themselves generalizing about the effects in societywide terms. Developing a similar case in the classroom, they might even see the advantages, "strategic" or otherwise, of making suspiciously structural arguments about "society's" overall trajectory across longer periods of time—for instance, since the 1950s or since the earlier twentieth century and

even the later nineteenth. Our grasp of these arguments is all the better—more subtle, more sophisticated, more effective—because of
everything we've learned through and since the cultural turn. Naturally, in such hypothetical debates, we'd want to talk about the discursive strategies involved and deconstruct the meanings they contain,
particularly for the gendered and racialized dimensions. In that sense,
we're hugely better equipped. But we may still want to talk about
class, about capitalism, about the structural distribution of inequalities, about the varying political capacities available to different social
categories of people depending on their access to resources, and so
forth.

In other words, a further answer to my question "What kind of history?" is that it all depends on the kinds of debates, the kinds of purposes, that happen to be in play. In my own experience of the exigencies of the time, the kinds of politics associated with the linguistic
turn—those interpellating it, those surrounding it, and those it helped
enable and sustain—were both unavoidable and a decisive good. They
were always intimately entwined with the accompanying new forms
of cultural history. History's priorities became refocused by decentering the discipline's established subject matters; by claiming the
neglected contexts of the personal, the local, and the everyday; and by
allowing historians to better face questions of political subjectivity.
But why should the earlier concerns of social historians be forgotten,
as opposed to fruitfully reengaged? Why should embracing the possibilities of microhistory require leaving macrohistory entirely behind?
Outside the immediate scholarly domain, those other forms and levels
of analysis are completely unavoidable: they're encountered in arguments over the dinner table, in classroom obligations, in public dispu-
tations (from Op-Ed page to television studio and beyond), in the
framing of public policy, and in the writing of popular histories. Others will certainly stay active on these fronts, whether new cultural historians care to or not.

Of course, some historians are trying to combine social and cultural
history with forms of generalizing abstraction about "society" in the
overarching contextual sense. Studies that show it can be done include
Carolyn Steedman's current work on servants and service during the
era of Thompson's *Making,* Catherine Hall's studies of the consequences of the dialectics of nation and empire for the nineteenth-century histories of citizenship, and Leora Auslander's melding of the his-

tories of state formation and everyday life through a study of French furniture and furnishing.[28] In practice, moreover, the "new cultural history" has generated far more pragmatics and a considerably richer eclecticism than its wilder enemies or the more generalized mutterings of the profession had ever been willing to allow. Far more than any extremist advocacy feared by such opponents—let alone the irresponsible junking of the historian's evidentiary rules and practices or the moral surrender of the historian's calling and the collapse of the discipline's "core" (as the worst anticulturalist jeremiads wanted to claim)—many were looking for creative ways of combining the new incitements of cultural history and the hard-won, but now established, gains of social history. Particularly in the work of the younger generations—those now publishing their books and working on their dissertations—the differences between social history and cultural history imply less an opposition than an opportunity.

Conclusion

My first point in concluding this book concerns the urgent need for a basic pluralism. I've deliberately avoided any detailed explicating of the various debates surrounding the big shift from social to cultural history that forms the subject of this book. Those battles lasted roughly a decade following the mid-1980s, often taking bitterly over-polemicized forms. Through them, "postmodernism" became a catchall name for a miscellany of culturalist influences, from Foucault, poststructuralism, and literary deconstruction to cultural studies, postcolonialism, and forms of feminist theory. Many social historians accused postmodernists of apostasy—of abandoning social history's calling and its implicit politics. Shouting back, self-described postmodernists accused their critics of clinging to obsolete concepts and approaches, especially materialist conceptions of class.[29] For a while, the discipline threatened to separate into mutually hostile camps, with convinced materialists and structuralists facing culturalists and "linguistic turners" across a hardening binary divide. Similar theoretical and epistemological polarities were repeated across other disciplines, variously linked to wider political debates.

By the later 1990s, passions had cooled. Desires for theoretical purity or some finality of resolution—by asserting the rival virtues of poststructuralist influences versus the established patterns of structuralist history, or modernization theory against postmodernist critique of grand narratives, or Weber against Foucault—were not getting us very far. Social history's amorphously aggrandizing desire for primacy in the discipline, so marked in the 1970s, was actually being superseded by a more eclectic repertoire of approaches and themes, for which the new cultural history had become the broadly accepted description. More to the point, the boundaries between different kinds of history became extraordinarily more blurred. Many social historians continued as before, reproducing the distinctive autonomies of their work, methodologically and topically. But many others now moved increasingly freely across the old distinctions between the social, the cultural, the political, the intellectual, and so forth, allowing new hybridities to form.

To a very great extent (in my view), the earlier, overheated polemics reflected the internecine agonies of a particular cluster of generations, consisting of those of us who were educated and trained in the 1960s and early 1970s and who were formed politically under the sign of 1968. In contrast, apart from a few students of the 1980s who were directly associated with some of the principals, younger people seemed markedly less excited about joining these battles. Students trained in the 1990s were interested less in the programmatic advocacy of one authorizing form of theory against another than in finding ways of combining social and cultural history, concretely and imaginatively. As I've mentioned, there were certainly more senior figures who were thinking their way through to a similar place—Carolyn Steedman and Catherine Hall, for example. But examples of recently published first books demonstrating such hybridity have become legion. These new studies specifically refuse the polarized division between the "social" and the "cultural," vesting recognizably social and political topics with a cultural analytic, responding to the incitements of cultural theory, and grounding these in as dense and imaginative a range of sources and interpretive contexts as possible.[30] On this very practical evidence, the division between "social" and "cultural" was always a false categorical separation. As I argued at the end of chapter 4, there's no need to choose.

My second point in this conclusion is that some confidence needs to be regained in the possibility of grasping society as a whole, of theorizing its bases of cohesion and instability, and of analyzing its forms of motion. The uncertainties surrounding the available terms of social and political theory by the end of the 1970s—above all, for theorizing the relations joining state, politics, and ideology to economy and social formation—may have driven such thinking among historians underground. But they haven't prevented sociologists and political scientists from continuing to do such work, often with strong historical claims. Moreover, neither skepticism about the persuasiveness of grand narratives nor critiques of Enlightenment thinking require altogether abandoning the project of societywide analysis or societal history. For my own part, I've continued thinking in terms of capitalism, class, the nation, social formation, and so forth. But I am far more cautious and uncertain about exactly what these grand-theoretical concepts can allow me to discuss and explain. I have a far clearer understanding of the degree to which all these terms—*nation, class, society,* and *social*—come heavily laden with contexts and histories of meaning, which historians need to uncover, specify, and locate. More than anything else, perhaps, the linguistic turn has allowed exactly these categories of modern social understanding to become historicized, so that such terms as *class* and *society* have become historically locatable and contingent.

My third point is that things change. In my lifetime, I've seen two huge reorientations of historical studies, which I've tried to describe here. Both were driven by interdisciplinarity. The popularity of social history was marked originally by the intellectual hegemony of the social or behavioral sciences, usually framed by some version of modernization theory—although it was increasingly inflected by an independently minded Marxist or Marxisant radicalism by the 1970s. Then, in the 1980s, the "new cultural history" and cultural studies became the natural site of innovation. I see absolutely no reason why the "cultural turn" should be the end of the story or the final chapter in some whiggish romance of ever-improving historiographical sophistication. Something else, I'm sure, is lying in wait. Furthermore, just as there are ways in which the earlier commitment to the "history of society" could be recuperated, certain features of the new cultural history "looped back," by the mid-1990s, to social history's founding influences. This was true, to a great extent, of Edward Thompson (particularly in his more "culturalist" eighteenth-century essays), but it applied most of all to the oeuvre of Raymond Williams. Whether via the influence of Said, the Subaltern Studies historians, and other postcolonial thinkers or through Steedman's running critiques and reflections, Williams's fundamental themes retain their active importance.[31]

My fourth point is that politics matters, in a doubled sense. On the one hand, the impetus for both shocks of innovation in my lifetime, the social history wave and the new cultural history, came from broader political developments extending way beyond the academy per se. Again, I see no reason why such political impetus should not recur, especially given the extraordinarily momentous and dangerous political time we've recently entered. On the other hand, each of the superb historians I've discussed at the end of chapters 2, 3, and 4— Edward Thompson, Tim Mason, and Carolyn Steedman—spent a large part of their careers outside the university, involved in one kind of public activity or another. That synergy of political and intellectual commitment, generated in the borderlands, invariably incites the best historical work.

If optimism, disappointment, and reflectiveness were the main registers of the radical historian's sensibility between the 1960s and the 1990s, perhaps defiance is the appropriate response for our new contemporary moment. For more than a decade now, we've been encouraged to see ourselves at "the end of history," in a world only describable through neoliberalism's redeployed languages of "modernity," through the relentlessly totalizing pressure of market principles, and through a new set of brutally demonizing rhetorics about good and evil in the world. But the effectiveness of grand narratives can't be contested by skepticism and incredulity alone, least of all when new or refurbished grand narratives are so powerfully reordering the globe. Grand narratives can't be contested by pretending they don't exist. That's why we need new "histories of society." In their respective times, both social history and the new cultural history were insurgent forms of knowledge, and the relevance of historical studies for the future will certainly require renewing an insurgent spirit again.

"All history is contemporary history: not in the ordinary sense of the word, where contemporary history means the history of the comparative recent past, but in the stricter sense: the consciousness of one's own activity as one actually performs it. History is thus the self-knowledge of the living mind. For even when the events which the historian studies are events that happened to the distant past, the condition of their being historically known is that they should vibrate in the historian's mind."

—R. G. Collingwood, The Idea of History

NOTES

Preface and Acknowledgments

1. These twin quotations come respectively from George Orwell, *Nineteen Eighty-Four* (London: Secker and Warburg, 1949), and George Santayana, *The Life of Reason* (New York: Charles Scribner, 1905). I've taken my versions from Anthony Jay, ed., *The Oxford Dictionary of Political Quotations,* 2nd ed. (Oxford: Oxford University Press, 2001), 276, 314.

2. The first quoted phrase is taken from the jacket description of Alun Munslow and Robert A. Rosenstone, eds., *Experiments in Rethinking History* (New York: Routledge, 2004); the second from the title of Richard J. Evans, *In Defence of History* (London: Granta, 1997).

3. Sylvia Thrupp (1903–97) was born in England but migrated to British Columbia with her family at the age of five. She received her Ph.D. from the University of London in 1931, returning to Canada in 1935 where she taught first at the University of British Columbia (1935–44) and then at the University of Toronto (1945). From 1945 to 1961 she taught at the University of Chicago. Together with many articles on guilds and historical demography, she published two major books, *The Worshipful Company of Bakers of London* (London: Galleon Press, 1933), and *The Merchant Class of Medieval London, 1300–1500* (Ann Arbor: University of Michigan Press, 1989; orig. pub. 1948). A collection of her essays was published as Raymond Grew and Nicholas H. Steneck, eds., *Society and History: Essays by Sylvia L. Thrupp* (Ann Arbor: University of Michigan Press, 1977).

4. Stuart Hall, "Notes on Deconstructing 'the Popular,'" in Raphael Samuel, ed., *People's History and Socialist Theory* (London: Routledge and Kegan Paul, 1981), 239.

Chapter 1

1. To take one small, but telling, example, at the end of my Oxford bachelor's degree program, in summer 1970, my history finals consisted of

eight three-hour sit-down exams covering the entirety of my studies during the previous three years, including a chosen period of European history. By distributing questions on either side of World War I, the examiners for "Europe, 1856–1939" contrived to end the first part of the exam in 1914 and open the second part in 1918, thereby conveniently abolishing the Russian Revolution. Yet I can't have been the only undergraduate during 1967–70 to have devoted a big part of my studies to understanding the crisis of czarism and the Bolshevik seizure of power. In general, the Oxford history curriculum of those years remained a chipped and crumbling monument to a dusty and cloistered lack of imagination, against which the efforts of the undergraduate History Reform Group, dating from 1961, made absolutely no impact. My proudest undergraduate accomplishment was to have been denounced to the faculty board by Regius Professor Hugh Trevor-Roper (aka Lord Dacre) in 1970 for editing the History Reform Group's duplicated journal, *The Oxford Historian*. For the forming of the group, see Tim Mason, "What of History?" *The New University* 8 (December 1961), 13–14. The occasion of Mason's article was a review of E. H. Carr's *What Is History?*—a key reference point for my generation of historians. See Richard J. Evans's useful introduction to the new edition, in Edward Hallett Carr, *What Is History?* (Houndmills: Palgrave, 2001), ix–xlvi.

2. Winston Churchill, *The Second World War*, 6 vols. (London: Cassell, 1948–54); Arthur Bryant, *The Years of Endurance, 1793–1892* (New York: Harper, 1942) and *The Years of Victory, 1802–1812* (New York: Harper, 1945). For the Churchill documentary, see *Winston Churchill: The Valiant Years* (Jack Le Vien, BBC, 1961).

3. See A. J. P. Taylor, *Politics in Wartime and Other Essays* (London: Hamish Hamilton, 1964) and *From Napoleon to Lenin: Historical Essays* (New York: Harper and Row, 1966). Books by Taylor that formed my first substantial introduction to German history include *The Course of German History: A Survey of the Development of Germany since 1815* (London: Methuen, 1961; orig. pub. 1946), *The Struggle for Mastery in Europe, 1848–1918* (Oxford: Clarendon Press, 1954), *Bismarck, the Man and the Statesman* (London: Hamish Hamilton, 1955), and *The Origins of the Second World War* (London: Hamish Hamilton, 1961).

4. The debate over Geoffrey R. Elton's *The Tudor Revolution in Government: Administrative Changes in the Reign of Henry VIII* (Cambridge: Cambridge University Press, 1953) and his edited volume *The Tudor Constitution: Documents and Commentary* (Cambridge: Cambridge University Press, 1960) was launched by G. L. Harriss and Penry Williams, in "A Revolution in Tudor History?" *Past and Present* 25 (July 1963), 3–58, followed by J. P. Cooper (26 [November 1963], 110–12), G. R. Elton (29 [December

1964], 26–49), Harriss and Williams (31 [July 1965], 87–96), and Elton (32 [December 1965], 103–9). The critique of A. J. P. Taylor's *Origins* appeared in Timothy W. Mason, "Some Origins of the Second World War," *Past and Present,* 29 (December 1964), 67–87, with response by Taylor in "War Origins Again" (30 [April 1965], 110–13). The articles on the general crisis of the seventeenth century were collected in Trevor H. Aston, ed., *Crisis in Europe, 1560–1660: Essays from Past and Present* (London: Routledge, 1965).

5. See Fernand Braudel, *La Méditerranée et le monde méditerranéen à l'époque de Philippe II,* 2nd ed., 2 vols. (Paris: Colin, 1966), translated as *The Mediterranean and the Mediterranean World in the Age of Philip II,* 2 vols. (London: Collins, 1972–73).

6. Valerie Walkerdine, "Dreams from an Ordinary Childhood," in Liz Heron, ed., *Truth, Dare or Promise: Girls Growing Up in the Fifties* (London: Virago, 1985), 77. Walkerdine captures the disjunction perfectly (64): "I didn't have an affair at fourteen, join the Communist Party at sixteen, go off to paint in Paris, or live in an ashram in India. Childhood fantasies of getting out, of being rich and famous abounded, but in the circles *I* moved in there had been only two ways to turn the fantasy into the dream-lived-as-real of bourgeois life, and they were to marry out or work my way out. It is the latter which, for that first moment of the fifties, lay open to me. For that moment of the postwar educational expansion fueled my puny and innocent little dreams as I grew up, the epitome of the hard-working, conservative and respectable working-class girl." I'm grateful to Frank Mort for reminding me of this essay. For the classic statement of this kind, see also Raymond Williams, "Culture Is Ordinary," *Resources of Hope: Culture, Democracy, Socialism* (London: Verso, 1989), 3–18.

7. Edward P. Thompson, *The Making of the English Working Class* (London: Gollancz, 1963; paperback ed., Harmondsworth: Penguin, 1968).

8. Paul Slack is now professor of early modern social history at Oxford and the principal of Linacre College. He came to play a key role in the journal *Past and Present* (prominently discussed in chapter 2), joining its editorial board in 1978 and acting as its editor from 1986 to 1994; in 2000, he became chairman of its board. See Paul Slack, *The Impact of Plague in Tudor and Stuart England* (London: Routledge and Kegan Paul, 1985); *Poverty and Policy in Tudor and Stuart England* (London: Longman, 1988); *From Reformation to Improvement: Public Welfare in Early Modern England* (Oxford: Clarendon Press, 1999). See also Paul Slack, ed., *Rebellion, Popular Protest, and the Social Order in Early Modern England* (Cambridge: Cambridge University Press, 1984); Terence Ranger and Paul Slack, eds., *Epidemics and Ideas: Essays on the Historical Perception of Pestilence* (Cambridge: Cambridge University Press,

1992); Peter Burke, Brian Harrison, and Paul Slack, eds., *Civil Histories: Essays Presented to Sir Keith Thomas* (Oxford: Oxford University Press, 2000).

9. Of course, this observation does not apply only to historians on the left. Since the 1970s, conservatives of many kinds, including not a few liberals, have spent inordinate time and energy opposing, dismissing, and regretting the arrival of women's history (and often the arrival of women themselves) in the discipline. My favorite example is of a former colleague at the University of Michigan, a relatively young and not terribly conservative full professor, who marked his departure from the department in the early 1990s with a letter to the dean in which the professor attacked his late home for turning into a department of gender history and cultural studies.

10. In making this argument, I'm very conscious of my own social and cultural hybridity, which travels back and forth between a set of lasting Anglo-British or European affiliations and those influences and exigencies far more specific to the United States.

11. See Joan Wallach Scott, "Gender: A Useful Category of Historical Analysis," *American Historical Review* 91 (1986), 1053–75, reprinted in *Gender and the Politics of History* (New York: Columbia University Press, 1988), 28–50.

12. Many autobiographical reflections by historians might be cited in illustration of my argument here. Recent memoirs by Eric Hobsbawm (*Interesting Times: A Twentieth-Century Life* [New York: Pantheon, 2002]) and Sheila Rowbotham (*Promise of a Dream: Remembering the Sixties* [London: Allen Lane, 2000]) are especially relevant to the contexts described in this book. The interview is likewise an extremely revealing contemporary form: see, for example, Henry Abelove et al., eds., *Visions of History: Interviews with E. P. Thompson, Eric Hobsbawm, Sheila Rowbotham, Linda Gordon, Natalie Zemon Davis, William Appleman Williams, Staughton Lynd, David Montgomery, Herbert Gutman, Vincent Harding, John Womack, C. L. R. James, Moshe Lewin* (New York: Pantheon, 1984). See also the regular "Historical Passions" feature in *History Workshop Journal,* especially Cora Kaplan, "Witchcraft: A Child's Story," 41 (spring 1996), 254–60; Denise Riley, "Reflections in the Archive?" 44 (autumn 1997), 238–42; Joan Thirsk, "Nature versus Nurture," 47 (spring 1999), 273–77. See, above all, Carlo Ginzburg's eloquent and moving reflections in "Witches and Shamans," *New Left Review* 200 (July–August 1993), 75–85.

13. Eric J. Hobsbawm, "From Social History to the History of Society," *Daedalus* 100 (1971), 20–45.

Chapter 2

1. Eric Hobsbawm, *Primitive Rebels: Studies in Archaic Forms of Social Movement in the Nineteenth and Twentieth Centuries* (Manchester: Manchester

University Press, 1959) and *Labouring Men: Studies in the History of Labour* (London: Weidenfeld and Nicolson, 1964); George Rudé, *The Crowd in the French Revolution* (Oxford: Oxford University Press, 1959) and *The Crowd in History: A Study of Popular Disturbances in France and England, 1730–1848* (New York: Wiley, 1964); Edward P. Thompson, *The Making of the English Working Class* (London: Gollancz, 1963; paperback ed., Harmondsworth: Penguin, 1968).

2. Eric Hobsbawm and George Rudé, *Captain Swing: A Social History of the Great English Agricultural Uprising of 1830* (London: Lawrence and Wishart, 1968).

3. See Geoff Eley, "John Edward Christopher Hill (1912–2003)," *History Workshop Journal* 56 (autumn 2003), 287–94.

4. Strictly speaking, this was Britain's "second New Left," identified generationally with the group around Perry Anderson, who assumed control of *New Left Review* in the early 1960s. The "first New Left" was an earlier realignment of the mid-1950s, through which a new generation of student leftists (including Stuart Hall, Charles Taylor, Gabriel Pearson, Raphael Samuel, and others) converged with an older cohort of Marxists leaving the Communist Party in 1956–57, among whom were Thompson, Hill, and some other historians. See Michael Kenny, *The First British New Left: British Intellectuals after Stalin* (London: Lawrence and Wishart, 1995).

5. Alexander Cockburn and Robin Blackburn, eds., *Student Power: Problems, Diagnosis, Action* (Harmondsworth: Penguin, 1969); Trevor Pateman, ed., *Counter Course: A Handbook in Course Criticism* (Harmondsworth: Penguin, 1972); Robin Blackburn, ed., *Ideology in Social Science: Readings in Critical Social Theory* (London: Fontana, 1972).

6. Gareth Stedman Jones, "The Pathology of English History," *New Left Review* 46 (November–December 1967), 29–43, reprinted as "History: The Poverty of Empiricism," in Blackburn, *Ideology in Social Science,* 96–115; Perry Anderson, "Components of the National Culture," in Cockburn and Blackburn, *Student Power,* 214–84, originally published in *New Left Review* 50 (July–August 1968), 3–57.

7. The first quotation is from Karl Marx, *Early Writings,* ed. Lucio Colletti (Harmondsworth: Penguin, 1975), 425; the second is from Friedrich Engels to Joseph Bloch, 21–22 September 1890, in Karl Marx and Friedrich Engels, *Selected Correspondence* (Moscow: Progress Publishers, 1965), 417.

8. I remember very well the first time I came out openly as a Marxist during my undergraduate years. In my final year, for a specialized seminar course entitled "Industrialism and the Growth of Governmental Power in the United States, 1865–1917," I presented an extended essay in which I

applied an explicitly Marxist analysis to Populism. For someone still fresh to Marxist theory, this seemed a very big deal.

9. It should also be acknowledged that the excitement generated by Marxist culture and historiography at this time was also founded on the membership of a relatively closed community. There was relatively little dialogue with the established traditions of history writing, except via stern negative critique.

10. This diffusion of European theory into the English language had a complicated intellectual history, whose details can't be gone into here. Some influences migrated westward from dissident circles in Eastern Europe, including those of the *Praxis* group of philosophers in Yugoslavia, Georg Lukács in Hungary, Leszek Kolakowski and others in Poland, Karel Koscik in Czechoslovakia, and new Marxist sociologists in Hungary and Poland. Others spread outward from Italy and France, where large Communist parties had secured relatively protected spaces for Marxist thinking inside the universities and the wider public sphere. In those countries without a large Communist Party, Marxism also acquired a few university footholds, as in West Germany with the influence of the Frankfurt School or Ernst Bloch in Tübingen. In much of continental Europe, in contrast to Britain, Communism's centrality for the antifascist resistance struggles of the 1940s had made a long-lasting space for Marxist ideas inside the national intellectual culture, despite the narrowing brought by the Cold War. This could be seen in France through the influence of such writers as Jean-Paul Sartre and such journals as *Les Temps modernes* and *Arguments* or in the wider prestige of structuralism. Trotskyism could also be a source of vitality, as could smaller intellectual networks, such as the French group *Socialisme ou Barbarie,* centered around Cornelius Castoriadis and Claude Lefort.

11. Laura Mulvey, quoted in Jonathan Green, *Days in the Life: Voices from the English Underground, 1961–1971* (London: Heineman Minerva, 1988), 11.

12. For a brief conspectus, see Robert Hewison, *Too Much: Art and Society in the Sixties, 1960–75* (Oxford: Oxford University Press, 1987), 25–34. See also John R. Cook, *Dennis Potter: A Life on Screen* (Manchester: Manchester University Press, 1995), 23–61; Peter Stead, *Dennis Potter* (Bridgend: Seren Books, 1993), 44–73; Stuart Laing, "Banging in Some Reality: The Original 'Z Cars,'" in John Corner, ed., *Popular Television in Britain: Studies in Cultural History* (London: BFI Publishing, 1991), 125–44.

13. See Perry Anderson, *Considerations on Western Marxism* (London: Verso, 1976).

14. The idea of an "epistemological break" separating Marx's mature thinking contained in *Capital* from the youthful philosophical critiques of the

early 1840s was proposed by the French Marxist philosopher Louis Althusser in his two works of 1965, *Pour Marx* and *Lire le Capital,* whose translation profoundly reshaped British Marxist discussion during the next decade. See Louis Althusser, *For Marx* (London: Allen Lane, 1969); Louis Althusser and Etienne Balibar, *Reading Capital* (London: New Left Books, 1970). Gregory Elliott provides detailed explication in *Althusser: The Detour of Theory* (London: Verso, 1987), 115–85. The pre-Althusserian temper of the times can be gauged from Erich Fromm, ed., *Socialist Humanism: An International Symposium* (Garden City, N.Y.: Doubleday, 1965), which divides its thirty-five contributions into five subsections: "Humanism," "Man," "Freedom," "Alienation," and "Practice." István Mészáros's *Marx's Theory of Alienation* (London: Merlin Press, 1970) remains the classic work of this type.

15. For the British New Left's efforts at finding a "third space" from which the existing traditions of orthodox Communism and reformist social democracy could be critiqued, see Geoff Eley, *Forging Democracy: The History of the Left in Europe, 1850–2000* (New York: Oxford University Press, 2002), 335–36, 353–56; Stuart Hall, "The 'First' New Left: Life and Times," in Robin Archer et al., eds., *Out of Apathy: Voices of the New Left Thirty Years On* (London: Verso, 1989), 11–38; Michael Kenny, *The First New Left: British Intellectuals after Stalin* (London: Lawrence and Wishart, 1995); Lin Chun, *The British New Left* (Edinburgh: Edinburgh University Press, 1993), 1–64.

16. Stuart Hall, quoted in Ronald Fraser et al., *1968: A Student Generation in Revolt* (New York: Pantheon, 1988), 30.

17. See Raymond Williams, *Culture and Society, 1780–1950* (London: Hogarth Press, 1958) and *The Long Revolution* (Harmondsworth: Penguin, 1961). The best introductions to Williams are Raymond Williams's *Politics and Letters: Interviews with New Left Review* (London: New Left Books, 1979) and John Higgins's *Raymond Williams: Literature, Marxism, and Cultural Materialism* (London: Routledge, 1999). Williams developed his idea of culture as "a whole way of life" initially in *Culture and Society,* 16. For "structures of feeling," see Higgins, *Raymond Williams,* 37–42, which traces it back to the book Williams published with Michael Orrom in 1954, *Preface to Film* (London: Film Drama Limited). The phrase "the best which has been thought and said" was coined in 1869 by Matthew Arnold in *Culture and Anarchy* (Cambridge: Cambridge University Press, 1963), 6. See Williams, *Culture and Society,* 120–36, and Lesley Johnson, *The Cultural Critics: From Matthew Arnold to Raymond Williams* (London: Routledge and Kegan Paul, 1979), 2–4, 27–34.

18. I was certainly inspired by some individual historians (including several of my immediate teachers), but the strongest impetus—in terms of theory, general interpretation, and examples of best intellectual practice—

owed very little to the official culture of the discipline or the profession, where those interests were, on the contrary, subject to ridicule or disapproval. In large part, my sources of inspiration came entirely from the outside.

19. See especially John McIlroy and Sallie Westwood, eds., *Border Country: Raymond Williams in Adult Education* (Leicester: National Institute of Adult Continuing Education, 1993); Stephen Woodhams, *History in the Making: Raymond Williams, Edward Thompson, and Radical Intellectuals, 1936–1956* (London: Merlin Press, 2001); Williams's first two novels, *Border Country* (London: Chatto and Windus, 1960) and *Second Generation* (London: Chatto and Windus, 1964). This trajectory from early marginality and exclusion to subsequent prestige was replicated during the 1970s and 1980s by the first generation of British feminists, who invented and then helped institutionalize women's history. Before the 1990s (if at all), most of the pioneers—for example, Sheila Rowbotham, Sally Alexander, Anna Davin, and Catherine Hall—did not receive appointments and other forms of recognition within history as a discipline. See Carolyn Steedman, "The Price of Experience: Women and the Making of the English Working Class," *Radical History Review* 59 (spring 1994), 110–11; Terry Lovell, ed., *British Feminist Thought: A Reader* (Oxford: Blackwell, 1990), 21–27.

20. Edward P. Thompson, *The Poverty of Theory and Other Essays* (London: Merlin Press, 1978), 183.

21. Raymond Williams, quoted in Michael Green, "Raymond Williams and Cultural Studies," *Working Papers in Cultural Studies* 6 (autumn 1974), 34.

22. Raymond Williams, "Base and Superstructure in Marxist Cultural Theory," *New Left Review* 82 (November–December 1973), 3–16; *Marxism and Literature* (Oxford: Oxford University Press, 1977).

23. Williams, *Marxism and Literature*, 82.

24. Williams, *Marxism and Literature*, 99, 82.

25. Antonio Gramsci, *Selections from the Prison Notebooks*, ed. Quintin Hoare and Geoffrey Nowell-Smith (London: Lawrence and Wishart, 1971).

26. The reference is to Alfred Cobban's *The Social Interpretation of the French Revolution* (Cambridge: Cambridge University Press, 1964). Cobban's critique rapidly became a general marker for anti-Marxist hostility among historians.

27. See Christopher Hill, review of *The Modern Prince and Other Writings*, by Antonio Gramsci, ed. Louis Marks, *New Reasoner* 4 (spring 1958), 107–30; Eric Hobsbawm, "The Great Gramsci," *New York Review of Books*, 4 April 1974, 39–44, and "Gramsci and Political Theory," *Marxism Today* 31 (July 1977), 205–13; Gwyn A. Williams, "The Concept of 'Egemonia' in

the Thought of Antonio Gramsci: Some Notes in Interpretation," *Journal of the History of Ideas* 21 (1960), 586–99.

28. Robbie Gray, "History," in Pateman, *Counter Course,* 280–93. See also Gray's subsequent monograph *The Labour Aristocracy in Victorian Edinburgh* (Oxford: Clarendon Press, 1976).

29. See Eugene D. Genovese, "Marxian Interpretations of the Slave South," in Barton J. Bernstein, ed., *Towards a New Past: Dissenting Essays in American History* (New York: Pantheon, 1968), 90–125; "On Antonio Gramsci," *Studies on the Left* 7 (March–April 1967), 83–108. Both were reprinted in Genovese's collection *In Red and Black: Marxian Explorations in Southern and Afro-American History* (London: Allen Lane, 1971), 315–53, 391–422. *In Red and Black* was one of the very few books (like Edward P. Thompson's *Making* and Hobsbawm's *Labouring Men*) that I acquired in hardback in those days. The quotation is taken from *In Red and Black,* 348.

30. See Aileen S. Kraditor, "American Radical Historians on their Heritage," *Past and Present* 56 (August 1972), 136–53. Interestingly, both Genovese and Kraditor eventually ended their careers disavowing Marxism and the Left altogether.

31. One of these new universities, Sussex, generated great intellectual excitement in the second half of the sixties and was my second choice after Oxford when I applied for university entrance in 1966. In fall 1970, after graduating from Oxford, I entered the Sussex graduate program, whose interdisciplinary atmosphere seemed like a bracing gust of fresh air.

32. For a striking instance of such hostility, see Maurice Cowling, "Mr. Raymond Williams," *Cambridge Review,* 27 May 1961, 546–51 (the lead article), denouncing Raymond Williams's appointment to the Cambridge English faculty. The author was a thirty-five-year-old right-wing historian, failed Conservative parliamentary candidate, and former journalist, who had recently moved to Peterhouse from Williams's new college, Jesus. Cowling attacked Williams contemptuously as a leader of the whole "group of English radicals, lapsed Stalinists, academic Socialists, and intellectual Trotskyites" who, "with others from the extra-mural boards, the community centers, and certain Northern universities," were politicizing and degrading national cultural life. Cowling concluded, "It should not be imagined that it is the function of the English scholar to engage in social criticism." Cowling emerged during the 1970s as a kind of *éminence grise* of Thatcherist intellectual Conservatism, helping found the Salisbury Group in 1977 and editing the emblematic volume *Conservative Essays* (Cambridge: Cambridge University Press, 1978). Among his many publications, see the bizarre, but erudite, *Religion and Public Doctrine in Modern England,* 3 vols. (Cambridge: Cam-

bridge University Press, 1980–2001). See also Maurice Cowling, "Raymond Williams in Retrospect," *New Criterion* 8 (February 1990).

33. See Steven Lukes, *Émile Durkheim, His Life and Work: A Historical and Critical Study* (New York: Harper and Row, 1972).

34. Eric J. Hobsbawm, "From Social History to the History of Society," *Daedalus* 100 (1971), 43.

35. The speed of social history's acceptance can easily be exaggerated. As I experienced, it certainly had little imprint in Oxford in the 1960s and early 1970s. In 1971, a perfectly competent survey of historical studies, Arthur Marwick's *The Nature of History* (London: Macmillan), avoided giving social history any treatment of its own.

36. *Social History* 1 (1976), 3.

37. Before leaving in 1961 for the new University of Sussex, Asa Briggs (born 1921) taught in Leeds, which was also the base of the Industrial Revolution historian Arthur J. Taylor and the Marxist Edward Thompson. Briggs originally worked on early nineteenth-century Birmingham and edited two volumes of pathbreaking local research, *Chartist Studies* (London: Macmillan, 1959) and (with John Saville) *Essays in Labour History* (London: Macmillan, 1960). The latter was a memorial volume for G. D. H. Cole, one of the earlier pioneers of labor history, going back to the interwar years. See also Adrian Wilson, "A Critical Portrait of Social History," in Adrian Wilson, ed., *Rethinking Social History: English Society, 1570–1920, and Its Interpretation* (Manchester: Manchester University Press, 1993), 1–24; Miles Taylor, "The Beginnings of Modern British Social History?" *History Workshop Journal* 43 (spring 1997), 155–76.

38. In what follows, my desire to hold bibliographical citations to manageable proportions is no reflection on the relative importance of the several individuals I've omitted. For Christopher Hill, see my obituary essay cited in note 3 above, together with Penelope J. Corfield, " 'We Are All One in the Eyes of the Lord': Christopher Hill and the Historical Meanings of Radical Religion," *History Workshop Journal* 58 (autumn 2004), 111–27. For Rodney Hilton, see Peter Coss, "R. H. Hilton," *Past and Present* 176 (August 2002), 7–10. For Dorothy Thompson, see her *Outsiders: Class, Gender, and Nation* (London: Verso, 1993) and "The Personal and the Political," *New Left Review* 200 (July–August 1993), 87–100.

39. See Eric Hobsbawm, "The Historians' Group of the Communist Party," in Maurice Cornforth, ed., *Rebels and Their Causes: Essays in Honour of A. L. Morton* (London: Lawrence and Wishart, 1979), 21–47; Bill Schwarz, " 'The People' in History: The Communist Party Historians' Group, 1946–56," in Richard Johnson et al., eds., *Making Histories: Studies in History-Writing and Politics* (London: Hutchinson, 1982), 44–95; Dennis Dworkin,

Cultural Marxism in Postwar Britain: History, the New Left, and the Origins of Cultural Studies (Durham: Duke University Press, 1997), 10–44; David Parker, "The Communist Party and Its Historians, 1946–89," *Socialist History* 12 (1997), 33–58; Harvey J. Kaye, *The British Marxist Historians: An Introductory Analysis* (Oxford: Polity Press, 1984). For Dona Torr, see her *Tom Mann and His Times* (London: Lawrence and Wishart, 1956); John Saville, ed., *Democracy and the Labour Movement: Essays in Honor of Dona Torr* (London: Lawrence and Wishart, 1954); David Renton, "Opening the Books: The Personal Papers of Dona Torr," *History Workshop Journal* 52 (autumn 2001), 236–45.

40. See the following works by Hobsbawm: *Labouring Men; Primitive Rebels; Captain Swing* (with George Rudé); *Bandits* (London: Weidenfeld and Nicolson, 1969); "Peasant Land Occupations," *Past and Present* 62 (February 1974), 120–52; *Nations and Nationalism since 1780: Programme, Myth, Reality* (Cambridge: Cambridge University Press, 1992); *The Age of Revolution, 1789–1848* (London: Weidenfeld and Nicolson, 1962); *The Age of Capital, 1848–1875* (London: Weidenfeld and Nicolson, 1975); *The Age of Empire, 1872–1914* (London: Weidenfeld and Nicolson, 1987); *The Age of Extremes: The Short Twentieth Century, 1914–1992* (London: Weidenfeld and Nicolson, 1994).

41. Kiernan's works include *British Diplomacy in China, 1880 to 1885* (Cambridge: Cambridge University Press, 1939), *The Revolution of 1854 in Spanish History* (Oxford: Clarendon Press, 1966), *The Lords of Human Kind: European Attitudes towards the Outside World in the Imperial Age* (London: Weidenfeld and Nicolson, 1969), *Marxism and Imperialism: Studies* (London: Routledge and Kegan Paul, 1974), *America, the New Imperialism: From White Settlement to World Hegemony* (London: Zed Press, 1978), *State and Society in Europe, 1550–1650* (Oxford: Blackwell, 1980), *The Duel in History: Honour and the Reign of Aristocracy* (Oxford: Oxford University Press, 1988), and *Tobacco: A History* (London: Radius, 1991).

42. See Rudé, *Crowd in the French Revolution; Wilkes and Liberty: A Social Study of 1763 to 1774* (Oxford: Oxford University Press, 1962); *Crowd in History; Captain Swing* (with Eric Hobsbawm); *Protest and Punishment: The Story of Social and Political Protestors Transported to Australia, 1788–1868* (Oxford: Oxford University Press, 1978).

43. See Raphael Samuel, ed., *Village Life and Labour* (London: Routledge and Kegan Paul, 1975) and *Miners, Quarrymen, and Salt Workers* (London: Routledge and Kegan Paul, 1977); Samuel, "History Workshop, 1966–80," in Raphael Samuel, ed., *History Workshop: A Collectanea, 1967–1991; Documents, Memoirs, Critique, and Cumulative Index to "History Workshop Journal"* (Oxford: History Workshop, 1991). For Edward Thompson, see his *Making of the English Working Class;* Edward Thompson and Eileen

Yeo, eds., *The Unknown Mayhew: Selections from the Morning Chronicle, 1849–1850* (London: Merlin Press, 1971); Thompson, *Whigs and Hunters: The Origin of the Black Act* (London: Allen Lane, 1975); Thompson with Douglas Hay et al., *Albion's Fatal Tree: Crime and Society in Eighteenth-Century England* (London: Allen Lane, 1975); Thompson, *Customs in Common: Studies in Traditional Popular Culture* (London: Merlin Press, 1991).

44. See Arthur Leslie Morton, *A People's History of England* (London: Lawrence and Wishart, 1938). See also Harvey J. Kaye, "Our Island Story Retold: A. L. Morton and 'the People' in History," in *The Education of Desire: Marxists and the Writing of History* (New York: Routledge, 1992), 116–24; Margot Heinemann and Willie Thompson, eds., *History and Imagination: Selected Writings of A. L. Morton* (London: Lawrence and Wishart, 1990).

45. See the citations in notes 37–41 above. The easiest general introduction is in Kaye, *British Marxist Historians.*

46. Edward P. Thompson, "The Peculiarities of the English," in *Poverty of Theory,* 35–91. The relevant *New Left Review* articles are Perry Anderson's "Origins of the Present Crisis" (23 [January–February 1964], 26–54) and "The Myths of Edward Thompson, or Socialism and Pseudo-Empiricism" (35 [January–February 1966], 2–42) and Tom Nairn's "The English Working Class" (24 [March–April 1964], 45–57) and "The Anatomy of the Labour Party" (27 [September–October 1964], 38–65; 28 [November–December 1964], 33–62).

47. Both Saville and Harrison were movers of the Society for the Study of Labour History. With Asa Briggs, Saville coedited the volumes *Essays in Labour History* (London: Macmillan, 1960–71; Croom Helm, 1977). Between the 1950s and 1990s, he published prolifically on labor history. He edited the *Dictionary of Labour Biography,* which began in 1972 and reached its tenth volume by 2000 (London: Macmillan). On publishing his first book, *Before the Socialists: Studies in Labour and Politics, 1861–1881* (London: Routledge and Kegan Paul, 1965), Harrison became a reader in politics at Sheffield University, having previously taught in the Extra-Mural Department. In 1970, he moved to the Warwick Center for the Study of Social History (created five years before by Edward Thompson), where he founded the Modern Records Center. He also became the official biographer for the Webbs, publishing the first volume, *Life and Times of Sydney and Beatrice Webb, 1858–1905: The Formative Years* (Basingstoke: Macmillan, 2000), shortly before he died.

48. Arthur J. Taylor, ed., *The Standard of Living in Britain in the Industrial Revolution* (London: Methuen, 1975).

49. John Saville, *Rural Depopulation in England and Wales, 1851–1951* (London: Routledge and Kegan Paul, 1957); G. E. Mingay, *English Landed*

Society in the Eighteenth Century (London: Routledge and Kegan Paul, 1963); F. M. L. Thompson, *English Landed Society in the Nineteenth Century* (London: Routledge and Kegan Paul, 1963); Hobsbawm and Rudé, *Captain Swing.*

50. The great works of Beatrice (1858–1943) and Sidney Webb (1859–1947) included the nine-volume *English Local Government from the Revolution to the Municipal Corporations Act* (London: Longmans, 1906–29), *The History of Trade Unionism* (London: Longmans, 1894), and *Industrial Democracy* (London: Longmans, 1897). G. D. H. Cole (1889–1959) published countless works between the early twentieth century and the 1950s, including the multivolume *History of Socialist Thought* (London: Macmillan, 1953–60); he coauthored, with Raymond Postgate, what remained for many years the best general history of British popular movements, *The Common People, 1746–1938* (London: Methuen, 1938). R. H. Tawney (1880–1962) published, among other works, *The Agrarian Problem in the Sixteenth Century* (London: Longmans, 1912), the edited volume (with Eileen Power) *Tudor Economic Documents* (London: Longmans, 1924), *Religion and the Rise of Capitalism: A Historical Study* (London: Murray, 1926), *Land and Labour in China* (London: G. Allen and Unwin, 1932), and "The Rise of the Gentry, 1558–1640," *Economic History Review* 11 (1941), 1–38. Tawney's hugely influential political tracts include *The Acquisitive Society* (London: G. Bell and Sons, 1920) and *Equality* (London: Unwin, 1931). John (1872–1949) and Barbara Hammond (1873–1961) published a pioneering trilogy of works on the human costs of industrialization. Their *The Village Labourer, 1760–1832* (London: Longmans, 1911), *The Town Labourer, 1760–1832* (London: Longmans, 1917), and *The Skilled Labourer, 1760–1832* (London: Longmans, 1919) exercised enormous influence on Thompson's project. In general, see David Sutton, "Radical Liberalism, Fabianism, and Social History," in Johnson et al., *Making Histories,* 15–43.

51. Anne Summers, "Thomas Hodgkin (1910–1982)," *History Workshop Journal* 14 (autumn 1982), 180–82. See especially Thomas Hodgkin, *Nationalism in Colonial Africa* (London: F. Muller, 1956); *Nigerian Perspectives: An Historical Anthology* (Oxford: Oxford University Press, 1960); *Vietnam: The Revolutionary Path* (London: Macmillan, 1981).

52. See especially Hobsbawm, *Primitive Rebels; Bandits;* "Peasants and Politics," *Journal of Peasant Studies* 1 (1973), 1–??.

53. See Christopher Hill, Rodney Hilton, and Eric Hobsbawm, "*Past and Present:* Origins and Early Years," *Past and Present* 100 (August 1983), 3–14. In the previous year (1957), the social anthropologist Max Gluckman, the sociologist Philip Abrams, and the agrarian historian Joan Thirsk had also joined the board.

54. Trevor Aston, ed., *Crisis in Europe, 1560–1660* (London: Routledge and Kegan Paul, 1965).

55. Aston, *Crisis in Europe,* 5.

56. See John H. Elliott, "The Decline of Spain," *Past and Present* 20 (November 1961), 52–75; *The Revolt of the Catalans* (Cambridge: Cambridge University Press, 1963); *Imperial Spain, 1469–1716* (London: Edward Arnold, 1963); "Revolution and Continuity in Early Modern Europe," *Past and Present* 42 (February 1969), 35–56; "Self-Perception and Decline in Early Seventeenth-Century Spain," *Past and Present* 74 (February 1977), 41–61. For the subsequent course of the general debate, see Geoffrey Parker and Lesly M. Smith, eds., *The General Crisis of the Seventeenth Century* (London: Routledge and Kegan Paul, 1978).

57. See especially Philip Abrams, *Historical Sociology* (Ithaca: Cornell University Press, 1982).

58. Worsley's first book was *The Trumpet Shall Sound: A Study of "Cargo" Cults in Melanesia* (London: MacGibbon and Kee, 1957), in some ways a parallel text to Hobsbawm's *Primitive Rebels.* He then published *The Third World* (London: Weidenfeld and Nicolson, 1964), followed two decades later by *The Three Worlds: Culture and Development* (London: Weidenfeld and Nicolson, 1984), together with diverse other publications, including *Marx and Marxism* (London: Tavistock, 1982). He held the chair of sociology at Manchester since 1964 and was president of the British Sociological Association in 1971–74.

59. Georges Lefebvre, in *Les Paysans du Nord pendant la Revolution francaise* (Bari: Laterza, 1959; orig. pub. 1924) and *The Great Fear of 1789: Rural Panic in Revolutionary France* (Paris: A. Colin, 1932), and Albert Soboul, in *Les Sans-culottes Parisiens en l'An II* (Paris: Librairie Clavreuil, 1958), produced innovative and inspiring classics of social history.

60. See Ernest Labrousse, *La crise de l'économie francaise à la fin de l'Ancien Régime et au début de la Revolution* (Paris: Presses universitaires de France, 1944).

61. See Peter Burke, *Sociology and History* (London: Allen and Unwin, 1980), 25.

62. Marc Bloch, *The Royal Touch: Sacred Monarchy and Scrofula in England and France* (London: Routledge and Kegan Paul, 1973; orig. pub., in French, 1924).

63. Lucien Febvre, *Un destin: Martin Luther* (Paris: Rieder, 1928); *The Problem of Unbelief in the Sixteenth Century: The Religion of Rabelais* (Cambridge: Harvard University Press, 1982; orig. pub., in French, 1942).

64. Marc Bloch, *French Rural History: An Essay on Its Basic Characteristics* (Berkeley: University of California Press, 1966; orig. pub., in French,

1931); *Feudal Society* (Chicago: University of Chicago Press, 1961; orig. pub., in French, 1939–40).

65. Braudel, *Mediterranean; Civilization and Capitalism, 15th–18th Century,* 3 vols. (New York: Harper and Row, 1981–84; orig. pub., in French, pub. 1979).

66. See Olivia Harris, "Braudel: Historical Time and the Horror of Discontinuity," *History Workshop Journal* 57 (spring 2004), 161–74.

67. See especially John L. Harvey's fascinating article "An American *Annales*? The AHA and the *Revue internationale d'historie economique* of Lucien Febvre and Marc Bloch," *Journal of Modern History* 76 (2004), 578–621.

68. François Furet and Adeline Daumard in 1959, quoted in Georg G. Iggers, *New Directions in European Historiography* (Middletown, Conn.: Wesleyan University Press, 1984), 66.

69. See Peter Burke, ed., *Economy and Society in Early Modern Europe: Essays from "Annales"* (London: Routledge and Kegan Paul, 1972). For the reception of Braudel's work, see, above all, John A. Marino, "The Exile and His Kingdom: The Reception of Braudel's *Mediterranean,*" *Journal of Modern History* 76 (2004), 622–52. Interestingly in light of my own argument about the externality of impulses toward historiographical innovation, Marino stresses Braudel's time spent in Algeria (1923–32), Brazil (1935–38), and German prisoner-of-war camps (1940–45). See also Howard Caygill, "Braudel's Prison Notebooks," *History Workshop Journal* 57 (spring 2004), 151–60.

70. For the details of the reception, see Peter Burke, *The French Historical Revolution: The "Annales" School, 1919–1989* (Cambridge: Polity Press, 1999); François Dosse, *New History in France: The Triumph of "Annales"* (Urbana: University of Illinois Press, 1984); Traian Stoianovich, *French Historical Method: The "Annales" Paradigm* (Ithaca: Cornell University Press, 1976); Stuart Clark, ed., *The "Annales" School: Critical Assessments,* 4 vols. (London: Routledge, 1999); Carole Fink, *Marc Bloch: A Life in History* (Cambridge: Cambridge University Press, 1989); Matthias Middell, "The *Annales,*" in Stefan Berger, Heiko Feldner, and Kevin Passmore, eds., *Writing History: Theory and Practice* (London: Arnold, 2003), 104–17.

71. See especially the testimony of Eric Hobsbawm's "British History and the *Annales:* A Note" and "Marx and History," in *On History* (New York: New Press, 1997), 178–85, 187. Labrousse worked at the school's core, where Lefebvre's relationship to *Annales* was more oblique. See especially Labrousse, *La crise de l'économie française; "*1848, 1830, 1789: Comment naissant les révolutions?" in *Actes du congrès historique du centenaire de la Révolution de 1848* (Paris, 1948), 1–21. Simultaneously sympathetic to Marxism and close to *Annales,* Lefebvre held the chair of the history of the French Revolu-

tion at the Sorbonne from 1937 to 1945 and formed the strongest bridge between the two traditions. See Richard Cobb, "Georges Lefebvre," in *A Second Identity* (Oxford: Oxford University Press, 1969), 84–100. At the core of the *Annales* school, the medievalist Guy Bois and the Catalan historian Pierre Vilar were also Marxists. See Guy Bois, *The Crisis of Feudalism: Economy and Society in Eastern Normandy c. 1300–1550* (Cambridge: Cambridge University Press, 1984; orig. pub., in French, 1976); Pierre Vilar, *La Catalogne dans l'Espagne moderne: Recherches sur les fondements économiques des structures nationales* (Paris: S.E.V.P.E.N., 1962) and *A History of Gold and Money, 1450–1920* (London: New Left Books, 1976).

72. Quoted in Martine Bondois Morris, "Ernest Labrousse, 1895–1988," in Kelly Boyd, ed., *Encyclopedia of Historians and Historical Writing* (London: Fitzroy Dearborn, 1999), 1:677. For the next generation of *Annalistes,* this spelled a belief in social science and quantification every bit as dogmatic as the rigidified Marxism of the Stalinist era—not surprisingly, perhaps, as several of the generation's leading voices (including François Furet, Emmanuel Le Roy Ladurie, and Denis Richet) began their adult lives in the French Communist Party in the late 1940s and early 1950s, as loyal Stalinists. See Dosse, *New History in France,* 182–98.

73. See here the reflections of Pierre Vilar, a Marxist member of the *Annales* school, in "Marxist History, a History in the Making: Towards a Dialogue with Althusser," *New Left Review* 80 (July–August 1973), 65–106. See also Gregor McLennan, *Marxism and the Methodologies of History* (London: Verso, 1981), 129–51; Christopher Lloyd, *Explanation in Social History* (Oxford: Blackwell, 1986), 243–60. Hobsbawm's recent restatement of Marxism's foundational standpoint reflects this materialist convergence with the classical *Annaliste* perspectives: "Such a framework must be based on the one element of directional change in human affairs which is observable and objective, irrespective of our subjective or contemporary wishes and value-judgments, namely the persistent and increasing capacity of the human species to control the forces of nature by means of manual and mental labor, technology, and the organization of production" ("What Can History Tell Us about Contemporary Society?" in *On History,* 31).

74. A good example was the flourishing of Marxology, or the more academic criticism of Marxist thought, which, in these years, escaped from the publishing houses of the Communist parties and the larger ultra-left-wing sects. The most widely circulated anthologies and commentaries were published by non-Marxist or, at least, nonaffiliated progressives, with commercial publishers. See, for example, Lewis B. Feuer, ed., *Marx and Engels: Basic Writings on Politics and Philosophy* (London: Fontana, 1969); Arthur P. Mendel, ed., *Essential Works of Marxism* (New York: Bantam, 1961); T. B.

Bottomore and Maximilien Rubel, eds., *Karl Marx: Selected Writings in Sociology and Social Philosophy* (Harmondsworth: Penguin, 1963); C. Wright Mills, *The Marxists* (Harmondsworth: Penguin, 1963); Karl Marx and Friedrich Engels, *The Communist Manifesto,* with an introduction by A. J. P. Taylor (Harmondsworth: Penguin, 1967). The culmination came with David McLellan's biography *Karl Marx: His Life and Thought* (London: Macmillan, 1973) and the launching of the Pelican Marx Library (in association with *New Left Review*), whose first title was Martin Nicolaus's long awaited edited volume *Grundrisse: Foundations of the Critique of Political Economy (Rough Draft)* (Harmondsworth: Penguin, 1973).

75. See Eric Hobsbawm, *Interesting Times: A Twentieth-Century Life* (New York: Pantheon, 2002), 347.

76. See especially Seymour Martin Lipset and Richard Hofstadter, eds., *Sociology and History: Methods* (New York: Basic Books, 1968); Robert F. Berkhofer, Jr., *A Behavioral Approach to Historical Analysis* (New York: Free Press, 1969). One of the best critical surveys of this enduring syndrome is Terrence J. McDonald's "What We Talk about When We Talk about History: The Conversations of History and Sociology," in Terrence J. McDonald, ed., *The Historic Turn in the Human Sciences* (Ann Arbor: University of Michigan Press, 1996), 91–118.

77. Several other journals, such as *Politics and Society* and *Theory and Society* (launched in 1970 and 1974, respectively), had less involvement by historians (by formal disciplinary affiliation) but shared the same intellectual moment.

78. Peter Laslett, *The World We Have Lost,* 2nd ed. (London: Methuen, 1971), 241–52, 20.

79. An excellent example would be Michael Anderson's devastating critique of Neil J. Smelser's influential and impressive *Social Change in the Industrial Revolution: An Application of Theory to the British Cotton Industry* (Chicago: University of Chicago Press, 1959). See Michael Anderson, "Sociological History and the Working-Class Family: Smelser Revisited," *Social History* 1 (1976), 317–34.

80. The two biggest monuments to the Cambridge Group's program of "social structural history" were the proceedings of a conference organized by Laslett in 1969, which assembled twenty-two international demographers in Cambridge to assess the idea of progressive nucleation, and the massively erudite general history of British population published by Wrigley and Schofield in 1981, which formed the apogee of the group's achievement. In each case, the broader implications remained unclear. See Peter Laslett, ed., *Household and Family in Past Time: Comparative Studies in the Size and Structure of the Domestic Group over the Last Three Centuries in England, France, Serbia, Japan,*

and Colonial North America, with Further Materials from Western Europe (Cambridge: Cambridge University Press, 1972); E. A. Wrigley and Roger Schofield, *The Population History of England, 1541–1871: A Reconstruction* (Cambridge: Cambridge University Press, 1981).

81. Emmanuel Le Roy Ladurie, *The Peasants of Languedoc* (Urbana: University of Illinois Press, 1974). See Robert Brenner's classic critique "Agrarian Class Structure and Economic Development in Pre-Industrial Europe," *Past and Present* 70 (February 1976), 30–74; "The Origins of Capitalist Development: A Critique of Neo-Smithian Marxism," *New Left Review* 104 (July–August 1977), 25–92; "The Agrarian Roots of European Capitalism," *Past and Present* 97 (November 1982), 16–113. The surrounding debates were collected in Trevor H. Aston and C. H. E. Philpin, eds., *The Brenner Debates: Agrarian Class Structure and Economic Development in Pre-Industrial Europe* (Cambridge: Cambridge University Press, 1985).

82. See Edward Shorter, *The Making of the Modern Family* (London: Fontana, 1976); Lawrence Stone, *The Family, Sex, and Marriage in England, 1500–1800* (London: Weidenfeld and Nicolson, 1977).

83. See Peter Kriedte, Hans Medick, and Jürgen Schlumbohm, *Industrialization before Industrialization: Rural Industry in the Genesis of Capitalism* (Cambridge: Cambridge University Press, 1981; orig. pub., in German, 1977). The term *protoindustry* was a coinage of the economic historian Franklin Mendel: see his "Proto-Industrialization: The First Phase of the Industrialization Process," *Journal of Economic History* 32 (1972), 241–61.

84. Edward P. Thompson, "Under the Same Roof-Tree," *Times Literary Supplement,* 4 May 1973. For Thompson's critique of Lawrence Stone and Edward Shorter, see his "Happy Families," *New Society,* 8 September 1977, reprinted in Thompson, *Making History: Writings on History and Culture* (New York: New Press, 1994), 299–309.

85. See especially David Levine, *Family Formation in an Age of Nascent Capitalism* (New York: Academic Press, 1977) and *Reproducing Families: The Political Economy of English Population History* (Cambridge: Cambridge University Press, 1987); Charles Tilly, ed., *Historical Studies of Changing Fertility* (Princeton: Princeton University Press, 1978); Tilly, "Demographic Origins of the European Proletariat," in David Levine, ed., *Proletarianization and Family History* (Orlando: Academic Press, 1984), 1–85; Wally Seccombe, "Marxism and Demography," *New Left Review* 137 (January–February 1983), 22–47; Seccombe, *A Millennium of Family Change: Feudalism to Capitalism in Northwestern Europe* (London: Verso, 1992); Seccombe, *Weathering the Storm: Working-Class Families from the Industrial Revolution to the Fertility Decline* (London: Verso, 1993).

86. For Medick's work, see also "The Proto-Industrial Family Econ-

omy: The Structural Function of Household and Family during the Transition from Peasant Society to Industrial Capitalism," *Social History* 1 (1976), 291–315; "Plebeian Culture in the Transition to Capitalism," in Raphael Samuel and Gareth Stedman Jones, eds., *Culture, Ideology and Politics: Essays for Eric Hobsbawm* (London: Routledge and Kegan Paul, 1983), 84–113.

87. Peter Laslett, *Family Life and Illicit Love in Earlier Generations* (Cambridge: Cambridge University Press, 1977).

88. See H. J. Dyos, ed., *The Study of Urban History* (London: Edward Arnold, 1968).

89. See Derek Fraser and Anthony Sutcliffe, eds., *The Pursuit of Urban History* (London: Edward Arnold, 1983); and for Dyos's posthumously collected essays, David Cannadine and David Reeder, eds., *Exploring the Urban Past: Essays in Urban History by H. J. Dyos* (Cambridge: Cambridge University Press, 1982). See also the two-volume showcase Dyos edited with Michael Wolff, *The Victorian City: Images and Realities* (London: Routledge and Kegan Paul, 1973), which assembled scholars from many disciplines to analyze all aspects of nineteenth-century urbanization, from economic, social, political, institutional, and cultural points of view.

90. See Philippe Ariès, *Centuries of Childhood* (London: Jonathan Cape, 1962; orig. pub., in French, 1960). Much pioneering work was subsumed in studies of the family, especially in U.S. history, where demographic and psychoanalytic approaches held early sway: for the former, see John Demos, *A Little Commonwealth: Family Life in Plymouth Colony* (London: Oxford University Press, 1970); for the latter, Lloyd DeMause, ed., *The History of Childhood* (New York: Psychohistory Press, 1974). Early surveys included John R. Gillis, *Youth in History* (New York: Academic Press, 1974); C. John Somerville, "Toward a History of Childhood and Youth," *Journal of Interdisciplinary History* 3 (1972), 438–47; and J. H. Plumb, "The New World of Children in Eighteenth-Century England," *Past and Present* 58 (May 1975), 64–95. For an intermediate taking of stock, see Harry Hendrick, "The History of Childhood and Youth," *Social History* 9 (1984), 87–96. Current surveys include Hugh Cunningham, *Children and Childhood in Western Society since 1500* (London: Longman, 1995), and Harry Hendrick, *Children, Childhood, and English Society, 1880–1990* (Cambridge: Cambridge University Press, 1997).

91. The classic and hugely influential volume was Stuart Hall and Tony Jefferson, eds., *Resistance through Rituals: Youth Subcultures in Post-War Britain* (London: Hutchinson, 1976). For the sociology of deviance and radical criminology, see Stanley Cohen, ed., *Images of Deviance* (Harmondsworth: Penguin, 1971); Ian Taylor and Laurie Taylor, eds., *Politics and Deviance* (Harmondsworth: Penguin, 1973); Ian Taylor, Paul Walton, and Jock

Young, *The New Criminology* (London: Routledge and Kegan Paul, 1973). Early historical work included Natalie Zemon Davis, "The Reasons of Misrule: Youth Groups and Charivaris in Sixteenth-Century France," *Past and Present* 50 (February 1971), 41–75; Susan Magarey, "The Invention of Juvenile Delinquency in Early Nineteenth-Century England," *Labour History* 34 (1978), 11–27; Stephen Humphries, *Hooligans or Rebels? An Oral History of Working-Class Childhood and Youth, 1889–1939* (Oxford: Blackwell, 1981); and Dieter Dowe, ed., *Jugendprotest und Generationenkonflikt in Europa im 20. Jahrhundert: Deutschland, England, Frankreich und Italien im Vergleich* (Bonn: Verlag Neue Gesellschaft, 1986).

92. The pioneering work was by Edward Thompson. See Thompson, *Whigs and Hunters;* Hay et al., *Albion's Fatal Tree.* For histories of imprisonment, the key work was Michael Ignatieff's *A Just Measure of Pain: The Penitentiary in the Industrial Revolution, 1750–1850* (London: Macmillan, 1978). For the wider research, see J. S. Cockburn, ed., *Crime in England, 1550–1800* (London: Methuen, 1977); V. A. C. Gatrell, Bruce Lenman, and Geoffrey Parker, eds., *Crime and the Law: The Social History of Crime in Western Europe since 1500* (London: Europa, 1980); John Brewer and John Styles, eds., *An Ungovernable People: The English and Their Law in the Seventeenth and Eighteenth Centuries* (New Brunswick, N.J.: Rutgers University Press, 1980); Stanley Cohen and Andrew Scull, eds., *Social Control and the State: Historical and Comparative Essays* (Oxford: Robertson, 1983).

93. See especially Charles Tilly, *The Vendée* (Cambridge: Harvard University Press, 1964); Charles Tilly and Edward Shorter, *Strikes in France, 1830–1968* (Cambridge: Cambridge University Press, 1974); Charles Tilly, Louise Tilly, and Richard Tilly, *The Rebellious Century, 1830–1930* (Cambridge: Harvard University Press, 1975); Charles Tilly, "Reflections on the History of European Statemaking" and "Food Supply and Public Order in Modern Europe," in Charles Tilly, ed., *The Formation of National States in Western Europe* (Princeton: Princeton University Press, 1975), 3–83, 380–455; Tilly, "Getting it Together in Burgundy, 1675–1975," *Theory and Society* 4 (1977), 479–504; Tilly, *From Mobilization to Revolution* (Reading, Mass.: Addison-Wesley, 1978); Tilly, "Did the Cake of Custom Break?" in John M. Merriman, ed., *Consciousness and Class Experience in Nineteenth-Century Europe* (New York: Holmes and Meier, 1979), 17–44.

94. See Charles Tilly, *The Contentious French* (Cambridge, Mass.: Belknap Press, 1986); *Popular Contention in Great Britain, 1758–1834* (Cambridge, Mass: Harvard University Press, 1995).

95. There are signs of recent change. See Charles Tilly, ed., *Citizenship, Identity, and Social History* (Cambridge: Cambridge University Press, 1995); *Stories, Identities, and Political Change* (Lanham, Md.: Rowman and Littlefield, 2002).

96. Charles Tilly, *Contentious French,* 403–4.

97. See Edward P. Thompson, *William Morris: From Romantic to Revolutionary* (New York: Pantheon, 1976; orig. pub. 1955); Edward P. Thompson and T. J. Thompson, *There Is a Spirit in Europe: A Memoir of Frank Thompson* (London: Gollancz, 1947); Edward P. Thompson, ed., *The Railway: An Adventure in Construction* (London: British-Yugoslav Association, 1948); Thompson, "Socialist Humanism: An Epistle to the Philistines," *New Reasoner* 1, no. 1 (summer 1957), 105–43; Thompson, "Agency and Choice," *New Reasoner* 1, no. 5 (summer 1959), 89–106; Thompson, ed., *Out of Apathy* (London: Stevens and Sons/New Left Books, 1960).

98. See Hobsbawm, *Interesting Times,* 214; Gwyn A. Williams, *Artisans and Sans-Culottes: Popular Movements in France and Britain during the French Revolution* (London: Edward Arnold, 1968), 118.

99. Hobsbawm, *Interesting Times,* 214.

100. See Edward P. Thompson, ed., *Warwick University Ltd.* (Harmondsworth: Penguin, 1970).

101. Edward P. Thompson, *Making of the English Working Class,* 12.

102. Edward P. Thompson, *Making of the English Working Class,* 9.

103. Edward P. Thompson, *Whigs and Hunters;* Hay et al., *Albion's Fatal Tree.*

104. The original sources for Thompson's essays were as follows: "Time, Work-Discipline, and Industrial Capitalism," *Past and Present* 38 (December 1967), 56–97; "The Moral Economy of the English Crowd in the Eighteenth Century," *Past and Present* 50 (February 1971), 76–136; "Rough Music: Le charivari anglais," *Annales: E.S.C.* 27 (1972), 285–312. "The Sale of Wives" was published for the first time in Thompson, *Customs in Common,* 404–66.

105. Hay et al., *Albion's Fatal Tree,* 13. For the wider interest in social histories of crime, see Cockburn, *Crime in England;* Gatrell, Lenman, and Parker, *Crime and the Law;* Brewer and Styles, *Ungovernable People.*

106. See Raphael Samuel, "The Social History Group, 1965–1974," in Samuel, *History Workshop: A Collectanea,* 85–91. Having formed among graduate students in British history at Nuffield College, the group moved to St. Anthony's in 1968, internationalizing its composition and interests in the process. Original members included Gillian Sutherland, Brian Harrison, Gareth Stedman Jones, Angus Hone, Roderick Floud, Nuala O'Faolain, Peter Lowbridge, Raphael Samuel, Peter Burke (on sabbatical from Sussex), and Patricia Hollis. Also taking an interest was a lone senior member of the university, the eighteenth-century religious historian John Walsh.

107. See Stuart Hall, "Raphael Samuel, 1934–96," and Sheila Rowbotham, "Some Memories of Raphael," *New Left Review* 221 (January–February 1997), 119–27, 128–32.

108. Editorial introduction in Samuel, *History Workshop: A Collectanea,* IV–V.

109. For the inception of women's history in Britain, see Lovell, *British Feminist Thought,* 21–27; see also the reminiscences of Sheila Rowbotham, Anna Davin, Sally Alexander, and Catherine Hall, in Michelene Wandor, ed., *Once a Feminist: Stories of a Generation* (London: Virago, 1990), 28–42, 55–70, 81–92, 171–82. For Sheila Rowbotham's pioneering works, see *Resistance and Revolution* (Harmondsworth: Penguin, 1972); *Hidden from History: 300 Years of Women's Oppression and the Fight against It* (London: Pluto Press, 1973); *Women's Consciousness, Man's World* (Harmondsworth: Penguin, 1973). See also Sally Alexander, *Becoming a Woman and Other Essays in Nineteenth and Twentieth-Century Feminist History* (New York: New York University Press, 1995), xi–xxi, 97–125, 249–53.

110. See Thompson's magisterial review of responses and appropriations of the "moral economy" argument in the two decades after the article's publication: Edward P. Thompson, "The Moral Economy Reviewed," in *Customs in Common,* 259–351. See also Roger Wells, "E. P. Thompson, 'Customs in Common' and 'Moral Economy,'" *Journal of Peasant Studies* 21 (1994), 263–307. For Thompson's influence in India, see, above all, Sumit Sarkar, "The Relevance of E. P. Thompson," in *Writing Social History* (New Delhi: Oxford University Press, 1997), 50–81; Rajnarayan Chandavarkar, "'The Making of the Working Class': E. P. Thompson and Indian History," *History Workshop Journal* 43 (spring 1997), 177–96. Thompson's personal relationship to India ran through his father, Edward John Thompson (1886–1946). A Methodist missionary and man of Indian letters, the elder Thompson taught in West Bengal during 1910–22; developed close friendships with Rabindranath Tagore, Jawaharlal Nehru, and other Indian intellectuals; and published widely on Indian history and Bengali culture. See Edward P. Thompson, *"Alien Homage": Edward Thompson and Rabindranath Tagore* (Delhi: Oxford University Press, 1993); Sumit Sarkar, "Edward Thompson and India: The Other Side of the Medal," in Sarkar, *Writing Social History,* 109–58. For a careful and well-founded critique of this relationship, see Robert Gregg and Madhavi Kale, "The Empire and Mr. Thompson: Making of Indian Princes and English Working Class," *Economic and Political Weekly* 32, no. 36 (6 September 1997), 2273–88. See also Frederick Cooper, "Work, Class, and Empire: An African Historian's Retrospective on E. P. Thompson," *Social History* 20 (1995), 235–41.

111. By the later meetings, the international range of the invited participation had greatly broadened. The long-term core included David William Cohen, Alf Lüdtke, Hans Medick, and Gerald Sider. The first roundtable, on "work processes" and held in Göttingen in 1978, produced a volume edited

by Robert Berdahl et al., *Klassen und Kultur: Sozialanthropologische Perspektiven in der Geschichtsschreibung* (Frankfurt am Main: Syndikat, 1982); the second met in Paris in 1980, leading to an edited volume by Hans Medick and David Sabean, *Interest and Emotion: Essays on the Study of Family and Kinship* (Cambridge: Cambridge University Press, 1984); the third and fourth, meeting in Bad Homburg in 1982–83, considered issues of "domination/*Herrschaft*" and culminated in Alf Lüdtke's edited volume *Herrschaft als soziale Praxis: Historische und social-anthropologische Studien* (Göttingen: Vandenhoeck und Ruprecht, 1991); the fifth and sixth extended through 1985–89 and eventually led to an edited volume by Gerald Sider and Gavin Smith, *Between History and Histories: The Making of Silences and Commemorations* (Toronto: University of Toronto Press, 1997). For an account of this particular history, see David William Cohen, *The Combing of History* (Chicago: University of Chicago Press, 1994), 1–23.

112. For the less appealing side of this characteristic, see Jonathan Rée, "E. P. Thompson and the Drama of Authority," *History Workshop Journal* 47 (spring 1999), 211–21.

113. Williams, *Politics and Letters,* 97–98. In this respect, Thompson's literary interests are especially pertinent. See Edward P. Thompson, *Witness against the Beast: William Blake and the Moral Law* (New York: New Press, 1993); *The Romantics: England in a Revolutionary Age* (New York: New Press, 1997). See also Marilyn Butler, "Thompson's Second Front," and Iain A. Boal, "The Darkening Green," *History Workshop Journal* 39 (spring 1995), 71–78, 124–35.

114. The part of his book with the most impact for me personally in this respect was its extraordinary reading of Methodism—although, after four intervening decades of encounters with psychoanalytic theory, feminism, histories of sexuality, and debates about subjectivity, my response now would doubtless be slightly different. See Barbara Taylor, "Religion, Radicalism, and Fantasy," *History Workshop Journal* 39 (spring 1995), 102–12.

115. Interview with E. P. Thompson, in Henry Abelove et al., eds., *Visions of History* (New York: Pantheon, 1984), 21.

116. The other contemporary text that deserves to be mentioned in this regard is Richard Hoggart's *Uses of Literacy: Aspects of Working-Class Life, with Special References to Publications and Entertainments* (London: Chatto and Windus, 1957).

117. Richard Johnson, "Edward Thompson, Eugene Genovese, and Socialist-Humanist History," *History Workshop Journal* 6 (autumn 1978), 85.

118. Equally inspiring were two essays by Natalie Zemon Davis (with a place of publication that was no accident): "The Reasons of Misrule: Youth Groups and Charivaris in Sixteenth-Century France," *Past and Present* 50

(February 1971), 41–47 (in the same issue in which Edward P. Thompson's article "Moral Economy" appeared); and "The Rites of Violence: Religious Riot in Sixteenth-Century France," *Past and Present* 59 (May 1973), 51–91. By the mid-1970s things were starting to change. See Keith Thomas, *Religion and the Decline of Magic: Studies in Popular Beliefs in Sixteenth and Seventeenth-Century England* (London: Weidenfeld and Nicolson, 1971); Christopher Hill, *The World Turned Upside Down: Radical Ideas during the English Revolution* (London: Maurice Temple Smith, 1972). A little later came Natalie Zemon Davis, *Society and Culture in Early Modern France: Eight Essays* (Stanford: Stanford University Press, 1975). See also Keith Thomas, "History and Anthropology," *Past and Present* 24 (April 1963), 3–24. Thomas was a student of Christopher Hill. Edward P. Thompson's own writings on this score include "Rough Music," in *Customs in Common*, 467–538; "Anthropology and the Discipline of Historical Context," *Midland History* 1 (1972), 41–55; *Folklore, Anthropology, and Social History* (Brighton: John L. Noyes, 1979); and "History and Anthropology," in *Making History*, 200–225.

119. See Williams, *Marxism and Literature*, 82; Edward Thompson, "Folklore, Anthropology, and Social History," *Indian Historical Review* 3 (January 1977), 265.

120. Edward P. Thompson, "Introduction: Custom and Culture," in *Customs in Common*, 7.

121. See Kaye, *British Marxist Historians*, 12–13. See also Hobsbawm, "Historians' Group of the Communist Party"; Schwarz, "'The People' in History"; Parker, "The Communist Party and Its Historians"; Dworkin, *Cultural Marxism*, 10–44.

122. See the volume Thompson edited for *New Left Review* at the height of the first New Left, *Out of Apathy*, to which he contributed one of his best polemical essays, "Outside the Whale," a ringing call for the necessity of dissent against the conformities of national and "Natopolitan" culture, framed by the ethics of commitment initiated in the 1930s, in the name of socialist humanism. By the end of the sixties, many within the second New Left viewed apathy as itself a political statement about the rottenness of the political system. Thompson's essay was reprinted in his *Poverty of Theory*, 1–33.

Chapter 3

1. See Geoff Eley and James Retallack, eds., *Wilhelminism and Its Legacies: German Modernities, Imperialism, and the Meanings of Reform, 1890–1930; Essays for Harmut Pogge von Strandmann* (New York: Berghahn Books, 2003).

2. I assiduously read all six volumes of Churchill's war memoirs, for example, as well as the Alanbrooke war diaries and a variety of other memoirs (a confession I'm still slightly embarrassed to make). See Winston

Churchill, *The Second World War,* 2nd ed., 6 vols. (London: Cassell, 1948–54); Arthur Bryant, *The Turn of the Tide, 1939–1943* (London: Collins, 1957) and *Triumph in the West: A History of the War Years Based on the Diaries of Field-Marshall Lord Alanbrooke, Chief of the Imperial General Staff* (London: Collins, 1959). See also Julia Stapleton, *Sir Arthur Bryant and National History in Twentieth-Century Britain* (Lanham, Md.: Lexington Books, 2005).

3. I also thought of working on the social history of English football and even wrote to the Manchester anthropologist Max Gluckman, who'd given a BBC radio talk on the ethnography of football some years before. For a reminiscence of Gluckman and Manchester United, whom I also supported, see Eric Hobsbawm, *Interesting Times: A Twentieth-Century Life* (New York: Pantheon, 2003), 347.

4. I was disposed toward Germany for personal reasons, too. Going to Germany in 1964 was my first trip away from home, an extremely liberating experience. In one way or another, "Germany" framed a large part of my transition to adult life.

5. Hans-Ulrich Wehler, *Bismarck und der Imperialismus* (Cologne: Kiepenheuer und Witsch, 1969).

6. See especially Werner Conze, *Die Strukturgeschichte des technisch-industriellen Zeitalters als Aufgabe für Forschung und Unterricht* (Cologne: Westdeutscher Verlag, 1957). See also Irmline Veit-Brause, "Werner Conze (1910–1986): The Measure of History and the Historian's Measures," and James Van Horn Melton, "From Folk History to Structural History: Otto Brunner (1898–1982) and the Radical-Conservative Roots of German Social History," in Hartmut Lehmann and James Van Horn Melton, eds., *Paths of Continuity: Central European Historiography from the 1930s to the 1950s* (Cambridge: Cambridge University Press, 1994), 299–343, 263–92.

7. Full and detailed references to even the most important works of these individuals and to their influence would hopelessly overburden these footnotes. The Webbs's works included, most famously, *The History of Trade Unionism* (1894), *Industrial Democracy* (1897), and the nine-volume *English Local Government from the Revolution to the Municipal Corporations Act* (1906–29); among Tawney's key works was *Religion and the Rise of Capitalism* (1926); the Hammonds's trilogy embraced *The Village Labourer, 1760–1832* (1911), *The Town Labourer, 1760–1832* (1917), and *The Skilled Labourer, 1760–1832* (1919); among Cole's later works was a multivolume international *History of Socialist Thought* (1953–60). I've sketched these intellectual histories in more detail in Geoff Eley, "The Generations of Social History," in Peter N. Stearns, ed., *Encyclopedia of European Social History: From 1350 to 2000* (New York: Charles Scribner's Sons, 2001), 1:3–29. For full citations, see chapter 2, note 50, in the present book.

8. Eric Hobsbawm (*Interesting Times*, 115) offers a succinct summary: "Founded by the great Fabians Sidney and Beatrice Webb, devoted exclusively to the political and social sciences, led by the later architect of the British social security system, William Beveridge, with a faculty whose most prominent and charismatic teachers were nationally known socialists— Harold Laski, R. H. Tawney—it stood on some kind of left almost *ex officio*. That is what attracted foreigners from inside and outside the empire. If that was not what necessarily attracted its British students, overwhelmingly an elite of first-generation scholarship-winning boys and girls from London families on the borderline between working and lower middle classes, it was likely to influence them once they had arrived."

9. See especially Tawney's *The Acquisitive Society* (1921) and *Equality* (1931).

10. Later in the twentieth century, these left-wing political influences became easily effaced by processes of professionalization, which allowed the story of social history's origins to be written entirely as a sequence of academic developments internal to the universities. Social history's British pioneers included a number of women who likewise tended to disappear from the main historiographical record, such as the medievalist Eileen Power (1889–1940), the seventeenth-century historian Alice Clark (1874–1934), and the female members of several famous partnerships, including Beatrice Webb, Barbara Hammond, and Alice Stopford Green (1847–1929). The wife of J. R. Green (author of the *Short History of the English People* [London: Macmillan, 1874]), Alice Green published a long series of popular Irish histories after her husband's early death. Such voices reflected both the social and educational advancement of women in the early twentieth century and the political struggles needed to attain it. They were invariably connected to political activism through Fabianism, the Labour Party, and feminist suffrage politics. See especially Billie Melman, "Gender, History, and Memory: The Invention of Women's Past in the Nineteenth and Early Twentieth Centuries," *History and Memory* 5 (1993), 5–41.

11. See Gustav Mayer, *Radikalismus, Sozialismus und bürgerliche Demokratie,* ed. Hans-Ulrich Wehler (Frankfurt am Main: Suhrkamp, 1969), and *Arbeiterbewegung und Obrigkeitsstaat,* ed. Hans-Ulrich Wehler (Bonn: Verlag Neue Gesellschaft, 1972); Hans Speier, *German White-Collar Workers and the Rise of Hitler* (London and New Haven: Yale University Press, 1986).

12. See especially M. Rainer Lepsius, ed., *Soziologie in Deutschland und Österreich 1918–1945: Materialien zur Entwicklung, Emigration und Wirkungsgeschichte, Kölner Zeitschrift für Soziologie und Soizialpsychologie,* Sonderheft 23/1981 (Opladen: Westdeutscher Verlag, 1981). See also Volker Meja,

Dieter Misgeld, and Nico Stehr, eds., *Modern German Sociology* (New York: Columbia University Press, 1987).

13. This also applied to preuniversity generations yet to enter the profession. Eric Hobsbawm (born 1917) left Berlin in 1933 (at sixteen years old). Sidney Pollard (1925–98), another important figure in the growth of social history during the 1950s and 1960s and a founding member of the Society for the Study of Labour History, left Vienna on a *Kindertransport* in 1938; he trained at the LSE and taught for most of his career at the University of Sheffield. In 1980, he took a position at Bielefeld, the main center of social science history in West Germany, retiring back to Sheffield in 1990. See Colin Holmes, "Sidney Pollard, 1925–1998," *History Workshop Journal* 49 (spring 2000), 277–78.

14. In painting this picture with a broad brush, I certainly don't mean to efface the importance of these detailed intellectual and institutional histories. One obvious case would be the extraordinarily ramified influence of Werner Conze, both in his immediate context at the University of Heidelberg and in the wider circuits of research funding and scholarly discussion in the West German profession.

15. Fritz Fischer's *Germany's Aims in the First World War* (London: Chatto and Windus, 1967, orig. pub., in German, 1961) was followed by *War of Illusions: German Policies, 1911–1914* (London: Chatto and Windus, 1975; orig. pub., in German, 1969). See also Fritz Fischer, *From Kaiserreich to Third Reich: Elements of Continuity in German History, 1871–1945* (London: Allen and Unwin, 1986); John A. Moses, *The Politics of Illusion: The Fischer Controversy in German Historiography* (London: George Prior, 1975).

16. See the following collections edited by Hans-Ulrich Wehler: Eckart Kehr, *Der Primat der Innenpolitik: Gesammelte Aufsätze zur preußisch-deutsche Sozialgeschichte im 19. Jahrhundert* (Berlin: W. de Gruyter, 1965); Arthur Rosenberg, *Demokratie und Klassenkampf: Ausgewählte Studien* (Frankfurt am Main: Ullstein, 1974); Mayer, *Radikalismus, Sozialismus und bürgerliche Demokratie* and *Arbeiterbewegung und Obrigkeitsstaat*. See also Hans-Ulrich Wehler, "Staatsgeschichte oder Gesellschaftsgeschichte? Zwei Außenseiter der deutschen Historikerzunft: Veit Valentin und Ludwig Quidde," in Helmut Berding et al., eds., *Vom Staat des Ancien Régime zum modernen Parteienstaat: Festschrift für Theodor Schieder* (Munich: Oldenbourg, 1978), 349–68. Wehler's writings of this kind are conveniently collected in Hans-Ulrich Wehler, *Historische Sozialwissenschaft und Geschichtsschreibung: Studien zu Aufgaben und Traditionen deutscher Geschichtswissenschaft* (Göttingen: Vandenhoeck und Ruprecht, 1980). See also Hans-Ulrich Wehler, ed., *Deutsche Historiker,* 9 vols. (Göttingen: Vandenhoeck und Ruprecht, 1971–82).

17. Hans-Ulrich Wehler, "Historiography in Germany Today," in Jürgen Habermas, ed., *Observations on the Spiritual Situation of the Age* (Cambridge: MIT Press, 1984), 230–31.

18. For the most pertinent of innumerable programmatic writings, see Hans-Ulrich Wehler, *Geschichte als historische Sozialwissenschaft* (Frankfurt am Main: Suhrkamp, 1973) and *Modernisierungstheorie und Geschichte* (Göttingen: Vandenhoeck und Ruprecht, 1975); Jürgen Kocka, *Sozialgeschichte: Begriff, Entwicklung, Probleme* (Göttingen: Vandenhoeck und Ruprecht, 1977) and "Theoretical Approaches to the Social and Economic History of Modern Germany," *Journal of Modern History* 47 (1975), 101–19. For a similar reflection by a leading student of Fritz Fischer, see Arnold Sywottek, *Geschichtswissenschaft in der Legitimationskrise: Ein Überblick über die Diskussion um Theorie und Didaktik der Geschichte in der Bundesrepublik Deutschland 1969–1973* (Bonn: Verlag Neue Gesellschaft, 1974). See also Jürgen Kocka, ed., *Theorien in der Praxis des Historikers: Forschungsbeispiele und ihre Diskussion* (Göttingen: Vandenhoeck und Ruprecht, 1977).

19. See Jürgen Kocka, *Unternehmensverwaltung und Angestelltenschaft am Beispiel Siemens 1847–1914: Zum Verhältnis von Kapitalismus und Bürokratie in der deutschen Industrialisierung* (Stuttgart: Klett, 1969); *Facing Total War: German Society, 1914–1918* (Leamington Spa: Berg, 1984; orig. pub., in German, 1973); *White-Collar Workers in America, 1890–1940: A Social-Political History in International Perspective* (London: Sage, 1980; orig. pub., in German, 1977). Kocka's essays relating to his first book have been translated as *Industrial Culture and Bourgeois Society: Business, Labor, and Bureaucracy in Modern Germany* (New York: Berghahn Books, 1999). See also Volker R. Berghahn's helpful portrait in the same volume, "Introduction: The Quest for an Integrative History of Industrial Society," ix–viii.

20. Karl Dietrich Bracher, "The Nazi Takeover," *History of the Twentieth Century* 48 (London: Purnell, 1969), 1339.

21. Wehler, "Historiography in Germany Today," 243–44.

22. By 1976, James J. Sheehan, a leading U.S. German historian, described Wehler's ideas as the "new orthodoxy" in German historiography (review in *Journal of Modern History* 48 [1976], 566–67). At various times, Wehler's supporters have been called "the Kehrites" (after Eckart Kehr, whose ideas they adopted), the "Bielefeld school" (after the new university where Wehler, Kocka, and others were based), or simply the "critical historians." In the mid-1970s, the cohesion and influence of this network were certainly sometimes exaggerated, but it seems foolish to deny its existence altogether. Wehler and his allies definitely shaped perceptions of German history across the Atlantic, for instance, partly by their closeness to such leading U.S. German historians as Sheehan (Northwestern and then Stan-

ford), Gerald Feldman (Berkeley), and Charles Maier (Harvard). The main traffic of people and ideas diversified mainly during the 1990s. One of the best discussions can be found in Robert G. Moeller, "The Kaiserreich Recast? Continuity and Change in Modern German Historiography," *Journal of Social History* 17 (1984), 655–80. Both the common ground and the relatively diverse points of view can be sampled in Michael Stürmer's edited volume *Das kaiserliche Deutschland: Politik und Gesellschaft, 1871–1918* (Düsseldorf: Droste, 1970).

23. The best example would be Hartmut Kaelble (born 1940), who followed a study of industrial politics before 1914 with long-term research on social mobility and social inequality during industrialization, increasingly on a comparative European footing: see *Industrielle Interessenpolitik in der Wilhelminischen Gesellschaft: Zentralverband Deutscher Industrieller 1895–1914* (Berlin: W. de Gruyter, 1967); *Social Mobility in the 19th and 20th Centuries: Europe and North America in Comparative Perspective* (Leamington Spa: Berg, 1985); *Industrialization and Social Inequality in 19th Century Europe* (Leamington Spa: Berg, 1986); *A Social History of Western Europe, 1880–1980* (New York: Barnes and Noble, 1990). See also Hartmut Kaelble et al., *Probleme der Modernisierung in Deutschland: Sozialhistorische Studien zum 19. und 20. Jahrhundert* (Opladen: Westdeutscher Verlag, 1978).

24. Wolfgang J. Mommsen, the twin brother of the equally influential Hans Mommsen, published a pioneering study of Max Weber's thought, various works on imperialism, and innumerable studies and commentaries on the historiography of the *Kaiserreich*. Between 1978 and 1985, he became the first full director of the German Historical Institute in London, inaugurating its activities with an international conference in Mannheim in 1978 on the historiography of the *Kaiserreich*. See Wolfgang J. Mommsen, *Max Weber and German Politics, 1890–1920* (Chicago: University of Chicago Press, 1985; orig. pub., in German, 1959); *The Age of Bureaucracy: Perspectives on the Political Sociology of Max Weber* (Oxford: Blackwell, 1974); *The Political and Social Theory of Max Weber: Collected Essays* (Chicago: University of Chicago Press, 1989).

25. The anthologies *Geschichte und Psychoanalyse* (1971), *Geschichte und Soziologie* (1972), and *Geschichte und Ökonomie* (1973) were edited by Hans-Ulrich Wehler for the Neue Wissenschaftliche Bibliothek series of the Cologne publisher Kiepenheuer und Witsch. In the 1960s and 1970s, the Neue Wissenschaftliche Bibliothek, for which Wehler was also the general history editor, was the premier series of academic anthologies aimed at students. He also edited the anthologies *Moderne deutsche Sozialgeschichte* (1966) and *Imperialismus* (1969) in that series.

26. The series title is Kritische Studien zur Geschichtswissenschaft.

Most of the early titles were republished works, collected essays, or conference volumes, but by 1976, the Bielefeld dissertation students were also publishing their own books. By 2003, 160 titles had appeared.

27. See, for example, the volume edited by Heinrich August Winkler, *Organisierter Kapitalismus: Voraussetzungen und Anfänge* (Göttingen: Vandenhoeck und Ruprecht, 1974), which brought together papers originally prepared for a session at the Regensburg Historians' Conference in October 1972. Among the ten contributors were Wehler, Kocka, and Puhle. The session's discussion of "organized capitalism" was a good example of Wehler's project in operation: the concept was proposed in a "heuristic" spirit in the interests of "theory formation and theory critique" on the new ground of a "comparative social history"; the essays covered France, Italy, Britain, and the United States as well as Germany; and the concept was advanced as an explicit alternative to the rival Marxist-Leninist concept of "state monopoly capitalism." See Winkler's preface to the edited volume (*Organisierter Kapitalismus*, 7).

28. See Hans-Ulrich Wehler, *Das Deutsche Kaiserreich 1871–1918* (Göttingen: Vandenhoeck und Ruprecht, 1973), translated as *The German Empire, 1871–1918* (Leamington Spa: Berg, 1985). The main responses included Andreas Hillgruber's "Politische Geschichte in moderner Sicht" (*Historische Zeitschrift* 216 [1973], 529–52), Hans-Günther Zmarzlik's "Das Kaiserreich in neuer Sicht" (222 [1976], 105–26), Lothar Gall's "Bismarck und der Bonapartismus" (222 [1976], 618–37), and Klaus Hildebrand's "Geschichte oder 'Gesellschaftsgeschichte': Die Notwendigkeit einer politischen Geschichtsschreibung von den internationalen Beziehungen" (223 [1976], 328–57). A more measured but equally conservative response came from Thomas Nipperdey, "Wehlers Kaiserreich: Eine kritische Auseinandersetzung," *Geschichte und Gesellschaft* 1 (1975), 538–60.

29. Hans-Ulrich Wehler, ed., *Sozialgeschichte Heute: Festschrift für Hans Rosenberg* (Göttingen: Vandenhoeck und Ruprecht, 1974).

30. Hans-Ulrich Wehler, ed., *Arbeitsbücher zur modernen Geschichte* (Göttingen: Vandenhoeck und Ruprecht, 1976–).

31. The outer limits of serious dialogue with Marxism were reached in Kocka's 1973 book on "class society" during World War I. There, to show the relationship between increased class tensions and the political breakdown of 1918, he skillfully used "as a heuristic device" a class-analytic model of social structure and social conflict deriving from Marx. But in so doing, he rejected what he regarded as the Marxist teleology of rising class consciousness, disputing any direct correlation between increasing economic hardship and propensity for political protest. He likewise disputed a simplistic Marxist view of the state as the instrument of the economically dominant classes.

All that was well and good. But the crudest orthodox Marxist-Leninist think-ing about those two relationships—class conflict and class consciousness, capitalism and the state—was invoked to dispose of any possible Marxist approach, whereas the early 1970s were actually a time of extremely ramified Marxist debates about precisely these questions. See Kocka, *Facing Total War*. For extended discussion, see Geoff Eley, "Capitalism and the Wil-helmine State: Industrial Growth and Political Backwardness, 1890–1918," in *From Unification to Nazism: Reinterpreting the German Past* (London: Allen and Unwin, 1986), 42–58.

32. For a succinct example, see Wehler, "Historiography in Germany Today," 246–49.

33. *Berufsverbot* was the generic name for a range of government decrees and practices that, beginning in 1972, severely compromised civil liberties in West Germany for anyone who had a record of "extremist" polit-ical involvement and held or applied for a civil service job. That category of employment included schoolteachers (both at and below the university level), railway and postal workers, and doctors and nurses in state hospitals, as well as civil servants in the narrower sense—in other words, some 16 per-cent of total West German employment. Thus, the measures became a pow-erful device for tightening the public ideological climate and delegitimizing Marxist and other radical ideas.

34. Interestingly, Kocka and Wehler embraced some of the British Marxist historians, such as Eric Hobsbawm, whose work was admitted to the repertoire of important influences and with whom close contacts developed. This exception was manageable partly because so much of Hobsbawm's Marxism was empirically embedded rather than being forcefully explicated as such, whereas such figures as Edward Thompson and Raymond Williams were consistently ignored. Certain East German historians also received genuine recognition, usually where methodological originality provided a suitable alibi—most notably in the case of Hartmut Zwahr. See especially Zwahr's *Zur Konstituierung des Proletariats als Klasse: Strukturuntersuchung über das Leipziger Proletariat während der industriellen Revolution* (Berlin: Akademie-Verlag, 1978).

35. Chris Lorenz, "Jürgen Kocka," in Kelly Boyd, ed., *Encyclopedia of Historians and Historical Writing* (London: Fitzroy Dearborn, 1999), 1:650. See also Chris Lorenz, "Beyond Good and Evil? The German Empire of 1871 and Modern German Historiography," *Journal of Contemporary History* 30 (1995), 729–67.

36. Helmut Böhme, *Deutschlands Weg zur Großmacht: Studien zum Ver-hältnis von Wirtschaft und Staat während der Reichsgründungszeit 1848–1881* (Cologne: Kiepenheuer und Witsch, 1966).

37. Hans Rosenberg, *Große Depression und Bismarckzeit: Wirtschaftsablauf, Gesellschaft und Politik in Mitteleuropa* (Berlin: W. de Gruyter, 1967). Rosenberg first advanced this argument in "Political and Social Consequences of the Great Depression of 1873-1896 in Central Europe," *Economic History Review* 13 (1943), 58-73.

38. See Hans-Jürgen Puhle, *Agrarische Interessenpolitik und preußischer Konservatismus in wilhelminischen Reich 1893-1914* (Hanover: Verlag für Literature und Zeitgeschehen, 1966); Kaelble, *Industrielle Interessenpolitik;* Peter-Christian Witt, *Die Finanzpolitik des Deutschen Reiches von 1903-1913* (Lübeck: Matthiesen, 1970); Volker R. Berghahn, *Der Tirpitz-Plan. Genesis und Verfall einer innenpolitischen Krisenstrategie unter Wilhelm II* (Düsseldorf: Droste, 1971); Dirk Stegmann, *Die Erben Bismarcks: Parteien und Verbände in der Spätphase des Wilhelminischen Deutschlands; Sammlungspolitik 1897-1918* (Cologne: Kiepenheuer und Witsch, 1970); Eckart Kehr, *Primat der Innenpolitik,* and *Schlachtflottenbau und Parteipolitik 1894-1901. Versuch eines Querschnitts durch die innenpolitischen, sozialen und ideologischen Voraussetzungen des deutschen Imperialismus* (Berlin: Matthiesen Verlag, 1930).

39. See Helmut Böhme, ed., *Probleme der Reichsgründungszeit 1848-1879* (Cologne: Kiepenheuer und Witsch, 1968); Wehler, *Moderne deutsche Sozialgeschichte;* Stürmer, *Das kaiserliche Deutschland.*

40. Wehler, *Bismarck,* 115.

41. Hans-Ulrich Wehler, "Industrial Growth and Early German Imperialism," in Roger Owen and Bob Sutcliffe, eds., *Studies in the Theory of Imperialism* (London: Longman, 1972), 89, 87.

42. Wehler, "Industrial Growth," 88.

43. Wehler, "Industrial Growth," 89.

44. Hans-Ulrich Wehler, "Probleme des Imperialismus," in *Krisenherde des Kaiserreichs 1871-1918: Studien zur deutschen Sozial- und Verfassungsgeschichte* (Göttingen: Vandenhoeck und Ruprecht, 1970), 131.

45. For example, in December 1906, after protracted conflicts over colonial policy with a parliamentary opposition led by the Catholic Center Party and the SPD, Chancellor Bernhard von Bülow dissolved the Reichstag and called fresh elections, using the slogan "Struggle against Ultramontanes, Guelfs, Socialists, and Poles." The name *Ultramontane* was the common pejorative used by Protestant nationalists for supporters of the Center Party, implying a primary political allegiance to Rome; Guelfs were the Hanoverian Particularists who wished to reverse the annexation of Hanover by Prussia in 1866. See Witt, *Finanzpolitik,* 152-57.

46. For foundational statements of this argument, see Wolfgang Sauer, "Das Problem des deutschen Nationalstaats," in Wehler, *Moderne deutsche Sozialgeschichte,* 407-36; Michael Stürmer, "Konservatismus und Revolution

in Bismarcks Politik," in Stürmer, *Das kaiserliche Deutschland,* 143–67; Wehler, *Das Deutsche Kaiserreich,* 118–31.

47. Wehler, *Das Deutsche Kaiserreich,* 238–39, 226.

48. See Geoff Eley, introduction and "*Sammlungspolitik,* Social Imperialism, and the Navy Law of 1898," in *From Unification to Nazism,* 8–11, 110–53.

49. See Geoff Eley, "Social Imperialism in Germany: Reformist Synthesis or Reactionary Sleight of Hand?" in *From Unification to Nazism,* 154–67; "Defining Social Imperialism: Use and Abuse of an Idea," *Social History* 1 (1976), 265–90.

50. See Ralf Dahrendorf, *Society and Democracy in Germany* (London: Weidenfeld and Nicolson, 1968), 404.

51. Turning on its head a famous anticapitalist aphorism of Max Horkheimer's ("Whoever does not want to talk about fascism should keep quiet about capitalism"), Kocka argued, "Whoever does not want to talk about pre-industrial, pre-capitalist, and pre-bourgeois traditions should keep quiet about fascism" ("Ursachen des Nationalsozialismus," *Aus Politik und Zeitgeschichte,* 21 June 1980, 11). Winkler agreed: "The reasons why democracy was liquidated in Germany in the course of the world economic crisis and not in the other developed industrial societies have less to do with the course of the crisis itself than with the different pre-industrial histories of these countries. The conditions for the rise of fascism have at least as much to do with feudalism and absolutism as with capitalism" ("Die 'neue Linke' und der Faschismus: Zur Kritik neomarxistischen Theorien über den Nationalsozialismus," in *Revolution, Staat, Faschismus: Zur Revision des Historischen Materialismus* [Göttingen: Vandenhoeck und Ruprecht, 1978], 83). In this way, the stakes for the *Sonderweg* thesis were set extremely high.

52. For me, the damning early critiques were Noam Chomsky's *American Power and the New Mandarins* (Harmondsworth: Penguin, 1969) and Andre Gunder Frank's *Sociology of Development and Underdevelopment of Sociology* (London: Pluto Press, 1971). See also Dean C. Tipps, "Modernization Theory and the Comparative Study of Societies: A Critical Perspective," *Comparative Studies in Society and History* 15 (1973), 199–266; Anthony D. Smith, *The Concept of Social Change: A Critique of the Functionalist Theory of Social Change* (London: Routledge and Kegan Paul, 1973); John G. Taylor, *From Modernization to Modes of Production: A Critique of Sociologies of Development and Underdevelopment* (London: Macmillan, 1979). For a cogent defense from this period, see Raymond Grew, "Modernization and Its Discontents," *American Behavioral Scientist* 21 (1977), 289–312; "More on Modernization," *Journal of Social History* 14 (1981), 179–87.

53. The forward-moving unity of values implied by this conception of

"modernity" is conveniently expressed, in all its glorious simplicity, by the preface to a Festschrift honoring Lawrence Stone, an influential practitioner of modernization theory among historians: "How and why did Western Europe change itself during the sixteenth, seventeenth and eighteenth centuries so as to lay the social, economic, scientific, political, ideological, and ethical foundations for the rationalist, democratic, individualistic, technological industrialized society in which we now live? England was the first country to travel along this road" (A. L. Beier, David Cannadine, and James M. Rosenheim, eds., *The First Modern Society: Essays in English History in Honour of Lawrence Stone* [Cambridge: Cambridge University Press, 1989], vii).

54. Hans-Ulrich Wehler, "Geschichte und Zielutopie der deutschen 'bürgerlichen Gesellschaft,'" in *Aus der Geschichte Lernen? Essays* (Munich: C. H. Beck, 1988), 251.

55. Hans-Ulrich Wehler, "Wie 'bürgerlich' war das Deutsche Kaiserreich?" in *Aus der Geschichte Lernen?* 199.

56. Wehler, "Geschichte und Zielutopie," 252.

57. Dahrendorf, *Society and Democracy,* 397.

58. Hobsbawm was always an important supporter of social-structural analysis, economic history, and quantitative methods. Another close collaborator of Kocka and Wehler was the Sheffield economic historian Sidney Pollard, who was briefly a member of the Communist Party Historians' Group and was Hobsbawm's colleague in the Economic History and Labour History Societies. Pollard also taught at Bielefeld during the 1980s. Of course, both Hobsbawm and Pollard also had German-speaking origins. Like Williams, Edward Thompson was entirely ignored.

59. Richard J. Evans, "Introduction: Wilhelm II's Germany and the Historians," in Richard J. Evans, ed., *Society and Politics in Wilhelmine Germany* (London: Croom Helm, 1978), 23. The volume edited by Evans, to which I contributed, was conceived partly as a specifically British response to the new West German work, drawing explicitly on some distinctive social history perspectives. The image of the puppet theater was used by Zmarzlik in "Das Kaiserreich in neuer Sicht."

60. As a budding German historian, I consciously resisted my first inclination to study some aspect of the history of the labor movement, on the grounds that left-wing historians seemed drawn too easily to the history of their own tradition. To me, helping illuminate the origins of fascism seemed equally important. My first book was *Reshaping the German Right: Radical Nationalism and Political Change after Bismarck* (London and New Haven: Yale University Press, 1980; 2nd ed., Ann Arbor: University of Michigan Press, 1991).

61. Erich Matthias, "Kautsky und der Kautskyanismus: Die Funktion

der Ideologie in der deutschen Sozialdemokratie vor dem Ersten Weltkrieg," *Marxismusstudien,* 2nd ser., vol. 2, 1957, 151–97; Susanne Miller, *Das Problem der Freiheit im Sozialismus: Freiheit, Staat und Revolution in der Programmatik der Sozialdemokratie von Lasalle bis zum Revisionismusstreit* (Frankfurt am Main: Europäische Verlaganstalt, 1964); Werner Conze and Dieter Groh, *Die Arbeiterbewegung in der nationalen Bewegung: Die deutsche Sozialdemokratie vor, während und nach der Reichsgründung* (Stuttgart: Klett Cotta, 1966); Guenther Roth, *The Social Democrats in Imperial Germany* (New York: Arno Press, 1963); Gerhard A. Ritter, *Die Arbeiterbewegung im Wilhelminischen Reich: Die Sozialdemokratische Partie und die Freien Gewerkschaften 1890–1900* (Berlin: Colloquium, 1959).

62. See the handsome commemorative volume edited by Georg Eckert, *1863–1963: Hundert Jahre deutsche Sozialdemokratie; Bilder und Dokumente* (Hanover: J. H. W. Dietz Nachf., 1963), in which Conze and one of his earliest students, Frolinde Balser, were centrally involved. The Conze school was the key scholarly grouping emphasizing the labor movement's historic affinities with the mid-nineteenth-century "national movement" for German unification. The other key voice of Conze's generation, Theodor Schieder, was less concerned directly with the SPD but shared the perspective. See *Das deutsche Kaiserreich von 1871 als Nationalstaat* (Cologne: Westdeutscher Verlag, 1961). Significantly, Schieder also supervised Wehler's doctoral thesis on Social Democracy's attitudes toward nationality questions, which was published in this first wave of academic studies of the pre-1914 SPD. See Hans-Ulrich Wehler, *Sozialdemokratie und Nationalstaat: Die deutsche Sozialdemokratie und die Nationalitätenfragen in Deutschland von Karl Marx bis zum Ausbruch des Ersten Weltkrieges* (Würzburg: Holzner-Verlag, 1962).

63. In addition to his important *Die Strukturgeschichte des technisch-industriellen Zeitalters* (see note 6 above), Conze published a groundbreaking article in 1954 on the relationship between the new language of class and the social changes of industrialization: see Werner Conze, "From 'Pöbel' to 'Proletariat': The Socio-Historical Preconditions of Socialism in Germany," in Georg Iggers, ed., *The Social History of Politics: Critical Perspectives in West German Historical Writing since 1945* (New York: St. Martin's Press, 1985), 49–80. In 1957, he formed the Arbeitskreis für moderne Sozialgeschichte (Working Group for Modern Social History), which convened regular meetings among a compact interdisciplinary network of historians, sociologists, economists, lawyers, and anthropologists, eventually sponsoring larger-scale conferences. From 1962, it also sponsored the book series Industrielle Welt. By the 1970s, these activities were overlapping with those of the Wehler network.

64. See Gustav Mayer, "Die Trennung der proletarischen von der

bürgerlichen Demokratie in Deutschland, 1863–1870," in *Radikalismus, Sozialismus und bürgerliche Demokratie,* 108–78.

65. Werner Conze, "Der Beginn der deutschen Arbeiterbewegung," in Waldomar Besson and Friedrich von Gaertringen, eds., *Geschichte und Gegenwartsbewußtsein: Historische Betrachtungen und Untersuchungen; Festschrift für Hans Rothfels zum 70. Geburtstag* (Göttingen: Vandenhoeck und Ruprecht, 1963), 323–38, quotation from 337–38.

66. Conze and Groh, *Die Arbeiterbewegung in der nationalen Bewegung,* 124.

67. The quote is from Wolfgang Schieder, "Das Scheitern des bürgerlichen Radikalismus und die sozialistische Parteibildung in Deutschland," in Hans Mommsen, ed., *Sozialdemokratie zwischen Klassenbewegung und Volkspartei* (Frankfurt am Main: Fischer Taschenbuchverlag, 1974), 21. Conze's causal focus on the split between liberals and labor in Germany rather neglected the opening of comparable divisions elsewhere in Europe during the later nineteenth century. In that respect, Britain was more exceptional than Germany.

68. For example, aside from the monographs, Conze's Industrielle Welt series (published by Klett-Cotta in Stuttgart) published a sequence of thick conference volumes convening small legions of scholars working on relevant themes: Werner Conze and Ulrich Engelhardt, eds., *Arbeiter im Industrialisierungsprozeß: Herkunft, Lage und Verhalten* (1979; conference in 1978); Werner Conze and Ulrich Engelhardt, eds., *Arbeiterexistenz im 19. Jahrhundert: Lebensstandard und Lebensgestaltung deutscher Arbeiter und Handwerker* (1981; conference in 1980); Ulrich Engelhardt, ed., *Handwerker in der Industrialisierung: Lage, Kultur und Politik vom späten 18. bis ins frühe 20. Jahrhundert* (1984; conference in 1982); Klaus Tenfelde, ed., *Arbeiter im 20. Jahrhundert* (1991; conference in 1989).

69. The following volumes have appeared so far, all published by J. H. W. Dietz Nachf. in Bonn: Jürgen Kocka, *Weder Stand noch Klasse: Unterschichten um 1800* (1990) and *Arbeitsverhältnisse und Arbeiterexistenzen: Grundlagen der Klassenbildung im 19. Jahrhundert* (1990); Gerhard A. Ritter and Klaus Tenfelde, *Arbeiter im Deutschen Kaiserreich 1871–1914* (1992); Heinrich August Winkler, *Von der Revolution zur Stabilisierung: Arbeiter und Arbeiterbewegung in der Weimarer Republik 1918 bis 1924* (1984), *Der Schein der Normalität: Arbeiter und Arbeiterbewegung in der Weimarer Republik 1924 bis 1930* (1985), and *Der Weg in die Katastrophe: Arbeiter und Arbeiterbewegung in der Weimarer Republik 1930 bis 1933* (1987); Michael Schneider, *Unterm Hakenkreuz: Arbeiter und Arbeiterbewegung 1933 bis 1939* (1999). Still to be published are two further volumes by Kocka on class formation and the rise of the labor movement up to 1875; one by Ritter on the labor movement between 1875

and 1890; two by Tenfelde on the years up to 1914 and World War I; and a further volume by Schneider on World War II. The series will also be carried past 1945.

70. See also Kocka's book-length essay on the theory and methodologies of writing working-class history for nineteenth-century Germany, *Lohnarbeit und Klassenbildung: Arbeiter und Arbeiterbewegung in Deutschland 1800–1875* (Bonn: J. H. W. Dietz Nachf., 1983), which offered a sketch for the full-scale studies to come. The argument was introduced and framed by a critique of East German Marxist-Leninist historiography. For a distilled version of this book, see Jürgen Kocka, "Problems of Working-Class Formation in Germany: The Early Years, 1800–1875," in Ira Katznelson and Aristide R. Zolberg, eds., *Working-Class Formation: Nineteenth-Century Patterns in Western Europe and the United States* (Princeton: Princeton University Press, 1986), 279–351.

71. This applies somewhat less to the three volumes by Winkler (see note 69 above), which adopt more of an overall narrative frame.

72. Some analytical separation is clearly unavoidable and needn't imply a causal hierarchy. The organizational difficulty of writing a general history from this point of view is handled best by Schneider in the volume on the pre 1933 Third Reich. See Schneider, *Unterm Hakenkreuz.*

73. Ritter, *Die Arbeiterbewegung im Wilhelminischen Reich.*

74. Margaret R. Somers, "Class Formation and Capitalism: A Second Look at a Classic," *Archives européennes de sociologie* 38 (1996), 198. This essay is an incisive critique of Katznelson and Zolberg, *Working-Class Formation.* See also Somers, "Workers of the World, Compare!" *Contemporary Sociology* 18 (1989), 325–29.

75. There was a specifically German language for reconciling these two theoretical worlds. In a commentary on the German historiographical debates about the *Sonderweg* in the early 1980s, a friend and I argued that one solution was "to combine individualizing and hermeneutic methods with systematic analysis of the social structures and processes in which history takes place" (David Blackbourn and Geoff Eley, *The Peculiarities of History: Bourgeois Society and Politics in Nineteenth-Century Germany* [Oxford: Oxford University Press, 1984], 33). A strong argument to this effect was made by Wolfgang J. Mommsen in *Geschichtswissenschaft jenseits des Historismus* (Düsseldorf: Droste, 1971).

76. Antonio Gramsci, *Selections from the Prison Notebooks,* ed. Quintin Hoare and Geoffrey Nowell Smith (London: Lawrence and Wishart, 1971); "Gramsci's Letters from Prison," ed. Hamish Henderson, *New Edinburgh Review* 25 (1974), 3–47, and 26 (1974), 1–44; Lynne Lawner, ed., *Letters from Prison* (New York: Harper and Row, 1975). For the English-language

reception of Gramsci, see Geoff Eley, "Reading Gramsci in English: Observations on the Reception of Antonio Gramsci in the English-Speaking World, 1957–82," *European History Quarterly* 14 (1984), 441–78.

77. See especially Louis Althusser, "Contradiction and Overdetermination," in *For Marx* (London: Allen Lane, 1969), 87–128, and "Ideology and Ideological State Apparatuses," in *Lenin and Philosophy and Other Essays* (London: NLB, 1971), 121–73; Nicos Poulantzas, *Political Power and Social Classes* (London: NLB, 1973), *Fascism and Dictatorship* (London: NLB, 1974), *Classes in Contemporary Capitalism* (London: NLB, 1975), and *State, Power, Socialism* (London: NLB, 1978).

78. For this important context, see Terry Lovell, ed., *British Feminist Thought: A Reader* (Oxford: Blackwell, 1990). By "increasingly unassimilable," I mean a challenge becoming harder and harder to ignore, defuse, or contain.

79. Center for Contemporary Cultural Studies, ed., "On Ideology," *Working Papers in Cultural Studies* 10 (1977); Ernesto Laclau, *Politics and Ideology in Marxist Theory* (London: Verso, 1977). See also the works of Göran Therborn: *Science, Class, and Society: On the Formation of Sociology and Historical Materialism* (London: NLB, 1976); *What Does the Ruling Class Do When It Rules? State Apparatuses and State Power under Feudalism, Capitalism, and Socialism* (London: NLB, 1978); *The Ideology of Power and the Power of Ideology* (London: Verso, 1980).

80. Elizabeth Fox-Genovese and Eugene Genovese, "The Political Crisis of Social History: A Marxian Perspective," *Journal of Social History* 10 (1976), 205–20; Gareth Stedman Jones, "From Historical Sociology to Theoretical History," *British Journal of Sociology* 27 (1976), 295–305.

81. See Richard Johnson, "Thompson, Genovese, and Socialist-Humanist History," *History Workshop Journal* 6 (autumn 1978), 96–119.

82. The essay appeared in shorter and longer versions. See, respectively, Gareth Stedman Jones, "The Languages of Chartism," in James Epstein and Dorothy Thompson, eds., *The Chartist Experience: Studies in Working-Class Radicalism and Culture, 1830–60* (London: Macmillan, 1982), 3–58; "Rethinking Chartism," in Stedman Jones, *Languages of Class: Studies in English Working-Class History, 1832–1982* (Cambridge: Cambridge University Press, 1983), 90–178.

83. William H. Sewell, Jr., *Work and Revolution in France: The Language of Labor from the Old Regime to 1848* (Cambridge: Cambridge University Press, 1980). Sewell recently reflected, "In 1971 . . . , I was a fresh Ph.D. and a practitioner of what we then called 'the new social history'; when I left the Institute after a five-year appointment stretching from 1975 to 1980, I had taken the 'linguistic turn' and was writing in the style that later came to

be dubbed 'the new cultural history'" ("Whatever Happened to the 'Social' in Social History?" in Joan W. Scott and Debra Keates, eds., *Schools of Thought: Twenty-Five Years of Interpretive Social Science* [Princeton: Princeton University Press, 2001], 209).

84. Lutz Niethammer and Franz Brüggemeier, "Wie wohnten Arbeiter im Kaiserreich?" *Archiv für Sozialgeschichte* 16 (1976), 61–134; "Bedürfnisse, Erfahrung und Verhalten," special issue, *SOWI* 6 (1977), 147–96 (see especially Alf Lüdtke's guide to reading, "Fundstellen zur historischen Rekonstruktion des 'Alltagslebens,'" 188–89); Jürgen Reulecke and Wolfhard Weber, eds., *Fabrik—Familie—Feierabend: Beiträge zur Sozialgeschichte des Alltags im Industriezeitalter* (Wuppertal: Hammer, 1978). See also Detlev Puls, ed., *Wahrnehmungsformen und Protestverhalten: Studien zur Lage der Unterschichten im 18. und 19. Jahrhundert* (Frankfurt am Main: Suhrkamp, 1979); Dieter Groh, "Base-Processes and the Problem of Organization: Outline of a Social History Research Project," *Social History* 4 (1979), 265–83.

85. Alf Lüdtke, "Zur Einleitung," *SOWI* 6 (1977), 147.

86. For Marx's famous 1859 preface to *A Contribution to the Critique of Political Economy*, see Marx, *Early Writings*, 424–28.

87. See Alaine Touraine, *L'après socialisme* (Paris: Grasset, 1983); André Gorz, *Farewell to the Working Class* (London: Pluto Press, 1982); Rolf Ebbighausen and Friedrich Tiemann, eds., *Das Ende der Arbeiterbewegung in Deutschland? Ein Diskussionsband zum sechzigsten Geburtstag von Theo Pirker* (Opladen: Westdeutscher Verlag, 1984); Michael Schneider, "In Search of a 'New' Historical Subject: The End of Working-Class Culture, the Labor Movement, and the Proletariat," *International Labor and Working-Class History* 32 (fall 1987), 46–58.

88. Eric Hobsbawm, "The Forward March of Labour Halted?" in Martin Jacques and Francis Mulhern, eds., *The Forward March of Labour Halted?* (London: Verso, 1981), 1–19.

89. See Julius Gould, *The Attack on Higher Education: Marxist and Radical Penetration* (London: Institute for the Study of Conflict, 1977). The Birmingham conference met on 17 September 1977.

90. Chaired by Raymond Williams in King's College, Cambridge, on 23 February 1978, this meeting was called to protest the politics of *Berufsverbot* in West Germany and to launch a Cambridge branch of the Campaign for Academic Freedom and Democracy.

91. For contemporary analyses that were decisive for me at the time, see Stuart Hall, "Living with the Crisis" and "The Great Moving Right Show" (orig. pub. 1978), in *The Hard Road to Renewal: Thatcherism and the Crisis of the Left* (London: Verso, 1988), 19–38, 39–56.

92. See Richard J. Evans and W. R. Lee, eds., *The German Family: Essays*

on the Social History of the Family in Nineteenth- and Twentieth-Century Germany (London: Croom Helm, 1981); Richard J. Evans, ed., *The German Working Class, 1888–1933: The Politics of Everyday Life* (London: Croom Helm, 1982) and "Religion and Society in Germany," special issue, *European Studies Review* 13 (1982); Richard J. Evans and W. R. Lee, eds., *The German Peasantry: Conflict and Community in Rural Society from the Eighteenth to the Twentieth Centuries* (London: Croom Helm, 1986); Richard J. Evans and Dick Geary, eds., *The German Unemployed: Experiences and Consequences of Mass Unemployment from the Weimar Republic to the Third Reich* (London: Croom Helm, 1987); Richard J. Evans, ed., *The German Underworld: Deviants and Outcasts in German History* (London: Routledge, 1988); David Blackbourn and Richard J. Evans, eds., *The German Bourgeoisie: Essays on the Social History of the German Middle Class from the Late Eighteenth to the Early Twentieth Century* (London: Routledge, 1991).

93. Contrast, for example, the Norwich volume edited by Evans and Lee on *The German Peasantry* and the equally valuable parallel volume edited by Robert G. Moeller, *Peasants and Lords in Modern Germany: Recent Studies in Agricultural History* (London: Allen and Unwin, 1986). Whereas the former drew its collaborators as much from East as West Germany and, in disciplinary terms, as much from ethnology and "empirical cultural studies" as from history per se, the Moeller volume drew only on West Germans from Bielefeld. Likewise, despite its subtitle, Richard J. Evans's volume *The German Working Class* was surprisingly unalive to the emerging energy and potentials of *Alltagsgeschichte* (see especially Evans's "Introduction: The Sociological Interpretation of German Labour History," 31–33).

94. I emigrated to the United States in the summer of 1979 and so was personally absent from most of the group's later meetings. For the flavor of the first two sessions, see David F. Crew and Eve Rosenhaft, "SSRC Research Group on Modern German Social History, First Meeting: History of the Family, U.E.A., Norwich, 7–8 July 1978," *Social History* 4 (1979), 103–9; Geoff Eley and Keith Nield, "Why Does Social History Ignore Politics?" *Social History* 5 (1980), 249–71 (for commentary on the discussions in the second meeting, held 12–13 January 1979).

95. The allusions are to Annette Kuhn and AnneMarie Wolpe's edited volume *Feminism and Materialism: Women and Modes of Production* (London: Routledge, 1978) and Heidi Hartmann's "The Unhappy Marriage of Marxism and Feminism: Towards a More Progressive Union," *Capital and Class* 8 (1979), 1–33.

96. Tim Mason, "Intention and Explanation: A Current Controversy about the Interpretation of National Socialism," in Mason, *Nazism, Fascism, and the Working Class,* ed. Jane Caplan (Cambridge: Cambridge University Press, 1995), 230.

97. Tim Mason, "The Workers' Opposition in Nazi Germany," *History Workshop Journal* 11 (spring 1981), 121.

98. See Tim Mason, "Some Origins of the Second World War," *Past and Present* 29 (December 1964), 67–87, reprinted in *Nazism, Fascism, and the Working Class,* 33–52; "Labour in the Third Reich, 1933–39," *Past and Present* 33 (1966), 112–41. Mason's work here was a complex critique of A. J. P. Taylor's potboiling *The Origins of the Second World War* (London: Hamish Hamilton, 1961). Taylor had appealed to me through his controversialism, antiestablishment radicalism, and general pithiness of style. He was known as "the man who likes to stir things up" (A. J. P. Taylor, *A Personal History* [London: Hodder and Stoughton, 1984]).

99. Anne Summers, "Appreciation: Tim Mason. Growing the New History," *The Guardian,* 13 March 1990.

100. He was also virtually alone in engaging seriously with the East German scholarship of the 1960s. See especially Tim Mason, "The Primacy of Politics: Politics and Economics in National Socialist Germany," in Stuart J. Woolf, ed., *The Nature of Fascism* (London: Weidenfeld and Nicolson, 1968), 165–95, reprinted in Mason, *Nazism, Fascism, and the Working Class,* 53–76.

101. See Tim Mason, "Women in Germany, 1925–1940: Family, Welfare, and Work," parts 1 and 2, *History Workshop Journal* 1 (spring 1976), 74–113, and 2 (autumn 1976), 5–32, reprinted in Mason, *Nazism, Fascism, and the Working Class,* 131–212. This ground-laying essay originated, memorably, in the seventh annual History Workshop, "Women in History," held at Ruskin College, Oxford, on 4–6 May 1973.

102. See Tim Mason, "The Great Economic History Show," *History Workshop Journal* 21 (spring 1986), 3–35; "Italy and Modernization," *History Workshop Journal* 25 (spring 1988), 127–47; "The Turin Strikes of March 1943," in Mason, *Nazism, Fascism, and the Working Class,* 274–94.

103. Mason, "Workers' Opposition," 120.

104. Discussion here is complicated by the difficulties of translation. The usual German word for "resistance" in the sense of the illegal underground is *Widerstand,* which, after 1945, carried connotations of ethical commitment and organized preparation inseparably linked with the myth of the 1944 July assassination plot. Broszat's concept of *Resistenz* (explicitly distinguished from *Widerstand*) took its meanings from medicine and physics, suggesting elements of "immunity" or a countervailing ability to impede the flow of a current. It signified those elements of social life (actions, practices, structures, relations) "limiting the penetration of Nazism and blocking its total claim to power and control" (Ian Kershaw, *The Nazi Dictatorship: Problems and Perspectives of Interpretation,* 4th ed. [London: Arnold, 2000], 194).

105. Kershaw, *Nazi Dictatorship,* 204. In Kershaw's exposition, resis-

tance "embraced all forms of limited and partial rejection, whatever the motives, of specific aspects of Nazi rule." Kershaw explained, "Instead of dealing in images of black and white, resistance was portrayed in shades of grey; as a part of the everyday reality of trying to adjust to, and cope with, life in a regime impinging on practically all aspects of daily existence, posing a total claim on society, but—as a direct consequence—meeting numerous blockages and restrictions in its attempt to make good this claim" (193). Kershaw himself was part of the Bavaria Project. See Ian Kershaw, *Popular Opinion and Political Dissent in the Third Reich, 1933–1945* (Oxford, 1983; new ed., 2002) and *The "Hitler Myth": Image and Reality in the Third Reich* (Oxford, 1987).

106. See also especially the works of Detlev Peukert, *Die KPD im Widerstand: Verfolgung und Untergrundarbeit an Rhein und Ruhr 1933 bis 1945* (Wuppertal, 1980); *Ruhrarbeiter gegen den Faschismus: Dokumentation über den Widerstand im Ruhrgebiet 1933–1945* (Frankfurt am Main, 1976); *Die Edelweisspiraten: Protestbewegungen jugendlicher Arbeiter im Dritten Reich* (Cologne, 1980); *Inside Nazi Germany: Conformity and Opposition in Everyday Life* (New Haven, 1987).

107. Martin Broszat, "Resistenz und Widerstand: Eine Zwischenbilanz des Forschungsprojekts 'Widerstand und Verfolgung in Bayern 1933–1945,'" in Broszat, *Nach Hitler: Der schwierige Umgang mit unserer Geschichte; Beiträge von Martin Broszat*, ed. Hermann Graml and Klaus-Dietmar Henke (Munich, 1987), 75–76.

108. See, above all, Ulrich Herbert, *Hitler's Foreign Workers: Enforced Foreign Labour in Germany under the Third Reich* (Cambridge: Cambridge University Press, 1998; orig. pub., in German, 1986); Herbert, ed., *Europa und der "Reichseinsatz": Ausländische Zivilarbeiter, Kriegsgefangene und KZ-Häftlinge in Deutschland 1938–1945* (Essen: Klartext, 1991); Herbert, "Labour and Extermination: Economic Interest and the Primacy of *Weltanschauung* in National Socialism," *Past and Present* 138 (February 1993), 144–95.

109. Mary Nolan, "Rationalization, Racism, and *Resistenz*: Recent Studies of Work and the Working Class in Nazi Germany," *International Labor and Working-Class History* 48 (fall 1995), 132. Other studies of industrial "rationalization" emphasize continuities between the Third Reich and similar histories of the 1920s and 1950s, thereby further displacing German workers as agents. Such research stresses their objectification and disempowerment rather than the scope for self-assertion that interested Mason or the room for modest negotiation expressed by *Resistenz*. See especially Tilla Siegel, *Leistung und Lohn in der nationalsozialistischen "Ordnung der Arbeit"* (Opladen: Westdeutscher Verlag, 1989); Rüdiger Hachtmann, *Industriearbeit im "Dritten Reich": Untersuchungen zu den Lohn- und Arbeitsbedingungen in Deutschland*

1933–1945 (Göttingen: Vandenhoeck und Ruprecht, 1989); Tilla Siegel and Thomas von Freyberg, *Industrielle Rationalisierung unter dem Nationalsozialismus* (Frankfurt am Main: Campus, 1991); Dagmar Reese, Eve Rosenhaft, Carola Sachse, and Tilla Siegel, eds., *Rationale Beziehungen? Geschlechterverhältnisse im Rationalisierungsprozeß* (Frankfurt am Main: Suhrkamp, 1993).

110. Tim Mason, "Introduction to the English Edition," in *Social Policy in the Third Reich: The Working Class in the "National Community,"* ed. Jane Caplan (Providence: Berg, 1993), 3–4.

111. Jane Caplan, introduction to Mason, *Nazism, Fascism, and the Working Class,* 5.

112. Tim Mason, epilogue to *Social Policy,* 285. The ninety-four-page epilogue was composed during 1988–89, shortly before Mason died, eleven to twelve years after publication of the original German edition of the book.

113. Mason, epilogue to *Social Policy,* 285.

114. Mason's central involvement in the History Workshop collective vitally influenced his thinking in these respects. By issue 13 (spring 1982), *History Workshop Journal* had renamed itself "a journal of Socialist and Feminist Historians." See the Editorial, "History Workshop Journal and Feminism." The same issue carried an article signaling Mason's personal shift in that direction: Tim Mason, "Comrade and Lover: Rosa Luxemburg's Letters to Leo Jogiches," *History Workshop Journal* 13 (spring 1982), 94–109. I'm grateful to Frank Mort for pushing me to emphasize this point.

115. Mason, epilogue to *Social Policy,* 316.

116. See, for example, Alf Lüdtke, "What Happened to the 'Fiery Red Glow'? Workers' Experiences and German Fascism," in Lüdtke, ed., *The History of Everyday Life: Reconstructing Historical Experiences and Ways of Life* (Princeton: Princeton University Press, 1995), 198–251; "The Appeal of Exterminating 'Others': German Workers and the Limits of Resistance," in Michael Geyer and John W. Boyer, eds., *Resistance against the Third Reich, 1933–1990* (Chicago: University of Chicago Press, 1994), 53–74. See also Adelheid von Saldern, "Victims or Perpetrators? Controversies about the Role of Women in the Nazi State," in David Crew, ed., *Nazism and German Society, 1933–1945* (London: Routledge, 1994), 141–65; Atina Grossmann, "Feminist Debates about Women and National Socialism," *Gender and History* 3 (1991), 350–58.

117. Mason, epilogue to *Social Policy,* 275, 282–83.

118. The proceedings of this conference were edited by Thomas Childers and Jane Caplan as *Reevaluating the Third Reich* (New York: Holmes and Meier, 1993). Tim Mason's written reflections on the conference—in "Whatever Happened to 'Fascism'?" *Radical History Review* 49 (1991), 89–98, reprinted as an appendix to Childers and Caplan's *Reevaluating*

(253–62) and in Mason's *Nazism, Fascism, and the Working Class* (323–31)—do not reproduce this particular formulation's centrality to his comments at the conference.

119. Mason, epilogue to *Social Policy*, 285.

Chapter 4

1. All three initiatives were launched in 1976. The twelve-person editorial collective of *History Workshop Journal* was avowedly socialist and feminist. Two members bridged to earlier moments of left-wing British social history: Raphael Samuel (1938–96), a schoolboy member of the Communist Party Historians' Group and a moving spirit in the first New Left, and Tim Mason (1940–90), an assistant editor at *Past and Present* during 1967–71. With a third member of the collective, Gareth Stedman Jones (born 1943), a leading light of the second New Left, they convened the Oxford Social History Seminar in the later 1960s. Anna Davin (born 1940) and Sally Alexander (born 1943) were founders of women's history in Britain. The collective was heavily Oxford-centered, comprising either ex-students of the nonuniversity trade union–sponsored Ruskin College (plus Samuel, who taught there) or academic historians educated in Oxford. The youngest member was in his midtwenties; everyone was under forty. *Social History*'s editorial board was entirely academic but less dominated by Oxbridge and London and generally more mixed in complexion, extending from Marxists of various kinds, through non-Marxist specialists in the history of social policy and the history of education, to fervent social science historians. While most board members were in their thirties, a few were older, and the youngest was twenty-seven. In goals, purposes, contents, and potential contributors, the two journals shared many interconnections. For example, Tim Mason had originally been recruited for the *Social History* board until *History Workshop Journal* was conceived, whereupon he left the former and was replaced as the German historian (as it happens) by me. The Social History Society was a straightforward professionalizing initiative, somewhat centered around Harold Perkin (1926–2004), who had been both the first lecturer (at Manchester in 1951) and the first professor (Lancaster in 1967) in social history at British universities. He was the author of *The Origins of Modern English Society, 1780–1880* (London: Routledge and Kegan Paul, 1969), an early and influential general history written from the social history standpoint.

2. Elizabeth Fox-Genovese and Eugene Genovese, "The Political Crisis of Social History: A Marxian Perspective," *Journal of Social History* 10 (1976), 205–20. *Marxist Perspectives* was launched in 1978 on an extremely broad and elaborate base of support and with great hopes attached. It envisaged forms of dialogue between Marxists and non-Marxists in the profes-

sion, not dissimilar, mutatis mutandis, from the purposes of *Past and Present* in the 1950s. In a remarkable act of self-immolation, it ceased publishing after nine issues, essentially destroyed by its primary creators.

3. Gareth Stedman Jones, "From Historical Sociology to Theoretical History," *British Journal of Sociology* 27 (1976), 295–305. See also the editorial by Stedman Jones and Raphael Samuel, "Sociology and History" in the inaugural issue of *History Workshop Journal* (1 [spring 1976], 6–8).

4. By "politics," Judt meant "the means and purposes by which civil society is organized and governed." See Tony Judt, "A Clown in Regal Purple: Social History and the Historians," *History Workshop Journal* 7 (spring 1979), 89, 88, 68. The intemperate language of the polemic made constructive discussion among Judt's fellow French historians in North America unlikely. Judt's article began: ". . . social history is suffering a severe case of pollution. The subject has become a gathering place for the unscholarly, for historians bereft of ideas and subtlety" (67). It continued in the same vein: ". . . bereft of any social or theoretical value . . . complete epistemological bankruptcy . . . ludicrous . . . fundamentally unscholarly approach . . . mediocrity . . . blind belief . . . twaddle . . .unscholarly, stupid, or historically illiterate . . . shoddy work . . . the slow strangulation of social history." These phrases are taken from pp. 14, 15, 77, 78, 79, 81, 86, 88, 88, 89 respectively. As Judt acknowledged me as having suggested "the theme" of this article, the coincidence of its publication with my arrival in North America made for an interesting induction.

5. By working directly on history per se, Foucault offered historians readier access to poststructuralist thinking than did some other theorists (such as Jacques Derrida). Likewise, it was no accident that Foucault's studies of particular sites and practices—such as the treatment of the insane, the practice of medicine, and especially the changing forms of punishment and incarceration—attracted more interest from historians than the purer epistemological works. Foucault's *Madness and Civilization: A History of Insanity in the Age of Reason* (1965), *The Birth of the Clinic: An Archaeology of Medical Perception* (1973), and *Discipline and Punish: The Birth of the Prison* (1977) fell into the first category; *The Order of Things: An Archaeology of the Human Sciences* (1970) and *The Archaeology of Knowledge* (1972) fell into the second (all of Foucault's works here cited were published by Pantheon in New York). See also Hayden V. White, *Metahistory: The Historical Imagination of Nineteenth-Century Europe* (Baltimore: Johns Hopkins University Press, 1973); Clifford Geertz, *The Interpretation of Cultures* (New York: Basic Books, 1973).

6. See "Two Interviews with Raymond Williams," *Red Shift* 2 (1977), 12–17, and 3 (1977), 13–15 (*Red Shift* was a small local journal produced by the Cambridge Communist Party); Raymond Williams, *Marxism and Litera-*

ture (Oxford: Oxford University Press, 1977); Stuart Hall, "Living with the Crisis" and "The Great Moving Right Show" (both orig. pub. 1978), in *The Hard Road to Renewal: Thatcherism and the Crisis of the Left* (London: Verso, 1988), 19–38, 39–56; Edward Said, *Orientalism* (New York: Random House, 1978). For the Gramsci reception, see David Forgacs, "Gramsci and Marxism in Britain," *New Left Review* 176 (July–August 1989), 70–88; Geoff Eley, "Reading Gramsci in English: Observations on the Reception of Antonio Gramsci in the English-Speaking World, 1957–1982," *European History Quarterly* 14 (1984), 441–78.

7. During this time, Taussig also taught an anthropology graduate course based around Edward P. Thompson's *Making of the English Working Class* (London: Gollancz, 1963; paperback ed., Harmondsworth: Penguin, 1968), and I spoke to his class.

8. Fox-Genovese and Genovese, "Political Crisis"; Stedman Jones, "From Historical Sociology"; Judt, "Clown in Regal Purple"; Lawrence Stone, "History and the Social Sciences in the Twentieth Century," in Charles F. Delzell, ed., *The Future of History* (Nashville: Vanderbilt University Press, 1976), 3–42.

9. Louise and Chuck Tilly, "To Prospective Participants in a Discussion of WHENCE AND WHITHER SOCIAL HISTORY?" Center for Research on Social Organization of the University of Michigan, 7 October 1979. The conference convened on 21 October 1979. I'm quoting from my own file on the subject. The comment on the impact of econometricians referred, in particular, to the huge controversy ignited during the mid-1970s by the publication of Robert William Fogel and Stanley L. Engerman's *Time on the Cross: The Economics of American Negro Slavery* (Boston: Little, Brown, 1974). The resulting debates concerned not only the substantive claims about the economics of slavery but the relevance of quantitative methods for historians. During the mid-1970s, the general advocacy of the latter, sometimes with evangelical zeal, was at its height. See, for example, William O. Aydelotte, Allen G. Bogue, and Robert William Fogel, eds., *The Dimensions of Quantitative Research in History* (Princeton: Princeton University Press, 1972); Roderick Floud, *An Introduction to Quantitative Methods for Historians* (London: Methuen, 1973); Floud, ed., *Essays in Quantitative Economic History* (Oxford: Clarendon Press, 1974).

10. Geoff Eley, "The State of Social History," paper presented at the conference "Whence and Whither History?" University of Michigan, Ann Arbor, October 1979.

11. Richard Johnson, "Edward Thompson, Eugene Genovese, and Socialist-Humanist History," *History Workshop Journal* 6 (autumn 1978),

79–100; Edward P. Thompson, *The Poverty of Theory and Other Essays* (London: Merlin Press, 1978).

12. See Raphael Samuel's edited volume *People's History and Socialist Theory* (London: Routledge, 1981), 376–408, for the Oxford debate between Stuart Hall ("In Defense of Theory"), Richard Johnson ("Against Absolutism"), and Edward P. Thompson ("The Politics of Theory"). See also Martin Kettle, "The Experience of History," *New Society,* 6 December 1979, reprinted in Raphael Samuel, ed., *History Workshop: A Collectanea, 1967–1991; Documents, Memoirs, Critique, and Cumulative Index to "History Workshop Journal"* (Oxford: History Workshop, 1991), 107; Susan Magarey, "That Hoary Old Chestnut, Free Will and Determinism: Culture vs. Structure, or History vs. Theory in Britain," *Comparative Studies in Society and History* 29 (1987), 626–39.

13. The short position papers written for the occasion of the conference were subsequently collected for publication by the Tillys under the rubric "Problems in Social History: A Symposium," in *Theory and Society* 9 (1980), 667–81. They include papers by Louise Tilly, Edward Shorter, Francis G. Couvares, David Levine, and Charles Tilly. The only such paper not solicited was my own. None of the intensity of the event itself or its concluding explosiveness is hinted at in that published account. There is another reference to the occasion in William H. Sewell, Jr., "Whatever Happened to the 'Social' in Social History?" in Joan W. Scott and Debra Keates, eds., *Schools of Thought: Twenty-Five Years of Interpretive Social Science* (Princeton: Princeton University Press, 2001), 213: "Taking on the anthropological study of culture was therefore an exciting but also profoundly troubling step for an adept of the new social history. In my case (and I think in others as well) taking this step amounted to a sort of conversion experience, a sudden and exhilarating reshaping of one's intellectual and moral world. I can also testify that going over to anthropological methods and theories could attract considerable hostility from one's erstwhile new social history colleagues—especially in my subfield of labor history, where anything smacking of 'idealism' was taken as evidence of political as well as intellectual apostasy."

14. Frances G. Couvares, "Telling a Story in Context; or, What's Wrong with Social History?" *Theory and Society* 9 (1980), 675.

15. Charles Tilly, "Two Callings of Social History," *Theory and Society* 9 (1980), 681.

16. Louise Tilly, "Social History and Its Critics," *Theory and Society* 9 (1980), 67.

17. Louise Tilly and Joan W. Scott, *Women, Work, and Family* (New York: Holt, Rinehart, and Winston, 1978); Joan W. Scott, *Gender and the*

Politics of History (New York: Columbia University Press, 1988). The former of these titles appeared the year before the Ann Arbor conference and took a strongly social science approach in offering the first general account of modern European social history from a women's history standpoint; the latter provided benchmark advocacy for the so-called cultural turn, taking an avowedly poststructuralist approach.

18. This reflected British feminists' crucial reassessment of Freud and the psychoanalytic tradition, undertaken during the later 1970s and early 1980s by way of Jacques Lacan. Key texts included Juliet Mitchell, *Psychoanalysis and Feminism* (Harmondsworth: Penguin, 1974); Juliet Mitchell and Jacqueline Rose, eds., *Feminine Sexuality* (London: Macmillan, 1982); Jacqueline Rose, "Femininity and Its Discontents," *Feminist Review* 14 (1983), 5–21, reprinted in *Sexuality in the Field of Vision* (London: Verso, 1986), 83–103. For a succinct introduction, see Terry Lovell, ed., *British Feminist Thought: A Reader* (Oxford: Blackwell, 1990), 187–94. See also Sally Alexander, "Women, Class, and Sexual Difference in the 1830s and 1840s: Some Reflections on the Writing of a Feminist History," *History Workshop Journal* 17 (spring 1984), 125–49, reprinted in *Becoming a Woman and Other Essays in Nineteenth and Twentieth-Century Feminist History* (New York: New York University Press, 1995), 97–125.

19. Note also the retrospective editorial "Ten Years After" (*History Workshop Journal* 20 [autumn 1985], 1–4), which situated the journal's development politically in relation to Thatcherism. A similar trajectory occurred at *Radical History Review,* running from the theme issue on British Marxist history (19 [winter 1978–79]), through the issue entitled "The Return of Narrative" (31 [1985]), to one entitled "Language, Work, and Ideology" (34 [1986]). One key early article was Donald Reid's "The Night of the Proletarians: Deconstruction and Social History" (28–30 [1984], 445–63), a discussion of Jacques Rancière. Interestingly, *Radical History Review*'s issue entitled "Sexuality in History" (20 [spring–summer 1979]) contained very little evidence of the new perspectives. By the time the follow-up volume was published ten years later, however, that field was already being transformed. See Kathy Peiss and Christina Simmons, eds., *Passion and Power: Sexuality in History* (Philadelphia: Temple University Press, 1989). See also John C. Fout and Maura Shaw Tantillo, eds., *American Sexual Politics: Sex, Gender, and Race since the Civil War* (Chicago: University of Chicago Press, 1993), which includes articles from the *Journal of the History of Sexuality,* newly founded in 1991.

20. This was hardly less true of Tilly and Scott's *Women, Work, and Family* than of Carl Degler's synthetic survey "Women and the Family," in

Michael Kammen, ed., *The Past before Us* (Ithaca: Cornell University Press, 1980), 308–26.

21. It's impossible to provide very extensive references here. For the history of work in Britain, see especially Sally Alexander, "Women's Work in Nineteenth-Century London" (orig. pub. 1974) and "Women, Class, and Sexual Difference," in *Becoming a Woman*, 3–55, 97–125; Sonya O. Rose, "Gender at Work: Sex, Class, and Industrial Capitalism," *History Workshop Journal* 21 (spring 1986), 113–31, and *Limited Livelihoods: Gender and Class in Nineteenth-Century England* (Berkeley: University of California Press, 1991); "Gender and Employment," special issue, *Social History* 13 (1988). Two key works on middle-class formation were Mary P. Ryan's *Cradle of the Middle Class: Family and Community in Oneida County, New York, 1780–1865* (Cambridge: Cambridge University Press, 1981) and Leonore Davidoff and Catherine Hall's *Family Fortunes: Men and Women of the Middle Class, 1780–1850* (London: Hutchinson, 1987). Impetus for new thinking about popular culture came through the range of new journals in cultural studies, including *Media, Culture, and Society* (1978–), *Block* (1979–89), *Social Text* (1982–), *Representations* (1983–), *Cultural Critique* (1985–), *Cultural Studies* (1987–), and *New Formations* (1987–). For a feminist critique of Edward Thompson, Raymond Williams, and the British "culturalist" classics, see Julia Swindells and Lisa Jardine, *What's Left? Women in Culture and the Labour Movement* (London: Routledge, 1990). Of course, we shouldn't exaggerate the speed of the impact of gender analysis in the 1980s. Among twenty mainly thematic essays in one imposing handbook of international research in labor history, Klaus Tenfelde's edited volume *Arbeiter und Arbeiterbewegung im Vergleich. Berichte zur internationalen historischen Forschung* (Historische Zeitschrift Sonderheft 15 [Munich: Oldenbourg, 1986]), there is not a single entry on women. Aside from a lame exculpatory footnote on the second page of the introduction, gender relations are likewise glaringly absent from Ira Katznelson and Aristide R. Zolberg's edited volume *Working-Class Formation: Nineteenth-Century Patterns in Western Europe and the United States* (Princeton: Princeton University Press, 1986).

22. The first of Foucault's works, *Madness and Civilization*, was translated in 1965, followed by *The Order of Things* in 1970 and *Archaeology of Knowledge* in 1972. By the end of the 1970s, all his works were available in English except volumes 2 and 3 of *The History of Sexuality*, which were yet to be published in France: see *The History of Sexuality*, vol. 1, *An Introduction;* vol. 2, *The Use of Pleasure;* and vol. 3, *The Care of the Self* (New York: Random House, 1978–1986). See also Michel Foucault, *Language, Counter-Memory, Practice: Selected Essays and Interviews*, ed. D. F. Bouchard (Oxford: Blackwell,

1977); Colin Gorden, ed., *Power/Knowledge: Selected Interviews and Other Writings, 1972–1977, by Michel Foucault* (Brighton: Harvester, 1980). For the early social histories of crime and imprisonment in Britain, see chapter 2, note 92, in the present book. The West German reception of Foucault followed similar tracks, initially occurring very much on the margins of the academy. See Uta Schaub, "Foucault, Alternative Presses, and Alternative Ideology in West Germany," *German Studies Review* 12 (1989), 139–53. One early text that registered Foucault's influence, via Gaston Bachelard and the French history and philosophy of science, is Keith Tribe's *Land, Labour, and Economic Discourse* (London: Routledge and Kegan Paul, 1978).

23. Peter Linebaugh, *The London Hanged: Crime and Civil Society in the Eighteenth Century* (London: Allen Lane, 1991); V. A. C. Gatrell, *The Hanging Tree: Execution and the English People, 1770–1868* (Oxford: Oxford University Press, 1994); Richard J. Evans, *Rituals of Retribution: Capital Punishment in Germany, 1600–1987* (Oxford: Oxford University Press, 1996).

24. See Richard J, Evans, ed., *The German Underworld: Deviants and Outcasts in German History* (London: Routledge, 1988). For another general collection lacking Foucault's influence, see Francis Snyder and Douglas Hay, eds., *Labour, Law, and Crime: An Historical Perspective* (London: Tavistock, 1987).

25. Michel Foucault, "Nietzsche, Genealogy, History," in *Language, Counter-Memory, Practice,* 146. Foucault also states, "The end of a genealogically directed history is not to rediscover the roots of our identity but, on the contrary, to strive to dissipate them; it does not attempt to locate the unique home from whence we come, that first homeland to which, the metaphysicians promise us, we will return; it attempts to reveal all the discontinuities that traverse us" (162). I've used a different translation of this passage.

26. Michel Foucault, "A Question of Method: An Interview with Michel Foucault," *Ideology and Consciousness* 8 (1981), 6.

27. Robert Darnton, "Intellectual and Cultural History," in Kammen, *Past Before Us,* 332.

28. See Samuel Kinser, "Annaliste Paradigm? The Geohistorical Structure of Fernand Braudel," *American Historical Review* 86 (1981), 63–105; Patrick Hutton, "The History of Mentalities: The New Map of Cultural History," *History and Theory* 20 (1981), 413–23; Gregor McLennan, "Braudel and the *Annales* Paradigm," in *Marxism and the Methodologies of History* (London: Verso, 1981), 129–51; Stuart Clark, "French Historians and Early Modern Popular Culture," *Past and Present* 100 (August 1983), 62–99; Michael Gismondi, " 'The Gift of Theory': A Critique of the *histoire des mentalités*," *Social History* 10 (1985), 211–30; Dominick LaCapra, "Is Everyone a *Mentalité* Case? Transference and the 'Culture' Concept," in *History and Crit-*

icism (Ithaca: Cornell University Press, 1985), 71–94; Lynn Hunt, "French History in the Last Twenty Years: The Rise and Fall of the *Annales* Paradigm," *Journal of Contemporary History* 21 (1986), 209–24. For a key critique from inside the tradition, see Roger Chartier, "Intellectual History or Socio-Cultural History? The French Trajectories," in Dominick LaCapra and Steven L. Kaplan, eds., *Modern European Intellectual History: Reappraisals and New Perspectives* (Ithaca: Cornell University Press, 1982), 13–46.

29. See Tony Bennett, *Formalism and Marxism* (London: Methuen, 1979); Robert Stam, "Mikhail Bakhtin and Left Cultural Critique," in E. Ann Kaplan, ed., *Postmodernism and Its Discontents: Theories, Practices* (London: Verso, 1988), 116–45; Peter Stallybrass and Alon White, *The Politics and Poetics of Transgression* (Ithaca: Cornell University Press, 1986).

30. In the new histories of consumption, there was an older strand of social history descending from J. H. Plumb and his students, which kept a powerful progressivist understanding of economic development and social improvement in Britain since industrialization. See especially Neil Mc-Kendrick, John Brewer, and J. H. Plumb, *The Birth of a Consumer Society: The Commercialization of Eighteenth-Century England* (London: Europa, 1982). Pioneering works with similar social history derivation in other fields include Michael B. Miller's *The Bon Marché: Bourgeois Culture and the Department Store, 1869–1920* (Princeton: Princeton University Press, 1981), Rosalind Williams's *Dream Worlds: Mass Consumption in Late Nineteenth-Century France* (Berkeley: University of California Press, 1982), and Richard Wightman Fox and T. Jackson Lears's edited volume *The Culture of Consumption: Critical Essays in American History, 1880–1980* (New York: Pantheon, 1983).

31. See Lawrence Grossberg, Cary Nelson, and Paula Treichler, eds., *Cultural Studies* (New York: Routledge, 1992). Of the four historian contributors, two (James Clifford and Lata Mani) taught in the History of Consciousness Program at the University of California, Santa Cruz; Catherine Hall was a senior lecturer in cultural studies at the Polytechnic of East London; and Carolyn Steedman was a senior lecturer in arts education at the University of Warwick.

32. Geertz, "Thick Description: Toward an Interpretive Theory of Culture," in *Interpretation of Cultures*, 3–30; Edward P. Thompson, "Anthropology and the Discipline of Historical Context," *Midland History* 1 (1972), 41–55.

33. Sherry B. Ortner, introduction to Ortner, ed., *The Fate of "Culture": Geertz and Beyond* (Berkeley: University of California Press, 1999), 11. For a critical explication of Geertzian ethnography, see, in the same volume, William H. Sewell, Jr., "Geertz, Cultural Systems, and History: From Synchrony to Transformation," 35–55.

34. See especially Sherry B. Ortner, "Theory in Anthropology since the Sixties," *Comparative Studies in Society and History* 26 (1984), 126–66. Compare the later discussion of culture in the introduction to the anthology in which Ortner's article was republished ten years later: Nicholas B. Dirks, Geoff Eley, and Sherry B. Ortner, eds., *Culture/Power/History: A Reader in Contemporary Social Theory* (Princeton: Princeton University Press, 1995), especially 3–6, 22–27, 36–39 (see 372–411 for Ortner's article).

35. Quoted by Nicholas B. Dirks, "Introduction: Colonialism and Culture," in Dirks, ed., *Colonialism and Culture* (Ann Arbor: University of Michigan Press, 1992), 1. See the brilliant reflections in Fernando Coronil's "Beyond Occidentalism toward Nonimperial Geohistorical Categories" (*Cultural Anthropology* 11 [1996], 51–87) and Couze Venn's "Occidentalism and Its Discontents" (in Phil Cohen, ed., *New Ethnicities, Old Racisms?* [London: Zed Books, 1999], 37–62), which may stand in for the huge literatures involved.

36. James Clifford and George E. Marcus, eds., *Writing Culture: The Poetics and Politics of Ethnography* (Berkeley: University of California Press, 1986); James Clifford, *The Predicament of Culture: Twentieth-Century Ethnography, Literature, and Art* (Cambridge: Harvard University Press, 1988); Clifford Geertz, *Works and Lives: The Anthropologist as Author* (Stanford: Stanford University Press, 1988).

37. The quotations are from Dirks, Eley, and Ortner, "Introduction," in *Culture/Power/History*, 37.

38. See Fernando Coronil, *The Magical State: Nature, Money, and Modernity in Venezuela* (Chicago: University of Chicago Press, 1997); Deborah Poole, *Vision, Race, and Modernity. A Visual Economy of the Andean Image World* (Princeton: Princeton University Press, 1997); E. Valentine Daniel, *Charred Lullabies: Chapters in an Anthropology of Violence* (Princeton: Princeton University Press, 1996); Liisa H. Malkki, *Purity and Exile: Violence, Memory, and National Cosmology among Hutu Refugees in Tanzania* (Chicago: University of Chicago Press, 1995); Roger Rouse, "Thinking through Transnationalism: Notes on the Cultural Politics of Class Relations in the Contemporary United States," *Public Culture* 7, no. 2 (winter 1995), 353–402, and "Questions of Identity: Personhood and Collectivity in Transnational Migration to the United States," *Critique of Anthropology* 15 (1995), 353–80; Susan Harding, "The Born-Again Telescandals," in Dirks, Eley, and Ortner, *Culture/Power/History*, 539–57, and *The Book of Jerry Fallwell: Fundamentalist Language and Politics* (Princeton: Princeton University Press, 2000); Sherry B. Ortner, "Reading America: Preliminary Notes on Class and Culture," in Richard G. Fox, ed., *Recapturing Anthropology: Working in the Present* (Santa Fe: School of American Research Press, 1991), 163–89, and *New Jersey Dreaming:*

Capital, Culture, and the Class of '58 (Durham: Duke University Press, 2003). With the exception of Poole, each of these authors has been associated with the Anthropology and History Program and the Program in the Comparative Study of Social Transformations at the University of Michigan.

39. See David R. Roediger, *The Wages of Whiteness: Race and the Making of the American Working Class* (London: Verso, 1991), 7. In the passage quoted in text, Roediger paraphrases the argument of an essay by Barbara J. Fields, "Ideology and Race in American History" (in J. Morgan Kousser and James M. McPherson, eds., *Region, Race, and Reconstruction: Essays in Honor of C. Vann Woodward* [Oxford: Oxford University Press, 1982], 143–77)—an argument reiterated in Fields, "Slavery, Race, and Ideology in the United States of America," *New Left Review* 181 (May–June 1990), 95–118. Roediger's own critique of this standpoint pioneered the case for histories of "whiteness." An analogous syndrome occurred in South African historiography, where social historians broadly "schooled in the traditions of historical materialism" likewise found it hard to deal with race per se: see Saul Dubow, *Scientific Racism in Modern South Africa* (Cambridge: Cambridge University Press, 1995), ix–x, 1 5, 284–91. For one U.S. historian who has always maintained analysis of class and race brilliantly together, see the various works of Robin D. G. Kelley, beginning with his remarkable study of Communism in Alabama: *Hammer and Hoe: Alabama Communists during the Great Depression* (Chapel Hill: University of North Carolina Press, 1990); *Race Rebels: Culture, Politics, and the Black Working Class* (New York: Free Press, 1994); *Yo' Mama's Disfunktional! Fighting the Culture Wars in Urban America* (Boston: Beacon Press, 1997); *Freedom Dreams: The Black Radical Imagination* (Boston: Beacon Press, 2002).

40. Fields, "Ideology and Race," 165.

41. Fields, "Slavery, Race, and Ideology," 118. Fields also stated: "The ritual repetition of the appropriate social behavior makes for the continuity of ideology, not the 'handing down' of the appropriate 'attitudes.' There, too, lies the key to why people may suddenly appear to slough off an ideology to which they had appeared subservient. Ideology is not a set of attitudes that people can 'have' as they have a cold, and throw off the same way. Human beings live in human societies by negotiating a certain social terrain, whose map they keep alive in their minds by the collective, ritual repetition of the activities they must carry out in order to negotiate the terrain. If the terrain changes, so must their activities, and therefore so must the map" (113).

42. Roediger, *Wages of Whiteness*, 7.

43. See Barbara J. Fields, "Whiteness, Racism, and Identity," *International Labor and Working-Class History* 60 (fall 2001), 54.

44. See Roediger, *Wages of Whiteness* and *Towards the Abolition of Whiteness: Essays on Race, Politics, and Working-Class History* (London: Verso, 1994). The concept of whiteness sparked burgeoning interest across the interdisciplinary field of American studies. Another historical work, Alexander Saxton's *The Rise and Fall of the White Republic: Class Politics and Mass Culture in Nineteenth-Century America* (London: Verso, 1990), appeared just before Roediger's book. There followed anthropologist Ruth Frankenberg's *White Women, Race Matters: The Social Construction of Whiteness* (Minneapolis: University of Minnesota Press, 1993) and Toni Morrison's *Playing in the Dark: Whiteness and the Literary Imagination* (Cambridge: Harvard University Press, 1992). Later monographs included Noel Ignatiev's *How the Irish Became White* (New York: Routledge, 1995), Neil Foley's *The White Scourge: Mexicans, Blacks, and Poor Whites in Texas Cotton Culture* (Berkeley: University of California Press, 1997), and Matthew Frye Jacobson's *Whiteness of a Different Color: European Immigrants and the Alchemy of Race* (Cambridge: Harvard University Press, 1998). For the wider cross-disciplinary literature, see Mike Smith, ed., *Whiteness: A Critical Reader* (New York: New York University Press, 1997); Michael Rogin, *Blackface, White Noise: Jewish Immigrants in the Hollywood Melting Pot* (Berkeley: University of California Press, 1996); Richard Dyer, *White* (London: Routledge, 1997). The usefulness of the concept was assailed by Eric Arnesen in "Whiteness and the Historians' Imagination," *International Labor and Working-Class History* 60 (fall 2001), 3–32, with responses by James R. Barrett, David Brody, Barbara J. Fields, Eric Foner, and Adolph Reed, Jr. (33–80), and a rejoinder from Arnesen, "Assessing Whiteness Scholarship" (81–92).

45. The quote is from David Roediger's afterword to the revised edition of *Wages of Whiteness* (London: Verso, 1999), 188. Eric Foner has remarked that this new interest in whiteness "cannot be separated from perceived white working-class conservatism from George Wallace voters of the 1960s to Ronald Reagan Democrats, or from the persistence of racial inequality despite the dismantling of the legal structure of discrimination" ("Response to Eric Arnesen," *International Labor and Working-Class History* 60 [fall 2001], 59).

46. The key work criticized by Roediger is Sean Wilentz, *Chants Democratic: New York City and the Rise of the American Working Class, 1788–1850* (New York: Oxford University Press, 1984). See also Sean Wilentz, "Against Exceptionalism: Class Consciousness and the American Labor Movement," *International Labor and Working-Class History* 26 (fall 1984), 1–24, with responses by Nick Salvatore (25–30) and Michael Hanagan (31–36). For Roediger's critique of Wilentz, see *Wages of Whiteness*, 43–92; *Towards the Abolition*, 27–34.

47. Roediger, *Wages of Whiteness,* 13.

48. Roediger's book closed with an analysis of racism's contribution to the formation of the Irish-American working class, who laundered their own stigmatizing as an inferior race ("Irish niggers") into an ideology of superiority over blacks, vilifying the latter as their own ticket into whiteness. See *Wages of Whiteness,* 133–63.

49. See Gary Gerstle, "Liberty, Coercion, and the Making of America," *Journal of American History* 79 (1987), 556–57.

50. See Stuart Hall, "A Torpedo Aimed at the Boiler-Room of Consensus," *New Statesman,* 17 April 1998, 14–19, which also reproduces the text of Enoch Powell's speech.

51. Stuart Hall, Chas Critcher, Tony Jefferson, John Clarke, and Brian Roberts, *Policing the Crisis: Mugging, the State, and Law and Order* (London: Macmillan, 1978).

52. Of course, the intellectual history of CCCS was far more elaborate than that. The best introduction is through the retrospective anthology edited by Stuart Hall, Dorothy Hobson, Andrew Lowe, and Paul Willis, *Culture, Media, Language: Working Papers in Cultural Studies, 1972–79* (London: Hutchinson, 1980), especially Stuart Hall's introduction, "Cultural Studies and the Center: Some Problematics and Problems" (15–47).

53. Center for Contemporary Cultural Studies, ed., *The Empire Strikes Back: Race and Racism in 70s Britain* (London: Hutchinson, 1982). The book's opening sentence read: "The central theme of this book is that the construction of an authoritarian state in Britain is fundamentally intertwined with the elaboration of popular racism in the 1970s." See, in the same volume, John Solomos, Bob Findlay, Simon Jones, and Paul Gilroy, "The Organic Crisis of British Capitalism and Race: The Experience of the Seventies," 9.

54. Paul Gilroy, "One Nation under a Groove: The Cultural Politics of 'Race' and Racism in Britain," in Geoff Eley and Ronald Grigor Suny, eds., *Becoming National: A Reader* (New York: Oxford University Press, 1996), 367.

55. In a sustained series of writings beginning in the late 1970s, Stuart Hall worked this argument into a theory of "Thatcherism." By this, he meant a new form of "authoritarian populism" built on the ruins of the postwar social democratic consensus, which established itself during the 1980s (and three successive election victories). A quite virulent discourse of the nation, sharpened via the Falklands/Malvinas War in 1982 and then turned against the striking coal miners during 1984–85 as the "enemy within," was vital to the cementing of that achievement. Constant evocations of Englishness, drawing on older imperial memories as well as the racist antagonisms of the postimperial present, were crucial. See especially Hall, *Hard Road to Renewal.*

56. See, for example, Paul Gilroy, "Nothing But Sweat inside My Hand: Diaspora Aesthetics and Black Arts in Britain," in Institute for Contemporary Arts, ed., *Black Film, British Cinema,* ICA Document 7 (London: ICA, 1988), 44–46, and "It Ain't Where You're From, It's Where You're At," *Third Text* 13 (winter 1990–91), 3–16; Kobena Mercer, "Diasporic Culture and the Dialogic Imagination: The Aesthetics of Black Independent Film in Britain," in Mbye Cham and Claire Andrade-Watkins, eds., *Blackframes: Critical Perspectives on Black Independent Film* (Boston: MIT Press, 1988), 50–61. See also Benita Parry, "Overlapping Territories and Intertwined Histories: Edward Said's Postcolonial Cosmopolitanism," in Michael Sprinker, ed., *Edward Said: A Critical Reader* (Oxford: Blackwell, 1992), 23.

57. See the preface to Robert Colls and Philip Dodd, eds., *Englishness: Politics and Culture, 1880–1920* (London: Croom Helm, 1986): "Because we could not find a suitable or willing contributor, there is no account of what 'the Empire,' or a part of it, thought of the English." See also Bill Schwarz, "Englishness and the Paradox of Modernity," *New Formations* 1 (spring 1987), 147–53. There were some exceptions to historians' neglect. For example, John MacKenzie began a long series of studies of the popular culture of imperialism, which approached "Englishness . . . as a complex of historical, moral and heroic values which justified the possession of an empire" (quoted in Parry, "Overlapping Territories," 42 n. 7). As Parry argues, the study of "ephemeral writing such as popular fiction, text-books for use in non-elite schools, advertizing, as well as official works on colonial policy . . . would enable one to construct a language of ascendancy in self-definitions of Englishness, valorizing masculinity, encouraging notions of 'supermen,' inflecting patriotism with racism, and underwriting both exercise of and deferral to authority." First published in 1972, Parry's own *Delusions and Discoveries: India in the British Imagination, 1880–1930* (London: Verso, 1998), was an early pioneering study from a literary standpoint (see her new preface, 1–28). See John M. MacKenzie, *Propaganda and Empire: The Manipulation of British Public Opinion, 1880–1960* (Manchester: Manchester University Press, 1984); MacKenzie, ed., *Imperialism and Popular Culture* (Manchester: Manchester University Press, 1984). See also John A. Mangan, *The Games Ethic and Imperialism* (Harmondsworth: Penguin, 1986); Michael Rosenthal, *The Character Factory: Baden-Powell and the Origins of the Boy Scout Movement* (New York: Pantheon, 1986).

58. Parry, "Overlapping Territories," 23.

59. Parry, "Overlapping Territories," 24.

60. The classic works are by the historical anthropologist Ann Laura Stoler, *Carnal Knowledge and Imperial Power: Race and the Intimate in Colonial Rule* (Berkeley: University of California Press, 2002) and *Race and the Educa-*

tion of Desire: Foucault's History of Sexuality and the Colonial Order of Things (Durham: Duke University Press, 1995). The essays incorporated into *Carnal Knowledge* extend back to the late 1980s. While they presuppose all the intellectual radicalism summarized under the rubric of the "cultural turn," including an intense running conversation with sympathetic historians, Stoler's analysis is meticulously grounded in the kind of archival research and dense empirical knowledge celebrated during the heyday of social history. In fact, Stoler's earlier book *Capitalism and Confrontation in Sumatra's Plantation Belt, 1870–1979* (New Haven and London: Yale University Press, 1985) was organized around a strongly materialist political economy perspective. See also Lora Wildenthal, *German Women for Empire, 1884–1945* (Durham: Duke University Press, 2001).

61. The six founding members of the Subaltern Studies collective were Shahid Amin, David Arnold, Partha Chatterjee, David Hardiman, Gyanendra Pandey, and Guha (who edited the first six volumes, between 1982 and 1989). For *Subaltern Studies II* (1983), Dipesh Chakrabarty and Gautam Bhadra joined the collective. With the exception of Sumit Sukar, a member in 1984–94, the collective remained the same until 1996, when the editorial group considerably expanded. From *Subaltern Studies VII* (1992), editorship of the volumes rotated among the collective. Until *Subaltern Studies XI: Community, Gender, and Violence* (New York: Columbia University Press, 2000), edited by Partha Chatterjee and Pradeep Jenagathan, all the volumes were published by Oxford University Press in Delhi. For detailed histories of the project, see Vinayak Chaturvedi, ed., *Mapping Subaltern Studies and the Postcolonial* (London: Verso, 2000); David Ludden, ed., *Reading Subaltern Studies: Critical History, Contested Meaning, and the Globalization of South Asia* (London: Anthem Press, 2002). For Guha, see Shahid Amin and Gautam Bhadra, "Ranajit Guha: A Biographical Sketch," in David Arnold and David Hardiman, eds., *Subaltern Studies VIII: Essays in Honour of Ranajit Guha* (Delhi: Oxford University Press, 1994), 222–25; Dipesh Chakrabarty, "Ranajit Guha, 1922–," in Kelly Boyd, ed., *Encyclopedia of Historians and Historical Writing* (London: Fitzroy Dearborn Publishers, 1999), 1:494.

62. For details, see Chaturvedi, introduction to *Mapping Subaltern Studies, viii–ix.* See also Aijaz Ahmad, "Fascism and National Culture: Reading Gramsci in the Days of *Hindutva,*" in *Lineages of the Present: Ideology and Politics in Contemporary South Asia* (London: Verso, 2000), 129–66.

63. For the "wrestling" with theory, see Hall's answer to a question about the nature of "theoretical gains" following his talk to the April 1990 Urbana-Champaign Cultural Studies Conference, "Cultural Studies and Its Theoretical Legacies," in Grossberg, Nelson, and Treichler, *Cultural Studies,* 289.

64. Aside from Hall et al., *Policing the Crisis,* see especially the following essays by Hall: "Race, Articulation, and Societies Structured in Dominance," in United Nations Educational, Scientific, and Cultural Organization, ed., *Sociological Theories: Race and Colonialism* (Paris: UNESCO, 1980), 305–45; "The Whites of Their Eyes: Racist Ideologies and the Media," in George Bridges and Ros Brunt, eds., *Silver Linings* (London: Lawrence and Wishart, 1981), 28–52; "Gramsci's Relevance for the Study of Race and Ethnicity," *Journal of Communication Inquiry* 10 (1986), 5–27. In 1988–89, Hall began publishing intensively on the subject of migration, identity, "new ethnicities," and diaspora, including his own relationship to the Caribbean. See especially "Diasporic Questions: 'Race,' Ethnicity, and Identity," in David Morley and Kuan-Hsing Chen, eds., *Stuart Hall: Critical Dialogues in Cultural Studies* (London: Routledge, 1996), 411–503 (Morley and Chen's volume contains essays on and by Hall); "When Was 'the Post-Colonial'? Thinking at the Limit," in Iain Chambers and Lidia Curti, eds., *The Post-Colonial Question: Common Skies, Divided Horizons* (London: Routledge, 1996), 242–60. The shifts in Hall's writings can be tracked through the detailed bibliography in Morley and Chen, *Stuart Hall,* 504–14.

65. For an early instance, see Francis Barker et al., eds., *Europe and Its Others: Proceedings of the Essex Conference on the Sociology of Literature, July 1984* (Colchester: University of Essex, 1985), including Edward Said's "Orientalism Reconsidered" (14–27).

66. To take a telling example, Partha Chatterjee's *Nationalist Thought and the Colonial World: A Derivative Discourse?* (London: Zed Books, for the United Nations University, 1986), though conceived in direct dialogue with current Western theorists of the subject (notably, Anthony J. Smith, Ernest Gellner, and Benedict Anderson), was barely noticed by European historians; in contrast, his later *The Nation and Its Fragments: Colonial and Postcolonial Histories* (Princeton: Princeton University Press, 1993) became a central item of discussion. The shift of publishers was in itself symptomatic.

67. At the University of Michigan, this happened under the aegis of the Program in the Comparative Study of Social Transformations, a new interdisciplinary program launched in September 1987 and initially based on history, anthropology, and sociology. The cross-disciplinary constituency quickly broadened toward humanities departments, with a growing stress on cultural studies. Equally crucial was a strong international commitment drawing on most non-Western parts of the world. I've discussed this local history in Geoff Eley, "Between Social History and Cultural Studies: Interdisciplinarity and the Practice of the Historian at the End of the Twentieth Century," in Joep Leerssen and Ann Rigney, eds., *Historians and Social Values* (Amsterdam: Amsterdam University Press, 2000), 96–98.

68. Paul Gilroy, *The Black Atlantic: Modernity and Double Consciousness* (Cambridge; Harvard University Press, 1993); Mary Louise Pratt, *Imperial Eyes: Travel Writing and Transculturation* (London: Routledge, 1992); "Colonial and Post-Colonial History," special issue, *History Workshop Journal* 36 (autumn 1993); Andrew Parker, Mary Russo, Doris Sommer, and Patricia Yeagar, eds., *Nationalisms and Sexualities* (New York: Routledge, 1992); Michael Sprinker, ed., *Edward Said: A Critical Reader* (Oxford: Blackwell, 1992); Edward Said, *Culture and Imperialism* (New York: Knopf, 1993).

69. We should never underestimate the earlier separation of discussions and their discrete circuits of influence or how slowly they managed to come together. To take Stuart Hall as an example, I remember standing in a group of highly well-informed sociologists at Michigan in spring 1986, none of whom had heard of Hall, then professor of sociology at the British Open University; within several years, his name had entered full U.S. currency. Hall exemplifies the shift in thematics I'm describing: when he spoke at Michigan under the auspices of the Program in the Comparative Study of Social Transformations in 1990, his topic was theories of power from Althusser through Gramsci to Foucault; when he spoke in 1999, his topic was the problem of "the postcolonial."

70. See the Latin American Subaltern Studies Group's "Founding Statement," *Boundary 2*, no. 20 (fall 1993), 110–21, and the journal *Nepantla: Views from the South* (2000–2003), whose first issue contains a forum entitled "Cross-Genealogies and Subaltern Knowledges" (1 [2000], 9–89), with contributions by Dipesh Chakrabarty, John Beverley, Ileana Rodriguez, and Lawrence Grossberg. See also Florencia E. Mallon, "The Promise and Dilemma of Subaltern Studies: Perspectives from Latin American History," and Frederick Cooper, "Conflict and Connection: Rethinking Colonial African History," *American Historical Review* 99 (1994), 1491–1515, 1516–45.

71. See Sanjay Seth, *Marxist Theory and Nationalist Politics: The Case of Colonial India* (London: Sage, 1995).

72. Antonio Gramsci, "Notes on Italian History," in Quintin Hoare and Geoffrey Nowell Smith, eds. and trans., *Selections from the Prison Notebooks of Antonio Gramsci* (London: Lawrence and Wishart, 1971), 55, quoted by Ranajit Guha in his preface to Guha, ed., *Subaltern Studies I: Writings on South Asian History and Society* (Delhi: Oxford University Press, 1982), vii.

73. See Ranajit Guha, *A Rule of Property for Bengal: An Essay on the Idea of Permanent Settlement* (Paris: Mouton, 1963); "Neel Darpan: The Image of a Peasant Revolt in a Liberal Mirror," *Journal of Peasant Studies* 2 (1974), 1–46; *Elementary Aspects of Peasant Insurgency in Colonial India* (Delhi: Oxford University Press, 1983); "The Prose of Counter-Insurgency," in Guha, ed., *Sub-*

altern Studies II (Delhi: Oxford University Press, 1983), 1–42, reprinted in Dirks, Eley, and Ortner, *Culture/Power/History*, 336–71.

74. Chakrabarty, "Ranajit Guha," 494.

75. Gayatri Chakravorty Spivak, "Can the Subaltern Speak?" in Cary Nelson and Lawrence Grossberg, eds., *Marxism and the Interpretation of Culture* (Urbana and Chicago: University of Illinois Press, 1988), 271–313. This volume's thirty-nine contributors had assembled for a conference at the University of Illinois in Urbana-Champaign in the summer of 1983. That conference's successor was the still larger Cultural Studies Conference in the spring of 1990, the proceedings of which appeared as Grossberg, Nelson, and Treichler's *Cultural Studies*. The shifting tenor and thematics of these two conferences were themselves an allegory of the movement from "the social" to "the cultural."

76. These disagreements reflected acrimonious political divisions, themselves linked to the so-called culture wars of the early 1990s, centered around "postmodernism." See the following attacks by Sumit Sarkar: "The Decline of the Subaltern in *Subaltern Studies,*" in *Writing Social History* (Delhi: Oxford University Press, 1996), 82–108, reprinted in Chaturvedi, *Mapping Subaltern Studies*, 300–323; and "Orientalism Revisited: Saidian Frameworks in the Writing of Modern Indian History," in Chaturvedi, *Mapping Subaltern Studies*, 239–55. Careful rejoinders can be found in Dipesh Chakrabarty's "Radical Histories and Question of Enlightenment Rationalism: Some Recent Critiques of *Subaltern Studies*" and Gyanendra Pandey's "Voices from the Edge: The Struggle to Write Subaltern Histories," in Chaturvedi, *Mapping Subaltern Studies*, 256–80, 281–99. Sarkar was a member of the Subaltern Studies collective from 1984 to 1994; Pandey was a founding member; Chakrabarty joined soon after the launch. See also David Ludden, "A Brief History of Subalternity," in *Reading Subaltern Studies*, 1–39.

77. See Ranajit Guha, *An Indian Historiography of India: A Nineteenth-Century Agenda and Its Implications* (Calcutta: K. P. Bagchi, 1988), given as the S. G. Deuskar Lectures on Indian History in 1987; "Chandra's Death," in Guha, ed., *Subaltern Studies V* (Delhi: Oxford University Press, 1987), 135–65. This general point may be illustrated in many particular ways. See, for instance, the reconfigured problematic linking Shahid Amin's "Small Peasant Commodity Production and Rural Indebtedness: The Culture of Sugarcane in Eastern UP, c. 1880–1920" (in Guha, *Subaltern Studies I*, 39–87) with his "Gandhi as Mahatma: Gorakhpur District, Eastern UP, 1921–2" (in Guha, ed., *Subaltern Studies III: Writings on South Asian History and Society* [Delhi: Oxford University Press, 1984], 1–61) and "Approver's Testimony, Judicial Discourse: The Case of Chauri Chaura" (in Guha, *Subaltern Studies V*, 166–202).

78. See Edward W. Said, "Narrative, Geography, and Interpretation," *New Left Review* 180 (March–April 1990), 81–85 (containing Said's remarks from the first Raymond Williams Memorial Lecture, London, 10 October 1989); "Intellectuals in the Post-Colonial World," *Salmagundi* 70–71 (spring–summer 1986), 44–64; "Jane Austen and Empire," in Terry Eagleton, ed., *Raymond Williams: Critical Perspectives* (Oxford: Polity Press, 1989), 150–64. See also Gauri Viswanathan, "Raymond Williams and British Colonialism: The Limits of Metropolitan Cultural Theory," in Dennis L. Dworkin and Leslie G. Roman, eds., *Views beyond the Border Country: Raymond Williams and Cultural Politics* (New York: Routledge, 1993), 217–30.

79. Nor was he particularly interested in poststructuralist thinkers, such as Derrida or Foucault. Williams remained firmly implanted in an extremely catholic range of more-centered Marxist traditions.

80. See especially "When Was Modernism?" "Metropolitan Perceptions and the Emergence of Modernism," and "The Politics of the Avant-Garde," in Raymond Williams, *The Politics of Modernism: Against the New Conformists,* ed. Tony Pinkney (London: Verso, 1989), 31–36, 37–48, 49–63.

81. Raymond Williams, *The Country and the City* (London: Chatto and Windus, 1973). See also Raymond Williams and Edward Said, "Media, Margins, and Modernity," in Williams, *The Politics of Modernism,* 177–97; Edward W. Said, "Traveling Theory," in *The World, the Text, and the Critic* (Cambridge: Harvard University Press, 1983), 226–47.

82. See especially Dipesh Chakrabarty, *Provincializing Europe: Postcolonial Thought and Historical Difference* (Princeton: Princeton University Press, 2000) and *Habitations of Modernity: Essays in the Wake of Subaltern Studies* (Chicago: University of Chicago Press, 2002); Gyan Prakash, *Another Reason: Science and the Imagination of Modern India* (Princeton: Princeton University Press, 1999), Ranajit Guha, *History at the Limit of World History* (New York: Columbia University Press, 2003) and *Dominance without Hegemony: History and Power in Colonial India* (Cambridge: Harvard University Press, 1997); Partha Chatterjee, *Nation and Its Fragments* and *A Possible India: Essays in Political Criticism* (Delhi: Oxford University Press, 1997). See also, in general, the contents of the two most recent Subaltern Studies volumes: Gautam Bhadra, Gyan Prakash, and Susie Tharu, eds., *Subaltern Studies X: Writings on South Asian History and Society* (Delhi: Oxford University Press, 1999), and Partha Chatterjee and Pradeep Jeganathan, eds., *Subaltern Studies XI: Community, Gender and Violence* (New York: Columbia University Press, 2000).

83. Said, *Orientalism,* 14.

84. Said, *Orientalism,* 19.

85. For an incisive reflection on contemporary postcoloniality, see Nicholas B. Dirks, "Postcolonialism and Its Discontents: History, Anthro-

pology, and Postcolonial Critique," in Scott and Keates, *Schools of Thought*, 227–51. For a brilliant demonstration of the profound implications for writing the history of the metropolis, see the following essays by Bill Schwarz: "Not Even Past Yet," *History Workshop Journal* 57 (spring 2004), 101–15; "Crossing the Seas," in Schwarz, ed., *West Indian Intellectuals in Britain* (Manchester: Manchester University Press, 2003), 1–30; and "Becoming Postcolonial," in Paul Gilroy, Lawrence Grossberg, and Angela McRobbie, eds., *Without Guarantees: In Honour of Stuart Hall* (London: Verso, 2000), 268–81. See also Schwarz's interview with Stuart Hall, "Breaking Bread with History: C. L. R. James and *The Black Jacobins*," *History Workshop Journal* 46 (autumn 1998), 17–31.

86. I should perhaps give myself more credit in this respect. For example, I learned a great deal directly from the work of my first doctoral student at the University of Michigan in the early 1980s, who explored the influence of popular perceptions of empire inside English society in the nineteenth century: see Susan Thorne, *Congregational Missions and the Making of an Imperial Culture in Nineteenth-Century England* (Stanford: Stanford University Press, 1999). Lora Wildenthal's *German Women for Empire* also began as a dissertation in the mid-1980s.

87. "Nostalgia for the Present" is the title of a chapter focused around film in Fredric Jameson's *Postmodernism, or The Cultural Logic of Late Capitalism* (Durham: Duke University Press, 1991), 279–96.

88. See Pierre Nora, *Les lieux de mémoire*, 7 vols. (Paris, 1984–92), translated as *The Realms of Memory: The Construction of the French Past*, 3 vols. (New York: Columbia University Press, 1997–), and *Rethinking France*, 4 vols. (Chicago: University of Chicago Press, 2001–). For the genesis of a German counterpart, see Etienne François, Hannes Siegrist, and Jakob Vogel, eds., *Nation und Emotion: Deutschland und Frankreich im Vergleich 19. und 20. Jahrhundert* (Göttingen: Vandenhoeck und Ruprecht, 1995). For a searching critique, see Peter Carrier, "Places, Politics, and the Archiving of Contemporary Memory in Pierre Nora's *Les lieux de mémoire*," in Susannah Radstone, ed., *Memory and Methodology* (Oxford: Berg, 2000), 37–57.

89. This paragraph is deliberately composed from the buzzwords of contemporary social theory and cultural commentary. See, in particular, David Harvey, *The Condition of Postmodernity* (Oxford: Blackwell, 1989); Roland Robertson, *Globalization: Social Theory and Global Culture* (London: Sage, 1992); Alain Lipietz, *Towards a New Economic Order: Post-Fordism, Ecology, and Democracy* (Cambridge: Polity Press, 1992). The phrase "the postmodern condition" originates with Jean-François Lyotard (*The Postmodern Condition* [Manchester: Manchester University Press, 1984]); the phrase "the end of history" was launched into public discourse by Francis Fukuyama (*The*

End of History and the Last Man [New York: Free Press, 1992]); the phrase "cultural logic" comes from Jameson (*Postmodernism, or The Cultural Logic of Late Capitalism*). The best early handbook of commentary on these transitions is still Stuart Hall and Martin Jacques's edited volume *New Times: The Changing Face of Politics in the 1990s* (London: Lawrence and Wishart, 1991). See also Ash Amin, ed., *Post-Fordism: A Reader* (Oxford: Blackwell, 1994).

90. See Jameson's important argument about "cognitive mapping," in *Postmodernism*, 45–54, 408–18.

91. See especially Steven L. Kaplan, *Farewell Revolution: Disputed Legacies, France, 1789/1989* (Ithaca: Cornell University Press, 1995) and *Farewell, Revolution: The Historians' Feud, France, 1789/1989* (Ithaca: Cornell University Press, 1995); Geoff Eley, "Finding the People's War: Film, British Collective Memory, and World War II," *American Historical Review* 105 (2001), 818–38.

92. See especially Martin Evans and Ken Lunn, eds., *War and Memory in the Twentieth Century* (Oxford, 1997).

93. Raphael Samuel, *Theatres of Memory*, vol. 1, *Past and Present in Contemporary Culture* (London: Verso, 1994), 443–44. This understanding of history as an organic form of knowledge is again anticipated by Raymond Williams, who was also a nonhistorian by discipline.

94. See, in particular, Lynn Hunt's edited volume *The New Cultural History* (Berkeley: University of California Press, 1989) and the later retrospective edited by Victoria E. Bonnell and Lynn Hunt, *Beyond the Cultural Turn: New Directions in the Study of Society and Culture* (Berkeley. University of California Press, 1999). If the first of these volumes expressed what seems in retrospect far more a set of local Berkeley preoccupations, the second opens a very partial window onto the intervening discussions.

95. See Charles Tilly, *Big Structures, Large Processes, Huge Comparisons* (New York: Russell Sage, 1984).

96. The best-known representative of this group is Carlo Ginzburg: see *The Cheese and the Worms: The Cosmos of a Sixteenth-Century Miller* (Baltimore: Johns Hopkins University Press, 1980; orig. pub., in Italian, 1976); *The Night Battles: Witchcraft and Agrarian Cults in the Sixteenth and Seventeenth Centuries* (London: Routledge and Kegan Paul, 1983; orig. pub., in Italian, 1966); *Clues, Myth, and the Historical Method* (Baltimore: Johns Hopkins University Press, 1989; orig. pub., in Italian, 1986); *Ecstacies: Deciphering the Witches' Sabbath* (New York: Pantheon, 1991; orig. pub., in Italian, 1989); *The Judge and the Historian: Marginal Notes on a Late Twentieth-Century Miscarriage of Justice* (London: Verso, 1999). Other representatives include Eduardo Grendi, Carlo Poni, and Giovanni Levi. See Giovanni Levi, "On Micro-History," in Peter Burke, ed., *New Perspectives on Historical Writing*

(University Park: Pennsylvania State University Press, 1992), 93–113; Edward Muir and Guido Ruggiero, eds., *Microhistory and the Lost Peoples of Europe* (Baltimore: Johns Hopkins University Press, 1991).

97. For an excellent showcase of this work, see Alf Lüdtke, ed., *The History of Everyday Life: Reconstructing Historical Experiences and Ways of Life* (Princeton: Princeton University Press, 1995); for my own commentary, see Geoff Eley, "Labor History, Social History, *Alltagsgeschichte:* Experience, Culture, and the Politics of the Everyday; A New Direction for German Social History?" *Journal of Modern History* 61, no. 2 (June 1989), 297–343.

98. See Natalie Zemon Davis, *Society and Culture in Early Modern France* (Stanford: Stanford University Press, 1975); *The Return of Martin Guerre* (Cambridge: Harvard University Press, 1983); *Fiction in the Archives: Pardon Tales and Their Tellers in Sixteenth-Century France* (Stanford: Stanford University Press, 1987). See also Robert Darnton, *The Great Cat Massacre and Other Episodes in French Cultural History* (New York: Basic Books, 1984).

99. Beginning with *The Making of the English Working Class* (London: Gollancz, 1963; paperback ed., Harmondsworth: Penguin, 1968), Thompson conducted a running debate with historical sociologies of various kinds, as well as angry polemics against the ahistorical varieties. For an excellent example, see Edward P. Thompson, "On History, Sociology, and Historical Relevance," *British Journal of Sociology* 27 (1976), 387–402.

100. Joan W. Scott, "Gender: A Useful Category of Historical Analysis," *American Historical Review* 91 (1986), 1053–75. This essay was reprinted two years later in the same author's hugely influential volume *Gender and the Politics of History* (28–50). The specific quote is taken from *Gender and the Politics of History,* 42.

101. For instance, debate surrounded Joan W. Scott's "On Language, Gender, and Working-Class History," which appeared in *International Labor and Working-Class History* 31 (spring 1987), 1–13, with responses by Bryan D. Palmer (14–23), Christine Stansell (24–29), and Anson Rabinbach (30–36); see also Scott's "Reply to Criticism" (32 [1987], 39–45). Unfortunately, Scott initiated much of the acrimony accompanying these discussions. See her debate with Laura Lee Downs over Downs's "If 'Woman' Is Just an Empty Category, Then Why Am I Afraid to Walk Alone at Night? Identity Politics Meets the Postmodern Subject," *Comparative Study in Society and History* 35 (1993), 414–37: Joan W. Scott, "The Tip of the Volcano," 438–43; Downs, "Reply to Joan Scott," 444–51. See also Bryan D. Palmer, *Descent into Discourse: The Reification of Language and the Writing of Social History* (Philadelphia: Temple University Press, 1990), 172–86. For the key constructive response, see Kathleen Canning, "Gender and the Politics of

Class Formation: Rethinking German Labor History," *American Historical Review* 97 (1992), 736–68, and "Feminist History after the Linguistic Turn: Historicizing Discourse and Experience," *Signs* 19 (1994), 368–404.

102. An important exception during this period was Judith R. Walkowitz, whose *City of Dreadful Delight: Narratives of Sexual Danger in Late-Victorian London* (Chicago: University of Chicago Press, 1992) carefully negotiated the challenges of culturalism, building on her earlier *Prostitution and Victorian Society: Women, Class, and the State* (New York: Cambridge University Press, 1980), which was firmly located in social history. See also her early articles, which managed to register the possibilities of the cultural turn without repudiating social history: "Male Vice and Feminist Virtue: Feminism and the Politics of Prostitution in Nineteenth-Century Britain," *History Workshop Journal* 13 (spring 1982), 79–93, with Jane Caplan's Introduction, "The Politics of Prostitution," 77–78; and "Science, Feminism and Romance: The Men and Women's Club 1885–1889," *History Workshop Journal* 21 (spring 1986), 37–59.

103. See also Eley, "Finding the People's War," 818. Although it has clear affinities, this is not the same as the other distinction, often attributed to "postmodernists" but actually an axiom of self-conscious historical writing for many years, which separates "history as the past" from "history as the processes through which historians endow the past with meaning." Where the one comprises the never attainable reservoir of everything that has ever happened, the other encompasses the rules and methods, narratives and interpretations, and theories and intuitions required to give it shape. My own point is that professional historians are by no means the only people engaging in that task.

104. One of the best short descriptions of this feminist intellectual history in Britain is Lovell's introduction to *British Feminist Thought,* especially 21–22. See also Michele Barrett's new introduction to the revised 1988 edition of her *Women's Oppression Today: Problems in Marxist Feminist Analysis* (London, 1980), whose subtitle was changed to *The Marxist/Feminist Encounter.* The author's intervening reflections marked the challenge of poststructuralisms of various kinds to the earlier certainties of materialism, while foregrounding the profoundly differing political context of the 1980s as opposed to the 1970s, especially the now inescapable salience of "race," racism, and ethnicity. In the meantime, the specifically British coordinates of the discussion have become clearer. See Imelda Whelehan, *Modern Feminist Thought: From the Second Wave to "Post-Feminism"* (New York: New York University Press, 1995).

105. Ginzburg, *The Cheese and the Worms;* Jacques Rancière, *The Nights of*

Labor: The Workers' Dream in Nineteenth-Century France (Philadelphia: Temple University Press, 1989); Wolfgang Schivelbusch, *The Railway Journey: Trains and Travel in the Nineteenth Century* (New York: Urizen Books, 1979).

106. Ginzburg was taken up extremely quickly in *History Workshop Journal*. See Carlo Ginzburg, "Morelli, Freud, and Sherlock Holmes: Clues and Scientific Method," *History Workshop Journal* 9 (spring 1980), 5–36; Keith Luria, "The Paradoxical Carlo Ginzburg" and (with Romulo Gandolfo) "Carlo Ginzburg: An Interview," *Radical History Review* 35 (1986), 80–111. I remember my friend and coauthor David Blackbourn enthusing about Schivelbusch in the early 1980s: see David Blackbourn and Geoff Eley, *The Peculiarities of German History: Bourgeois Society and Politics in Nineteenth-Century Germany* (Oxford: Oxford University Press, 1984), 186, 214. For Rancière, see Reid, "The Night of the Proletarians."

107. Benedict Anderson, *Imagined Communities: Reflections on the Origin and Spread of Nationalism* (London: Verso, 1983); Ronald Fraser, *In Search of a Past: The Manor House, Amnersfield, 1933–1945* (London: Verso, 1984); Patrick Wright, *On Living in an Old Country: The National Past in Contemporary Britain* (London: Verso, 1985); Stallybrass and White, *The Politics and Poetics of Transgression;* Carolyn Steedman, *Landscape for a Good Woman: A Story of Two Lives* (London: Virago, 1986); Denise Riley, *"Am I That Name?" Feminism and the Category of "Women" in History* (Minneapolis: University of Minnesota Press, 1988).

108. Said, *Orientalism;* Guha, *Subaltern Studies I;* Center for Contemporary Cultural Studies, *The Empire Strikes Back;* Paul Gilroy, *"There Ain't No Black in the Union Jack": The Cultural Politics of Race and Nation* (London: Hutchinson, 1987); Spivak, "Can the Subaltern Speak?"; Homi Bhabha, "The Other Question: The Sterotype and Colonial Discourse," *Screen* 24 (1983), 18–36; Hall, "Race, Articulation, and Societies," "Whites of Their Eyes," and "Gramsci's Relevance"; James C. Scott, *Weapons of the Weak: Everyday Forms of Peasant Resistance* (New Haven: Yale University Press, 1985) and *Domination and the Arts of Resistance: Hidden Transcripts* (New Haven: Yale University Press, 1990); Said, *Culture and Imperialism.*

109. For early instances of more densely grounded historical accounts, see especially Stoler, *Carnal Knowledge* and *Race and the Education of Desire;* Catherine Hall, *White, Male, and Middle-Class: Explorations in Feminism and History* (Cambridge: Polity Press, 1992); Anne McClintock, *Imperial Leather: Race, Gender, and Sexuality in the Colonial Conquest* (New York: Routledge, 1995). Significantly, none of these three authors was a historian in the full disciplinary sense: Stoler is an anthropologist, McClintock is a literary scholar, and Hall is a historian who taught successively in departments of cultural studies and sociology until 1998.

110. Strictly speaking, Steedman's book comes in three parts: "Stories" is a single chapter setting out the overall approach; "Exiles" assembles two chapters of autobiographical materials (or stories) about her memories of her mother and father, for use as the case study; and "Interpretations" situates those materials through a set of five historical reflections ("Living outside the Law," "Reproduction and Refusal," "Childhoods," "Exclusions," and "Histories").

111. Elton believed, bizarrely, that aspirant historians could go naked into the archive. See Geoffrey R. Elton, *The Practice of History* (London: Fontana, 1967); see also his later diatribe against the linguistic turn, *Return to Essentials: Some Reflections on the Present State of Historical Study* (Cambridge: Cambridge University Press, 1991). To affirm the importance of the historian's apprenticeship is another matter entirely. Cf. Carolyn Steedman, "History and Autobiography," in *Past Tenses: Essays on Writing, Autobiography, and History* (London: Rivers Oram Press, 1992), 45–46: "I really do believe, as a result of my education and socialization as a historian, that nothing can be said to have happened in the past until you have spent three years at it (three years at least), got on many trains, opened many bundles in the archives, stayed in many flea-bitten hotels. This is the craft-romance of historical practice, and I fall for it all the way." I agree.

112. See Carolyn Steedman, *Dust: The Archive and Cultural History* (New Brunswick, N.J.: Rutgers University Press, 2002), especially chapter 4, "The Space of Memory: In an Archive" (66–88).

113. Steedman, *Dust,* 68.

114. Thomas Richards, *The Imperial Archive: Knowledge and the Fantasy of Empire* (London: Verso, 1993), 11.

115. Steedman, *Dust,* 81.

116. For further pushing of the envelope, see Natalie Zemon Davis, *Women on the Margins: Three Seventeenth-Century Lives* (Cambridge: Harvard University Press, 1995); *Slaves on Screen: Film and Historical Vision* (Cambridge: Harvard University Press, 2000).

117. Rather than calling this new area of work "biography" in the received sense, a better way of posing the possibilities would be to focus on the treatment of lives as complex and fragmentary texts, whose reading requires placement in a rich variety of settings. For brilliant reflections to this effect, see Kali Israel, *Names and Stories: Emilia Dilke and Victorian Culture* (New York: Oxford University Press, 1999). Three superb examples of "unbiography" in this sense are Regina Morantz-Sanchez's *Conduct Unbecoming a Woman: Medicine on Trial in Turn-of-the-Century Brooklyn* (New York: Oxford University Press, 1999), Carolyn Steedman's *Childhood, Culture, and Class in Britain: Margaret McMillan, 1860–1931* (London: Virago, 1990), and Israel's

Names and Stories. For further reflections, see Carolyn Steedman, "Forms of History, Histories of Form," in *Past Tenses,* 159–70; Steedman, *Dust,* 149–50; Luisa Passerini, "Transforming Biography: From the Claim of Objectivity to Intersubjective Plurality," *Rethinking History* 4 (2000), 413–16.

118. See my detailed commentary in Geoff Eley, "Is All the World a Text? From Social History to the History of Society Two Decades Later," in Terrence J. McDonald, ed., *The Historic Turn in the Human Sciences* (Ann Arbor: University of Michigan Press, 1996), 193–243.

119. The quotation is from Olivia Harris, "Of All His Exploring," *History Workshop Journal* 20 (autumn 1985), 176 (a review of Ronald Fraser's *In Search of a Past*).

120. Timothy G. Ashplant, "Fantasy, Narrative, Event: Psychoanalysis and History," *History Workshop Journal* 23 (spring 1987), 168.

121. This point was made by Jacqueline Rose in "A Comment," *History Workshop Journal* 28 (autumn 1989), 152.

122. For a fascinating illustration of the new interest in psychoanalytic theory, both as a vector for the new cultural history and in sharp contrast to the kind of questions it was possible to ask thirty years ago, during the height of the social history wave, see Saul Dubow and Jacqueline Rose's new edition of Wulf Sachs's *Black Hamlet* (Baltimore: Johns Hopkins University Press, 1996; orig. pub. 1937). This book was the record of a psychoanalytic encounter during 1933–35 between Sachs, a Jewish South African psychiatrist, and John Chavafambira, a Manyika *nganga* (healer-diviner), who arrived in Johannesburg in 1927. Based formally on the mutual exchange of contrasting medical expertise, but predicated around obvious disparities of power and position, Sachs's account now stands as a remarkable sociocultural document. In their preface, Dubow and Rose describe a "modern readership with interests in the construction of social identity, the relationship between knowledge and power, and the interconnections between psychoanalytic, literary, and historical thought" (x–xi). This readership could not have been postulated until recently. It is entirely an artifact of the period since the 1980s.

123. Steedman, *Landscape,* 21.

124. Carolyn Steedman, *Policing the Victorian Community: The Formation of English Provincial Police Forces, 1856–80* (London: Routledge, 1984).

125. *Landscape* was published in 1986. It was preceded by *The Tidy House: Little Girls Writing* (London: Virago, 1982), which received the Fawcett Society Book Prize for 1983, and by Carolyn Steedman, Cathy Urwin, and Valerie Walkerdine, eds., *Language, Gender, and Childhood* (London: Routledge and Kegan Paul, 1985), a volume of papers originating in the "Lan-

guage and Learning" stream of the fourteenth History Workshop, which was entitled "Language and History" and held at Brighton in November 1980. Then came *The Radical Soldier's Tale: John Pearman, 1819–1908* (London: Routledge, 1988); *Childhood, Culture, and Class;* and *Past Tenses.* The *Language, Gender, and Childhood* volume bears revealingly on the themes of this chapter in two respects. First, the fourteenth History Workshop was conceived very much with the aim of healing the divisiveness of the previous workshop (the last one held in Oxford, in November 1979). As the three editors remark, the latter had been "a dividing place for more than the Workshop itself." They explain: "It brought a tradition of people's history and workers' writing into direct confrontation with new sources of socialism from Europe, and there was a dramatic enactment of this confrontation in the darkness of a deconsecrated church in Walton Street, where titanic figures of the left boomed the struggle in imperious male voices; and the only woman on the platform stood up to say that, excluded from the form and rhetoric of the debate, she could only stay silent" (7). (For the thirteenth History Workshop, see note 12 above.) Second, the affiliations of the eight contributors illustrate yet again the provenance of innovative historical work coming from outside the discipline during the 1980s: only one contributor was in a history department; one came from English, one from child care and development, two from education, and three from cultural studies. In the meantime, three now hold professorial appointments in history.

126. In the fall of 1992, she taught in the History Department at the University of Michigan. In 1993, she was appointed to a readership in the Warwick Center for the Study of Social History, founded by Edward Thompson in 1965 and since closed down.

127. Steedman, *Landscape,* 7.

128. Steedman, *Landscape,* 5.

129. Mary Chamberlain, "Days of Future Past," *New Socialist,* April 1986, 43.

130. Steedman, "History and Autobiography," 47.

131. Steedman, "History and Autobiography," 50.

132. Steedman, introduction to *Past Tenses,* 10.

133. Steedman, "History and Autobiography," 48–49. Cf. Carolyn Steedman, "Culture, Cultural Studies, and the Historians," in Grossberg, Nelson, and Treichler, *Cultural Studies,* 614: "This is to say that history is the most impermanent of written forms: it is only ever an account that will last a while. The very practice of historical work, the uncovering of new facts, the endless reordering of the immense detail that makes the historian's map of the past, performs this act of narrative destabilization, on a daily basis. The written history does, of course, reach narrative closure all the time, for man-

uscripts have to be delivered to publishers and papers given; but that is only its formal closure. Soon, the written history rejoins—has to rejoin—the insistent, tireless, repetitive beat of a cognitive form that has no end"; "the written history is not just *about* time, doesn't just *describe* time, or *take time as its setting;* rather, it embeds time in its narrative structure."

134. Steedman, introduction to *Past Tenses,* 11. Elsewhere, Steedman describes "a large-scale cultural shift in understanding of the self that had to do with ideas and theories of development and growth in the human subject and a new relationship to time." According to Steedman, "'The child' (that is, real children and child-figures) embodied this understanding that was conceptualized across a wide variety of public forms at the turn of the [twentieth] century." Steedman similarly maintains that "the state of childhood came to be understood as an extension of the self: an extension in time, into the future, and an extension of depth and space, of individual interiority—a way of describing the space lying deep within the individual soul; always a lost place, but at the same time, *always there.*" See Carolyn Steedman, *"La Théorie qui n'en est pas une;* or, Why Clio Doesn't Care," in Ann-Louise Shapiro, ed., *Feminists Revision History* (New Brunswick, N.J.: Rutgers University Press, 1994), 86, 88.

135. Steedman, *Childhood, Culture, and Class,* 259.

136. See Carolyn Steedman, "The Watercress Seller," in *Past Tenses,* 193–202.

137. The opening of her brief essay "Women's Biography and Autobiography: Forms of History, Histories of Form" (in Helen Carr, ed., *From My Guy to Sci-Fi: Genre and Women's Writing in the Postmodern World* [London: Pandora, 1989], 99) provides a useful prospectus for this aspect of her work: "This essay, then, involves a discussion of literary form, of what literary forms permit and what they prevent in particular historical contexts."

138. The Punjabi girl, named Amarjit, was an English-born nine-year-old whose family came originally from rural Punjab. Steedman taught her sometime in the late 1970s, in a group needing extra help with reading and writing. After taking home a particular book the previous day, Amarjit made up a song from a considerable portion of the text. Steedman recorded the song. For Steedman's reflections on the reaction of the school and the wider cultural, historical, and theoretical meanings of the story, see the remarkable essay "'Listen, How the Caged Bird Sings': Amarjit's Song," in Steedman, Urwin, and Walkerdine, *Language, Gender, and Childhood,* 137–63, reprinted, in a shortened version, in Steedman, *Past Tenses,* 90–108. See also Steedman's commentary on the *Memoir* of John Pearman, in *The Radical Soldier's Tale,* 1–106. *The Tidy House* was Steedman's account of a story composed by three working-class eight-year-old girls in 1976 about the lives they expected themselves to lead. Apart from the acuteness of its reading of the

emergent imaginary of the small child, in all its gendered and class-ridden complexities, this book contains a brilliant sustained reflection on the relationship between cognition and writing.

139. This is one of the major themes of Steedman's *Childhood, Culture, and Class*. For a reconsideration, see Carolyn Steedman, "Fictions of Engagement: Eleanor Marx, Biographical Space," in John Stokes, ed., *Eleanor Marx (1855–1898): Life—Work—Contacts* (Aldershot: Ashgate, 2000), especially 35–39.

140. See Carolyn Steedman, "A Weekend with Elektra," *Literature and History,* 3rd ser., 6 (1997), 25.

141. Steedman, "Weekend with Elektra," 18.

142. Steedman, "Weekend with Elektra," 26. See Steedman's related discussions in "Culture, Cultural Studies, and the Historians" and "The Price of Experience: Women and the Making of the English Working Class," *Radical History Review* 59 (spring 1994), 109–19.

143. As Steedman notes, this telling "happened somewhere else, in a piece of writing that Thompson published two years after *The Making . . .* came out." In a short story called "The Rising Cost of Righteousness," published in 1965 in the short-lived New Left magazine *Views* (1963–66), Thompson "does appear to use the suffering self embodied in a woman to tell of social and political relationships." Set in contemporary Yorkshire, the story centers on a young woman's bid for independence, her defeated return to a loveless lower-middle-class marriage, and the act of marital rape that ensues. Steedman's reading of this text allows her to "place Thompson more securely than anything else could, within the radical tradition that was inaugurated in the early eighteenth century, of telling the story of political power and political relations, as sexual domination and exploitation." See Steedman, "Weekend with Elektra," 26, 28.

144. Steedman, "Culture, Cultural Studies, and the Historians," 613–14. The quotation inside the quotation is from a W. H. Auden poem, "Musée Des Beaux Arts," which, as it happens, was chosen by Stuart Hall to be read at Raphael Samuel's funeral. See W. H. Auden, *Collected Shorter Poems, 1927–1957* (London: Faber and Faber, 1966), 123; "Raphael Samuel, 1938–1996," *History Workshop Journal* 43 (spring 1997), vi–vii.

145. Steedman admits, "I see now that I have spent all my life resisting the account of class formation that I was given in that teaching, *not* because it excludes women, but because it is a heroic tale, which most experiences do not fit (which even most of the experiences of the men named in the epic do not fit)" ("Price of Experience," 108).

146. Joseph Bristow, "Life Stories: Carolyn Steedman's History Writing," *New Formations* 13 (1991), 114.

147. Carolyn Steedman, "Englishness, Clothes, and Little Things," in Christopher Breward, Becky Conekin, and Caroline Cox, eds., *The Englishness of English Dress* (Oxford: Berg, 2002), 29–44; "What a Rag Rug Means," in *Dust,* 112–41.

148. See Carolyn Steedman, "Lord Mansfield's Women," *Past and Present* 176 (August 2002), 105–43; "The Servant's Labour: The Business of Life, England, 1760–1820," *Social History* 29 (2004), 1–29.

Chapter 5

1. See Alf Lüdtke, *The History of Everyday Life: Reconstructing Historical Experiences and Ways of Life* (Princeton: Princeton University Press, 1995); Geoff Eley, "Labor History, Social History, *Alltagsgeschichte:* Experience, Culture, and the Politics of the Everyday; A New Direction for German Social History?" *Journal of Modern History* 61, no. 2 (June 1989), 297–343.

2. For evidence of greater pluralism, see Winfried Schulze, ed., *Sozialgeschichte, Alltagsgeschichte, Mikro-Historie. Eine Diskussion* (Göttingen: Vandenhoeck und Ruprecht, 1994). For a recent anthology, which constructs the German genealogies of cultural history largely without the battles of the 1980s, while effacing the pioneering contribution of *Alltagsgeschichte,* see Ute Daniel, *Kompendium Kulturgeschichte: Theorien, Praxis, Schlüsselwörter* (Frankfurt am Main: Suhrkamp, 2001), which also ignores Raymond Williams and the British-American lines of cultural studies. I reviewed these partialities in Geoff Eley, "Problems with Culture: German History after the Linguistic Turn," *Central European History* 31 (1998), 197–227.

3. See Joan Wallach Scott, "Gender: A Useful Category of Historical Analysis," *American Historical Review* 91 (1986), 1053–75, reprinted in *Gender and the Politics of History* (New York: Columbia University Press, 1988), 28–50; Lawrence Stone, "History and Post-Modernism," *Past and Present* 131 (May 1991), 217–18, with later responses by Patrick Joyce and Catriona Kelly (133 [November 1991], 204–9, 209–13), Stone and Gabrielle M. Spiegel (135 [May 1992], 189–94, 194–208; David Mayfield and Susan Thorne, "Social History and Its Discontents: Gareth Stedman Jones and the Politics of Language," *Social History* 17 (1992), 165–88, with responses from Jon Lawrence and Miles Taylor (18 [1993], 1–15), Patrick Joyce (18 [1993], 81–85; 20 [1995], 73–91; 21 [1996], 96–98), Mayfield and Thorne (18 [1993], 219–33), Anthony Easthope (18 [1993], 235–49), James Vernon and Neville Kirk (19 [1994], 81–97, 221–40), Kelly Boyd and Rohan McWilliam (19 [1994], 93–100), Geoff Eley and Keith Nield (19 [1994], 355–64), and Marc W. Steinberg (19 [1994], 193–214).

4. For this wider context, see Paul Berman's edited volume *Debating P.C.: The Controversy over Political Correctness on College Campuses* (New York:

Laurel, 1992), which anthologizes the primary commentaries, and Sarah Dunant's edited volume *The War of the Words: The Political Correctness Debate* (London: Virago, 1994), which collects British reactions. See also Christopher Newfield and Ronald Strickland, eds., *After Political Correctness: The Humanities and Society in the 1990s* (Boulder: Westview Press, 1995); Cary Nelson and Dilip Parameshwar Gaonkar, eds., *Disciplinarity and Dissent in Cultural Studies* (New York: Routledge, 1996); Amitava Kumar, ed., *Class Issues: Pedagogy, Cultural Studies, and the Public Sphere* (New York: New York University Press, 1997); Michael Berubé, *Public Access: Literary Theory and American Cultural Politics* (London: Verso, 1994). Interestingly, with the singular exception of Joan Scott, historians by discipline were virtually never involved in these wider debates.

5. Bryan D. Palmer, *Descent into Discourse: The Reification of Language and the Writing of Social History* (Philadelphia: Temple University Press, 1990), 188.

6. In my own view, that crisis of "class-political understanding" bespoke an actually occurring sociopolitical transition of genuinely epochal dimensions. In other words, together with the larger political and theoretical rethinking it connoted, the cultural turn represented a necessary struggling with contemporary problems, for which the loyal reaffirming of classical materialist positions afforded little help. For further discussion, see Geoff Eley and Keith Nield, "Farewell to the Working Class?" *International Labor and Working-Class History* 57 (spring 2000), 1–30; Geoff Eley, *Forging Democracy: The History of the Left in Europe, 1850–2000* (New York: Oxford University Press, 2002), especially 341–504. The current status of the class concept in historiography, theory, and politics will be addressed by Keith Nield and myself in our forthcoming book on the subject (Ann Arbor: University of Michigan Press).

7. Michael Hardt and Antonio Negri, *Empire* (Cambridge: Harvard University Press, 2001). For critical responses, see also Gopal Balakrishnan, ed., *Debating Empire* (London: Verso, 2003). Among the burgeoning self-analytical literatures generated by the antiglobalization movement, one of the most suggestive is Joel Schalit's edited volume *The Anti-Capitalism Reader: Imagining a Geography of Opposition* (New York: Akashic Books, 2002).

8. For Bryan Palmer's own subsequent recognition of this, see his *Culture of Darkness: Night Travels in the Histories of Transgression* (New York: Monthly Review Press, 2000), an eloquent and imaginative tour de force of historiographical synthesis, deploying the insights and findings of the new cultural histories across a dazzling variety of settings between the medieval era and now.

9. My implicit reference here is to Richard J. Evans, *In Defence of History* (New York: Norton, 2000).

10. Edward P. Thompson, "Anthropology and the Discipline of Historical Context," *Midland History* 1 (1972), 41-55.

11. Charles Tilly, *Big Structures, Large Processes, Huge Comparisons* (New York: Russell Sage, 1984). For a good insight into one field of contemporary debate, see Keith Jenkins, ed., *The Postmodern History Reader* (London: Routledge, 1997).

12. Eric J. Hobsbawm, "From Social History to the History of Society," *Daedalus* 100 (1971), 20-45.

13. Such superb studies as those of Chakrabarty, Prakash, and other Subaltern Studies historians aren't immune from this tendency. Likewise, in Harootunian's sophisticated reflections on the understandings of history shaping Japanese and European conceptions of modernity, some remarkably simplified allusions to the West do service. But I mean neither to diminish the importance of these works nor to question the need for abstract theorizing of the West. See Gyan Prakash, *Another Reason: Science and the Imagination of Modern India* (Princeton: Princeton University Press, 1999); Dipesh Chakrabarty, *Provincializing Europe: Postcolonial Thought and Historical Difference* (Princeton: Princeton University Press, 2000); Harry Harootunian, *History's Disquiet: Modernity, Cultural Practice, and the Question of Everyday Life* (New York: Columbia University Press, 2000). For careful and levelheaded reflections on these matters, see Nicholas B. Dirks, *Castes of Mind: Colonialism and the Making of Modern India* (Princeton: Princeton University Press, 2001), 303-15; "Postcolonialism and Its Discontents: History, Anthropology, and Postcolonial Critique," in Joan W. Scott and Debra Keates, eds., *Schools of Thought: Twenty-Five Years of Interpretive Social Science* (Princeton: Princeton University Press, 2001), 227-51.

14. Dipesh Chakrabarty, "Postcoloniality and the Artifice of History," in *Provincializing Europe,* 27.

15. Among the most useful of the proliferating discussions of Europe's meanings, see Anthony Pagden, ed., *The Idea of Europe from Antiquity to the European Union* (Cambridge: Cambridge University Press, 2002).

16. The quotation comes from Terry Eagleton, *Ideology: An Introduction* (London: Verso, 1991), 28. See also Raymond Williams, "Culture is Ordinary," in *Resources of Hope: Culture, Democracy, Socialism* (London: Verso, 1989), 3-18. This barely scratches the surface of the full range of definitions and usages of the term *culture.* Thus, social science historians tend to treat culture as a separable domain of study (as in forms of systems theory, including Habermasian conceptions of the "lifeworld") or else approach it discretely as "values" via consumer preferences, rational actor models, neo-institutional approaches, and so forth. See, for instance, Joseph Melling and

Jonathan Barry, eds., *Culture in History: Production, Consumption, and Values in Historical Perspective* (Exeter: Exeter University Press, 1992).

17. Carolyn Steedman, "Culture, Cultural Studies, and the Historians," in Lawrence Grossberg, Cary Nelson, and Paula A. Treichler, eds., *Cultural Studies* (New York: Routledge, 1992), 617.

18. Steedman, "Culture, Cultural Studies, and the Historians," 616–17. For the source of the joke (at Robert Darnton's expense), see Dominick LaCapra, "Is Everyone a *Mentalité* Case? Transference and the 'Culture' Concept," in *History and Criticism* (Ithaca: Cornell University Press, 1985), 71–94. See also LaCapra, "Chartier, Darnton, and the Great Symbol Massacre," in *Soundings in Critical Theory* (Ithaca: Cornell University Press, 1989), 67–83. An important essay that addresses the unease expressed here is Richard Biernacki's "Method and Metaphor after the New Cultural History," in Victoria E. Bonnell and Lynn Hunt, eds., *Beyond the Cultural Turn: New Directions in the Study of Society and Culture* (Berkeley: University of California Press, 1999), 62–92.

19. Early influential texts were Vron Ware's *Beyond the Pale; White Women, Racism, and History* (London: Verso, 1992) and the essays collected in Ann Laura Stoler's *Carnal Knowledge and Imperial Power: Race and the Intimate in Colonial Rule* (Berkeley: University of California Press, 2002). For a key recent anthology, see Antoinette Burton, ed., *After the Imperial Turn: Thinking with and through the Nation* (Durham: Duke University Press, 2003). For British history, the pioneering essays were by Catherine Hall, in *White, Male and Middle Class: Explorations in Feminism and History* (New York: Routledge, 1992), 205–95. See also Susan Thorne, *Congregational Missions and the Making of an Imperial Culture in Nineteenth-Century England* (Stanford: Stanford University Press, 1999); Clare Midgley, ed., *Gender and Imperialism* (Manchester: Manchester University Press, 1998); Bill Schwarz, *Memories of Empire in Twentieth-Century England* (forthcoming); Antoinette Burton, "Who Needs the Nation? Interrogating 'British' History," in Catherine Hall, ed., *Cultures of Empire: Colonizers in Britain and the Empire in the Nineteenth and Twentieth Centuries. A Reader* (New York: Routledge, 2000), 138–39, and "Thinking Beyond the Boundaries: Empire, Feminism, and the Domains of History," *Social History* 26 (2001), 6–71; Simon Gikandi, *Maps of Englishness: Writing Identity in the Culture of Colonialism* (New York: Columbia University Press, 1996); Raphael Samuel, "Empire Stories: The Imperial and the Domestic," in *Theatres of Memory*, vol. 2, *Island Stories: Unravelling Britain* (London: Verso, 1998); Kathleen Wilson, *The Sense of the People: Politics, Culture, and Imperialism in England, 1715–1785* (Cambridge: Cambridge University Press, 1995); Catherine Hall, "The Nation Within and Without," in Catherine Hall, Keith

McClelland, and Jane Rendall, *Defining the Victorian Nation: Class, Race, Gender, and the Reform Act of 1867* (Cambridge: Cambridge University Press, 2000), 179–233; Catherine Hall, *Civilizing Subjects: Colony and Metropole in the English Imagination, 1830–1867* (Chicago: University of Chicago Press, 2002). For France, see Gary Wilder, "Unthinking French History: Colonial Studies beyond National Identity," in Burton, *After the Imperial Turn,* 125–43; Sue Peabody and Tyler Stovall, eds., *The Color of Liberty: Histories of Race in France* (Durham: Duke University Press, 2003). For Germany, see Lora Wildenthal, "Notes on a History of 'Imperial Turns' in Modern Germany," in Burton, *After the Imperial Turn,* 144–56; H. Glenn Penny and Matti Bunzl, eds., *Wordly Provincialism: German Anthropology in the Age of Empire* (Ann Arbor: University of Michigan Press, 2003); H. Glenn Penny, *Objects of Culture: Ethnology and Ethnographic Museums in Imperial Germany* (Chapel Hill: University of North Carolina Press, 2002).

20. The foundational study is Amy Kaplan and Donald Pease's edited volume *Cultures of United States Imperialism* (Durham: Duke University Press, 1993). Key genealogies include the new historiography of the West and internal colonialism: for example, Patricia Nelson Limerick, *The Legacy of Conquest: The Unbroken Past of the American West* (New York: Norton, 1988); Tomas Almaguer, *Racial Fault Lines: The Historical Origins of White Supremacy in California* (Berkeley: University of California, 1994). See also Robert R. Rydell, *All the World's a Fair: Visions of Empire at American International Expositions, 1876–1916* (Chicago: University of Chicago Press, 1984). For key recent monographs, see Louise Michelle Newman, *White Women's Rights: The Racial Origins of Feminism in the United States* (New York: Oxford University Press, 1999); Laura Wexler, *Tender Violence: Domestic Visions in an Age of U.S. Imperialism* (Chapel Hill: University of North Carolina Press, 2000); Mary A. Renda, *Taking Haiti: Military Occupation and the Culture of U.S. Imperialism, 1915–1940* (Chapel Hill: University of North Carolina Press, 2001); Laura Briggs, *Reproducing Empire: Race, Sex, Science, and U.S. Imperialism in Puerto Rico* (Berkeley: University of California Press, 2002); Maria E. Montoya, *Translating Property: The Maxwell Land Grant and the Conflict over Land in the American West, 1840–1900* (Berkeley: University of California Press, 2002); Susan Bernadin et al., *Trading Gazes: Euro-American Women Photographers and Native North Americans, 1880–1940* (New Brunswick, N.J.: Rutgers University Press, 2003).

21. Much of this seeks to reformulate the impact of empire, to contain and defuse its significance. This is true, in different ways, of both David Cannadine's simpleminded study *Ornamentalism: How the British Saw Their Empire* (London: Macmillan, 2001) and Linda Colley's more sophisticated work *Captives: Britain, Empire, and the World, 1600–1850* (New York: Random

House, 2002). See also Peter Mandler, "The Problem with Cultural History," *Cultural and Social History* 1 (2004), 94–117; Mandler's study purports to acknowledge the importance of the cultural turn in this respect, while proceeding to dismiss any effective contribution.

22. Among the vast and variegated recent literatures on empire, see Stephen Howe's *Empire: A Very Short Introduction* (Oxford: Oxford University Press, 2002) and *Ireland and Empire: Colonial Legacies in Irish History and Culture* (Oxford: Oxford University, 2000), each exemplary in their respective ways. See also Anthony Pagden, *Peoples and Empires: A Short History of European Exploration, Migration, and Conquest from Greece to the Present* (New York: Modern Library, 2001); Jürgen Osterhammel, *Colonialism: A Theoretical Overview* (Princeton: M. Wiener, 1997); Anthony G. Hopkins, *Globalization in World History* (New York: Norton, 2002); Robert J. C. Young, *Postcolonialism: An Historical Introduction* (Oxford: Blackwell, 2001).

23. See Trevor H. Aston and C. H. E. Philpin, eds., *The Brenner Debates: Agrarian Class Structure and Economic Development in Pre-Industrial Europe* (Cambridge: Cambridge University Press, 1985); Perry Anderson, *Passages from Antiquity to Feudalism* (London: NLB, 1974) and *Lineages of the Absolutist State* (London: NLB, 1974); Immanuel Wallerstein, *The Modern World-System*, 3 vols. (New York: Academic Press, 1974–89).

24. See Charles Tilly, ed., *The Formation of National States in Western Europe* (Princeton: Princeton University Press, 1975), *Coercion, Capital, and European States, AD 990–1990* (Oxford: Blackwell, 1990), and *European Revolutions, 1492–1992* (Oxford: Blackwell, 1993); Keith Thomas, *Religion and the Decline of Magic: Studies in Popular Beliefs in Sixteenth and Seventeenth-Century England* (London: Weidenfeld and Nicolson, 1971) and *Man and the Natural World: Changing Attitudes in England, 1500–1800* (London: Allen Lane, 1983).

25. See especially Michael Mann, *The Sources of Social Power*, vol. 1, *A History of Power from the Beginning to A.D. 1760*, and vol. 2, *The Rise of Classes and Nation States, 1760–1914* (Cambridge: Cambridge University Press, 1986–93); *States, War, and Capitalism: Studies in Political Sociology* (Oxford: Blackwell, 1988). See also Anthony Giddens, *A Contemporary Critique of Historical Materialism*, vol. 2, *The Nation-State and Violence* (Cambridge: Polity Press, 1985); John A. Hall, *Powers and Liberties: The Causes and Consequences of the Rise of the West* (Oxford: Blackwell, 1985); Evelyne Huber Stephens, John D. Stephens, and Dietrich Rueschemeyer, *Capitalist Development and Democracy* (Chicago: University of Chicago Press, 1992); Theda Skocpol, ed., *Democracy, Revolution, and History* (Ithaca: Cornell University Press, 1998). For suggestive commentary, see Perry Anderson, *English Questions* (London: Verso, 1992), 205–38.

26. Kenneth Pomeranz, *The Great Divergence: China, Europe, and the Making of the Modern World Economy* (Princeton: Princeton University Press, 2000) and "Beyond the East-West Binary: Resituating Development Paths in the Eighteenth-Century World," *Journal of Asian Studies* 61 (2002), 539–90; Victor B. Lieberman, *Strange Parallels: Southeast Asia in Global Context, c. 800–1830*, vol. 1, *Integration on the Mainland* (Cambridge: Cambridge University Press, 2003); Lieberman, ed., *Beyond Binary Histories: Reimagining Eurasia to c. 1830* (Ann Arbor: University of Michigan Press, 1999); Christopher A. Bayley, *The Birth of the Modern World, 1780–1914: Global Connections and Comparisons* (Oxford: Blackwell, 2004).

27. For especially powerful examples of social science articulation with politics and policymaking—one reactionary, the other liberal—see Samuel P. Huntington, *The Clash of Civilizations and the Remaking of World Order* (New York: Simon and Schuster, 1996), *Who Are We? The Challenges to America's National Identity* (New York: Simon and Schuster, 2004), and *The Third Wave: Democratization in the Late Twentieth Century* (Norman: University of Oklahoma Press, 1991); Robert D. Putnam, *Bowling Alone: The Collapse and Revival of American Community* (New York: Simon and Schuster, 2000), and Putnam, ed., *Democracies in Flux: The Evolution of Social Capital in Contemporary Society* (Oxford: Oxford University Press, 2002).

28. Carolyn Steedman, "Lord Mansfield's Women," *Past and Present* 176 (August 2002), 105–43, and "The Servant's Labour: The Business of Life, England, 1760–1820," *Social History* 29 (2004), 1–29; Catherine Hall, *Civilizing Subjects: Metropole and Colony in the English Imagination, 1830–1867* (Chicago: University of Chicago Press, 2002); Hall, McClelland, and Rendall, *Defining the Victorian Nation;* Leora Auslander, *Taste and Power: Furnishing Modern France* (Berkeley: University of California Press, 1996).

29. Much of the early polemics were fueled by the particular identities of Gareth Stedman Jones and Joan Wallach Scott. Each had been heavily associated, politically and historiographically, with the earlier breakthrough to social history, including a heavy stress on the axiomatic priority of social explanation, which has been self-consciously Marxist for Stedman Jones. By advocating forms of linguistic analysis and the primacy of discourse during the early to middle 1980s, they seemed to be disavowing their former materialism and everything it entailed. By the early 1990s, the most pronounced self-describing "postmodernist" was the British historian Patrick Joyce, who followed a similar trajectory out of social history. See Joyce, "The End of Social History?" *Social History* 20 (1995), 73–91; "The Return of History: Postmodernism and the Politics of Academic History in Britain," *Past and Present* 158 (February 1998), 207–35.

30. For a rather random selection of first-rate examples, see Becky E.

Conekin, *"The Autobiography of a Nation": The 1951 Festival of Britain* (Manchester: Manchester University Press, 2003); Matthew Hilton, *Smoking in British Popular Culture, 1800–2000* (Manchester: Manchester University Press, 2000); Jennifer Jenkins, *Provincial Modernity: Local Culture and Liberal Politics in Fin-de-Siècle Hamburg* (Ithaca: Cornell University Press, 2003); H. Glenn Penny, *Objects of Culture: Ethnology and Ethnographic Museums in Imperial Germany* (Chapel Hill: University of North Carolina Press, 2002).

31. See especially Steedman, "Culture, Cultural Studies, and the Historians," 613–22.

INDEX